AFRICAN AMERICANS

A CONCISE HISTORY

FOURTH EDITION
VOLUME 1

Darlene Clark Hine
NORTHWESTERN UNIVERSITY

William C. Hine
SOUTH CAROLINA STATE UNIVERSITY

Stanley Harrold
SOUTH CAROLINA STATE UNIVERSITY

Boston Columbus Indianapolis New York San Francisco Upper Saddle River
Amsterdam Cape Town Dubai London Madrid Milan Munich Paris Montréal Toronto
Delhi Mexico City São Paulo Sydney Hong Kong Seoul Singapore Taipei Tokyo

To
Carter G. Woodson & Benjamin Quarles

Editor-in-Chief: Dickson Musslewhite
Publisher: Charlyce Jones Owen
Editorial Assistant: Maureen Diana
Director of Marketing: Brandy Dawson
Senior Marketing Manager: Maureen E. Prado Roberts
Marketing Assistant: Samantha Bennett
Production Manager: Kathy Sleys
Creative Design Director: Jayne Conte
Interior Designer: Carmen DiBartolomeo
Cover Designer: Suzanne Behnke
Cartographer: International Mapping
Image Permission Coordinator: Beth Brenzel

Cover Art: Woodwork shop of Claflin University, Orangeburg, S.C., circa 1800s. Courtesy of the Library of Congress
Media Director: Brian Hyland
Lead Media Project Manager: Alison Lorber
Full-Service Project Management/ Composition: Suganya Karrupasamy/ Element, LLC
Printer/Binder: R.R. Donnelley & Sons, Crawfordsville
Cover Printer: Lehigh-Phoenix
Text Font: New Baskerville

Credits and acknowledgments borrowed from other sources and reproduced, with permission, in this textbook appear on pages C-1 to C-2.

Library of Congress Cataloging-in-Publication Data

Hine, Darlene Clark.
  African Americans : a concise history/Darlene Clark Hine, William C. Hine, Stanley Harrold.—4th ed.
    p. cm.
  "Combined volume."
  Includes bibliographical references and index.
  ISBN-13: 978-0-205-80627-0
  ISBN-10: 0-205-80627-9
  1. African Americans—History—Textbooks. I. Hine, William C. II. Harrold, Stanley. III. Title.
  E185.H534 2012
  973.0496073–dc23

2011022435

10 9 8 7 6 5 4 3 2 1

Combined Volume:
ISBN 13: 978-0-205-80627-0
ISBN 10: 0-205-80627-9
Volume 1:
ISBN 13: 978-0-205-80936-3
ISBN 10: 0-205-80936-7
Volume 2:
ISBN 13: 978-0-205-80626-3
ISBN 10: 0-205-80626-0

PEARSON

CONTENTS

PART II: Slavery, Abolition, and the Quest For Freedom: The Coming of the Civil War, *1793–1861*

6 Life in the Cotton Kingdom •• *1793–1861*   124

7 Free Black People in Antebellum America •• *1820–1861*   146

8 OPPOSITION TO SLAVERY •• *1730–1833*   170

9 LET YOUR MOTTO BE RESISTANCE •• *1833–1850*   188

13 THE MEANING OF FREEDOM: THE FAILURE OF RECONSTRUCTION •• *1868–1877* 282

PREFACE

O ne ever feels his two-ness,—an American, a Negro; two souls, two thoughts, two unreconciled strivings; two warring ideals in one dark body." So wrote W. E. B. Du Bois in 1897. African-American history, Du Bois maintained, was the history of this double-consciousness. Black people have always been part of the American nation that they helped to build. But they have also been a nation unto themselves, with their own experiences, culture, and aspirations. African-American history cannot be understood except in the broader context of American history. American history cannot be understood without African-American history.

Since Du Bois's time our understanding of both African-American and American history has been complicated and enriched by a growing appreciation of the role of class and gender in shaping human societies. We are also increasingly aware of the complexity of racial experiences in American history. Even in times of great racial polarity some white people have empathized with black people and some black people have identified with white interests.

It is in light of these insights that *African Americans: A Concise History* tells the story of African Americans. That story begins in Africa, where the people who were to become African Americans began their long, turbulent, and difficult journey, a journey marked by sustained suffering as well as perseverance, bravery, and achievement. It includes the rich culture—at once splendidly distinctive and tightly intertwined with a broader American culture—that African Americans have nurtured throughout their history. And it includes the many-faceted quest for freedom in which African Americans have sought to counter white oppression and racism with the egalitarian spirit of the Declaration of Independence that American society professes to embody.

Nurtured by black historian Carter G. Woodson during the early decades of the twentieth century, African-American history has blossomed as a field of study since the 1950s. Books and articles have appeared on almost every facet of black life. Yet this survey is the first comprehensive college textbook of the African-American experience. It draws on recent research to present black history in a clear and direct manner, within a broad social, cultural, and political framework. It also provides thorough coverage of African-American women as active builders of black culture.

African Americans: A Concise History balances accounts of the actions of African-American leaders with investigations of the lives of the ordinary men and women in black communities. This community focus helps make this a history of a people rather than an account of a few extraordinary individuals. Yet the book does not neglect important political and religious leaders, entrepreneurs, and entertainers. And it gives extensive coverage to African-American art, literature, and music.

African-American history started in Africa, and this narrative begins with an account of life on that continent to the sixteenth century and the beginning of the forced migration of millions of Africans to the Americas. Succeeding chapters present the struggle of black people to maintain their humanity during the slave trade and as slaves in North America during the long colonial period.

The coming of the American Revolution during the 1770s initiated a pattern of black struggle for racial justice in which periods of optimism alternated with times of repression. Several chapters analyze the building of black community institutions, the antislavery movement, the efforts of black people to make the Civil War a war for emancipation, their struggle for equal rights as citizens during Reconstruction, and the strong opposition these efforts faced. There is also substantial coverage of African-American military service, from the War for Independence through American wars of the nineteenth and twentieth centuries.

During the late nineteenth century and much of the twentieth century, racial segregation and racially motivated violence that relegated African Americans to second-class citizenship provoked despair, but also inspired resistance and commitment to change. Chapters on the late nineteenth and early twentieth centuries cover the Great Migration from the cotton fields of the South to the North and West, black nationalism, and the Harlem Renaissance. Chapters on the 1930s and 1940s—the beginning of a period of revolutionary change for African Americans—tell of the economic devastation and political turmoil caused by the Great Depression, the growing influence of black culture in America, the racial tensions caused by black participation in World War II, and the dawning of the civil rights movement.

The final chapters tell the story of African Americans during the second half of the twentieth century and beginning of the twenty-first century. They portray the successes of the civil rights movement at its peak during the 1950s and 1960s and the efforts of African Americans to build on those successes during the more conservative 1970s and 1980s. Finally, there are discussions of black life at the turn of the twenty-first century and of the continuing impact of African Americans on life in the United States.

In all, *African Americans: A Concise History*, tells a compelling story of survival, struggle, and triumph over adversity. It will leave students with an appreciation of the central place of black people and black culture in this country and a better understanding of both African-American and American history.

What's New in the Fourth Edition

In the fourth edition of *African Americans: A Concise History*, we have greatly expanded coverage of science and technology. We have added information concerning how these related aspects of life have impacted African-American history and have in turn been shaped by African Americans. In addition, every chapter has been thoroughly revised and improved with new special features as well as updated scholarship. A new feature, **Roots of Culture**, examines the cultural contributions of African Americans through the various lenses, including literature, politics, photography, journalism, dance, and music. A new section at the end of each chapter, **Myhistorylab Connections**, connects documents, audio and video clips, interactive maps, and activities available on the Myhistorylab Web site that relate to content in the text.

Highlights of the New Edition

- In the early chapters there are new sections on technology in West African civilization and in the ships that carried Africans across the Atlantic Ocean to slavery in America. Another section describes technology in British America's plantation life.
- There is more emphasis on the contribution of black scientist Benjamin Banneker to intellectual developments during the Revolutionary Era.

- In the chapters that deal with the nineteenth century, the relationship between technology, cotton production, and slavery receives extended coverage, as does the impact of technology on the underground railroad.
- There is additional coverage of black miners' use of technology during the California gold rush, of slaves who toiled at the Tredegar Ironworks during the Civil War, and of the tools and machinery employed by black families to cultivate and grow cotton during the decades following the war.
- A discussion of the black contribution to the 1893 Columbian World's Exposition in Chicago indicates the growing importance of science and technology as the nineteenth century ended.
- For the twentieth and twenty-first century chapters, there are new sections on W. E. B. Du Bois, the Talented Tenth and the *Souls of Black Folk;* on black inventors, and black social scientists.
- There is expanded discussion of radio during the 1930s, including African-American disc jockeys, jazz programs, and *Destination Freedom.*
- There is new coverage of the Tuskegee Airmen, especially in regard to aviation technology.
- Chapters 23 and 24 have been reorganized, with the text now ending with the election of 2008.
- There are new sections on the arrest of Claudette Colvin, on Shirley Chisholm's political career, and on the impact of the 2009 recession on employed black women.
- In Chapter 24 there is updated and expanded discussion of the presidential campaign of Obama and McCain and of the election of 2008.

SUPPLEMENTARY MATERIALS

SUPPLEMENTS FOR INSTRUCTORS	SUPPLEMENTS FOR STUDENTS
PEARSON **myhistorylab**	**PEARSON** **myhistorylab**
www.myhistorylab.com	**www.myhistorylab.com**
Save Time. Improve Results. MyHistoryLab provides a wealth of resources geared to meet the diverse teaching and learning needs of today's instructors and students.	**Save Time. Improve Results.** MyHistoryLab's many accessible tools will encourage you to read your text and help you improve your grade in your course.
Instructor's Resource Center	**www.coursesmart.com**
www.pearsonhighered.com/irc	CourseSmart eTextbooks offer the same content as the printed text in a convenient online format—with highlighting, online search, and printing capabilities. You **save 60% over the list price** of the traditional book.
The Instructor's Resource Center is a Web site where instructors can download the online supplements for *The African Americans: A Concise History.* Contact your local Pearson representative for access or request access online.	
Instructor's Manual with Tests	*African-American Biographies*
www.pearsonhighered.com/irc	This collection of brief biographical sketches of the many African American figures represented in the text serves as an indispensable companion to *African Americans: A Concise History.* Students can use this as a reference to learn more about the people who have helped to shape both American and African-American history. **Volume 1 ISBN: 0-13-193785-5; Volume 2 ISBN: 0-13-193794-4**
Available for download from the Instructor's Resource Center, the Instructor's Manual provides summaries, outlines, learning objectives, lecture and discussion topics, and audio/visual resources for each chapter. The Test Item File includes multiple choice, essay, identification and short-answer, chronology, and map questions.	

SUPPLEMENTS FOR INSTRUCTORS	SUPPLEMENTS FOR STUDENTS
MyTest www.pearsonmytest.com This test generator Web site contains over 1,200 multiple-choice and essay questions. Questions can be edited, and tests can be printed in several different formats.	**A Short Guide to Writing About History, 7/e** Written by Richard Marius, late of Harvard University, and Melvin E. Page, Eastern Tennessee State University, this engaging and practical text explores the writing and researching processes, identifies different modes of historical writing, including argument, and concludes with guidelines for improving style. **ISBN-10: 0205673708; ISBN-13: 9780205673704**
PowerPoint Presentations www.pearsonhighered.com/irc Available online for download from the Instructor's Resource Center, the PowerPoint Presentations include all of the images, maps, and figures from the text and text slides summarizing the content in each chapter.	**Penguin Valuepacks** www.pearsonhighered.com/penguin A variety of Penguin-Putnam texts are available at discounted prices when bundled with *African Americans: A Concise History*. Texts include works by Frederick Douglass, Martin Luther King, W. E. B. Du Bois and many others.
Transparency Acetates Over 100 transparency acetates are available for use in the classroom and include the maps, figures and charts from the text.	***Longman American History Atlas*** This full-color historical atlas designed especially for college students is a valuable reference tool and visual guide to American history. This atlas includes maps covering the scope of American history. **ISBN: 0321004868; ISBN-13: 9780321004864**
Retrieving the American Past Reader Program www.pearsoncustom.com, keyword search/rtap Available through the Pearson Custom Library, the *Retrieving the American Past* (RTAP) program lets you create a textbook or reader that meets your needs and the needs of your course. RTAP gives you the freedom and flexibility to add chapters from several best-selling Pearson textbooks, in addition to *African Americans: A Concise History* and/or 100 topical reading units written by the History Department of Ohio State University, all under one cover. Choose the content you want to teach in depth, in the sequence you want, at the price you want your students to pay.	

myhistorylab Connections

(www.myhistorylab.com)

At the end of each chapter is a new section, **MyHistoryLab Connections**, a list of documents, maps, videos, or additional resources that are included in the new MyHistoryLab Web site that accompanies the fourth edition of *African Americans*.

For Instructors and Students: MyHistoryLab

Save TIME. Improve Results.
MyHistoryLab is a dynamic website that provides a wealth of resources geared to meet the diverse teaching and learning needs of today's instructors and students. MyHistoryLab's many accessible tools will encourage students to read their text and help them improve their grade in their course.

- **Pearson eText**—An e-book version of *African Americans: A Concise History* is included in My HistoryLab. Just like the printed text, students can highlight and add their own notes as they read the book online.

- **Gradebook**—Students can follow their own progress and instructors can monitor the work of the entire class. Automated grading of quizzes and assignments helps both instructors and students save time and monitor their results throughout the course.

- **History Bookshelf**—Students may read, download, or print 100 commonly assigned history works.

- **Audio Files**—Full audio of the entire text is included to suit the varied learning styles of today's students.

- **MySearchLab**—This website provides students access to a number of reliable sources for online research, as well as clear guidance on the research and writing process.

ABOUT THE AUTHORS

Darlene Clark Hine is Board of Trustees Professor of African-American Studies and Professor of History at Northwestern University. She is a fellow of the American Academy of Arts and Sciences, and past President of the Organization of American Historians and of the Southern Historical Association. Hine received her BA at Roosevelt University in Chicago, and her MA and Ph.D. from Kent State University, Kent, Ohio. Hine has taught at South Carolina State University, Purdue University, and Michigan State University. She was a fellow at the Center for Advanced Study in the Behavioral Sciences at Stanford University and at the Radcliffe Institute for Advanced Studies at Harvard University. She is the author and/or co-editor of fifteen books, most recently *The Harvard Guide to African American History* (Cambridge: Harvard University Press, 2000), co-edited with Evelyn Brooks Higginbotham and Leon Litwack. She co-edited a two-volume set with Earnestine Jenkins, *A Question of Manhood: A Reader in Black Men's History and Masculinity* (Bloomington: Indiana University Press, 1999, 2001); and with Jacqueline McLeod, *Crossing Boundaries: Comparative History of Black People in Diaspora* (Bloomington: Indiana University Press, 2000). With Kathleen Thompson she wrote *A Shining Thread of Hope: The History of Black Women in America* (New York: Broadway Books, 1998), and edited with Barry Gaspar, *More Than Chattel: Black Women and Slavery in the Americas* (Bloomington: Indiana University Press, 1996). She won the Dartmouth Medal of the American Library Association for the reference volumes co-edited with Elsa Barkley Brown and Rosalyn Terborg-Penn, *Black Women in America: An Historical Encyclopedia* (New York: Carlson Publishing, 1993). She is the author of *Black Women in White: Racial Conflict and Cooperation in the Nursing Profession, 1890–1950* (Bloomington: Indiana University Press, 1989). Her forthcoming book is entitled *The Black Professional Class: Physicians, Nurses, Lawyers, and the Origins of the Civil Rights Movement, 1890–1955*.

William C. Hine received his undergraduate education at Bowling Green State University, his master's degree at the University of Wyoming, and his Ph.D. at Kent State University. He is a professor of history at South Carolina State University. He has had articles published in several journals, including *Agricultural History, Labor History,* and the *Journal of Southern History*. He is currently writing a history of South Carolina State University.

Stanley Harrold Professor of History at South Carolina State University, received his bachelor's degree from Allegheny College and his master's and Ph.D. degrees from Kent State University. He is co-editor with Randall M. Miller of *Southern Dissent,* a book series published by the University Press of Florida. During the 1990s, he received two National Endowment for the Humanities Fellowships to pursue research dealing with the antislavery movement. In 2005, he received a Faculty Research Award from the NEH in support of his current research on physical conflict along America's North-South sectional border from the 1780s to the Civil War. His books include: *Gamaliel Bailey and Antislavery Union* (Kent, OH: Kent State University Press, 1986), *The Abolitionists and the South* (Lexington: University Press of Kentucky, 1995), *Antislavery Violence: Sectional, Racial, and Cultural Conflict in Antebellum America* (co-edited with John R. McKivigan, Knoxville: University of Tennessee Press, 1999), *American Abolitionists* (Harlow, UK: Longman, 2001), *Subversives: Antislavery Community in Washington, D.C., 1828–1865* (Baton Rouge: Louisiana State University Press, 2003), *The Rise of Aggressive Abolitionism: Addresses to the Slaves* (Lexington: University Press of Kentucky, 2004), and *Civil War and Reconstruction:*

A Documentary Reader (Oxford, UK: Blackwell, 2007). He has published articles in *Civil War History, Journal of Southern, History, Radical History Review,* and *Journal of the Early Republic.*

ACKNOWLEDGMENTS

In preparing *African-Americans: A Concise History* we have benefited from the work of many scholars and the help of colleagues, librarians, friends, and family.

Many librarians provided valuable help tracking down important material. They include Aimee Berry James, Lakeshia Darby Dawson, Ruth Hodges, Doris Johnson, Minnie Johnson, Barbara Keitt the late, Andrew Penson, and Mary L. Smalls, all of Miller F. Whittaker Library, South Carolina State University; James Brooks and Jo Cottingham of the interlibrary loan department, Cooper Library, University of South Carolina; and Allan Stokes of the South Carolina Library at the University of South Carolina. Kathleen Thompson, Marshanda Smith, and Robbie Davine Clark provided important documents and other source material.

Seleta Simpson Byrd and Rosalind Hanson of South Carolina State University and Linda Werbish and Marshanda Smith of Northwestern University provided valuable administrative assistance.

Each of us also enjoyed the support of family members, particularly Barbara A. Clark, Robbie D. Clark, Emily Harrold, Judy Harrold, Carol A. Hine, Peter J. Hine, Thomas D. Hine, and Alma J. McIntosh. Finally, we gratefully acknowledge the essential help of the superb editorial and production team at Pearson: Charlyce Jones Owen, Publisher, whose vision got this project started and whose unwavering support saw it through to completion; Maureen Diana, Editorial Assistant; Carmen DiBartolomeo who created the book's design; Ann Marie McCarthy, Executive Managing Editor, and Kathy Sleys, Production Manager, who saw it efficiently through production and manufacturing; Maureen Prado Roberts, Senior Marketing Manager; and Pat McCarthy, Southern Editorial, who pulled together the book's supplementary , material.

Darlene Clark Hine
Northwestern University

William C. Hine
South Carolina State University

Stanley Harrold
South Carolina State University

African Americans

Hear the audio files for Chapter 1 at **www.myhistorylab.com.**

FOCUS QUESTIONS

WHAT ARE the geographical characteristics of Africa?

WHERE AND how did humans originate?

WHY ARE ancient African civilizations important?

WHY IS West Africa significant for African-American history?

HOW DID the legacies of West African society and culture influence the way African Americans lived?

West Africans were making iron tools long before Europeans arrived in Africa.

THE ANCESTRAL HOMELAND of most black Americans is West Africa. Other regions—Angola and East Africa—were caught up in the great Atlantic slave trade that carried Africans to the New World during a period stretching from the sixteenth to the nineteenth centuries. But West Africa was the center of the trade in human beings. Knowing the history of West Africa therefore is important for understanding the people who became the first African Americans.

That history is best understood within the larger context of the history and geography of the whole African continent. This chapter begins with a survey of the larger context. It then explores West Africa's unique heritage and the facets of its culture that have influenced the lives of African Americans from the Diaspora—the original forced dispersal of Africans from their homeland—to the present.

A HUGE AND DIVERSE LAND

From north to south, Africa is divided into a succession of climatic zones (see Map 1-1). Except for a fertile strip along the Mediterranean coast and the agriculturally rich Nile River valley, most of the northern third of the continent consists of the Sahara Desert. For thousands of years, the Sahara limited contact between the rest of Africa—known as sub-Saharan Africa—and the Mediterranean coast, Europe, and Asia. South of the Sahara is a semidesert region known as the Sahel, and south of the Sahel is a huge grassland, or savannah, stretching from Ethiopia westward to the Atlantic Ocean. Arab adventurers named this savannah *Bilad es Sudan*, meaning 'land of the black people.' Much of the habitable part of West Africa falls within the savannah. The rest lies within the northern part of a **rain forest** that extends eastward from the Atlantic coast over most of the central part of the continent. Another region of savannah borders the rain forest to the south, followed by another desert—the Kalahari—and another coastal strip at the continent's southern extremity.

THE BIRTHPLACE OF HUMANITY

Paleoanthropologists—scientists who study the evolution and prehistory of humans—have concluded that the origins of humanity lie in the savannah regions of Africa. All people today, in other words, are very likely descendants of beings who lived in Africa millions of years ago.

The first stone tools are associated with the emergence—about 2.4 million years ago—of *Homo habilis*, the earliest creature designated as within the *homo* (human) lineage. They butchered meat with stone cutting and chopping tools and built shelters with stone foundations. Like people in **hunting and gathering societies** today, they probably lived in small bands in which women foraged for plant food and men hunted and scavenged for meat. A more advanced human, *Homo erectus*, emerged in Africa about 1.6 million years ago, is associated with the first evidence of human use of fire. Modern humans, *Homo sapiens*, evolved from *Homo erectus*.

ANCIENT CIVILIZATIONS AND OLD ARGUMENTS

The earliest civilization in Africa and one of the two earliest civilizations in world history is that of ancient Egypt (see Map 1-1), which emerged in the Nile River valley in

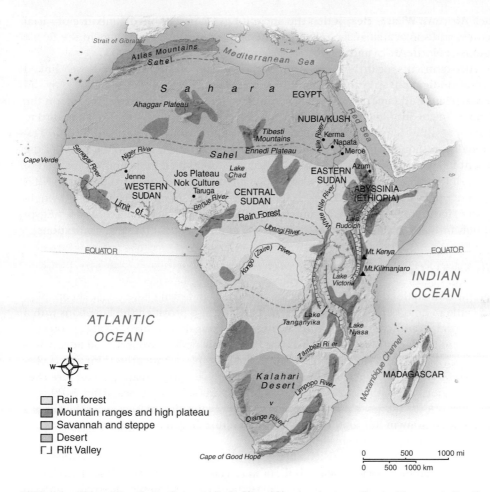

MAP 1-1 • Africa: Climatic Regions and Early Sites Africa is a large continent with several climatic zones. It is also the home of several early civilizations.

▶ **What impact** did the variety of climatic zones have on the development of civilization in Africa?

the fourth millennium BCE. Mesopotamian civilization, the other of the two, emerged in the valleys of the Tigris and Euphrates rivers in southwest Asia with the rise of the city-states of Sumer. In both regions, civilization appeared at the end of a long process in which hunting and gathering gave way to agriculture. The settled village life that resulted from this transformation permitted society to become increasingly **hierarchical** and specialized.

The race of the ancient Egyptians and the nature and extent of their influence on later Western civilizations have long been a source of controversy that reflects more about racial politics of recent history than it reveals about the Egyptians themselves. It is not clear whether they were an offshoot of their Mesopotamian contemporaries, whether they were representatives of a group of peoples whose origins were in both Africa and southwest Asia, or whether the ancestors of both the Egyptians and Mesopotamians were black Africans. What is clear is that the ancient Egyptians exhibited a mixture of racial features and spoke a language related to the languages spoken by others in the fertile regions of North Africa and southwest Asia.

Afrocentricists regard ancient Egypt as an essentially black civilization closely linked to other indigenous African civilizations to its south. They maintain that not only did the Egyptians influence later African civilizations but they had a decisive impact on the Mediterranean Sea region, including ancient Greece and Rome. Therefore in regard to philosophy and science black Egyptians were the originators of Western civilization. Traditionalists respond that modern racial categories have no relevance to the world of the ancient Egyptians. The ancient Greeks, they argue, developed the empirical method of inquiry and notions of individual freedom that characterize Western civilization. What is not under debate, however, is Egypt's contribution to the spread of civilization throughout the Mediterranean region. No one doubts that in religion, commerce, and art Egypt strongly influenced the development of Greece and subsequent Western civilizations.

Egyptian Civilization

A gentle annual flooding regularly irrigates the banks of leaving herd goats, sheep, pigs, and cattle in an otherwise desolate region. The Nile also provided the Egyptians with a transportation and communications artery, while their desert surroundings protected them from foreign invasion. Egypt became a unified kingdom around 3150 bce. A succession of 31 dynasties ruled it before the Roman Empire conquered it in 30 bce. Between 1550–1100 bce, Egypt expanded beyond the Nile valley, creating an empire over coastal regions of southwest Asia as well as Libya and Nubia in Africa. After 1100 bce, Egypt fell prey to a series of outside invaders. With the invasion of Alexander the Great's Macedonian army in 331 bce, Egypt's ancient culture began a long decline under the pressure of Greek ideas and institutions.

Before then, Egypt had resisted change for thousands of years. Kings presided over a strictly hierarchical society. Beneath them were classes of warriors, priests, merchants, artisans, and peasants. Scribes, who were masters of Egypt's complex **hieroglyphic** writing, staffed a large bureaucracy.

Egyptian society was also strictly **patrilineal** and **patriarchal.** Egyptian women nonetheless held a high status compared with women in much of the rest of the ancient world. They owned property independently of their husbands, oversaw household slaves, controlled the education of their children, held public office, served as priests, and operated businesses. There were several female rulers, one of whom, Hatshepsut, reigned for 20 years (1478–1458 bce).

A complex polytheistic religion shaped every facet of Egyptian life. Although there were innumerable gods, two of the more important were the sun god Re (or Ra), who represented the immortality of the Egyptian state, and Osiris, the god of the Nile, who embodied each person's immortality. Personal immortality and the immortality of the state merged in the person of the king, as expressed in Egypt's elaborate royal tombs. The most dramatic examples of those tombs, the Great Pyramids at Giza near the modern city of Cairo, were built more than 4,500 years ago to protect the bodies of three kings, so that their souls might successfully enter the life to come. The pyramids also dramatically symbolized the power of the Egyptian state and have endured as embodiments of the grandeur of Egyptian civilization.

KUSH, MEROË, AND AXUM

To the south of Egypt in the upper Nile River valley, in what is today the nation of Sudan, lay the ancient region known as Nubia. As early as the fourth millennium BCE, the black people who lived there interacted with the Egyptians. Archaeological evidence suggests that grain production and the concept of monarchy may have arisen in Nubia and then spread northward to Egypt. But Egypt's population was always much larger than that of Nubia, and during the second millennium BCE, Egypt used its military power to make Nubia an Egyptian colony and control Nubian copper and gold mines. Egyptians also required the sons of Nubian nobles to live in Egypt as hostages.

Egyptian religion, art, hieroglyphics, and political structure influenced Nubia. Then, with the decline of Egypt's decline during the first millennium BCE, the Nubians established an independent kingdom known as Kush, which had its capital at Kerma on the upper Nile River. During the eighth century BCE, the Kushites took control of upper (meaning southern, because the Nile flows south to North) Egypt, and in about 750, the Kushite king Piankhy added lower Egypt to his realm. Piankhy became pharaoh, the title used by Egyptian kings, and founded Egypt's twenty-fifth dynasty, which ruled until the Assyrians, who invaded Egypt from southwest Asia, drove the Kushites out in 663 BCE.

Kush itself remained independent for another thousand years. In 540 BCE a resurgent Egyptian army destroyed Kerma, and the Kushites moved their capital southward to Meroë. The new capital traded with East Africa, with regions to the west across the Sudan, and with the Mediterranean world by way of the Nile River. The development of

The ruined pyramids of Meroë on the banks of the upper Nile River are not as old as those at Giza in Egypt, and they differ from them stylistically. But they nonetheless attest to the cultural connections between Meroë and Egypt.

a smelting technology capable of exploiting local deposits of iron transformed the city into Africa's first industrial center.

Kush's wealth attracted powerful enemies, and in 23 BCE a Roman army invaded. But it was actually the decline of Rome and its Mediterranean economy that hurt Kush the most. As the Roman Empire grew weaker and poorer, its trade with Kush declined, and Kush, too, grew weakened. During the early fourth century CE, it fell to the neighboring Noba people, who in turn fell to the nearby kingdom of Axum, whose warriors destroyed Meroë.

Located in what is today Ethiopia, Axum emerged as a nation during the first century BCE as Semitic people from the Arabian Peninsula settled among a local black population. By the time it absorbed Kush during the fourth century CE, Axum had become the first Christian state in sub-Saharan Africa. By the eighth century, shifting trade patterns, environmental depletion, and Islamic invaders combined to reduce Axum's power. It nevertheless retained its unique culture and its independence.

WEST AFRICA

The immediate birthright of most African Americans, however, is to be found not in the ancient civilizations of the Nile valley—although those civilizations are part of the heritage of all Africans—but thousands of miles away among the civilizations that emerged in West Africa during the first millennium BCE.

Like Africa as a whole, West Africa is physically, ethnically, and culturally diverse. Much of West Africa south of the Sahara Desert falls within the **savannah** that spans the continent from east to west. West and south of the savannah, however, are extensive forests. These two environments—savannah and forest—were home to a great variety of cultures and languages. Patterns of settlement in the region ranged from isolated homesteads and hamlets to villages, towns, and cities.

West Africans began cultivating crops and tending domesticated animals between 1000 BCE and 200 CE. Those who lived on the savannah usually adopted settled village life well before those who lived in the forests. By 500 BCE, beginning with the Nok people of the forest region, some West Africans were producing iron tools and weapons.

From early times, the peoples of West Africa traded among themselves and with the peoples who lived across the Sahara Desert in North Africa. This extensive trade became an essential part of the region's economy and formed the basis for the three great western Sudanese empires that successively dominated the region from before 800 CE to the beginnings of the modern era.

ANCIENT GHANA

The first known kingdom in the western Sudan was Ghana. Founded by the Soninke people in the area north of the modern republic of Ghana, the kingdom's origins are unclear. It may have arisen as early as the fourth century CE or as late as the eighth century when Arab merchants began to praise its great wealth.

Because they possessed superior iron weapons, the Soninke were able to dominate their neighbors and forge an empire through constant warfare. Ghana's boundaries reached into the Sahara Desert to its north and modern Senegal to its south. But the empire's real power lay in commerce.

Ghana's kings were known in Europe and southwest Asia as the richest of monarchs, and trade produced their wealth. Ghana traded in several commodities. From North Africa came silk, cotton, glass beads, horses, mirrors, dates, and, especially, salt—a scarce necessity in the torridly hot western Sudan. In return, Ghana exported pepper, slaves, and, especially, gold.

Before the fifth century CE, Roman merchants and Berbers—the **indigenous** people of western North Africa—were West Africa's chief partners in the trans-Sahara trade. As Roman power declined and Islam spread across North Africa during the seventh and eighth centuries, Arabs replaced the Romans. Arab merchants settled in Saleh, the Muslim part of Kumbi Saleh, Ghana's capital, which by the twelfth century had become an impressive city. There were stone houses and tombs and as many as 20,000 people. Saleh had several mosques, and some Soninke converted to Islam, although it is unclear whether the royal family joined them. Muslims dominated the royal bureaucracy and in the process introduced Arabic writing to the region.

Commercial and religious rivalries led to Ghana's decline during the twelfth century. The Almoravids, who were Islamic Berbers from what is today Morocco, had been Ghana's principal competitors for control of the trans-Sahara trade. In 992 Ghana's army captured Awdaghost, the Almoravid trade center northwest of Kumbi Saleh. Driven as much by religious fervor as by economic interest, the Almoravids retaliated decisively in 1076 by conquering Ghana. The Soninke regained their independence in 1087, but a little over a century later fell to the Sosso, a previously tributary people.

THE EMPIRE OF MALI, 1230–1468

Following the defeat of Ghana by the Almorvids, many western Sudanese peoples competed for political and economic power. This contest ended in 1235 when the Mandinka, under their legendary leader Sundiata (c. 1210–1260), defeated the Sosso at the Battle of Kirina. Sundiata then forged the Empire of Mali.

Mali was socially, politically, and economically similar to Ghana. It was larger than Ghana, however, and centered farther south, in a region of greater rainfall and more abundant crops. Sundiata also gained direct control of the gold mines of Wangara, making his empire wealthier than Ghana had been. As a result, Mali's population grew to eight million.

Sundiata was also an important figure for western Sudanese religion. According to legend, he wielded magical powers to defeat his enemies. This suggests that he practiced an indigenous faith. But Sundiata was also a Muslim and helped make Mali—at least superficially—an Islamic state. West Africans had been converting to Islam since Arab traders arrived in the region centuries before, although many converts, like Sundiata, continued to practice indigenous religions as well. By his time, most merchants and bureaucrats were Muslims, and the empire's rulers gained stature among Arab states by converting to Islam.

To administer their vast empire at a time when communication was slow, Mali's rulers relied on personal and family ties with local chiefs. Commerce, bureaucracy, and scholarship also helped hold the empire together. Mali's most important city was Timbuktu, which had been established during the eleventh century beside the Niger River near the southern edge of the Sahara Desert. By the thirteenth century, Timbuktu had become a major hub for trade in gold, slaves, and salt. It attracted

VOICES

AL BAKRI DESCRIBES KUMBI SALEH AND GHANA'S ROYAL COURT

Nothing remains of the documents compiled by Ghana's Islamic bureaucracy. As a result, accounts of the civilization are all based on the testimony of Arab or Berber visitors. In this passage, written in the eleventh century, Arab geographer Al Bakri describes the great wealth and power of the king of Ghana and suggests there were tensions between Islam and the indigenous religion of the Soninke.

The city of Ghana [Kumbi Saleh] consists of two towns lying in a plain. One of these towns is inhabited by Muslims. It is large and possesses twelve mosques. . . . There are imams and muezzins, and assistants as well as jurists and learned men. Around the town are wells of sweet water from which they drink and near which they grow vegetables. The town in which the king lives is six miles from the Muslim one, and bears the name Al Ghaba [the forest]. . . . In the town where the king lives, and not far from the hall where he holds his court of justice, is a mosque where pray the Muslims who come on diplomatic missions. Around the king's town are domed buildings, woods, and copses where live the sorcerers of these people, the men in charge of the religious cult. . . .

Of the people who follow the king's religion, only he and his heir presumptive, who is the son of his sister, may wear sewn clothes. All the other people wear clothes of cotton, silk, or brocade, according to their means. All men shave their beards and women shave their heads. The king adorns himself like a woman, wearing necklaces and bracelets, . . . The court of appeal [for grievances against officials] is held in a domed pavilion around which stand ten horses with gold embroidered trappings. Behind the king stand ten pages holding shields and swords decorated with gold, and on his right are the sons of the subordinate kings of his country, all wearing splendid garments and their hair mixed with gold. . . . When the people professing the same religion as the king approach him, they fall on their knees and sprinkle their heads with dust, for this is their way of showing him their respect. As for the Muslims, they greet him only by clapping their hands.

- What does this passage indicate about life in ancient Ghana?
- According to Al Bakri, in what ways do customs in Kumbi Saleh differ from customs in Arab lands?

SOURCE: Roland Oliver and Caroline Oliver, *Africa in the Days of Exploration* (Upper Saddle River, NJ: Prentice Hall, 1965), 9–10.

merchants from throughout the Mediterranean world and became a center of Islamic learning.

The Mali Empire reached its peak during the reign of Mansa Musa (r. 1312–1337). One of the wealthiest rulers the world has known, Musa made himself and Mali famous when in 1324 he undertook a pilgrimage across Africa to the Islamic holy city of Mecca in Arabia. With an entourage of 60,000, a train of one hundred elephants,

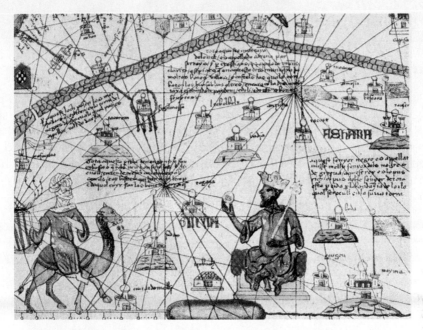

Mansa Musa, who ruled the West African Empire of Mali from 1312 to 1337, is portrayed at the bottom center of this portion of the fourteenth-century Catalan Atlas. Musa's crown, scepter, throne, and the huge gold nugget he displays symbolize his power and wealth.

and a propensity for distributing huge amounts of gold to those who greeted him along the way, Musa amazed the Islamic world. After his death, however, Mali declined. In 1468, one of the most powerful of its formerly subject peoples, the Songhai, captured Timbuktu, and their leader, Sunni Ali, founded a new West African empire.

THE EMPIRE OF SONGHAI, 1464–1591

Like the Mandinka and Soninke before them, the Songhai were great traders and warriors. The Songhai had seceded from Mali in 1375, and under Sunni Ali (r. 1464–1492), who reigned from 1464 to 1492, they built the last and largest of the western Sudanese empires.

When Sunni Ali died by drowning, Askia Muhammad Toure led a successful revolt against Ali's son to make himself king of Songhai. The new king, (r. 1492–1528), extended the empire northward into the Sahara, westward into Mali, and eastward to include the trading cities of Hausaland. A devout Muslim, Muhammad Toure used his power to spread the influence of Islam within the empire. During a pilgrimage to Mecca in 1497 he established diplomatic relations with Morocco and Egypt and recruited Muslim scholars to serve at the Sankore Mosque at Timbuktu. The mosque became a widely known center for the study of theology, law, mathematics, and medicine. Despite these efforts, by the end of Muhammad Toure's reign, Islamic culture remained weak in West Africa outside urban areas.

Songhai reached its peak of influence under Askia Daud (r. 1549–1582). But the political balance of power in West Africa was changing rapidly, and, lacking new leaders

The Ancient Manuscripts of Timbuktu

Timbuktu, ancient Mali's most important city, was an important center for a thriving trade in gold, salt, and slaves. It was also a city of spectacular intellectual and cultural achievements. Its many mosques and schools helped support a book trade that was famous throughout the region. The city took pride in its intellectual accomplishments. Many of the ancient manuscripts that exist today were carefully preserved as family treasures by the residents of the area over many generations. The manuscripts provide compelling evidence of the skill and sophistication of Mali's scientists, physicians, philosophers, and theologians. They also demonstrate the fact that Africa has a rich legacy of written culture, aspects of which crossed the Atlantic with the enslaved Africans who were transported to the Americas.

This text was written ▶ to train scholars in the field of astronomy. On this page, the text and diagram describe and demonstrate the rotation of the heavens.

▲ Islamic mystics played an important part in Timbuktu's religious life. This diagram explains the life of the mystics, which revolved around the teaching of their master.

▲ The manuscripts show Africa's rich legacy of written history. Such written records are believed to be crucial markers of civilization.

Islam was a powerful force in West Africa, but its practitioners were largely concentrated in cities like Timbuktu. What might explain this fact?

as resourceful as Sunni Ali or Muhammad Toure, Songhai failed to adapt. Since the 1430s, adventurers from the European country of Portugal had been establishing trading centers along the Guinea Coast, seeking gold and diverting it from the trans-Sahara trade. Their success threatened the Arab rulers of North Africa, Songhai's traditional partners in the trans-Sahara trade. In 1591 the king of Morocco, hoping to regain access to West African gold, sent an army of 4,000 mostly Spanish mercenaries armed with muskets and cannons across the Sahara to attack Gao, Songhai's capital. Only 1,000 of the soldiers survived the grueling march to confront Songhai's elite cavalry at Tondibi on the approach to Gao. But the Songhai forces were armed only with bows and lances, which were no match for firearms, and the mercenaries routed them. Its army destroyed, the Songhai empire fell apart. The Moroccans soon left the region, and West Africa was without a government powerful enough to intervene when the Portuguese, other Europeans, and the African kingdoms of the Guinea Coast became more interested in trading for human beings than for gold.

THE WEST AFRICAN FOREST REGION

The area called the forest region of West Africa, which includes stretches of savannah, extends 2,000 miles along the Atlantic coast from Senegambia in the northwest to the former kingdom of Benin (modern Cameroon) in the east. Significant migration into the forests began only after 1000 CE, as the western Sudanese climate became increasingly dry. Because people migrated southward from the Sudan in small groups over an extended period, the process brought about considerable cultural diversification.

Colonizing a region covered with thick vegetation was hard work. In some portions of the forest, agriculture did not supplant hunting and gathering until the fifteenth and sixteenth centuries. In more open parts of the region, however, several small kingdoms emerged centuries earlier. Although none of these kingdoms ever grew as large as the empires of the western Sudan, some were powerful.

The great mosque at the West African city of Jenne was first built during the fourteenth century CE. It demonstrates the importance of Islam in the region's trading centers. Roderick J. McIntosh, Rice University

The peoples of the forest region are of particular importance for African-American history because of the role they played in the Atlantic slave trade as both slave traders and as victims of the trade. Space limitations permit only a survey of the most important of these peoples, beginning with those of Senegambia in the northwest.

The inhabitants of Senegambia shared a common history and spoke closely related languages, but they were not politically united. Parts of the region had been incorporated within the empires of Ghana and Mali and had been exposed to Islamic influences. Senegambian society was strictly hierarchical, with royalty at the top and slaves at the bottom. Most people were farmers.

Southeast of Senegambia, the Akan states emerged during the sixteenth century as the gold trade provided local rulers with the wealth they needed to clear forests and initiate agricultural economies. The rulers traded gold from mines they controlled for slaves, who did the difficult work of cutting trees and burning refuse. Then settlers received open fields from the rulers in return for a portion of their produce and services. When Europeans arrived, they traded guns for gold. The guns in turn allowed the Akan states to expand, and during the late seventeenth century, one of them, the Ashantee, created a well-organized and densely populated kingdom, comparable in size to the modern country of Ghana. By the eighteenth century, this kingdom not only dominated the central portion of the forest region, but also used its army extensively to capture slaves for sale to European traders.

To the east of the Akan states (in modern Benin and western Nigeria) lived the people of the Yoruba culture. They gained ascendancy in the area as early as 1000 CE by trading kola nuts and cloth to the peoples of the western Sudan. During the seventeenth century, the Oyo people, employing a well-trained cavalry, imposed political unity on part of the Yoruba region. They, like the Ashantee, became extensively involved in the Atlantic slave trade. Located to the west of the Oyo were the Fon people, who formed the Kingdom of Dahomey, which rivaled Oyo as a center for the slave trade.

At the eastern end of the forest region was the Kingdom of Benin, which controlled much of what is today southern Nigeria. The people of this kingdom shared a common heritage with the Yoruba, who played a role in its formation during the thirteenth century. During the fifteenth century, after a reform of its army, Benin began to expand to the Niger River in the east, to the Gulf of Guinea to the south, and into Yoruba country to the west. The kingdom peaked during the late sixteenth century.

Benin remained little influenced by Islam or Christianity, but like other coastal kingdoms, it joined in the Atlantic slave trade. Beginning in the late fifteenth century, the Oba of Benin allowed Europeans to enter the country to trade for gold, pepper, ivory, and slaves. By the seventeenth century, Benin's prosperity depended on the slave trade.

This carved wooden ceremonial offering bowl is typical of a Yoruba art form that has persisted for centuries. It reflects religious practices as well as traditional hairstyle and dress.

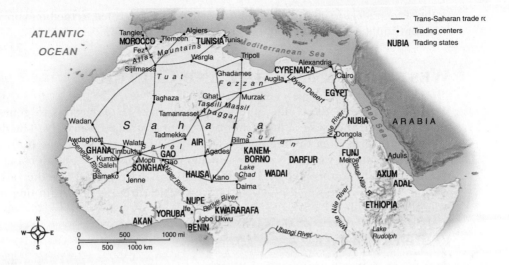

MAP 1-2 • Trans-Saharan Trade Routes Ancient trade routes connected sub-Saharan West Africa to the Mediterranean coast. Among the commodities carried southward were silk, cotton, horses, and salt. Among those carried northward were gold, ivory, pepper, and slaves.

▶ *What was the significance of the trans-Sahara trade in West African history?*

To Benin's east was Igboland, a densely populated but politically weak region stretching along the Niger River. The Igbo people lived in one of the stateless societies common in West Africa. In these societies, families rather than central authorities ruled. Village elders provided local government and life centered on family homesteads. Igboland had long exported field workers and skilled artisans to Benin and other kingdoms. When Europeans arrived, they expanded this trade, which brought many Igbos to the Americas (see Map 1-2).

KONGO AND ANGOLA

Although the forebears of most African Americans originated in West Africa, a large minority came from Central Africa. In particular they came from the area around the Congo River and its tributaries and the region to the south that the Portuguese called Angola. The people of these regions had much in common with those of the Guinea Coast. They divided labor by gender, lived in villages composed of extended families, and accorded semidivine status to their kings.

During the fourteenth and fifteenth centuries, much of the Congo River system, with its fertile valleys and abundant fish, came under the control of the Kingdom of Kongo. This kingdom's wealth also derived from its access to salt and iron and its extensive trade with the interior of the continent. Nzinga Knuwu, who was *Mani Kongo* (the Kongolese term for king) when Portuguese expeditions arrived in the region in the late fifteenth century, surpassed other African rulers in welcoming the intruders. His son Nzinga Mbemba tried to convert the kingdom to Christianity and remodel it along European lines. The resulting unrest, combined with Portuguese greed and the effects of the slave trade, undermined royal authority and ultimately led to the breakup of the kingdom and the disruption of the entire Kongo-Angola region.

WEST AFRICAN SOCIETY AND CULTURE

West Africa's great ethnic and cultural diversity makes it hazardous to generalize about the social and cultural background of the first African Americans. The dearth of written records from the region south of the Sudan compounds the difficulties. But working with a variety of sources, including oral histories, traditions, and archaeological and anthropological studies, historians have pieced together a broad understanding of the way the people of West Africa lived at the beginning of the Atlantic slave trade.

FAMILIES AND VILLAGES

By the early sixteenth century, most West Africans were farmers. They usually lived in hamlets or villages composed of extended families and clans called **lineages.** Generally, one lineage occupied each village, although some large lineages peopled several villages. Each extended family descended from a common ancestor, and each lineage claimed descent from a mythical personage. Depending on the ethnic group involved, extended families and lineages were either patrilineal or matrilineal.

In extended families, **nuclear families** (husband, wife, and children) or in some cases **polygynous families** (husband, wives, and children) acted as economic units. Nuclear and polygynous families existed in the context of a broader family community composed of grandparents, aunts, uncles, and cousins. Elders in the extended family had great power over the economic and social lives of its members.

Villages tended to be larger on the savannah than in the forest. In both regions, people used forced earth or mud to construct small houses. A nuclear or polygynous family unit might have several houses. In nuclear households, the husband occupied the larger house and his wife the smaller. In polygynous households, the husband had the largest house, and his wives lived in smaller ones.

Villagers' few possessions included cots, rugs, stools, and wooden storage chests. Their tools and weapons included bows, spears, iron axes, hoes, and scythes. Households used grinding stones, woven baskets, and a variety of ceramic vessels to prepare and store food. Villagers in both the savannah and forest regions produced cotton for clothing.

Farming in West Africa was not easy. Drought was common on the savannah. In the forest, where diseases carried by the tsetse fly sickened draft animals, agricultural plots were limited in size because they had to be cleared by hand. The fields surrounding forest villages averaged just two or three acres per family. Although there was private ownership of land in West Africa, people generally worked land communally, dividing tasks by gender.

WOMEN

In general, men dominated women in West Africa. As previously noted, men often had two or more wives, and, to a degree, custom held women to be the property of men. But West African women also enjoyed an amount of freedom that impressed Arabs and Europeans. In ancient Ghana, women sometimes served as government officials. Later, in the forest region, they sometimes inherited property and owned land—or at least controlled its income. Women—including enslaved women—in the royal court of Dahomey held high government posts. Ashantee noblewomen could own property, although they themselves could be considered inheritable property. The Ashantee queen held her own court to administer women's affairs.

Women retained far more sexual freedom in West Africa than was the case in Europe or southwest Asia. Sexual freedom in West Africa was, however, more apparent than real. Throughout the region secret societies instilled in men and women ethical standards of personal behavior. The most important **secret societies** were the women's *Sande* and the men's *Poro*. They initiated boys and girls into adulthood and provided sex education. They also established standards for personal conduct, especially in regard to issues of gender, by emphasizing female virtue and male honor. Other secret societies influenced politics, trade, medical practice, recreation, and social gatherings.

CLASS AND SLAVERY

Although many West Africans lived in stateless societies, most lived in hierarchically organized states headed by monarchs who claimed divine or semidivine status. Most of these monarchs' power was far from absolute, but they commanded armies, taxed commerce, and accumulated considerable wealth. Beneath the royalty were classes of landed nobles, warriors, peasants, and bureaucrats. Lower classes included blacksmiths, butchers, weavers, woodcarvers, and tanners.

Slavery had been part of this hierarchical social structure since ancient times. Although very common throughout West Africa, slavery was less so in the forest region than on the savannah. It took many forms and was not necessarily a permanent condition. Like people in other parts of the world, West Africans held war captives—including men, women, and children—to be without rights and suitable for enslavement. In Islamic regions, masters had obligations to their slaves similar to those of a guardian for a ward and were responsible for their slaves' religious well-being. In non-Islamic regions, the children of slaves acquired legal protections, such as the right not to be sold away from the land they occupied.

Slaves who served either in the royal courts of a West African kingdom or in a kingdom's armies often exercised power over free people and could acquire property. Also, the slaves of peasant farmers often had standards of living similar to those of their masters. Slaves who worked under overseers in gangs on large estates were far less fortunate. However, the children and grandchildren of these enslaved agricultural workers, gained employment and privileges similar to those of free people. Slaves retained a low social status, but in many respects slavery in West African societies functioned as a means of **assimilation.**

RELIGION

There were two religious traditions in fifteenth-century West Africa: Islamic and indigenous. Islam, which Arab traders introduced into West Africa, took root first in the Sudanese empires and remained more prevalent in the cosmopolitan savannah. Even there it was stronger in cities than in rural areas because it was the religion of merchants and bureaucrats. Islam fostered literacy in Arabic, the spread of Islamic learning, and the construction of mosques. Islam is resolutely monotheistic, asserting that Allah is the only God. It recognizes its founder, Muhammad, as well as Abraham, Moses, and Jesus, as prophets but regards none of them as divine.

West Africa's indigenous religions remained strongest in the forest region. They were **polytheistic** and **animistic,** recognizing many divinities and spirits. Beneath an all-powerful but remote creator god, lesser gods represented the forces of nature or were associated with particular mountains, rivers, trees, and rocks. Indigenous West African religion, in other words, saw the force of God in all things.

In part because practitioners of West African indigenous religions perceived the creator god to be unapproachable, they invoked the spirits of their ancestors and turned to magicians and oracles for divine assistance. These rituals were part of everyday life, making organized churches and professional clergy rare. Instead, family members with an inclination to do so assumed religious duties. These individuals encouraged their relatives to participate in ceremonies that involved music, dancing, and animal sacrifice in honor of deceased ancestors. Funerals were especially important because they symbolized the linkage between living and dead.

ART AND MUSIC

As was the case in other parts of the world, religious belief and practice influenced West African art. West Africans, seeking to preserve the images of their ancestors, excelled in woodcarving and sculpture in **terra-cotta,** bronze, and brass. Throughout the region, artists produced wooden masks representing in highly stylized manners ancestral spirits and gods. Wooden and terra-cotta figurines, sometimes referred to as 'fetishes,' were also extremely common.

West African music also served religion. Folk musicians employed such instruments as drums, xylophones, bells, flutes, and mbanzas (predecessor to the banjo) to produce a highly rhythmic accompaniment to the dancing associated with religious rituals. A **call-and-response** style of singing also played a vital role in ritual. Vocal music, produced in a full-throated, but often raspy, style, had polyphonic textures and sophisticated rhythms.

LITERATURE: ORAL HISTORIES, POETRY, AND TALES

West African literature was part of an oral tradition that passed from generation to generation. At its most formal, it was a literature developed by specially trained poets and musicians who served kings and nobles. But West African literature was also a folk art that expressed the views of the common people.

At a king's court there could be several poet-musicians who had high status and specialized in poems glorifying rulers and their ancestors by linking fact and fiction. The self-employed poets, called *griots*, who traveled from place to place were socially inferior to court poets, but they functioned in a similar manner. Both court poets and griots were men. Women were more involved in folk literature. They joined men in creating and performing work songs. They led in creating and singing dirges, lullabies, and satirical verses.

Just as significant for African-American history were the West African prose tales. Like similar stories told in other parts of Africa, these tales took two forms: those with human characters and those with animal characters who represented humans. The tales centered on human characters dealing with such subjects as creation, the origins of death, paths to worldly success, and romantic love.

The animal tales aimed to entertain and teach lessons. They focused on small creatures, often referred to as 'trickster characters,' who were pitted against larger beasts. In West Africa, these tales represented the ability of common people to counteract the power of kings and nobles. When the tales reached America, they became allegories for the struggle between enslaved African Americans and their powerful white masters.

TECHNOLOGY

West African technology was also distinctive and important. Although much knowledge about this technology has been lost, iron refining and forging, textile production, architecture, and rice cultivation helped shape life in the region.

As previously mentioned, iron technology had existed in West Africa since ancient times. Blacksmiths produced tools for agriculture, weapons for hunting and war, and ceremonial staffs and religious amulets. These products encouraged the development of cities and kingdoms.

Architecture embodied Islamic and indigenous elements, with the former predominant on the savanna and the latter in the forest region. Building materials consisted of stone, mud, and wood. Public buildings reached large proportions, and some mosques served 3,000 worshippers. Massive stone or mud walls surrounded cities and towns.

Handlooms for household production existed throughout Africa for thousands of years, and cloth made from pounding bark persisted in the forest region into modern times. But trade and Islamic influences led to commercial textile production. By the ninth century CE, large looms, some equipped with peddles, produced narrow strips of wool or cotton. Men, rather than women, made cloth and tailored it into embroidered robes, shawls, hats, and blankets, which Muslim merchants traded over wide areas.

Of particular importance for African-American history, West Africans living along rivers in coastal regions had produced rice since approximately 1000 bce. Portuguese who arrived during the fifteenth century CE reported large diked rice fields. Deliberate flooding of these fields, transplanting sprouts, and intensive cultivation were practices that reemerged in the colonial South Carolina low country.

CONCLUSION

Although all of Africa contributed to their background, the history of African Americans begins in West Africa, the region from which the ancestors of most of them were unwillingly wrested. Historians have discovered, as subsequent chapters will show, that West Africans taken to America and their descendants in America preserved much more of their ancestral way of life than scholars once believed possible. West African family organization, work habits, language structures and some words, religious beliefs, legends and stories, pottery styles, art, and music all reached America. These African legacies, although often sharply modified, influenced the way African Americans and other Americans lived in their new land and continue to shape American life.

This is an Ashantee sword from West Africa. It is sheathed in a ray-skin cover and has a gold handle. Although this sword dates to early modern times, it is likely that Ashantee craftsmen constructed similar swords much earlier.

Events in Africa	World Events

• 10 MILLION YEARS AGO •

5–10 million years ago	**1.6 million years ago**
Separation of hominids from apes	*Homo erectus* beginning to spread through Eurasia
4 million years ago	
Emergence of *australopithecines*	
2.4 million years ago	
Emergence of *Homo habilis*	
1.7 million years ago	
Emergence of *Homo erectus*	

• 1.5 MILLION YEARS AGO •

100,000–200,000 years ago	**8000 BCE**
Appearance of modern humans	Appearance of the first agricultural settlements in southwest Asia
6000 BCE	
Beginning of Sahara Desert formation	

• 5000 BCE •

5000 BCE	**3500 BCE**
First agricultural settlements in Egypt	Sumerian civilization in Mesopotamia
3800 BCE	
Predynastic period in Egypt	
c. 3150 BCE	
Unification of Egypt	

• 2500 BCE •

2700–2150 BCE	**2300 BCE**
Egypt's Old Kingdom	Beginning of Indus Valley civilization
2100–1650 BCE	
Egypt's Middle Kingdom	

• 1500 BCE •

1550–700 BCE	**1600–1250 BCE**
Egypt's New Kingdom	Mycenaean Greek civilization
	c. 1500
	Beginning of Shang dynasty in China

1000 bce

750–670 bce
Rule of Kushites over Egypt

540 bce
Founding of Meroë

c. 540 bce
Beginning of iron smelting in West Africa

50 ce
Destruction of Kush

600–336 bce
Classical Greek civilization

500 ce

632–750 ce
Islamic conquest of North Africa

c. 750–1076 ce
Empire of Ghana; Islam begins to take root in West Africa

204 bce–476 ce
Domination of Mediterranean by Roman Republic and Empire

500–1350 ce
European Middle Ages

c. 570 ce
Birth of Muhammad

1200 ce

1230–1468 ce
Empire of Mali

c. 1300 ce
Rise of Yoruba states

1400 ce

1434 ce
Start of Portuguese exploration and establishment of trading outposts on West African coast

c. 1450 ce
Centralization of power in Benin

1464–1591 ce
Empire of Songhai

1492 ce
Christopher Columbus and European encounter of America

1517 ce
Reformation begins in Europe

1600 ce

c. 1650 ce
Rise of Kingdom of Dahomey and the Akan states
Events in Africa

1610 ce
Scientific revolution begins in Europe

World Events

Events in Africa — **World Events**

REVIEW QUESTIONS

1. What was the role of Africa in the evolution of modern humanity?
2. Discuss the controversy concerning the racial identity of the ancient Egyptians. What is the significance of this controversy for the history of African Americans?
3. Compare and contrast the western Sudanese empires with the forest civilizations of the Guinea Coast.
4. Discuss the role of religion in West Africa. What was the African religious heritage of black Americans?
5. Describe West African society on the eve of the expansion of the Atlantic slave trade. What were the society's strengths and weaknesses?

PEARSON myhistorylab CONNECTIONS

Reinforce what you learned in this chapter by studying the many documents, images, maps, review tools, and videos available at **www.myhistorylab.com.**

READ AND REVIEW

✓•─│Study and **Review** on **myhistorylab.com** STUDY PLAN FOR CHAPTER 1

▢●─│Read the **Document** on **myhistorylab.com**

     A Tenth-Century Arab Description of the East African Coast

     Ghana and Its People in the Mid-Eleventh Century

     Herodotus on Carthaginian Trade and on the City of Meroe

     Job Hortop and the British Enter the Slave Trade, 1567

     Leo Africanus' Description of West Africa (1500)

     Muslim Reform in Songhai

🔍─│View the **Map** on **myhistorylab.com**

     Africa Climate Regions and Early Sites

RESEARCH AND EXPLORE

mysearchlab

     Consider these questions in a short research paper.

     What were the key features of West African society and culture? What place did slavery have in that society?

((•—Listen on **myhistorylab.com**

Ghana: Ewe-Atsiagbekor from Roots of Black Music in America

●—**Watch** the **Video** on **myhistorylab.com**

Africa as an Urban, Not Rural, Place

West African States

States, Societies, and Cities in Medieval West Africa

———————— ((•—**Listen** on **myhistorylab.com** ————————

Hear the audio files for Chapter 1 at
www.myhistorylab.com.

Middle Passage •• *1450–1809*

((•─Listen on **myhistorylab.com**

Hear the audio files for Chapter 2 at **www.myhistorylab.com.**

FOCUS QUESTIONS

HOW DID the arrival of the Europeans affect Africa?

HOW DID the slave trade in Africa differ from the Atlantic slave trade?

WHAT WAS the "Middle Passage"?

WHAT HAPPENED to Africans after they crossed the Atlantic?

HOW WERE slaves treated in the Americas?

WHY DID the Atlantic slave trade end?

After Great Britain banned the Atlantic slave trade in 1807, British warships enforced the ban. The people portrayed in this early nineteenth-century woodcut were rescued from a slave ship by the H.M.S. *Undine.*

The Atlantic slave trade inflicted great sorrow and loss on those Africans it tore from their homelands. This huge enterprise, which lasted for more than three centuries, brought millions of Africans 3,000 miles across the Atlantic Ocean to the Americas. It was the largest forced migration in history. By the eighteenth century, the voyage across the ocean in European ships called "slavers" had become known as the "**Middle Passage**." British sailors coined this innocuous phrase to describe the middle leg of a triangular journey first from England to Africa, then from Africa to the Americas, and finally from the Americas back to England. Yet today Middle Passage denotes an unbelievable descent into an earthly hell of cruelty and suffering. It was from the Middle Passage that the first African Americans emerged.

This chapter describes the Atlantic slave trade and the Middle Passage. It explores their origins both in European colonization in the Americas and in the slave trade that had existed in Africa itself for centuries. It focuses on the experience of the enslaved people whom the trade brought to America.

THE EUROPEAN AGE OF EXPLORATION AND COLONIZATION

The origins of the Atlantic slave trade and its long duration were products of Western Europe's expansion of power that began during the fifteenth century and continued into the twentieth century. For a variety of economic, technological, and demographic reasons, Portugal, Spain, the Netherlands, France, England, and other nations sought to explore, conquer, and colonize in Africa, Asia, and the Americas.

Portugal took the lead during the early 1400s when its ships reached Africa's western coast. Portuguese captains hoped to find Christian allies there against the Muslims of North Africa and to spread Christianity. But they were more interested in trade with African kingdoms, as were the Spanish, Dutch, English, and French who followed them.

Even more attractive than Africa to the Portuguese and their European successors as sources of trade and wealth were India, China, Japan, and the East Indies (modern Indonesia and Malaysia). In 1487 the Portuguese explorer Bartolomeu Dias discovered the Cape of Good Hope at the southern tip of Africa and thereby established that it was possible to sail around Africa to reach India and regions to its east. Ten years later Vasco da Gama initiated this route on behalf of Portuguese commerce. A similar desire to reach these eastern regions motivated the Spanish monarchy to finance Christopher Columbus's westward voyages that began in 1492.

Columbus, who believed the earth to be much smaller than it actually is, hoped to reach Japan or India by sailing west. Columbus's mistake led to his accidental landfall in the Americas. Columbus and those who followed him quickly enslaved indigenous Americans (American Indians) as laborers in fields and mines. Almost as quickly, many indigenous peoples either died of European diseases and overwork or escaped beyond the reach of European power. Consequently, European colonizers needed additional laborers. This demand for a workforce in the Americas caused the Atlantic slave trade.

THE SLAVE TRADE IN AFRICA

Slave labor was not peculiar to the European colonies in the Americas. Slavery and slave trading had existed in all cultures for thousands of years. As Chapter 1 indicates, slavery was common in West Africa, although it was usually less oppressive than it became in the Americas.

When Portuguese voyagers first arrived at Senegambia, Benin, and Kongo, they found a thriving commerce in slaves. These kingdoms represented the southern extremity of an extensive trade conducted by Islamic nations that involved the capture and sale of Europeans and North African Berbers, as well as black people from south of the Sahara Desert.

In West Africa, Sudanese horsemen conducted the Islamic slave trade. The horsemen invaded the forest region to capture people who could not effectively resist—often they belonged to stateless societies. The trade dealt mainly in women and children, who as slaves were destined for lives as concubines and domestic servants in North Africa and southwest Asia. This pattern contrasted with that of the later Atlantic slave trade, which primarily sought young men for agricultural labor in the Americas (Figure 2-1).

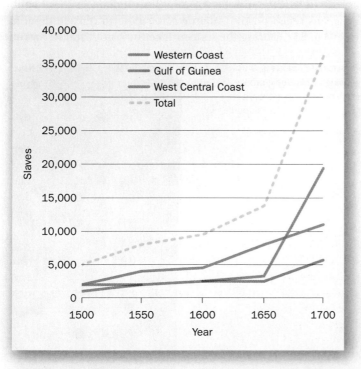

FIGURE 2-1 • Estimated Annual Exports of Slaves from Western Africa to the Americas, 1500–1700
Source: John Thornton, Africa and Africans in the Making of the Atlantic World, 1400–1680 (New York: Cambridge University Press, 1992), 118.

THE ORIGINS OF THE ATLANTIC SLAVE TRADE

When Portuguese ships first arrived off the **Guinea Coast**, their captains traded chiefly for gold, ivory, and pepper, but they also wanted slaves. Usually the Portuguese and the other European and white Americans who succeeded them did not capture and enslave people themselves. Instead they purchased slaves from African traders. This arrangement began formally in 1472 when the Portuguese merchant Ruy do Siqueira gained permission from the Oba (king) of Benin to trade for slaves, as well as gold and ivory, within the borders of the Oba's kingdom.

Interethnic rivalries in West Africa led to the warfare that produced these slaves during the sixteenth century. Although Africans were initially reluctant to sell members of their own ethnic group to Europeans, they did not at first consider it wrong to sell members of their own race to foreigners. In fact, neither Africans nor Europeans had yet developed a concept of racial solidarity. By the eighteenth century, however, at least the victims of the trade believed that such solidarity *should* exist. Ottobah Cugoano, who had been captured and sold during that century, wrote, "I must own to the shame of my countrymen that I was first kidnapped and betrayed by [those of] my own complexion."

Until the early sixteenth century, Portuguese seafarers conducted the Atlantic slave trade on a tiny scale to satisfy a limited market for domestic servants in Portugal and Spain. Other European countries had no demand for slaves because their workforces were already too large. But the impact of Columbus's voyages drastically changed the trade. The Spanish and the Portuguese—followed by the Dutch, English, and French—established colonies in the Caribbean, Mexico, and Central and South America. Because disease and overwork caused the number of American Indians in these regions rapidly to decline, Europeans relied on the Atlantic slave trade to replace them as a source of slave labor (see Map 2-1). During the sixteenth century, gold and silver mines

West African artists recorded the appearance of Europeans who came to trade in gold, ivory, and human beings. This Benin bronze relief sculpture, dating to the late sixteenth or early seventeenth century, portrays two Portuguese men. Werner Forman, Art Resource, NY

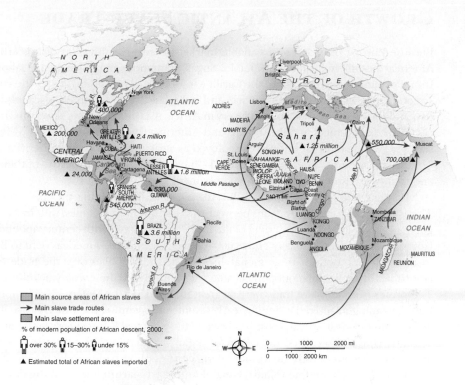

MAP 2-1 • The Atlantic and Islamic Slave Trades Not until 1600 did the Atlantic slave trade reach the proportions of the Islamic slave trade. The map shows the principal sources of slaves, primary routes, and major destinations.

▶ *According to* this map, which region in the Americas imported the most slaves?

TABLE 2.1 Estimated Slave Imports by Destination, 1451–1870

Destination	Total Slave Imports
British North America	500,000
Spanish America	2,500,000
British Caribbean	2,000,000
French Caribbean	1,600,000
Dutch Caribbean	500,000
Danish Caribbean	28,000
Brazil	4,000,000
Old World	200,000

SOURCE: Hugh Thomas, *The Slave Trade: The Story of the Atlantic Slave Trade,* 1440–1870 (New York: Simon & Schuster, 1997), 804.

in Spanish Mexico and Peru and especially sugar plantations in Portuguese Brazil produced an enormous demand for labor. The Atlantic slave trade grew to huge and tragic proportions to meet that demand (see Table 2-1).

GROWTH OF THE ATLANTIC SLAVE TRADE

Because Europe provided an insatiable market for sugar, cultivation of this crop in the Americas became extremely profitable. Sugar plantations employing slave labor spread from Portuguese-ruled Brazil to the Caribbean islands (West Indies). Later the cultivation of coffee in Brazil and of tobacco, rice, and **indigo** in British North America added to the demand for African slaves. Unlike slavery in Africa, Asia, and Europe, slavery in the Americas was based on race, as only Africans and American Indians were enslaved. Most of the slaves were men or boys, who were employed as agricultural laborers rather than soldiers or domestic servants. They became **chattel**—meaning personal property—of their masters and lost their customary rights as human beings.

Portugal and Spain dominated the Atlantic slave trade during the sixteenth century. They shipped about 2,000 Africans per year to their American colonies, with by far the most going to Brazil. From the beginning of the trade until its nineteenth-century abolition, about 6,500,000 of the approximately 11,328,000 Africans taken to the Americas went to Brazil and Spain's colonies. Both of these monarchies granted monopolies over the trade to private companies. In Spain the monopoly became known in 1518 as the *Asiento* (meaning contract). The profits from the slave trade were so great that by 1550 the Dutch, French, and English were becoming involved. During the early seventeenth century, the Dutch drove the Portuguese from the West African coast and became the principal European slave-trading nation.

The Dutch also shifted the center of sugar production to the West Indies. England and France followed, with the former taking control of Barbados and Jamaica and the latter taking Saint Domingue (Haiti), Guadeloupe, and Martinique. With the development of tobacco as a **cash crop** in Virginia and Maryland during the 1620s and with the continued expansion of sugar production in the West Indies, the demand for African slaves grew. The result was that England and France competed with the Dutch to control the Atlantic slave trade. After a series of wars, England emerged supreme. After 1713, English ships dominated the slave trade, carrying about 20,000 slaves per year from Africa to the Americas. At the peak of the trade during the 1790s, they transported 50,000 per year.

The profits from the Atlantic slave trade, together with those from the sugar and tobacco produced in the Americas by slave labor, were invested in England and helped fund the **Industrial Revolution** during the eighteenth century. In turn, Africa became a market for cheap English manufactured goods (see Map 2-2). Eventually, two triangular trade systems developed. In one, traders carried English goods to West Africa and exchanged the goods for slaves. Then the traders carried the slaves to the West Indies and exchanged them for sugar, which they took back to England on the third leg of the triangle. In the other triangular trade, white Americans from Britain's New England colonies carried rum to West Africa to trade for slaves. From Africa they took the slaves to the West Indies to exchange for sugar or molasses—sugar syrup—which they then took home to distill into rum.

THE AFRICAN-AMERICAN ORDEAL FROM CAPTURE TO DESTINATION

Recent scholarship indicates that the availability of large numbers of slaves in West Africa resulted from the warfare that accompanied the formation of states in that region. Captives suitable for enslavement were a by-product of these wars. The European traders

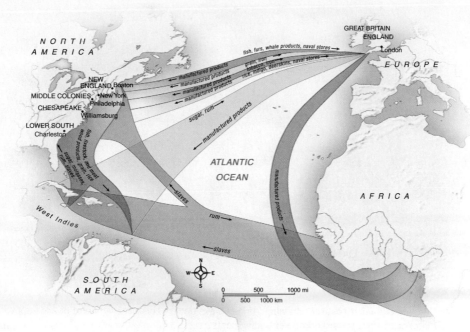

MAP 2-2 • Atlantic Trade among the Americas, Great Britain, and West Africa during the Seventeenth and Eighteenth Centuries Often referred to as a triangular trade, this map shows the complexity of early modern Atlantic commerce, of which the slave trade was a major part.

▶ *What does* this map suggest about the economy of the Atlantic world between 1600 and 1800?

provided the aggressors with firearms but did not instigate the wars. Instead they used the wars to enrich themselves.

Sometimes African armies enslaved the inhabitants of conquered towns and villages. At other times, raiding parties captured isolated families or kidnapped individuals. As warfare spread to the interior, captives had to march for hundreds of miles to the coast where European traders awaited them. Once the captives reached the coast, those destined for the Atlantic trade went to fortified structures called **factories**. Portuguese traders constructed the first factory at Elmina on the Guinea Coast in 1481—the Dutch captured it in 1637. Such factories contained the headquarters of the traders, warehouses for their trade goods and supplies, and dungeons or outdoor holding pens for the captives. In these pens, slave traders divided families and—as much as possible—ethnic groups to prevent rebellion. The traders stripped captives naked and inspected them for disease and physical defects. Those considered fit for purchase were branded like cattle with a hot iron bearing the symbol of a trading company.

THE CROSSING

After being held in a factory for weeks or months, captives faced the frightening prospect of leaving their native land for a voyage across an ocean that many of them had never before seen. Sailors rowed them out in large canoes to slave ships

In this late-eighteenth-century drawing, African slave traders conduct a group of bound captives from the interior of Africa toward European trading posts.

offshore. One English trader recalled that during the 1690s "the negroes were so wilful and loth to leave their own country, that they often leap'd out of the canoos, boat and ship, into the sea, and kept under water till they were drowned."

The passage normally lasted between two and three months. But the time required for the crossing varied widely. The larger ships were able to reach the Caribbean in 40 days, but voyages could take as long as six months. Both human and natural causes accounted for such delays. During the three centuries that the Atlantic slave trade endured, Western European nations often fought each other, and slave ships became prized targets. There were also such potentially disastrous natural forces as doldrums—long windless spells at sea—and hurricanes, which could destroy ships, crews, and cargoes.

THE SLAVERS AND THEIR TECHNOLOGY

Slave ships (called **slavers**) varied in size but grew larger over the centuries. A ship's size, measured in tonnage, determined how many slaves it could carry, with the formula being two slaves per ton. A ship of 200 tons might therefore carry 400 slaves. But captains often ignored the formula. Some kept their human cargo light, calculating that smaller loads lowered mortality and made revolt less likely. But most captains were "tight packers," who squeezed human beings together in hope that large numbers would offset increased deaths.

The slavers' cargo space was generally only five feet high. Ships' carpenters halved this vertical space by building shelves, so slaves might be packed above and below on planks that measured only 5.5 feet long and 1.3 feet wide. Consequently, slaves had only about 20 to 25 inches of headroom. To add to the discomfort, the crews chained male slaves together in pairs to help prevent rebellion and lodged them away from women and children.

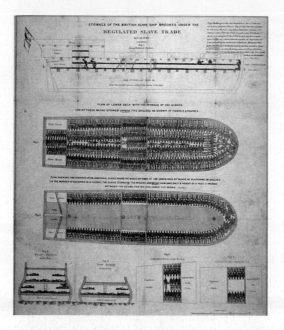

Plan of the British slave ship *Brookes*, 1788. This plan, which may undercount the human cargo the *Brookes* carried, shows how tightly Africans were packed aboard slave ships.

Mortality rates were high because the crowded, unsanitary conditions encouraged seaboard epidemics. Overall, one-third of the Africans subjected to the trade perished between their capture and their embarkation on a slave ship. Another third died during the Middle Passage or during "seasoning" on a Caribbean island. It would have been slight consolation to the enslaved to learn that because of the epidemics, the rate of death among slaver crews was proportionally higher than their own.

As historian Marcus Rediker notes, by the eighteenth century Europeans regarded slavers as "useful machines." The large three-masted, and full-rigged vessels, with their "cast-iron cannon ... harnessed unparalleled mobility, speed, and destructive power." By 1750 shipbuilders in Liverpool built slavers to order. The ships combined varieties of wood to produce strength, flexibility, and resistance to tropical ship worms that could bore into hulls. By 1800 they used copper sheathing to provide better protection below water. They used lattice doors, portholes, and fun-nels to ventilate slave quarters, which became healthier as time passed. They also maintained a special "hardware of bondage," including iron manacles, shackles, collars, branding implements, and thumbscrews.

A SLAVE'S STORY

In his book *The Interesting Narrative of the Life of Olaudah Equiano or Gustavus Vassa, the African*, published in 1789, former slave Olaudah Equiano provides a vivid account of a West African's capture, sale to traders, and voyage to America in 1755. Although recently discovered evidence suggests that Equiano *may* have been born in South Carolina rather than West Africa, scholars continue to respect the accuracy of his account. He tells the story of a young Igbo, the dominant ethnic group in what is today southern Nigeria. African slave raiders capture him when he is ten years old and force him to march along with other captives to the Niger River or one of its tributaries, where they trade

Portrait of a Negro man, Olaudah Equiano, 1780s (previously attributed to Joshua Reynolds) by English School (eighteenth century).

him to other Africans. His new captors take him to the coast and sell him to European slave traders whose ships sail to the West Indies.

The boy's experience at the coastal slave factory convinces him he has entered a sort of hell, peopled by evil spirits. The stench caused by forcing many people to live in close confinement makes him nauseated and emotionally agitated. His African and European captors try to calm him with liquor. But because he is not accustomed to alcohol, he becomes disoriented and more convinced of his impending doom. When the sailors lodge him with others below deck on the ship, he is so sick that he loses his appetite and hopes to die. Instead, because he refuses to eat, the sailors take him on deck and whip him.

During the time the ship is in port awaiting a full cargo of slaves, the boy spends much time on deck. After putting to sea, however, he usually remains below deck with the other slaves where "each had scarcely room to turn himself." There, the smells of unwashed bodies and of the toilet tubs, "into which the children often fell and were almost suffocated," create a loathsome atmosphere. The darkness, the chafing of chains on human flesh, the shrieks and groans of the sick and disoriented provide "a scene of horror almost inconceivable."

When slaves are allowed to get some fresh air and exercise on deck, the crew strings up nets to prevent them from jumping overboard. Even so, two Africans, who are chained together, evade the nets and jump into the ocean, preferring drowning to staying on board. The boy shares their desperation. Depression among the Africans led to a catatonia that contemporary observers called melancholy or extreme nostalgia. Alexander Falconbridge, a slave ship's surgeon, noted that the slaves had "a strong attachment to their native country" and a "just sense of the value of liberty."

Although the traders, seeking to lessen the possibility of shipboard conspiracy and rebellion, separated individuals who spoke the same language, the boy described by Equiano manages to find adults who speak Igbo. They explain to him the purpose of the voyage, which he learns is to go to the white people's country to labor for them. He does not realize that work on a West Indian island could be a death sentence.

Venture Smith

Born Broteer Furro, Venture Smith's journey in and out of slavery began in 1737 with his capture at age eight. Put on board a slave ship at Anomabu, in present-day Ghana, with some 260 other Africans, he was taken to Barbados. Almost a quarter of the slaves who began the voyage did not live to see the West Indies. If Smith had been sold in Barbados to the owner of a sugar plantation, as were many of his shipmates, we likely would have never heard from him again. Hardship, disease, and grinding labor meant that life expectancy for a slave in the cane fields was no more than a few years. As it happened, he was purchased by Robertson Mumford and taken to the Mumford's residence on Fishers Island in Connecticut.

◄ The title page of Venture Smith's narrative on his life. The Connecticut Historical Society, Hartford.

Smith did not settle easily into his new role as a slave in British North America. He married at age twenty-two and had three children, but as long as he was a slave his life had little stability. He was sold three times and made at least one escape attempt. However, by 1765 he had saved enough money to buy his freedom. Over the next ten years, he purchased the freedom of his wife and his children. His son, Cuff Smith, served as a soldier in the Continental Army during the Revolutionary War. In 1798, he told his remarkable life story

This detail from "A new and accurate map of ► the English empire in North America" (1755) includes the critical stops in the Atlantic trade, stops that were also part of venture Smith's journey.

to Elisha Niles, a Connecticut school teacher, who published it. Venture Smith died in 1805.

> The subject of the following pages, had he received only a common education, might have been a man of high respectability and usefulness; and had his education been suited to his genius, he might have been an ornament and an honor to human nature. It may perhaps, not be unpleasing to see the efforts of a great mind wholly uncultivated, enfeebled and depressed by slavery, and struggling under every disadvantage. The reader may here see a Franklin and a Washington, in a state of nature, or rather, in a state of slavery. Destitute as he is of all education, he still exhibits striking traces of native ingenuity and good sense.
>
> —Elisha Niles, from the Introduction

> I am now sixty nine years old. Though once strait and tall, measuring without shoes six feet one inch and an half, and every way well proportioned, I am now bowed down with age and hardship.... But amidst all my griefs and pains, I have many consolations; Meg, the wife of my youth, whom I married for love, and bought with my money, is still alive. My freedom is a privilege which nothing else can equal.... I am now possessed of more than one hundred acres of land, and three habitable dwelling houses. It gives me joy to think that I *have* and that I *deserve* so good a character, especially for *truth* and *integrity*. While I am now looking to the grave as my home, my joy for this world would be full-IF my children, Cuff for whom I paid two hundred dollars when a boy, and Solomon who was born soon after I purchased his mother—If Cuff and Solomon—O! that they had walked in the way of their father. But a father's lips are closed in silence and in grief!—Vanity of vanities, all is vanity!
>
> —Ventura Smith, last paragraph of his narrative

From "*A Narrative of the Life and Adventures of Venture, a Native of Africa, But Resident Above Sixty Years in the United States of America, Related By Himself, Venture Smith.*" (1798).

What lessons might Elisha Niles have hoped readers would draw from Smith's life story? Do we hear Smith's voice in the passage from his conclusion, or Niles'? How can we tell?

A CAPTAIN'S STORY

John Newton, a white captain of a slave ship, who was born in London in 1725, provides another perspective on the Middle Passage. In 1745 Newton, as an **indentured servant**, joined the crew of a slaver bound for Sierra Leone. Indentured servants lost their freedom for a specified number of years, either because they sold it or because they were being punished for debt or crime.

Newton was 25 when he became captain of the *Duke of Argyle*, an old 140-ton vessel that he converted into a slaver after it sailed from Liverpool on August 11, 1750. Near the Cape Verde Islands, off the coast of Senegambia, carpenters began making the alterations required for packing many Africans below deck. Newton also put the ship's guns and ammunition in order to protect against pirates or African resistance. On October 23 the *Duke of Argyle* reached Frenchman's Bay, Sierra Leone, where Newton observed other ships from England, France, and New England anchored offshore. Two days later, Newton purchased two men and a woman from traders at the port, but he had to sail to several other ports to accumulate a full cargo. Leaving West Africa on May 23, 1751, for the open sea, the ship delivered its slave to Antigua in the West Indies on July 3.

Poor health forced Newton to retire from the slave trade in 1754. Ten years later he became an Anglican priest, and from 1779 until his death in 1807 served as rector of St. Mary Woolnoth Church in London. By the late 1770s, Newton had repented his involvement in the slave trade and had become one of its leading opponents. Together with William Cowper—a renowned poet—Newton published the *Olney Hymns* in 1779. Among the selections included in this volume was "Amazing Grace," which Newton wrote as a reflection on divine forgiveness for his sins.

PROVISIONS FOR THE MIDDLE PASSAGE

Slave ships left Liverpool and other European ports provisioned with food supplies for their crews. When the ships reached the **Guinea Coast** in West Africa, their captains purchased pepper, palm oil, lemons, limes, yams, plantains, and coconuts. Because slaves were not accustomed to European foods, the ships needed these staples of the African diet. The crew usually fed the slaves twice per day in shifts. Cooks prepared vegetable pulps, porridge, and stews for the crew to distribute in buckets as the slaves assembled on deck during good weather or below deck during storms. At the beginning of the voyage, each slave received a wooden spoon for dipping into the buckets, which about ten individuals shared. But in the confined confusion below deck, slaves often lost their spoons. They then had to eat from the buckets with their unwashed hands, which spread disease.

Although slaver captains realized it was in their interest to feed their human cargoes well, they often skimped on supplies to save money and make room for more slaves. Therefore, the food on a slave ship was often insufficient to prevent malnutrition and weakened immune systems among people already traumatized by separation from their families and homelands. As a result, many Africans died during the Middle Passage from diseases amid the horrid conditions that were normal aboard the slave ships. Others died from depression: they refused to eat, despite the crews' efforts to force food down their throats.

Sanitation, Disease, and Death

Diseases such as malaria, yellow fever, measles, smallpox, hookworm, scurvy, and dysentery constantly threatened African cargoes and European crews during the Middle Passage. Death rates were astronomical on board the slave ships before 1750. Mortality dropped after that date because ships became faster and ships' surgeons knew more about hygiene and diet. There were also early forms of vaccinations against smallpox, which may have been the worst killer of slaves on ships. But, even after 1750, poor sanitation led to many deaths.

Usually slavers provided only three or four toilet tubs below deck for enslaved Africans to use during the Middle Passage. They had to struggle among themselves to get to the tubs, and children had a particularly difficult time. Those who were too ill to reach the tubs excreted where they lay, and diseases such as dysentery, which are spread by human waste, thrived. Alexander Falconbridge reported that during one dysentery epidemic, "The deck, that is, the floor of [the slaves'] rooms, was so covered with blood and mucus which had proceeded from them in consequence of the flux, that it resembled a slaughter-house.

John Newton's stark, unimpassioned records of slave deaths aboard the *Duke of Argyle* indicate even more about how the Atlantic slave trade devalued human life. Newton recorded deaths at sea only by number. He wrote in his journal, "Bury'd a man slave No. 84 ... bury'd a woman slave, No. 47." Yet Newton probably was more conscientious than other slaver captains in seeking to avoid disease. During his 1750 voyage, he noted only eleven deaths. These included ten slaves—five men, one woman, three boys, and one girl—and one crewman. Compared with the usual high mortality rates, this was an achievement.

What role ships' surgeons—general practitioners in modern terminology—played in preventing or inadvertently encouraging deaths aboard slave ships is difficult to determine. Many surgeons recognized that African remedies were more likely than European medications to alleviate the slaves' illnesses. The surgeons collected herbs and foods along the Guinea Coast. They also learned African nursing techniques, which they found more effective in treating on-board diseases than European procedures. What the surgeons did not understand, and regarded as superstition, was the holistic nature of African medicine. African healers maintained that body, mind, and spirit were interconnected elements of the totality of a person's well-being. The enslaved Africans were often just as dumbfounded by the beliefs and actions of their captors. They thought they had entered a world of bad spirits when they boarded a slaver, and they attempted to counteract the spirits with rituals from their homeland.

Resistance and Revolt at Sea

Because many enslaved Africans refused to accept their fate, slaver captains had to be vigilant. Uprisings were common. Most such rebellions took place while a ship prepared to set sail, the African coast was in sight, and the slaves could still hope to return home. But some revolts occurred on the open sea where it was unlikely the Africans, even if their revolt succeeded, could return to their homes or regain their freedom. Both sorts of revolt indicate that not even capture, forced march to the coast, imprisonment,

VOICES

DYSENTERY (OR THE BLOODY FLUX)

Alexander Falconbridge (d. 1792) served as ship's surgeon on four British slavers between 1780 and 1787. In 1788 he became an opponent of the trade and published An Account of the Slave Trade on the Coast of Africa. *Here he describes in gruesome detail conditions in slave quarters during a dysentery epidemic, which he mistakenly attributes to stale air and heat.*

Some wet and blowing weather having occasioned the port-holes to be shut, and the grating to be covered, fluxes and fevers among the Negroes ensued. While they were in this situation, my profession requiring it, I frequently went down among them, till at length their apartments became so extremely hot, as to be only sufferable for a very short time…. It is not in the power of the human imagination, to picture to itself a situation more dreadful or disgusting. Numbers of the slaves having fainted, they were carried upon deck, where several of them died, and the rest were, with great difficulty, restored….

The place allotted for the sick Negroes is under the half deck, where they lie on the bare planks. By this means, those who are emaciated, frequently have their skin, and even their flesh, entirely rubbed off, by the motion of the ship, from the prominent parts of the shoulders, elbows, and hips, so as to render the bones in those parts quite bare. And some of them, by constantly lying in the blood and mucus, that had flowed from those afflicted with the flux, and which … is generally so violent as to prevent their being kept clean, have their flesh much sooner rubbed off, than those who have only to contend with the mere friction of the ship. The excruciating pain which the poor sufferers feel from being obliged to continue in such a dreadful situation, frequently for several weeks, in case they happen to live so long, is not to be conceived or described. Few, indeed, are ever able to withstand the fatal effects of it. The utmost skill of the surgeon is here ineffectual….

The surgeon, upon going between decks, in the morning, to examine the situation of the slaves, frequently finds several dead; and among the men, sometimes a dead and living Negroe fastened by their irons together. When this is the case, they are brought upon the deck, and being laid on the grating, the living Negroe is disengaged, and the dead one thrown overboard….

Could slave traders have avoided the suffering described in this passage?

What impact would such suffering have had on those who survived it?

SOURCE: Alexander Falconbridge, *An Account of the Slave Trade on the Coast of Africa* (London: privately printed, 1788), in John H. Bracey Jr. and Manisha Sinha, *African American Mosaic: A Documentary History from the Slave Trade to the Twenty-first Century* (Upper Saddle River, NJ: Prentice Hall, 2004), 1: 24.

branding, and sale could break the spirit of many captives. These Africans preferred to face death rather than accept bondage.

Other slaves resisted their captors by drowning or starving themselves. Thomas Phillips, captain of the slaver *Hannibal* during the 1690s, commented, "We had about 12 negroes did wilfully drown themselves and others starved themselves to death; for 'tis their belief that when they die they return home to their own country and friends again." Captains used nets to prevent deliberate drowning. To deal with starvation, they used hot coals or a metal device called a *speculum oris* to force individuals to open their mouths for feeding.

CRUELTY

The Atlantic slave trade required more capital than any other maritime commerce during the seventeenth and eighteenth centuries. The investments for the ships, the exceptionally large crews they employed, the navigational equipment, the armaments, the purchase of slaves in Africa, and the supplies of food and water to feed hundreds of passengers were phenomenal. The aim was to carry as many Africans in healthy condition to the Americas as possible in order to make the large profits that justified such expenditures. Yet, as we have indicated, conditions aboard the vessels were abysmal.

Scholars have debated how much deliberate cruelty the enslaved Africans suffered from ships' crews. The West Indian historian Eric Williams asserts that the horrors of the Middle Passage have been exaggerated. Many writers, Williams contends, are led astray by the writings of those who, during the late eighteenth and early nineteenth centuries, sought to abolish the slave trade. In his view—and that of other historians—the difficulties of the Middle Passage were similar to those experienced by European indentured servants who suffered high mortality rates on the voyage to America.

From this perspective the primary cause of death at sea on all ships carrying passengers across the Atlantic Ocean to the Americas was epidemic disease, against which medical practitioners had few tools before the twentieth century. Contributing factors included inadequate means of preserving food from spoilage and failure to prevent fresh water from becoming contaminated during the long ocean crossing. According to Williams, overcrowding by slavers was only a secondary cause for the high mortality rates.

Such observations help place conditions aboard the slave ships in a broader perspective. Cruelty and suffering are, to some degree, historically relative in that practices acceptable in the past are now considered inhumane. Yet cruelty aboard slavers must also be placed in a cultural context. Cultures distinguish between what constitutes acceptable behavior to their own people, on the one hand, and to strangers, on the other. For Europeans, Africans were cultural strangers, and what became normal in the Atlantic slave trade was in fact exceptionally cruel compared to how Europeans treated each other. And as strangers, Africans were subject to brutalization by European crew members who often cared little about the physical and emotional damage they inflicted.

AFRICAN WOMµ SLAVE SHIPS

For similar reasons, African women did not enjoy the same protection against unwanted sexual attention from European men that European women received. Consequently,

This nineteenth-century engraving suggests the humiliation Africans endured as they were subjected to physical inspections before being sold.

sailors during long voyages attempted to sate their sexual appetites with enslaved women. African women caught in the Atlantic slave trade were worth half the price of African men in Caribbean markets, and as a result, captains took fewer of them on board their vessels. Perhaps because the women were less valuable commodities, crew members felt they had license to abuse them sexually. The separate below-deck compartments for women on slave ships also made them easier targets than they otherwise might have been.

LANDING AND SALE IN THE WEST INDIES

As a slaver neared the West Indies, the crew prepared its human cargo for landing and sale. They allowed the slaves to shave, wash with fresh water, and take more vigorous exercise. Those bound for the larger Caribbean islands or for the British colonies of southern North America often received some weeks of rest in the easternmost islands of the West Indies. French slave traders typically rested their slave passengers on **Martinique**. The English preferred **Barbados**. Sale to white plantation owners followed. Then began a period of what the planters called "seasoning," up to two years of acculturating slaves and breaking them in to plantation routines.

The process of landing and sale that ended the Middle Passage was often as protracted as the events that began it in Africa. After anchoring at one of the Lesser Antilles Islands—Barbados, St. Kitts, or Antigua—English slaver captains haggled with the agents of local planters over numbers and prices. They then determined whether to sell all their slaves at their first port of call, sell some of them, sail to another island, or sail to such North American ports as Charleston, Williamsport, or Baltimore.

Often, captains and crew had to do more to prepare slaves for sale than allow them to clean themselves and exercise. The ravages of cruelty, confinement, and disease could not be easily remedied. Slaves were required to oil their bodies to conceal blemishes, rashes, and bruises. Ships' surgeons used hemp to plug the anuses of those suffering from dysentery in order to block the bloody discharge the disease caused.

The humiliation continued as the slaves went to market. Once again they suffered close physical inspection from potential buyers. Unless a single purchaser agreed to buy an entire cargo of slaves, auctions took place either on deck or in sale yards on shore. However, some captains employed "the scramble." In these barbaric spectacles, the captain established standard prices for men, women, and children, herded the Africans together in a corral, and then allowed buyers to rush pell-mell among them to grab and rope together the slaves they desired.

SEASONING

Seasoning followed sale. On Barbados, Jamaica, and other Caribbean islands, planters divided slaves into three categories: **Creoles** (slaves born in the Americas), old Africans (those who had lived in the Americas for some time), and new Africans (those who had just survived the Middle Passage). Creole slaves were worth three times the value of unseasoned new Africans. Seasoning began the process of making new Africans more like Creoles.

In the West Indies, this process involved not only an apprenticeship in the work routines of the sugar plantations on the islands. It also prepared many slaves for resale to North American planters, who preferred "seasoned" slaves to "unbroken" ones who came directly from Africa. Seasoning was a disciplinary process intended to modify the behavior and attitude of slaves and make them effective laborers.

As part of this process, the slaves' new masters gave them new names: Christian names, generic African names, or names from classical Greece and Rome (such as Jupiter, Achilles, or Plato). The seasoning process also involved slaves learning European languages. Masters in the Spanish islands of the Caribbean were especially thorough teachers. Consequently, although Spanish-speaking African slaves and their descendants retained African words, they could be easily understood by any Spanish-speaking person. In the French and English Caribbean islands and in parts of North America, however, slave society produced Creole dialects that in grammar, vocabulary, and intonation had distinctive African linguistic features.

During seasoning, masters or overseers broke slaves into plantation work by assigning them to one of several work gangs. The strongest men joined the first gang, or "great gang," which did the heavy fieldwork of planting and harvesting. The second gang, including women and older men, did lighter fieldwork, such as weeding. The third gang, composed of children, worked shorter hours and performed such tasks as bringing food and water to the field gangs. Other slaves became domestic servants. New Africans served apprenticeships with old Africans from their same ethnic group or with Creoles. Some planters looked for cargoes of young people, anticipating that they might be more easily acculturated than older Africans.

Planters had to rely on old Africans and Creoles to train new recruits because white people were a minority in the Caribbean. Later, a similar demographic pattern developed in parts of the cotton-producing American South. In both regions, therefore, African custom shaped the cooperative labor of slaves in gangs. But the use of old Africans and Creoles as instructors and the appropriation of African styles of labor should not suggest leniency. Although the plantation overseers, who ran day-to-day operations, could be white, of mixed race, or black, they invariably imposed strict discipline. Drivers, who directed the work gangs, were almost always black, but they carried whips and frequently punished those who worked too slowly or showed disrespect. Planters assigned recalcitrant new Africans to the strictest overseers and drivers.

Planters housed slaves undergoing seasoning with the old Africans and Creoles who were instructing them. The instructors regarded such additions to their households as economic opportunities because the new Africans provided extra labor on the small plots of land that West Indian planters often allocated to slaves. Slaves could sell surplus root vegetables, peas, and fruit from their gardens and save to purchase freedom for themselves or others. Additional workers helped produce larger surpluses to sell at local markets, thereby reducing the time required to accumulate a purchase price.

New Africans also benefited from this arrangement. They learned how to build houses in their new land and cultivate vegetables to supplement the food the planter provided. Even though many Africans brought building skills and agricultural knowledge with them to the Americas, old Africans and Creoles helped teach them how to adapt what they knew to a new climate, topography, building materials, and social organization.

THE END OF THE JOURNEY: MASTERS AND SLAVES IN THE AMERICAS

By what criteria did planters assess the successful seasoning of new Africans? The first criterion was survival. Already weakened and traumatized by the Middle Passage, many Africans did not survive seasoning. A second criterion was that the Africans had to adapt to new foods and a new climate. The foods included salted codfish traded to the West Indies by New England merchants, Indian corn (maize), and varieties of squash not available in West Africa. The Caribbean islands like West Africa were tropical, but North America was much cooler. Even within the West Indies, an African was unlikely to find a climate exactly like the one he or she had left behind. A third criterion was learning a new language. Planters did not require slaves to speak the local language, which could be English, French, Spanish, Danish, or Dutch, perfectly. But slaves had to speak a creole dialect well enough to obey commands. A final criterion was psychological. When new Africans ceased to be suicidal, planters assumed they had accepted their status and their separation from their homeland.

It would have suited the planters if their slaves had met all these criteria. Yet that would have required the Africans to have been thoroughly desocialized by the Middle Passage, and they were not. As traumatic as that voyage was—for all the shock of capture, separation from loved ones, and efforts to dehumanize them—most of the Africans who entered plantation society in the Americas had not been stripped of their memories or their culture. When their ties to their villages and families were broken, they created bonds with shipmates that simulated blood relationships. Such bonds became the basis of new extended families.

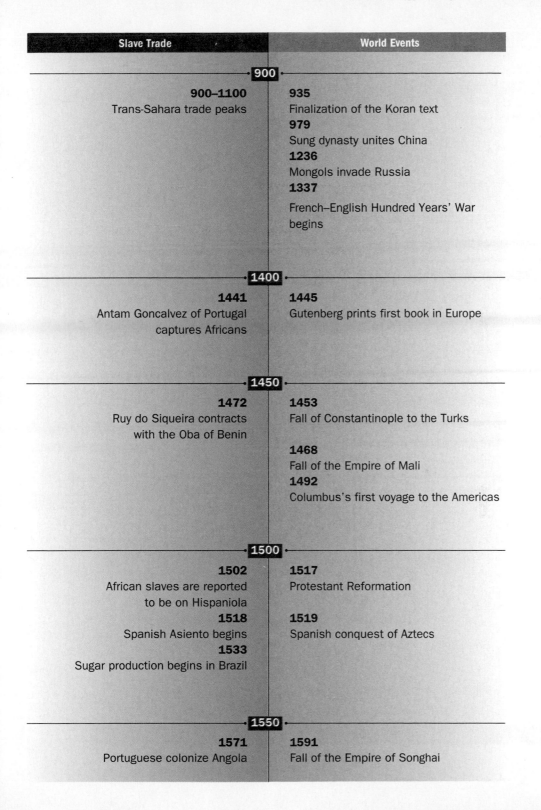

Slave Trade	World Events
	900
900–1100 Trans-Sahara trade peaks	**935** Finalization of the Koran text **979** Sung dynasty unites China **1236** Mongols invade Russia **1337** French–English Hundred Years' War begins
	1400
1441 Antam Goncalvez of Portugal captures Africans	**1445** Gutenberg prints first book in Europe
	1450
1472 Ruy do Siqueira contracts with the Oba of Benin	**1453** Fall of Constantinople to the Turks **1468** Fall of the Empire of Mali **1492** Columbus's first voyage to the Americas
	1500
1502 African slaves are reported to be on Hispaniola **1518** Spanish Asiento begins **1533** Sugar production begins in Brazil	**1517** Protestant Reformation **1519** Spanish conquest of Aztecs
	1550
1571 Portuguese colonize Angola	**1591** Fall of the Empire of Songhai

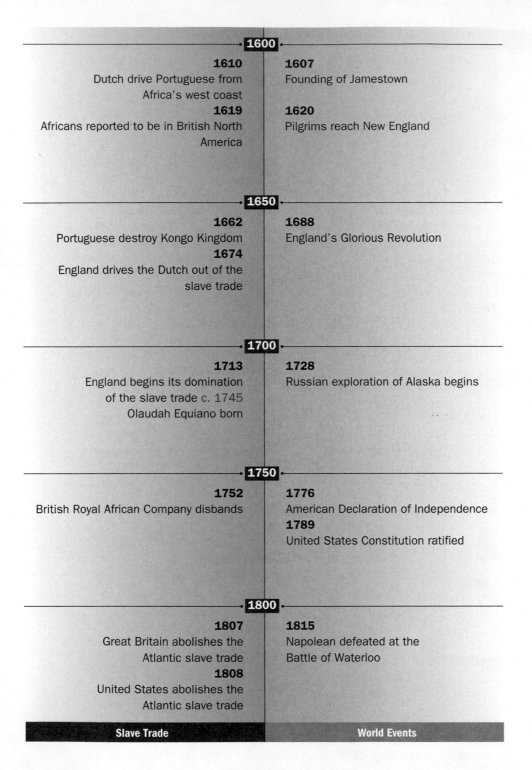

1600

1610
Dutch drive Portuguese from Africa's west coast

1607
Founding of Jamestown

1619
Africans reported to be in British North America

1620
Pilgrims reach New England

1650

1662
Portuguese destroy Kongo Kingdom

1688
England's Glorious Revolution

1674
England drives the Dutch out of the slave trade

1700

1713
England begins its domination of the slave trade c. 1745
Olaudah Equiano born

1728
Russian exploration of Alaska begins

1750

1752
British Royal African Company disbands

1776
American Declaration of Independence
1789
United States Constitution ratified

1800

1807
Great Britain abolishes the Atlantic slave trade

1815
Napolean defeated at the Battle of Waterloo

1808
United States abolishes the Atlantic slave trade

Slave Trade   **World Events**

As this suggests, African slaves did not lose all their culture during the Middle Passage and seasoning in the Americas. Their value system never totally replicated that of the plantation. Despite their ordeal, the Africans who survived the Atlantic slave trade and slavery in the Americas were resilient. Seasoning did modify behavior, yet the claim that it obliterated African Americans' cultural roots is incorrect.

The Ending of the Atlantic Slave Trade

The cruelties associated with the Atlantic slave trade contributed to its abolition in the early nineteenth century. During the late 1700s, English abolitionists led by Thomas Clarkson, William Wilberforce, and Granville Sharp began a religiously oriented moral crusade against slavery and the slave trade. Because the English had dominated the Atlantic trade since 1713, Britain's growing antipathy became crucial to the trade's destruction. But it is debatable whether moral outrage alone prompted this humanitarian effort. By the late 1700s, England's industrializing economy was less dependent on the slave trade and the entire plantation system than it had been previously. To maintain its prosperity, England needed raw materials and markets for its manufactured goods. Slowly but surely its ruling classes realized it was more profitable to invest in industry and other forms of trade and to leave Africans in Africa.

So morals and economic self-interest combined when Great Britain abolished the Atlantic slave trade in 1807 and tried to enforce that abolition on other nations through a naval patrol off the African coast. The following year, the U.S. Congress joined in outlawing the Atlantic trade. Although American, Brazilian, and Spanish slavers defied these prohibitions for many years, the forced migration from Africa to the Americas dropped to a tiny percentage of what it had been at its peak. Ironically, it was the coastal kingdoms of Guinea and western Central Africa that fought most fiercely to keep the trade going because their economies had become dependent on it. This persistence gave the English, French, Belgians, and Portuguese an excuse to establish colonial empires in Africa during the nineteenth century in the name of suppressing the slave trade.

Conclusion

Over more than three centuries, the Atlantic slave trade brought more than eleven million Africans to the Americas. Several million died in transit. Of those who survived, most came between 1701 and 1810, when more Africans than Europeans reached the New World. Most Africans went to the sugar plantations of the Caribbean and Brazil. Only 500,000 went to the British colonies of North America, either directly or after seasoning in the West Indies. From them have come the nearly 40 million African Americans alive today.

We are fortunate that a few Africans who experienced the Middle Passage recorded their testimony. Otherwise, we would find its horror even more difficult to comprehend. Even more important, however, is that so many survived the horrible experience of the Atlantic slave trade and carried on. Their struggle testifies to the human spirit that is at the center of the African-American experience.

REVIEW QUESTIONS

1. How did the Atlantic slave trade reflect the times during which it existed?

2. Think about Olaudah Equiano's experience as a young boy captured by traders and brought to a slave ship. What new and strange things did he encounter? How did he explain these things to himself? What kept him from descending into utter despair?

3. How could John Newton reconcile his Christian faith with his career as a slave-ship captain?

4. What human and natural variables could prolong the Middle Passage across the Atlantic Ocean? How could delay make the voyage more dangerous for slaves and crew?

5. How could Africans resist the dehumanizing forces of the Middle Passage and seasoning and use their African cultures to build black cultures in the New World?

myhistorylab CONNECTIONS

Reinforce what you learned in this chapter by studying the many documents, images, maps, review tools, and videos available at **www.myhistorylab.com.**

READ AND REVIEW

✔•┤**Study** and **Review** on **myhistorylab.com** STUDY PLAN FOR CHAPTER 2

▯•┤**Read** the **Document** on **myhistorylab.com**

  A Slave Ship Surgeon Writes about the Slave Trade in 1788

  A Slave Tells of His Capture in Africa in 1798

  An African Captive Tells the Story of Crossing the Atlantic in a Slave Ship

  England Asserts Her Dominion through Legislation in 1660

  From The Journal of Christopher Columbus (1492)

  Congress Prohibits Importation of Slaves (1807)

●┤**View** the **Map** on **myhistorylab.com**

  The Atlantic and Islamic Slave Trade

RESEARCH AND EXPLORE

mysearchlab

  Consider these questions in a short research paper.

  Why was the history of slavery repressed for so long? Why has interest in the subject grown in the past quarter of a century?

Read the **Document** on **myhistorylab.com**

Exploring America: Racism in American History

Watch the **Video** on **myhistorylab.com**

Atlantic Connections: Sugar, Smallpox and Slavery

From Triangular Trade to an Atlantic System: Rethinking the Links that Created the Atlantic World

What is Columbus's Legacy?

——————— ((•—Listen on **myhistorylab.com** ———————

Hear the audio files for Chapter 2 at

www.myhistorylab.com.

3

Black People in Colonial North America ·· *1526–1763*

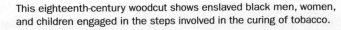

((•─Listen on **myhistorylab.com**

Hear the audio files for Chapter 3 at **www.myhistorylab.com.**

FOCUS QUESTIONS

WHO WERE the peoples of colonial North America?

HOW DID black servitude develop in the Chesapeake?

WHAT WERE the characteristics of plantation slavery from 1700 to 1750?

HOW DID the experience of African Americans under French and Spanish rule in North America compare to that in the British colonies?

HOW DID slavery affect black women in colonial America?

HOW DID African Americans resist slavery?

This eighteenth-century woodcut shows enslaved black men, women, and children engaged in the steps involved in the curing of tobacco.

THIS CHAPTER DESCRIBES the history of African-American life in colonial North America from the early sixteenth century to the end of the **French and Indian War** in 1763. It briefly covers the black experience in Spanish Florida, in New Spain's borderlands in the Southwest, and in French Louisiana, but concentrates on the British colonies that stretched along the eastern coast of the continent. During the seventeenth century, the plantation system that became a central part of black life in America for nearly two centuries took shape in the Chesapeake tobacco country and in the low country of South Carolina and Georgia. Unfree labor, which in the Chesapeake had originally involved both white and black people, solidified into a system of slavery based on race that also existed in the northern British colonies. African Americans responded to these conditions by intereacting with other groups, preserving parts of their African culture, seeking strength through religion, and resisting and rebelling against enslavement.

THE PEOPLES OF NORTH AMERICA

In the North American colonies during the seventeenth and eighteenth centuries, African immigrants gave birth to a new African-American people. Born in North America and forever separated from their ancestral homeland, they preserved a surprisingly large core of their African cultural heritage. Meanwhile, a new natural environment and contacts with people of American Indian and European descent helped African Americans shape a way of life within the circumstances that slavery forced on them. To understand the early history of African Americans, we must first briefly discuss the other peoples of colonial North America.

AMERICAN INDIANS

Historians and anthropologists group the original inhabitants of North America together as American Indians. But when the British began to colonize the Atlantic coastal portion of this huge region during the early seventeenth century, the indigenous peoples who lived there had no such all-inclusive name. They spoke many different languages, lived in diverse environments, and considered themselves distinct from one another.

In Mexico, Central America, and Peru, American Indian peoples developed complex, densely populated civilizations with hereditary monarchies, formal religions, armies, and social classes. They built stone temples and great cities, kept official records, and studied astronomy and mathematics. In the Southwest, the Anasazi and later Pueblo peoples developed sophisticated farming communities. Beginning around 900 CE, they produced pottery, studied astronomy, built large adobe towns, and struggled against a drying climate. Farther east in what is known as the Woodlands region, the Adena culture flourished in the Ohio River valley as early as 1000 BCE and attained the social organization required to construct large burial mounds. Between the tenth and fourteenth centuries CE, what is known as the Mississippian culture established a sophisticated civilization, marked by extensive trade routes, division of labor, and urban centers.

Climatic change and warfare destroyed the Mississippian culture during the fourteenth century, and only remnants of it existed when Europeans and Africans arrived in North America. By that time a diverse variety of American Indian cultures existed in what is today the eastern portion of the United States. Gravely weakened by diseases that settlers

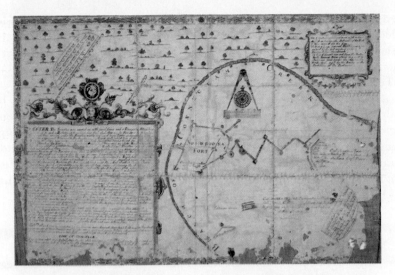

Escaping slaves in the Carolinas during the early eighteenth century sometimes found shelter with the Tuscaroras and other Indian tribes. This map, drawn during a colonial expedition against the Tuscaroras in 1713, shows a Tuscarora fort that escaped slaves probably helped design and build.

unwittingly brought from Europe, the woodlands Indians of North America's coastal regions were ineffective in resisting British settlers during the seventeenth century. Particularly in the Southeast, the British developed an extensive trade in Indian slaves.

Because American Indians were experts at living harmoniously with the natural resources of North America, they influenced the way people of African and European descent came to live there as well. Indian crops became staples of the newcomers' diets. On the continent's southeastern coast, British cultivation of tobacco, another Indian crop, secured the economic survival of the Chesapeake colonies of Virginia and Maryland and led to the enslavement of Africans in them.

The relationships between black people and American Indians during colonial times were complex. Although Indian nations often provided refuge to escaping black slaves, Indians sometimes became slaveholders and on occasion helped crush black revolts. Some black men assisted in the Indian slave trade and sometimes helped defend European colonists against Indian attacks. Although white officials attempted to keep them apart, social and sexual contacts between the two groups were frequent.

THE SPANISH EMPIRE

Following Christopher Columbus's voyage in 1492, the Spanish rapidly built a colonial empire in the Americas. But few Spaniards came to the Western Hemisphere, and Spain's colonial economy rested on the forced labor of the Indian population and, as the Indian population declined from disease and overwork, on enslaved Africans. Overseers in the mines and fields often brutally worked Africans and Indians to death. But because the Spanish were few, some of the African and Indians who survived were able to gain freedom and become tradesmen, small landholders, and militiamen. Often they were of mixed race and identified with their former masters rather than with the oppressed people beneath them in society. African, Indian, and Spanish customs in-termingled in what became a multicultural colonial society. Its center was in the West Indian islands of Cuba and Santo Domingo, Mexico, and northern South America. On its northern periphery were lands that are now part of the United States: South Carolina, Florida, Texas, Arizona, New Mexico, and California.

Africans came early to these borderlands. In 1526 Luis Vasquez de Ayllon brought one hundred African slaves with him from Hispaniola (modern Haiti and the Dominican Republic) in an attempt to establish a Spanish colony near what is now Georgetown, South Carolina. A decade later, slaves, who were either African or of African descent, accompanied Hernando de Soto on a Spanish expedition from Florida to the Mississippi River. In 1565 Africans helped construct the Spanish settlement of St. Augustine in Florida, which is now the oldest city in the continental United States.

THE BRITISH AND JAMESTOWN

While the powerful Spanish empire colonized warm, populous, and wealthy regions of the Americas, the relatively less powerful Britain (dominated by England). Acquired lands that were cooler, less populous, and deficient in easily acquired wealth. England's claim to the east coast of North America rested on the voyage of John Cabot, who sailed in 1497, just five years after Columbus's first westward voyage. But, unlike the Spanish who rapidly created an empire in the Americas, the English were slow to establish themselves in the region Cabot had reached. This was partly due to the harsher North American climate, with winters much colder than in England. In addition, the English monarchy was too poor to finance colonizing expeditions, and social turmoil associated with the Protestant Reformation absorbed its energies.

It took the English naval victory over the Spanish Armada in 1588 and money raised by **joint-stock companies** to produce in 1607 at Jamestown the first permanent British colony in North America. This settlement, established by the Virginia Company of London, was located in the Chesapeake region the British called Virginia. The company hoped to make a profit at Jamestown by finding gold, trading with Indians, cutting lum-ber, or raising crops, such as rice, sugar, or silk, that could not be produced in Britain.

None of these schemes was economically viable. Because of disease, hostility with the Indians, and especially economic failure, the settlement barely survived into the 1620s. By then, however, the experiments begun in 1612 by the English settler John Rolfe to cultivate a mild strain of tobacco that could be grown on the North American mainland began to pay off. Soon growing tobacco became the economic mainstay in Virginia and the neighboring colony of Maryland.

Sowing, cultivating, harvesting, and curing tobacco required considerable labor. Yet colonists in the Chesapeake could not follow the Spanish example of enslaving Indians to produce the crop. Disease had reduced the local Indian population, and those who survived eluded British conquest by retreating westward.

Unlike the West Indian sugar planters, however, the North American tobacco plant-ers did not immediately turn to Africa for laborers. British advocates of colonizing North America had always promoted it as a solution to unemployment, poverty, and crime in England. The idea was to send England's undesirables to America, where they could provide the cheap labor tobacco planters needed. Consequently, until 1700, white labor produced most of the tobacco in the Chesapeake colonies.

AFRICANS ARRIVE IN THE CHESAPEAKE

By early 1619, there were, nevertheless, 32 people of African descent—15 men and 17 women—living in the English colony at Jamestown. They were all "in the service of sev[er]all planters." The following August a Dutch warship, carrying 17 African men and three African women, moored at Hampton Roads at the mouth of the James River. Historians long believed these were the first black people in British North America.

The Africans became servants to the Jamestown officials and to favored planters. The colony's inhabitants, for two reasons, regarded the new arrivals and those black people who had been in Jamestown earlier to be *unfree*, but not slaves. First, unlike the Portuguese and the Spanish, the English had no law for slavery. Second, at least those Africans, who bore such names as Pedro, Isabella, Antoney, and Angelo, were Christians, and—according to English custom and morality in 1619—Christians could not be enslaved. So, once these individuals worked off their purchase price, they regained their freedom. In 1623, Antoney and Isabella married. The next year they became parents of William, whom their master had baptized in the local **Church of England (Anglican).**

During the following years, people of African descent remained a small minority in the expanding colonies of Maryland and Virginia. For example, a 1625 census reported only 23 black people living in the colony, compared with a combined total of 1,275 white people and Indians. This suggests that many of the first black inhabitants had either died or moved away. By 1649 the total Virginia population of about 18,500 included only 300 black people. The English, following the Spanish example, called them "negroes." (Negro means black in Spanish.)

BLACK SERVITUDE IN THE CHESAPEAKE

From the 1620s to the 1670s, black and white people worked in the tobacco fields together, lived together, and slept together (and also did these things with American Indians). They were all unfree indentured servants.

Indentured servitude had existed in Europe for centuries. In England, parents indentured—or, in other words, apprenticed—their children to "masters," who controlled their lives and had the right to their labor for a set number of years. In return, the masters supported the children and taught them a trade or profession.

As the demand for labor to produce tobacco in the Chesapeake expanded, indentured servitude came to include adults who sold their freedom for two to seven years in return for the cost of their voyage to North America. Instead of training in a profession, the servants could improve their economic standing by remaining as free persons in America after completing their period of servitude.

When Africans first arrived in Virginia and Maryland, they entered into similar contracts, agreeing to work for their masters until the proceeds of their labor recouped the cost of their purchase. Indentured servitude could be harsh in the tobacco colonies because masters sought to get as much labor as they could from their servants before the indenture ended. Most indentured servants died from overwork or disease before regaining their freedom.

The foremost example in early Virginia of a black man who emerged from servitude to become a tobacco planter himself is Anthony Johnson. But Johnson was not the only person of African descent who emerged from servitude to become a free property owner during the first half of the seventeenth century. Here and there, black men seemed to enjoy a status similar to their white counterparts. Free black men living in the Chesapeake participated fully in the commercial and legal life of the colonies. They owned land, farmed, lent money, sued in the courts, served as jurors and as minor officials, and at times voted.

This suggests that before the 1670s the English in the Chesapeake did not draw a strict line between white freedom and black slavery. Yet the ruling elite had since the early 1600s treated black servants differently from white servants. Over the decades, the region's British population gradually came to assume that persons of African descent were inalterably alien. This sentiment was the foundation of the establishment of **chattel slavery,** in which slaves were legally private property on a level with livestock, as the proper condition for Africans and those of African descent.

RACE AND THE ORIGINS OF BLACK SLAVERY

Between 1640 and 1700, the British tobacco-producing colonies stretching from Delaware to northern Carolina underwent a social and demographic revolution. An economy based primarily on the labor of white indentured servants became an economy based on the labor of black slaves. By 1700, slaves constituted at least 20 percent of Virginia's population. Probably most agricultural laborers were slaves.

Among the economic and demographic developments that led to the mass enslavement of people of African descent in the tobacco colonies was the precedent for enslaving Africans set in the British Caribbean sugar colonies during the second quarter of the seventeenth century. Also, African slaves became cheaper as white indentured servants became more expensive. This was because poor white people found better opportunities for themselves in other regions of British North America than in the tobacco colonies. Meanwhile, as fewer English men and women agreed to indenture themselves in return for passage to those colonies, Britain gained increased control over the Atlantic slave trade.

These changing circumstances provide the context for the beginnings of black slavery as a major phenomenon in British North America. Yet race and class were crucial in shaping the *character* of slavery in the British mainland colonies. From the first arrival of Africans in the Chesapeake, those English who exercised authority made decisions that qualified the apparent social mobility the Africans enjoyed. The English had historically distinguished between how they treated each other and how they treated those who were physically and culturally different from them. Such discrimination had been the basis of English colonial policies toward the Irish and the American Indians. Because the English considered Africans even more different from themselves than either the Irish or the Indians, they assumed from the beginning that Africans were generally inferior.

Therefore, although black and white servants residing in the Chesapeake during the early seventeenth century had much in common, their masters made distinctions between them based on race. The few women of African descent who arrived in the Chesapeake during those years worked in the tobacco fields with the male servants, while most white women performed domestic duties. Also, unlike white servants, black servants usually did not have surnames, and early census reports listed them separately from white people. By the 1640s, black people could not bear arms, and during the same decade, local Anglican priests (although not those in England itself) maintained that persons of

Negroes for Sale.

A Cargo of very fine ftout Men and Women, in good order and fit for immediate fervice, juft imported from the Windward Coaft of Africa, in the Ship Two Brothers.— Conditions are one half Cafh or Produce, the other half payable the firft of January next, giving Bond and Security if required.
The Sale to be opened at 10 o'Clock each Day, in Mr. Bourdeaux's Yard, at No, 48, on the Bay.
May 19, 1784.   JOHN MITCHELL.

Thirty Seafoned Negroes
To be Sold for Credit, at Private Sale.

AMONGST which is a Carpenter, none of whom are known to be difhoneft.
Alfo, to be fold for Cafh, a regular bred young Negroe Man-Cook, born in this Country, who ferved feveral Years under an exceeding good French Cook abroad, and his Wife a middle aged Wafher-Woman, (both very honeft) and their two Children. Likewife, a young Man a Carpenter.
For Terms apply to the Printer.

Sales like the one announced in this 1769 broadside were common since slavery had been established in the low country ninety years earlier. South Carolina and Georgia remained dependent on imported slaves for much longer than did the Chesapeake and the North.

African descent could not become Christians. Although sexual contacts among blacks, whites, and Indians were common, colonial authorities soon discouraged them.

These distinctions suggest that the status of black servants had never been the same as that of white servants. But only starting in the 1640s do records indicate a predilection toward making black people slaves rather than servants. During that decade, courts in Virginia and Maryland began to reflect an assumption that it was permissible for persons of African descent to serve their master for life rather than for a set term.

THE EMERGENCE OF CHATTEL SLAVERY

Legal documents and statute books reveal that, during the 1660s, other aspects of chattel slavery emerged in the Chesapeake colonies. Bills of sale began to stipulate that the children of black female servants would also be servants for life. In 1662 the House of Burgesses decreed that a child's condition—free or unfree—followed that of the mother. Just as significant, by the mid-1660s statutes in the Chesapeake colonies assumed servitude to be the natural condition of black people.

With these laws, slavery in British North America emerged in the form that it retained until the American Civil War: a racially defined system of perpetual involuntary servitude that compelled almost all black people to work as agricultural laborers. **Slave codes** enacted between 1660 and 1710 further defined American slavery as a system that sought as much to control persons of African descent as to exploit their labor. Slaves could not testify against white people in court, own property, leave their master's estate without a pass, congregate in groups larger than three or four, enter into contracts, marry, or, of course, bear arms. Profession of Christianity no longer protected a black person from enslavement, nor was conversion a cause for **manumission.** In 1669 the

House of Burgesses exempted from felony charges masters who killed a slave while administering punishment.

By 1700, just as the slave system began to expand in the southern colonies, enslaved Africans and African Americans had been reduced legally to the status of domestic animals except that, unlike animals (or masters who abused slaves), the law held slaves to be strictly accountable for their transgressions.

BACON'S REBELLION AND AMERICAN SLAVERY

The series of events that led to the enslavement of black people in the Chesapeake tobacco colonies preceded their emergence as the great majority of laborers in those colonies. The dwindling supply of white indentured servants, the growing availability of Africans, and preexisting white racial biases affected this transformation. But the key event in bringing it about was the rebellion led by Nathaniel Bacon in 1676.

Bacon was an English aristocrat who had recently migrated to Virginia. The immediate cause of his rebellion was a disagreement between him and the colony's royal governor William Berkeley over Indian policy. Bacon's followers were mainly white indentured servants and former indentured servants who resented the control the tobacco-planting elite exercised over the colony's resources and government. That Bacon also appealed to black slaves to join his rebellion indicates that poor white and black people still had a chance to unite against the **master class.**

Before such a class-based, biracial alliance could be realized, Bacon died of dysentery, and his rebellion collapsed. But the uprising convinced the colony's elite that continuing to rely on white agricultural laborers, who could become free and get guns, was dangerous. By switching from indentured white servants to an enslaved black labor force that would never become free or control firearms, the planters hoped to avoid class conflict among white people. Increasingly thereafter, white Americans perceived that both their freedom from class conflict and their prosperity rested on denying freedom to black Americans.

PLANTATION SLAVERY, 1700–1750

The reliance of Chesapeake planters on slavery to meet their labor needs was the result of racial prejudice, the declining availability of white indentured servants, the increasing availability of Africans, and fear of white class conflict. When, following the shift from indentured white to enslaved black labor, the demand for tobacco in Europe increased sharply, the newly dominant slave labor system expanded rapidly.

TOBACCO COLONIES

Between 1700 and 1770, some 80,000 Africans arrived in the tobacco colonies, and even more African Americans were born into slavery there (see Figure 3-1). Tobacco planting spread from Virginia and Maryland to Delaware and North Carolina and from the coastal plain to the foothills of the Appalachian Mountains. In the process, American slavery began to assume the form it kept for the next 165 years.

By 1750, 144,872 slaves lived in Virginia and Maryland, accounting for 61 percent of all the slaves in British North America. Another 40,000 slaves lived in the rice-producing

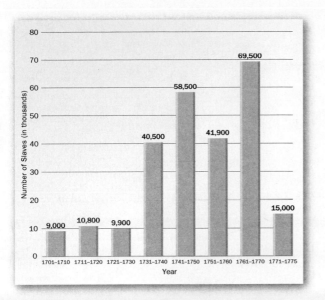

FIGURE 3-1 • Africans Brought as Slaves to British North America, 1701–1775 The rise in the number of captive Africans shipped to British North America during the early eighteenth century reflects the increasing dependence of British planters on African slave labor. The declines in slave imports during the periods 1751 to 1760 and 1771 to 1775 resulted from disruptions to commerce associated with the French and Indian War (or Seven Years' War) and the struggle between the colonies and Great Britain that preceded the American War for Independence. *Source:* Extract taken from *The American Colonies: From Settlement to Independence*, by R.C. Simmons (© R.C. Simmons, 1976) is reproduced by permission of PFD (www.pfd.co.uk) on behalf of R.C. Simmons.

regions of South Carolina and Georgia, accounting for 17 percent. Unlike the sugar colonies of the Caribbean, where white people were a tiny minority, they constituted a majority in the tobacco colonies and a large minority in the rice colonies. Also, most white southerners did not own slaves. Nevertheless the economic development of the region depended on enslaved black laborers.

The conditions under which those laborers lived varied. Most slaveholders farmed small tracts of land and owned fewer than five slaves. These masters and their slaves worked together and developed close personal relationships. Other masters owned thousands of acres of land and rarely saw most of their slaves. During the early eighteenth century, the great planters divided their slaves among several small holdings. They did this to avoid concentrating potentially rebellious Africans in one area. As the proportion of newly arrived Africans in the slave population declined later in the century, larger concentrations of slaves became more common.

Before the mid-eighteenth century, nearly all slaves—both men and women—worked in the fields. Like other agricultural workers, enslaved African Americans normally worked from sunup to sundown with breaks for food and rest. Even during colonial times, they usually had Sunday off.

From the beginnings of slavery in North America, masters tried to make slaves work harder and faster while slaves sought to conserve their energy, take breaks, and socialize with each other. African men regarded field labor as women's work and tried to avoid it if possible. But, especially if they had incentives, enslaved Africans could be efficient workers.

After 1750 some black men began to hold such skilled occupations on plantations as carpenter, smith, carter, cooper, miller, potter, sawyer, tanner, shoemaker, and weaver. Black women had, with the exception of weaving, less access to skilled occupations. When they did not work in the fields, they were domestic servants in the homes of their masters, cooking, washing, cleaning, and caring for children.

MAP 3-1 • Regions of Colonial North America, 1683–1763 The British colonies on the North American mainland were divided on to four regions. They were bordered on the south by Spanish Florida and to the west by regions claimed by France.

▶ *How did African Americans in the British colonies benefit from the close proximity of regions controlled by France and Spain?*

The dates in parentheses indicate when each British colony was established.

LOW-COUNTRY SLAVERY

South of the tobacco colonies, on the coastal plain or low country of Carolina and Georgia, a distinctive slave society developed (see Map 3-1). The influence of the West Indian plantation system was much stronger here than in the Chesapeake, and rice, not tobacco, became the staple crop.

The first British settlers who arrived in 1670 at Charleston (in what would later become South Carolina) were mainly immigrants from Barbados, rather than England. Many of them had been slaveholders on that island and brought slaves with them. Therefore, in the low country, black people were never indentured servants. They were chattel from the start. The region's subtropical climate discouraged white settlement and encouraged dependence on black labor the way it did in the sugar islands. By the early eighteenth century, more Africans had arrived than white people. By 1740 the Carolina low country had 40,000 slaves, who constituted 90 percent of the population in the region around Charleston.

During its first three decades, Carolina supplied Barbados with beef and lumber. Because West Africans from the Gambia River region were skilled herders, white settlers sought them out as slaves. Starting around 1700, however, the low-country planters concentrated on growing rice. Rice had been grown in West Africa for thousands of years, and many of the enslaved Africans who reached Carolina had the skill required to cultivate it in America. Economies of scale, in which an industry becomes more efficient as it grows larger, were more important in the production of rice than tobacco.

Although tobacco could be profitably produced on small farms, rice required large acreages. Therefore, large plantations on a scale similar to those on the sugar islands of the West Indies became the rule in the low country.

In 1732 King George II of England chartered the colony of Georgia to serve as a buffer between South Carolina and Spanish Florida. James Oglethorpe, who received the royal charter, wanted to establish a refuge for England's poor, who were expected to become virtuous through their own labor. Consequently, in 1734 he and the colony's other trustees banned slavery in Georgia. But economic difficulties combined with land hunger among white South Carolinians soon led to the ban's repeal. During the 1750s, rice cultivation and slavery spread into Georgia's coastal plain. By 1773 Georgia had as many black people—15,000—as white people.

Enslaved Africans on low-country plantations suffered from a high mortality rate from diseases, overwork, and poor treatment just as did their counterparts on Barbados and other sugar islands. Therefore, unlike the slave population in the Chesapeake colonies, the slave population in the low country did not grow by natural reproduction. Instead, until shortly before the American Revolution, it grew through continued arrivals from Africa.

Low-country slave society developed striking paradoxes in race relations. As the region's black population grew, white people became increasingly fearful of revolt, and by 1698 Carolina had the strictest slave code in North America. Yet, as the passage that begins this chapter indicates, black people in Carolina faced the quandary of being both feared and needed by white people. Even as persons of European descent grew fearful of black revolt, the colony in 1704 authorized the arming of enslaved black men when needed for defense against Indian and Spanish raids.

Of equal significance was the appearance in Carolina and to some extent in Georgia of distinct classes among people of color. Like the low-country society itself, such classes were more similar to those in the Caribbean sugar islands than in the mainland colonies to the north. A Creole population that had absorbed European values lived alongside white people in Charleston and Savannah. Members of this Creole population were frequently mixed-race relatives of their masters and enjoyed social and economic privileges denied to slaves who labored on the nearby rice plantations. Yet this urban mixed-race class was under constant white supervision.

In contrast, slaves who lived in the country retained considerable autonomy in their daily routines. The intense cultivation required to produce rice encouraged the evolution of a "task system" of labor on the low-country plantations. Rather than working in gangs as in the tobacco colonies, slaves on rice plantations had daily tasks. When they completed these tasks, they could work on plots of land assigned to them or do what they pleased without white supervision. Because black people were the great majority in the low-country plantations, they also preserved more of their African heritage than did black people who lived in the region's cities or in the more northerly British mainland colonies.

PLANTATION TECHNOLOGY

During the American colonial era, most people of African descent living on southern plantations employed technologies associated with raising and processing crops for distant markets. A minority gained technical skills associated with a variety of trades.

VOICES

A DESCRIPTION OF AN EIGHTEENTH-CENTURY VIRGINIA PLANTATION

The following eyewitness account of a large Virginia plantation in Fairfax County indicates the sorts of skilled labor slaves performed by the mid-eighteenth century. George Mason, one of Virginia's leading statesmen during the Revolutionary War era, owned this plantation, which he named Gunston Hall in 1758. The account is by one of Mason's sons.

My father had among his slaves carpenters, coopers, sawyers, blacksmiths, tanners, curriers, shoemakers, spinners, weavers and knitters, and even a distiller. His woods furnished timber and plank for the carpenters and coopers, and charcoal for the blacksmith, his cattle killed for his own consumption and for sale supplied skins for tanners, curriers, and shoemakers, and his sheep gave wool and his fields produced cotton and flax for the weavers and spinners, and his orchards fruit for the distiller. His carpenters and sawyers built and kept in repair all the dwelling-houses, barns, stables, ploughs, harrows, gates, &c., on the plantations and the outhouses at the home house. His coopers made the hogsheads the tobacco was prized in and the tight casks to hold the cider and other liquors. The tanners and curriers with the proper vats &c., tanned and dressed the skins as well for upper as for lower leather to the full amount of the consumption of the estate, and shoemakers made them into shoes for the negroes. . . . The blacksmith did all the iron work required by the establishment, as making and repairing ploughs, harrows, teeth chains, bolts, &c., &c. The spinners, weavers and knitters made all the coarse cloths and stockings used by the negroes, and nearly all worn by the children of it. The distiller made every fall a good deal of apple, peach and persimmon brandy. . . . Moreover, all the beeves and hogs for consumption or sale were driven up and slaughtered there at the proper seasons, and whatever was to be preserved was salted and packed away for after distribution.

- What does this passage indicate about plantation life in mid-eighteenth-century Virginia?

- How does the description of black people presented here compare to the passage from the South Carolina statute book that begins this chapter?

SOURCE: Edmond S. Morgan, *Virginians at Home: Family Life in the Eighteenth Century* (Williamsburg, VA: Colonial Williamsburg, 1952), 53–54.

In tobacco-growing regions, the harvest began a process of preparing leaves for market. Slaves hung plants in "tobacco houses," whose open construction kept out sunlight and rain, while allowing breezes to circulate and dry the leaves. On low-country rice plantations, slaves built, operated, and maintained irrigation systems. They threshed, winnowed, and pounded rice to remove the husks. At first they performed these labor-intensive operations by hand. By the mid-eighteenth century, however, masters introduced "winnowing fans and pounding mills" powered by draft animals. Also, during the eighteenth century, low-country slave artisans built vats, pumps, and structures required for turning indigo plants into a blue dye that was popular in Europe.

Enslaved carpenters used a variety of hand tools to construct the buildings required for all these processes. They also built other plantation buildings. Slave sawyers operated water-powered mills to cut lumber. Other slaves made barrels. They cut and prepared oak staves, trimmed the staves, soaked them, and bound them with iron hoops. Plantation blacksmiths formed the hoops from iron ingots and—using tongs and hammers—pounded the hoops into shape on anvils. They used a similar process to fashion nails, axe and hammer heads, hooks, horse shoes, hinges, and locks.

Like carpentry, tanning was essential. Slaves cooked deer and cow hides in lime to remove fur and then washed off the lime with a mixture of animal dung, salt, and water. They used tannin, a chemical found in tree bark, to cure the hides. After drying, softening, stretching, and trimming, slave craftsmen used the leather to make shoes, boots, garments, and other articles.

SLAVE LIFE IN EARLY AMERICA

Eighteenth-century housing for slaves was minimal and often temporary. In the Chesapeake, small log cabins predominated. They had dirt floors, brick fireplaces, wooden chimneys, and few, if any, windows. African styles of architecture were more common in coastal South Carolina and Georgia. In these regions, slaves built the walls of their houses with tabby—a mixture of lime, oyster shells, and sand—or, occasionally, mud. In either case, the houses had thatched roofs. Early in the eighteenth century, when single African men made up the mass of the slave population, these structures were used as dormitories. Later they housed generations of black families.

The amount of furniture and cooking utensils the cabins contained varied from place to place and according to how long the cabins were occupied. In some cabins, the only furniture consisted of wooden boxes for both storage and seating and planks for beds. As the eighteenth century progressed, slave housing on large plantations became more substantial, and slaves acquired tables, linens, chamber pots, and oil lamps. Yet primitive, poorly furnished log cabins persisted in many regions even after the abolition of slavery in 1865.

At first, slave dress was minimal during summer. Men wore breechcloths, women wore skirts, leaving their upper bodies bare, and children went naked until puberty. Later men wore shirts, trousers, and hats while working in the fields. Women wore shifts (loose, simple dresses) and covered their heads with handkerchiefs. In winter, masters provided heavier cotton and woolen clothing and cheap leather shoes. From the seventeenth century onward, slave women brightened clothing with dyes made from bark, decorated clothing with ornaments, and created African-style headwraps, hats, and hairstyles.

Food consisted of corn, yams, salt pork, and occasionally salt beef and salt fish. Slaves also caught fish and raised chickens and rabbits. When, during the eighteenth century, farmers in the Chesapeake began planting wheat, slaves baked biscuits. In the South Carolina low country, rice became an important part of African-American diets, but even there corn was the staple. During colonial times, slaves occasionally supplemented this limited diet with vegetables, such as cabbage, cauliflower, black-eyed peas, turnips, collard greens, and rutabagas, that they raised in their own gardens.

MISCEGENATION AND CREOLIZATION

When Africans first arrived in the Chesapeake during the early seventeenth century, they interacted culturally and physically with white indentured servants and with American Indians. This mixing of peoples changed all three groups. Interracial sexual contacts—miscegenation—produced people of mixed race. Meanwhile, cultural exchanges became an essential part of the process of creolization that led African parents to produce African-American children. When, as often happened, miscegenation and creolization occurred together, the change was both physical and cultural. However, the dominant British minority in North America during the colonial period defined persons of mixed race as black.

Miscegenation between blacks and whites and blacks and Indians was extensive throughout British North America during the seventeenth and eighteenth centuries. But it was less extensive and accepted than it was in the European sugar colonies in the Caribbean, in Latin America, or in French Canada, where many French men married Indian women. British North America was exceptional because many more white women migrated there than to Canada, Latin America, or the Caribbean. Therefore white men were far less likely to take black or Indian wives and concubines. Sexual relations between Africans and Indians were also more limited than they were elsewhere because the coastal Indian population had drastically declined before large numbers of Africans arrived. Yet miscegenation between black people and the remaining Indians was extensive, and there were instances of black-white marriage in seventeenth-century Virginia.

Colonial assemblies banned such interracial marriages mainly to keep white women from bearing mixed-race children. The assemblies feared that having free white mothers might allow persons of mixed race to sue and gain their freedom, thereby creating a legally recognized mixed-race class. Such a class, wealthy white people feared, would blur the distinction between the dominant and subordinate races and weaken white supremacy. The assemblies did far less to prevent white male masters from sexually exploiting their black female slaves—although they considered such exploitation immoral—because the children of such liaisons would be slaves.

THE ORIGINS OF AFRICAN-AMERICAN CULTURE

Creolization and miscegenation transformed the descendants of the Africans who arrived in North America into African Americans. Historians long believed that in this process the Creoles lost their African heritage. But scholars have found many African legacies not only in African-American culture but in American culture in general.

The preservation of the West African extended family was the basis of African-American culture. Because most Africans imported into the British colonies during the late seventeenth and early eighteenth centuries were males, most black men of that era could not have wives and children. It was not until the Atlantic slave trade declined briefly during the 1750s that sex ratios became more balanced and African-American family life began to flourish. Without that family life, black people could not have maintained as much of Africa as they did.

Even during the Middle Passage, enslaved Africans created "fictive kin relationships" for mutual support, and in dire circumstances, African Americans continued to improvise family structures. By the mid-eighteenth century, however, extended black families based on biological relationships dominated. Black people retained knowledge of their kinship ties to second and third cousins over several generations and wide stretches of territory. These extended families had roots in Africa, but were also a result of—and a reaction to—slavery. West African **incest taboos** encouraged slaves to pick mates who lived on plantations other than their own. The sale of slaves away from their immediate families also tended to extend families over wide areas. Once established, such far-flung kinship relationships helped others, who were forced to leave home, to adapt to new conditions under a new master. Kinfolk also sheltered escapees.

Extended families also influenced African-American naming practices, which reinforced family ties. Africans named male children after close relatives. Also when, early in the eighteenth century, more African Americans began to use surnames, they clung to the name of their original master. This reflected a West African predisposition to link a family name with a certain location.

The result was that African Americans preserved given and family names over many generations. Black men continued to bear such African names as Cudjo, Quash, Cuffee, and Sambo, and black women such names as Quasheba and Juba. Even when masters imposed demeaning classical names, such as Caesar, Pompey, Venus, and Juno, black Americans passed them on from generation to generation.

Bible names did not become common among African Americans until the mid-eighteenth century. This was because before that time masters often refused to allow slaves to be converted to Christianity. As a result, African religions—both indigenous and Islamic—persisted in parts of America well into the nineteenth century. Black Americans continued to perform an African circle dance known as the "ring shout" at funerals, and they decorated graves with shells and pottery in the West African manner. They looked to recently arrived Africans for religious guidance, held bodies of water to be sacred, remained in daily contact with their ancestors through **spirit possession,** and practiced **divination** and magic. When they became ill, they turned to "herb doctors" and "root workers."

THE GREAT AWAKENING

The major turning point in African-American religion came in conjunction with the religious revival known as the Great Awakening. This extensive social movement of the mid- to late-eighteenth century grew out of growing dissatisfaction among white Americans with a deterministic and increasingly formalistic style of Protestantism that seemed to deny most people a chance for salvation.

Some people of African descent had converted to Christianity before the Great Awakening. But two factors had prevented widespread black conversion. First, most masters feared that converted slaves would interpret their new religious status as a step toward freedom and equality. Second, many slaves remained devoted to their ancestral religions and were not attracted to Christianity.

West African Music in America

West African music played a key role in religious rituals and celebrations. The musical performance included three central elements. First, musicians used drums, xylophones, bells, flutes, and a predecessor of the banjo called the mbanzas to produce highly rhythmic music. Second, music provided the accompaniment for dancing that was also part of the event. Finally, music and dancing were matched with a call-and-response style of singing.

All three of these elements found their way into early African-American music. Slaves produced their own versions of West African instruments and made music, dances, and songs that reflected their West African heritage. And, like their African ancestors, slaves made music part of their religious life.

▲ This six-string wooden harp is a rare example of the type of instrument West African musicians and storytellers used to accompany themselves.

▶ **This photograph depicts two versions** of the African *mbanza*. They feature leather stretched across a gourd, a wooden neck, and strings made of animal gut. In America, such instruments became known as banjos.

◀ **This eighteenth-century painting of slaves** on a South Carolina plantation provides graphic proof of the continuities between West African culture and the emerging culture of African Americans.
Abby Aldrich, Rockefeller Folk Art Museum, Williamsburg, VA

How did music fit into the lives of slaves? Should it be considered a form of resistance?

With the Great Awakening, however, a process of general conversion began. African Americans did indeed link the spiritual equality preached by evangelical ministers with a hope for earthly equality. They tied salvation for the soul with liberation for the body. They recognized that the preaching style evangelicals adopted had much in common with West African "spirit possession." As in West African religion, eighteenth-century revivalism in North America emphasized personal rebirth, singing, movement, and emotion. The practice of total body immersion during baptism in rivers, ponds, and lakes that gave the Baptist church its name paralleled West African water rites.

Because it drew African Americans into an evangelical movement that helped shape American society, the Great Awakening increased mutual black-white acculturation. Revivalists appealed to the poor of all races and emphasized spiritual equality. Members of these biracial churches addressed each other as *brother* and *sister*. Black members took communion with white members, served as church officers, and both groups were subject to the same church discipline. By the late eighteenth century, black men were being ordained as priests and ministers and—often while still enslaved—preached to white congregations. They thereby influenced white people's perception of how services should be conducted.

Other factors, however, favored the development of a distinct African-American church. From the start, white churches seated black people apart from white people, belying claims to spiritual equality. Black members took communion *after* white members. Masters also tried to use religion to instill in their chattels such self-serving Christian virtues as meekness, humility, and obedience. Consequently, African Americans established their own churches when they could. Dancing, shouting, clapping, and singing became especially characteristic of their religious meetings. Black spirituals probably date from the eighteenth century, and like African-American Christianity itself, they blended West African and European elements.

African Americans also retained the West African assumption that the souls of the dead returned to their homeland and rejoined their ancestors. Reflecting this family-oriented view of death, African-American funerals were often loud and joyous occasions with dancing, laughing, and drinking. Perhaps most important, the emerging black church reinforced black people's collective identity and helped them persevere in slavery.

LANGUAGE, MUSIC, AND FOLK LITERATURE

Although African Americans did not retain their ancestral languages, those languages contributed to the **pidgins** and creolized languages that became **Black English** by the nineteenth century. It was in the low country, with its large and isolated black populations, that African-English creoles lasted the longest. In other regions, where black people were less numerous, the creole languages were less enduring. Nevertheless, they contributed many words to American—particularly southern—English. Among them are *yam, banjo* (from mbanza), *tote, goober* (peanut), *buckra* (white man), *cooter* (tortoise), *gumbo* (okra), *nanse* (spider), *samba* (dance), *tabby* (a form of concrete), and *voodoo*.

Music was another essential part of West African life, and it remained so among African Americans, who preserved an antiphonal, call-and-response style of singing with an emphasis on improvisation, complex rhythms, and a strong beat. Early on, masters banned drums and horns because of their potential for long-distance communication among slaves. But the African banjo survived in America, and African Americans quickly adopted the violin and guitar. Music may have been the most important aspect of African culture in the lives of American slaves. Eventually African-American music influenced all forms of American popular music.

West African folk literature also survived in North America. African tales, proverbs, and riddles—with accretions from American Indian and European stories—entertained, instructed, and united African Americans. Africans used tales of how weak animals like rabbits outsmarted stronger animals like hyenas and lions to symbolize the power of the common people over unjust rulers. African Americans used similar tales to portray the ability of slaves to outsmart and ridicule their masters.

THE AFRICAN-AMERICAN IMPACT ON COLONIAL CULTURE

African Americans also influenced the development of white culture. As early as the seventeenth century, black musicians performed English ballads for white audiences in a distinctively African-American style. Meanwhile, in the northern and Chesapeake colonies, people of African descent helped determine how all Americans celebrated. By the eighteenth century, slaves in these regions organized black election or coronation festivals that lasted for several days. Although dominated by African Americans, they attracted white observers and a few white participants.

The African-American imprint on southern diction and phraseology is especially clear. Because black women often raised their master's children, generations of white children acquired African-American speech patterns and intonations. Black people also influenced white notions about portents, spirits, and folk remedies. Black cooks in early America influenced both white southern and African-American eating habits. Preferences for barbecued pork, fried chicken, black-eyed peas, okra and collard and mustard greens owed much to West African culinary traditions.

African Americans also used West African culture and skills to shape the way work was done in the American South during and after colonial times. Africans accustomed to collective agricultural labor imposed the **"gang system"** on most American plantations. Masters learned that their slaves worked harder and longer in groups. By the mid-eighteenth century, masters often employed slaves as builders. As a result, African styles and decorative techniques influenced southern colonial architecture.

SLAVERY IN THE NORTHERN COLONIES

Organized religion played a much more important role in the foundation of most of the northern colonies than those of the South (except for Maryland). In New England religious utopianism shaped colonial life. The same was true in the West Jersey portion of New Jersey, where members of the English pietist Society of Friends (Quakers) settled during the 1670s, and Pennsylvania, which William Penn founded in 1682 as a Quaker colony. Quakers, like other pietists, emphasized nonviolence and a divine spirit within all humans. These beliefs disposed some Quakers to become early opponents of slavery.

Even more important than religion in shaping life in northern British North America were a cooler climate, sufficient numbers of white laborers, lack of a staple crop, and a diversified economy. All these circumstances made black slavery in the colonial North less extensive than and different from its southern counterparts.

Like all Americans during the colonial era, most northern slaves were agricultural laborers. But, in contrast to those in the South, slaves in the North typically lived in their master's house. They worked with their master, his family, and one or two other slaves on a small farm. In northern cities, which were often homeports for slave traders, enslaved people of African descent worked as artisans, shopkeepers, messengers, domestic servants, and general laborers.

Slave Codes

Consequently, most northern African Americans led lives that differed from their counterparts in the South. Mainly because New England had so few slaves, but also because of Puritan religious principles, slavery there was least oppressive. New England slaves could legally own, transfer, and inherit property. From the early seventeenth century onward, Puritans converted the Africans and African Americans who came among them to Christianity, recognizing their spiritual equality before God.

In the middle colonies of New York, New Jersey, and Pennsylvania, where black populations were larger and hence perceived by white people to be more threatening, the slave codes were stricter and penalties harsher. But even in these colonies, the curfews imposed on Africans and African Americans and restrictions on their ability to gather together were less well enforced than they were farther south.

These conditions encouraged rapid assimilation. Because of their small numbers, frequent isolation from others of African descent, and close association with their masters, northern slaves usually had fewer opportunities to preserve an African heritage.

SLAVERY IN SPANISH FLORIDA AND FRENCH LOUISIANA

Just as slavery in Britain's northern colonies differed from slavery in its southern colonies, slavery in Spanish Florida and French Louisiana—areas that later became parts of the United States—had distinctive characteristics. People of African descent, brought to Florida and Louisiana during the sixteenth, seventeenth, and eighteenth centuries, learned to speak Spanish or French rather than English, and they became Roman Catholics rather than Protestants. The routes to freedom were also more plentiful in the Spanish and French colonies than they were in Britain's plantation colonies.

The Spanish monarchy regarded the settlement it established at St. Augustine in 1565 as primarily a military outpost, and plantation agriculture was not significant in Florida under Spanish rule. Therefore, the number of slaves in Florida remained small, and black men were needed more as soldiers than as field workers. As militiamen, they gained power that eluded slaves in most of the British colonies, and as members of the Catholic Church, they acquired social status. When the British took control of Florida in 1763, local people of African descent retreated along with the city's white inhabitants to Cuba. It was with the British takeover that plantation slavery began to grow in Florida.

When the French in 1699 established their Louisiana colony in the lower Mississippi River valley, their objective, like that of the Spanish in Florida, was primarily military. In 1720 few black people (either slave or free) lived in the colony. During the following decade, Louisiana imported about 6,000 slaves, most of whom were male and from Senegambia. By 1731 black people outnumbered white people in the colony. Some of the Africans worked on plantations growing tobacco and indigo. But most lived in the port city of New Orleans, where many became skilled artisans, lived away from their masters, became Roman Catholics, and gained freedom. Unfortunately, New Orleans early in its history also became a place where it was socially acceptable for white men to exploit black women sexually. This custom eventually created a sizable mixed-race population with elaborate social gradations based on the amount of white ancestry a person had and the lightness of his or her skin.

AFRICAN AMERICANS IN NEW SPAIN'S NORTHERN BORDERLANDS

What is today the southwestern portion of the United States was from the sixteenth century to 1821 the northernmost part of New Spain. Centered on Mexico, this Spanish colony reached into Texas, California, New Mexico, Colorado, and Arizona. The first people of African descent who entered this huge region were members of Spanish exploratory expeditions. Some black or mulatto women also joined in Spanish military expeditions.

During the colonial era, however, New Spain's North American borderlands had far fewer black people than there were in the British colonies. In part this was because the total non-Indian population in the borderlands was extremely small. As late as 1792, for example, only around 3,000 colonists lived in Texas, including about 450 described as black or mulatto. There were even fewer colonists in New Mexico and California, where people of mixed African, Indian, and Spanish descent were common. Black men in the borderlands gained employment as sailors, soldiers, tradesmen, cattle herders, and day laborers. Some of them were slaves, but others had limited freedom. In contrast to the British colonies, in New Spain's borderlands most slaves were Indians.

Also in contrast to the British mainland colonies, where no formal aristocracy existed but where white insistence on racial separation gradually grew in strength, both hereditary rank and racial fluidity existed in New Spain's borderlands. In theory, throughout the Spanish empire in the Americas, "racial purity" determined social status, with Spaniards of "pure blood" at the top and Africans and Indians at the bottom. But almost all of the Spaniards who moved north from Mexico were themselves of mixed race, and people of African and Indian descent could more easily acquire status than they could in the British colonies. In the borderlands some black men held responsible positions at Roman Catholic missions. A few acquired large land holdings called *ranchos*.

In this painting, men, women and children await sale to slave traders, who stand at the doorway on the left.

BLACK WOMEN IN COLONIAL AMERICA

The lives of black women in early North America varied according to the colony in which they lived. The differences between Britain's New England colonies and its southern colonies are particularly clear. In New England, where religion and demographics made the boundary between slavery and freedom permeable, black women distinguished themselves in a variety of ways. The thoroughly acculturated Lucy Terry Prince of Deerfield, Massachusetts, published poetry during the 1740s and gained her freedom in 1756. Other black women succeeded as bakers and weavers. But in the South, where most black women of the time lived, they had few opportunities for work beyond the tobacco and rice fields and domestic labor in the homes of their masters.

During the late seventeenth and the eighteenth centuries, approximately 90 percent of southern black women worked in the fields, as was customary for women in West Africa. Black women also mothered their children and cooked for their families, a chore that involved lugging firewood and water and tending fires as well as preparing meals. Like other women of their time, colonial black women suffered from inadequate medical attention while giving birth. But because black women worked until the moment they delivered, they were more likely than white women to experience complications in giving birth and to bear low-weight babies.

As the eighteenth century passed, more black women became house servants. Yet most jobs as maids, cooks, and body servants went to the young, the old, or the infirm. Black women also wet-nursed their master's children. None of this was easy work. Those who did it were under constant white supervision and were particularly subject to the sexual exploitation that characterized chattel slavery.

European captains and crews molested and raped black women during the Middle Passage. Masters and overseers similarly used their power to force themselves on female slaves. The results were evident in the large mixed-race populations in the colonies and in the psychological damage it inflicted on African-American women and their mates. In particular, the sexual abuse of black women by white men disrupted the emerging black families in North America because black men usually could not protect their wives from it.

BLACK RESISTANCE AND REBELLION

That masters regularly used their authority to abuse black women sexually and thereby humiliate black men dramatizes the oppressiveness of a slave system based on race and physical force. Masters often rewarded black women who became their mistresses, just as masters and overseers used incentives to get more labor from field hands. But slaves who did not comply in either case faced a beating. Slavery in America was always a system that relied ultimately on physical force to deny freedom to African Americans. From its start, black men and women responded by resisting their masters as well as they could.

Such resistance ranged from sullen goldbricking (shirking assigned work) to sabotage, escape, and rebellion. Before the late eighteenth century, however, resistance and rebellion were not part of a coherent antislavery effort. Before the spread of ideas about natural human rights and universal liberty associated with the American and French revolutions, slave resistance and revolt did not aim to destroy slavery as a social system.

African men and women newly arrived in North America openly defied their masters. They frequently refused to work and often could not be persuaded by punishment to change their behavior. Africans tended to escape in groups of individuals who shared a common homeland and language. When they succeeded, they usually became "outliers," living nearby and stealing from their master's estate. Less frequently, they headed west where they found some safety among white frontiersmen, Indians, or interracial banditti. In some instances, escaped slaves, known as *maroons*—a term derived from the Spanish word *cimarron*, meaning wild—established their own settlements in inaccessible regions.

The most durable of such maroon communities in North America existed in the Spanish colony of Florida. In 1693 the Spanish king officially made this colony a refuge for slaves escaping from the British colonies, although he did not free slaves who were already there. Many such escapees joined the Seminole Indian nation and thereby gained protection during the period between 1763 and 1783 when the British ruled Florida and after 1821 when the United States took control. It was in part to destroy this refuge for former slaves that the United States fought the Seminole War from 1835 to 1842.

As slaves became acculturated, forms of slave resistance changed. To avoid punishment, African Americans replaced open defiance with more subtle day-to-day obstructionism. They malingered, broke tools, mistreated domestic animals, destroyed crops, poisoned their masters, and stole. Not every slave who acted this way, of course, was consciously resisting enslavement, but masters assumed that they were. Acculturation also brought different escape patterns. Increasingly, the more assimilated slaves predominated among escapees. Most of them were young men who left on their own and relied on their knowledge of American society to pass as free. Although some continued to head for maroon settlements, most sowught safety among relatives, in towns, or in the North Carolina piedmont where there were few slaves.

Rebellions were far rarer in colonial North America than resistance or escape. More and larger rebellions broke out during the early eighteenth century in Jamaica and Brazil. This discrepancy resulted mainly from demographics: in the sugar-producing colonies, black people outnumbered white people by six or eight to one, but in British North America black people were a majority only in the low country. Also, by the mid-eighteenth century, most male slaves in the British mainland colonies were Creoles with families, who had more to lose from a failed rebellion than did the single African men who made up the bulk of the slave population farther south.

Nevertheless, there were waves of rebellion in British North America during the years from 1710 to 1722 and 1730 to 1741. Men born in Africa took the lead in these revolts. In New York, 27 Africans, taking revenge for "hard usage," set fire to an outbuilding. When white men arrived to put out the blaze, the rebels attacked them with muskets, hatchets, and swords. They killed nine of the white men and wounded six. Shortly thereafter, local militia units captured the rebels, six of whom killed themselves. The other 21 were executed—some brutally. In 1741 another revolt conspiracy in New York led to another mass execution. Authorities put to death 30 black people and four white people convicted of helping them.

Even more frightening for most white people was the rebellion that began at Stono Bridge within 20 miles of Charleston in September 1739. Under the leadership of a man named Jemmy or Tommy, 20 slaves, who had recently arrived from Angola, broke into a "weare-house, & then plundered it of guns & ammunition." They killed the warehousemen, left their severed heads on the building's steps, and fled toward Florida. Other slaves joined the Angolans until their numbers reached one hundred. They sacked plantations and killed approximately 30 more white people. But when they stopped to celebrate their victories and beat drums to attract other slaves, planters on horseback aided by Indians routed them, killing 44 and dispersing the rest. Many of the rebels, including their leader, remained at large for up to three years, as did the spirit of insurrection. In 1740 Charleston authorities arrested 150 slaves and hanged ten daily to quell that spirit.

In South Carolina and other southern colonies, white people never entirely lost their fear of slave revolt. Whenever slaves rebelled or were rumored to rebel, the fear became intense. As the quotation that begins this chapter indicates, the unwillingness of many Africans and African Americans to submit to enslavement pushed white southerners into a siege mentality that became a determining factor in American history.

African-American Events	National Events
	1450
	1492 Columbus reaches the West Indies **1497** John Cabot's voyage to North America for England
	1500
1526 One hundred African slaves arrive at failed Spanish colony in present-day South Carolina	**1519** Spanish conquest of Aztecs
1529 Esteban shipwrecked on Texas coast	**1532** Spanish conquest of Incas
	1550
1565 Africans help establish St. Augustine	**1565** St. Augustine established **1587** Roanoke colony established
	1600
1619 Twenty-two Africans reported to be living in Jamestown; 20 more arrive	**1607** Jamestown established
1624 First documented African-American child born at Jamestown	**1612** Tobacco cultivated in Virginia by John Rolfe
	1650
1640–1670 Evidence of emergence of black slavery in Virginia	**1670** Carolina established
1693 Spanish Florida welcomes escaped slaves from the British colonies	**1676** Bacon's Rebellion
	1699 Louisiana established

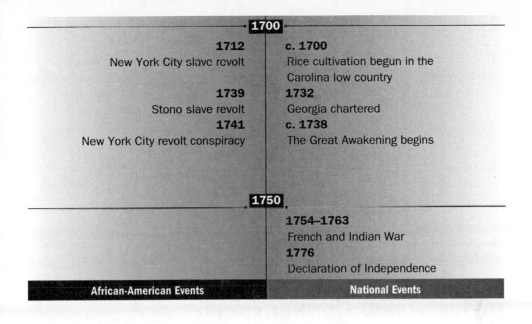

African-American Events	National Events
	1700
1712	**c. 1700**
New York City slave revolt	Rice cultivation begun in the Carolina low country
1739	**1732**
Stono slave revolt	Georgia chartered
1741	**c. 1738**
New York City revolt conspiracy	The Great Awakening begins
	1750
	1754–1763
	French and Indian War
	1776
	Declaration of Independence

CONCLUSION

Studying the history of black people in early America is both painful and exhilarating. It is painful to learn of their enslavement, the emergence of racism in its modern form, and the loss of so much of the African heritage. But it is exhilarating to learn how much of that heritage Africans and African Americans preserved, how they resisted their oppressors and forged strong family bonds, and how an emerging African-American culture began to influence all aspects of American society.

The varieties of black life during the colonial period also help us understand the complexity of African-American society later in American history. Although they had much in common, black people in the Chesapeake, in the low country, in Britain's northern colonies, in Spanish Florida, in French Louisiana, and in New Spain's borderlands had different experiences, different relationships with white people and Indians, and different prospects. Those who lived in the fledgling colonial towns and cities differed from those who were agricultural laborers. The lives of those who worked on small farms were quite different from the lives of those who served on large plantations.

Finally, African-American history during the colonial era raises fundamental issues about contingency and determinism in human events. Was the development of chattel slavery in the Chesapeake inevitable? Or had things gone otherwise (e.g., if Bacon's Rebellion had not occurred or had turned out differently) might African Americans in that region have retained more rights and access to freedom? What would have been the impact of that freedom on the colonies to the north and south of the Chesapeake?

REVIEW QUESTIONS

1. Based on your reading of this chapter, do you believe racial prejudice among British settlers in the Chesapeake led them to enslave Africans? Or did the unfree condition of the first Africans to arrive at Jamestown lead to racial prejudice among the settlers?

2. Why did vestiges of African culture survive in British North America? Did these vestiges help or hinder African Americans in dealing with enslavement?

3. Compare and contrast eighteenth-century slavery as it existed in the Chesapeake, in the low country of South Carolina and Georgia, and in the northern colonies.

4. What were the strengths and weaknesses of the black family in the eighteenth century?

5. How did enslaved Africans and African Americans preserve a sense of their own humanity?

myhistorylab CONNECTIONS

Reinforce what you learned in this chapter by studying the many documents, images, maps, review tools, and videos available at **www.myhistorylab.com**.

READ AND REVIEW

✓•─Study and **Review** on **myhistorylab.com** STUDY PLAN FOR CHAPTER 3

📖•─Read the **Document** on **myhistorylab.com**

A Virginian Describes the Difference between Servants and Slaves in 1722

Declaration against the Proceedings of Nathaniel Bacon (1676)

James Oglethorpe to The Trustees

James Oglethorpe, The Stono Rebellion (1739)

Lucy Terry Prince, "Bars Fight," (1746)

Maryland Addresses the Status of Slaves in 1664

Runaway Notices from The South Carolina Gazette (1732 and 1737)

The Selling of Joseph (1700)

The Slaves Revolt in South Carolina in 1739

🔍─View the **Map** on **myhistorylab.com**

Regions of Colonial North America, 1683-1763

The Colonies to 1740

RESEARCH AND EXPLORE

mysearch**lab**

Consider this question in a short research paper.

How did the evolving economy of the British colonies come to depend on a race-based system of slavery?

Read the **Document** on **myhistorylab.com**

Exploring America: Jamestown

Exploring America: The Great Awakening

Listen on **myhistorylab.com**

"Bars Fight" poem by Lucy Terry; read by Arna Bontemps

———————— **Listen** on **myhistorylab.com** ————————

Hear the audio files for Chapter 3 at
www.myhistorylab.com.

CHAPTER

4

Rising Expectations

*African Americans and the Struggle for
Independence • • 1763 –1783*

Listen on **myhistorylab.com**

Hear the audio files for Chapter 4 at **www.myhistorylab.com.**

FOCUS QUESTIONS

WHAT WAS the crisis in the British Empire?

WHAT DID the Declaration of Independence mean to African Americans?

HOW DID African Americans contribute to the Enlightenment?

WHAT ROLES did African Americans play in the war for Independence?

HOW DID the American Revolution weaken slavery?

African Americans fought on both sides in the American War for Independence. In this nineteenth-century painting, a black Patriot aims his pistol at a British officer during the Battle of Cowpens, fought in South Carolina in 1781.
William Ranney, "The Battle of Cowpens." Oil on Canvas. Photo by Sam Holland. Courtesy of South Carolina State House.

IN THIS CHAPTER we explore the African-American quest for liberty during the 20 years between 1763, when the French and Indian War ended, and 1783, when Britain recognized the independence of the United States. During this period, African Americans exercised an intellectual and political leadership that had far-ranging implications. A few black writers and scientists emerged, black soldiers fought in battle, black artisans proliferated, and—particularly in the North—black activists publicly argued against enslavement. Most important, many African Americans used the War for Independence to gain their freedom. Some were Patriots fighting for American independence. Others were Loyalists fighting for the British. Still others simply used the dislocations war caused to escape their masters.

THE CRISIS OF THE BRITISH EMPIRE

The great struggle for empire between Great Britain and France created the circumstances within which an independence movement and rising black hopes for freedom developed in America. This great conflict climaxed during the French and Indian War that began in North America in 1754, spread in 1756 to Europe, where it was called the Seven Years' War, and from there spread to other parts of the world.

The war sprang from competing British and French efforts to control the Ohio River valley and its lucrative **fur trade**. In 1754 and 1755, the French and their Indian allies defeated Virginian and British troops in this region and then attacked the western frontier of the British colonies. Not until 1758 did Britain undertake a vigorous and expensive military effort that by 1763 had forced France to withdraw from North America. Britain took Canada from France and Florida from France's ally Spain. In compensation, Spain received New Orleans and the huge French province of Louisiana in central North America (see Map 4-1).

These changes had momentous consequences. Deprived of their ability to play off Britain against France and Spain, American Indian nations east of the Mississippi River had great difficulty resisting white encroachment. Although the Florida swamps remained a refuge for escaping slaves, fugitives lost their Spanish protectors. Americans no longer had to face French and Spanish threats on their frontiers. The bonds between Britain and the thirteen colonies rapidly weakened.

These last two consequences were closely linked. The colonial assemblies had not always supported the war effort against the French. American merchants had traded with the enemy. Therefore, after the war ended, British officials decided Americans should be taxed to pay their share of the costs of empire and their commerce should be more closely regulated. During the 1760s Parliament repeatedly passed laws that many Americans considered oppressive. The Proclamation Line of 1763 aimed to placate Britain's Indian allies by forbidding American settlement west of the crest of the Appalachian Mountains. The Sugar Act of 1764 levied import duties designed, for the first time in colonial history, to raise revenue for Britain rather than simply to regulate American trade. In 1765 the Stamp Act, also passed to raise revenue, heavily taxed printed materials, such as deeds, newspapers, and playing cards.

In response, Americans at the Stamp Act Congress held in New York City in October 1765 took a first step toward united resistance. By agreeing not to import British goods, the congress forced Parliament in 1766 to repeal the Stamp Act. But the Sugar Act and

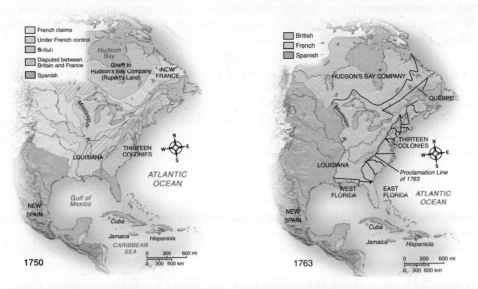

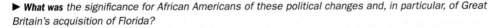

MAP 4-1 • European Claims in North America, 1750 (Left) and 1763 (Right) These maps illustrate the dramatic change in the political geography of North America that resulted from the British victory in the French and Indian War (1754–1763). It eliminated France as a North American power. France surrendered Canada and the Ohio River valley to Britain. Spain ceded Florida to Britain and, as compensation, received Louisiana from France.

▶ *What was the significance for African Americans of these political changes and, in particular, of Great Britain's acquisition of Florida?*

Proclamation Line remained in force, and Parliament soon indicated that it remained determined to exercise greater control in America.

In 1767 it forced the New York assembly to provide quarters for British troops and enacted the Townshend Acts, which taxed glass, lead, paint, paper, and tea imported into the colonies from Britain. Resistance to these taxes in Boston led the British government to station two regiments of troops there in 1768. The volatile situation this created led in 1770 to the Boston Massacre when a small detachment of British troops fired into an angry crowd, killing five Bostonians. Among the dead was a black sailor named Crispus Attucks, who had taken the lead in accosting the soldiers and became a martyr to the Patriot cause.

As it turned out, Parliament had repealed the Townshend duties, except the one on tea, before the massacre. This parliamentary retreat and a reaction against the bloodshed in Boston reduced tension between the colonies and Britain. A period of calm lasted until May 1773 when Parliament passed the Tea Act.

The Tea Act gave the financially insecure British East India Company a monopoly over all tea sold in the American colonies. Parliament hoped the tea monopoly would save the company from bankruptcy, but American merchants assumed the act was the first step in a plot to bankrupt them. Because it had huge tea reserves, the East India Company could sell its tea much more cheaply than colonial merchants could. Other

Americans believed the Tea Act was a trick to get them to pay the tax on tea by lowering its price. They feared that once Americans paid the tax on tea, British leaders would use it as a precedent to raise additional taxes.

To prevent this, Boston's radical Sons of Liberty in December 1773 dumped a shipload of tea into the city's harbor. In response Britain in early 1774 sent more troops to Boston and punished the city economically, sparking resistance throughout the colonies that eventually led to American independence. **Patriot** leaders organized the Continental Congress, which met in Philadelphia in September 1774 and demanded the repeal of all "oppressive" legislation. By November, Massachusetts Minutemen—members of an irregular militia—had begun to stockpile arms in the villages surrounding Boston.

In April 1775 Minutemen clashed with British troops at Lexington and Concord near Boston. This was the first battle in what became a war for independence. After a year during which other armed clashes occurred and the British rejected a compromise, Congress in July 1776 declared the colonies to be independent states, and the war became a revolution.

THE DECLARATION OF INDEPENDENCE AND AFRICAN AMERICANS

The declaration of Independence that the Continental Congress adopted on July 4, 1776, was drafted by a slaveholder in a slave-holding country. When Thomas Jefferson wrote "that all men are created equal; that they are endowed by their Creator with certain unalienable rights; that among these are life, liberty, and the pursuit of happiness," he was not supporting black claims for freedom. So convinced were Jefferson and his colleagues that black people could not claim the same rights as white people that they felt no need to qualify their words proclaiming universal liberty.

Yet, although Jefferson and the other delegates did not mean to encourage African Americans to hope the American War for Independence could become a war against slavery, that is what African Americans believed. Black people heard Patriot speakers make unqualified claims for human equality and natural rights. They read accounts of such speeches and listened as white people discussed them. In response African Americans began to assert that such principles logically applied as much to them as to the white population. They forced white people to confront the contradiction between the new nation's professed ideals and its reality. White citizens therefore had to choose between accepting the literal meaning of the Declaration, which meant changing American society, or rejecting the revolutionary ideology that supported their claims for independence.

THE IMPACT OF THE ENLIGHTENMENT

At the center of that ideology was the European Enlightenment. The roots of this intellectual movement, also known as the Age of Reason, lay in Renaissance secularism and humanism dating back to the fifteenth century. But it was Isaac Newton's *Principia Mathematica*, published in England in 1687, that shaped a new way of perceiving human beings and their universe.

Newton used mathematics to portray an orderly, balanced universe that ran according to natural laws that humans could discover through reason. Newton's insights

Because of southern opposition, the Declaration of Independence was edited to exclude criticism of the slave trade. Instead, the Declaration accused the British of inciting slaves to revolt against their masters.

supported the rationalized means of production and commerce associated with the Industrial Revolution that began in England during the early eighteenth century. But what made the Enlightenment of particular relevance to the **Age of Revolution** was John Locke's application of Newton's ideas to politics.

In his essay "Concerning Human Understanding," published in 1690, Locke maintained that human society—like the physical universe—ran according to natural laws. He contended that at the base of human laws were natural rights all people shared. Human beings, according to Locke, created governments to protect their natural individual rights to life, liberty, and private property. If a government failed to perform this basic duty and became oppressive, he insisted, the people had the right to overthrow it. Locke also maintained that the human mind at birth was a *tabula rasa* (i.e., knowledge and wisdom were not inherited but were acquired through experience). Locke saw no contradiction between these principles and human slavery, but during the eighteenth century, that contradiction became increasingly clear.

Most Americans became acquainted with Locke's ideas through pamphlets that a radical English political minority produced during the early eighteenth century. This literature portrayed the British government of the day as a conspiracy aimed at depriving British subjects of their natural rights, reducing them to slaves, and establishing tyranny. After the French and Indian War, Americans, both black and white, interpreted British policies and actions from this same perspective.

AFRICAN AMERICANS IN THE REVOLUTIONARY DEBATE

During the 1760s and 1770s when powerful slaveholders such as George Washington talked of liberty, natural rights, and hatred of enslavement, African Americans listened. The greatest source of optimism for African Americans was the expectation that white Patriot leaders would realize their revolutionary principles were incompatible with slavery. Those in England who believed white Americans must submit to British authority pointed out the contradiction. Samuel Johnson, the most famous writer in London,

The drawing portrays a black youngster joining in a Boston demonstration against the Stamp Act of 1765.

asked, "How is it that we hear the loudest yelps for liberty among the drivers of negroes?" But white Americans made similar comments. As early as 1763, James Otis of Massachusetts warned that "those who every day barter away other mens['] liberty, will soon care little for their own."

Such principled misgivings among white people about slavery helped improve the situation for black people in the North and Upper South during the war, but African Americans acting on their own behalf were key. In January 1766 slaves marched through Charleston, South Carolina, shouting "Liberty!" In the South Carolina and Georgia low country and in the Chesapeake, slaves escaped in massive numbers throughout the revolutionary era.

Rumors of slave uprisings spread throughout the southern colonies. However, it was in New England—the heartland of anti-British radicalism—that African Americans formally made their case for freedom. As early as 1701, a Massachusetts slave won his liberty in court. As the revolutionary era began, such cases multiplied. In addition, although slaves during the seventeenth and early eighteenth centuries had based their **freedom suits** on contractual technicalities, during the revolutionary period, they increasingly sued on the basis of principles of universal liberty.

African Americans in Massachusetts, New Hampshire, and Connecticut also petitioned their colonial or state legislatures for gradual emancipation. These petitions indicate that the black men who signed them were familiar with revolutionary rhetoric. African Americans learned this rhetoric as they joined white radicals to confront British authority.

In 1765 black men demonstrated against the Stamp Act in Boston. They rioted against British troops there in 1768 and joined Crispus Attucks in 1770. Black Minutemen stood with their white comrades at Lexington and Concord. In 1773 black petitioners

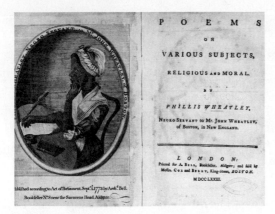

A frontispiece portrait of Phillis Wheatley precedes the title page of her first book of poetry, which was published in 1773. The portrait suggests Wheatley's small physique and studious manner.

from Boston told a delegate to the colonial assembly, "We expect great things from men who have made such a noble stand against the designs of their *fellow-men* to enslave them. . . . The divine spirit of *freedom*, seems to fire every human breast."

BLACK ENLIGHTENMENT

Besides influencing radical political discourse during the revolutionary era, the Enlightenment also shaped the careers of America's first black intellectuals. Because it emphasized human reason, the Enlightenment led to the establishment of colleges, academies, and libraries in Europe and America. These institutions usually served a tiny elite, but newspapers and pamphlets made science and literature available to the masses. The eighteenth century was also an era in which amateurs could make serious contributions to human knowledge. Some of these amateurs, such as Thomas Jefferson and Benjamin Franklin, were rich and well educated. What is striking is that some African Americans, whose advantages were far more limited, also became scientists and authors.

Because they had easier access to evangelical Protestantism than to secular learning, most African Americans who gained intellectual distinction during the late eighteenth century owed more to the Great Awakening than to the Enlightenment. The best known of these is Jupiter Hammon, a Long Island slave who published religious poetry in the 1760s. But Phillis Wheatley and Benjamin Banneker, who were directly influenced by the Enlightenment, became the most famous black intellectuals of their time.

PHILLIS WHEATLEY AND POETRY

In 1761, at age seven or eight, Wheatley came to Boston from Africa aboard a slaver. John Wheatley, a wealthy merchant, purchased her as a servant for his wife. Although Phillis spoke no English when her ship docked, she was soon reading and writing in that language and studying Latin. She pored over the Bible and became a fervent Christian. She also read the fashionable poetry of British author Alexander Pope and became a poet herself by the age of thirteen.

For the rest of her short life, Wheatley wrote poems to celebrate important events. Like Pope's, Wheatley's poetry reflected the aesthetic values of the Enlightenment. She aimed to blend thought, image, sound, and rhythm to provide a perfectly

VOICES

PHILLIS WHEATLEY ON LIBERTY AND NATURAL RIGHTS

Phillis Wheatley wrote the following letter to Samson Occom, an American-Indian minister, in 1774 after her return from England and as tensions between Britain and its American colonies intensified. In it, she links divine order, natural rights, and an inner desire for personal liberty. She expresses optimism that Christianity and the emergence of order in Africa will lead to the end of the Atlantic slave trade. And she hopes that God will ultimately overcome the avarice of American slaveholders ("Our modern Egyptians") and let them see the contradiction between their words and deeds.

February 11, 1774

Rev'd and honor'd Sir, I have this Day received your obliging kind Epistle, and am greatly satisfied with your Reasons respecting the Negroes, and think highly reasonable what you offer in Vindication of their natural Rights. Those that invade them cannot be insensible that the divine Light is chasing away the thick Darkness which broods over the Land of Africa; and the Chaos which has reign'd so long, is converting into beautiful Order, and reveals more and more clearly, the glorious Dispensation of civil and religious Liberty, which are so inseparably united, that there is little or no Enjoyment of one without the other. Otherwise, perhaps, the Israelites had been less solicitous for their Freedom from Egyptian Slavery; I don't say they would have been contented without it. By no Means, for in every human Breast, God has implanted a Principle, which we call Love of Freedom; it is impatient of Oppression, and pants for Deliverance. And by the leave of our modern Egyptians, I will assert that the same principle lives in us. God grant Deliverance in his own Way and Time, and get him honor upon all those whose Avarice impels them to countenance and help forward the Calamities of their fellow Creatures. This I desire not for their Hurt, but to convince them of the strange Absurdity of their Conduct whose Words and Actions are so diametrically opposite. How well the cry for Liberty, and the reverse Disposition for the exercise of oppressive Power over others agree, I humbly think it does not require the Penetration of a Philosopher to determine.

Phillis Wheatley

- How does this letter reflect principles associated with the Enlightenment?
- What insights does this letter provide into Wheatley's views on slavery and its abolition?

SOURCE: Roy Finkenbine, ed., *Sources of the African-American Past: Primary Sources in American History* (New York: Longman, 1997), 22–23.

---

balanced composition. In 1773 the Wheatleys sent her to London where her first book of poems—the first book ever by an African-American woman and the second by any American woman—was published under the title *Poems on Various Subjects, Religious and Moral.* The Wheatleys freed Phillis after her return to Boston, although she continued to live in their house until both of them died.

Wheatley was an advocate and symbol of the adoption of white culture by black people. Before her marriage in 1778 to John Peters, a black grocer, she lived almost exclusively among white people and absorbed their values. For example, although she lamented the sorrow her capture had caused her parents, she was grateful to have been brought to America and been given the opportunity to become a Christian.

But Wheatley did not simply copy her masters' views. Although the Wheatleys were loyal to Britain, she became a fervent Patriot. She attended Boston's Old North Church, a hotbed of anti-British sentiment, and wrote poems supporting the Patriot cause.

Wheatley also became an advocate and symbol of John Locke's ideas concerning the influence of environment on human beings. White leaders of the Revolution and intellectuals debated whether black people were inherently inferior in intellect to white people or whether this perceived black inferiority was the result of enslavement. Those who favored an environmental perspective considered Wheatley an example of what people of African descent could achieve if freed from oppression.

BENJAMIN BANNEKER AND SCIENCE

In the breadth of his achievement, Benjamin Banneker is even more representative of the Enlightenment than Phillis Wheatley. Like hers, his life epitomizes a flexibility concerning race that the revolutionary era briefly promised to expand.

Banneker was born free in Maryland in 1731 and died in 1806. The son of a mixed-race mother and an African father, he inherited a farm near Baltimore from his white grandmother. As a child, Banneker attended a racially integrated school. Later his farm gave him a steady income and the leisure to study literature and science.

With access to the library of his white neighbor George Ellicott, Banneker "mastered Latin and Greek and had a good working knowledge of German and French." Like Jefferson, Franklin, and others of his time, Banneker was fascinated with mechanics and in 1770 constructed a clock. He also wrote a treatise on bees. However, he gained international fame as a mathematician and astronomer. Because of his knowledge in these disciplines, he became a member of the survey commission for Washington, D.C. This made him the first black civilian employee of the U.S. government. Between 1791 and 1796, he used his astronomical observations and mathematical calculations to publish an almanac predicting the positions in the earth's night sky of the sun, moon, and constellations.

Like Wheatley, Banneker had thoroughly assimilated white culture and well understood the fundamental issues of human equality raised by the American Revolution. In 1791 he sent Thomas Jefferson, who was then U.S. secretary of state, a copy of his almanac to refute Jefferson's claim in *Notes on the State of Virginia* that black people were inherently inferior intellectually to white people. Noting Jefferson's commitment to the biblical statement that God had created "us all of one flesh," and Jefferson's words in the Declaration of Independence, Banneker called the great man to account concerning slavery.

AFRICAN AMERICANS IN THE WAR FOR INDEPENDENCE

When it come to fighting between Patriots on one side and the British and their Loyalist American allies on the other, African Americans joined the side that offered freedom. In the South, where the British held out the promise of freedom in exchange for military service, black men eagerly fought on the British side as **Loyalists**. In the North,

Benjamin Banneker

Benjamin Banneker was a true man of the Enlightenment. Like his peers on both sides of the Atlantic, Banneker was committed to a rational view of the universe. For him, the universe was a place of order, a place governed by the unchanging laws of logic and mathematics. And, as important, he believed human reason was capable of discovering those laws. These commitments were the common threads that connected his various interests: clocks, mechanics, astronomy, and mathematics.

It should not surprise us that Banneker applied the same searching rationality to the place of black people in the emerging American nation. He believed that the possession of a rational mind was at the heart of what it meant to be human. Therefore, when Thomas Jefferson asserted that blacks were intellectually inferior to whites, he was implying that they were less human as well. Banneker himself stood as strong evidence of the falsity of Jefferson's claim. By presenting clear proof of his rational mind to Jefferson in the form of his *Almanac*, Banneker was directly challenging Jefferson's commitment to the Enlightenment principles they both claimed to believe in.

◄ Portrait of Benjamin Banneker on the frontispiece of *Benjamin Banneker's Pennsylvania, Delaware, Maryland, and Virginia Almanack, for the Year of Our Lord, 1795.*

▶ This plan of the city of Washington, D.C. from 1791 shows Banneker's work as surveyor of our country's capital.

▲ We see Banneker's mind at work in his *Astronomical Journal, 1798,* in his solution to a mathematical puzzle called Trigonometry.

What common qualities tie together the images of Banneker's work?

where white Patriots were more consistently committed to human liberty than in the South, black men just as eagerly fought on the Patriot side.

The war began in earnest in August 1776 when the British landed a large army at Brooklyn, New York, and drove Washington's **Continental Army** across New Jersey into Pennsylvania. The military and diplomatic turning point in the war came the following year at Saratoga, New York, when a poorly executed British strategy to take control of the Hudson River led British general John Burgoyne to surrender his entire army to Patriot forces. This victory led France and other European powers to enter the war against Britain. Significant fighting ended in October 1781 when Washington and the French forced Lord Cornwallis to surrender another British army at Yorktown, Virginia.

When Washington had organized the Continental Army in July 1775, he forbade the enlistment of new black troops and the reenlistment of black men who had served at Lexington and Concord, Bunker Hill, and other early battles. Shortly thereafter, all thirteen states followed Washington's example. Several reasons account for Washington's decision and its ratification by the **Continental Congress**. Although several black men had served during the French and Indian War, the colonies had traditionally excluded African Americans from militia service. Patriot leaders feared that if they enlisted African-American soldiers, it would encourage slaves to leave their masters without permission. White people also feared that armed black men would endanger the social order. Paradoxically, white people simultaneously believed black men were too cowardly to be effective soldiers.

BLACK LOYALISTS

By mid-1775 the British had taken the initiative in recruiting African Americans. Many slaves escaped and sought British protection as Loyalists. The British employed most black men who escaped to their lines as laborers and foragers. During the siege at Yorktown in 1781, the British used the bodies of black laborers, who had died of smallpox, in a primitive form of biological warfare to try to infect the Patriot army. Even so, many black refugees fought for British or Loyalist units.

The most famous British appeal to African Americans to fight for the empire in return for freedom came in Virginia. On November 7, 1775, Lord Dunmore, the last royal governor of the Old Dominion, issued a proclamation offering to liberate slaves who joined "His Majesty's Troops . . . for the more speedily reducing this Colony to a proper sense of their duty to His Majesty's crown and dignity." Among those who responded to Dunmore's offer was Ralph Henry, a twenty-six-year-old slave of Patrick Henry. Perhaps Ralph Henry recalled his famous master's "Give me liberty or give me death" speech.

Dunmore recruited black soldiers out of desperation, then became the strongest advocate—on either the British or American side—of their fighting ability. When he issued his appeal, Dunmore had only 300 British troops and had been driven from Williamsburg, Virginia's colonial capital. Mainly because Dunmore had to seek refuge on British warships, only about eight hundred African Americans managed to reach his forces. Defeat by the Patriots at the Battle of Great Bridge in December 1775 curtailed his efforts.

But Dunmore's proclamation and the black response to it struck a tremendous psychological blow against his enemies. Of Dunmore's 600 troops at Great Bridge, half were African Americans whose uniforms bore the motto "Liberty to Slaves." Throughout the war, other British and Loyalist commanders followed his example, recruiting thousands of black men who worked and sometimes fought in exchange for their freedom.

BLACK PATRIOTS

Washington's July 1775 policy to the contrary, black men fought on the Patriot side from the very beginning of the Revolutionary War to its conclusion. Before Washington's arrival in Massachusetts, there were black Minutemen at Lexington and Concord, and some of the same men distinguished themselves at Bunker Hill. It was Dunmore's use of African-American soldiers that prompted Washington to reconsider his ban on black enlistment. "If that man, Dunmore," he wrote in late 1775, "is not crushed before the Spring he will become the most dangerous man in America. His strength will increase like a snowball running down hill. Success will depend on which side can arm the Negro faster." After receiving encouragement from black veterans, Washington, on December 30, 1775, allowed African-American reenlistment in the Continental Army. By the end of 1776 troop shortages forced Congress and the state governments to recruit black soldiers in earnest for the Continental Army and state militias. Even then, South Carolina and Georgia refused to permit black men to serve in regiments raised within their boundaries, although black men from these states joined other Patriot units.

Except for Rhode Island's black regiment and some companies in Massachusetts, black Patriots served in integrated military units. Enrollment officers often did not specify a man's race when he enlisted, so it is difficult to know precisely how many black men were involved. The figure usually given is 5,000 black soldiers out of a total Patriot force of 300,000.

Black men fought on the Patriot side in nearly every major battle of the war. Prince Whipple and Oliver Cromwell crossed the Delaware River with Washington on Christmas night 1776 to surprise Hessian mercenaries (German troops hired to fight on the British side) at Trenton, New Jersey. Others fought at Monmouth, Saratoga, Savannah, Princeton, and Yorktown. In 1777 a Hessian officer reported, "No [Patriot] regiment is to be seen in which there are not Negroes in abundance, and among them are able bodied, strong and brave fellows." Black women also supported the Patriot cause. Like white women, black women sometimes accompanied their soldier husbands into army camps, if not into battle.

THE REVOLUTION AND ANTISLAVERY

The willingness of African Americans to risk their lives in the Patriot cause encouraged northern legislatures to emancipate slaves within their borders. By the late 1770s, most of these legislatures were debating abolition. Petitions and lawsuits initiated by black people in Massachusetts, Connecticut, New Hampshire, and elsewhere encouraged such consideration. But an emerging market economy, the Great Awakening, and the Enlightenment established the cultural context in which people who believed deeply in the sanctity of private property could consider such a momentous change. Economic, religious, and intellectual change had convinced many that slavery should be abolished.

Enlightenment rationalism was a powerful antislavery force. In the light of reason, slavery appeared to be inefficient, barbaric, and oppressive. But rationalism alone could

A free African American from New England, Lemuel Haynes enlisted as a minuteman in 1774 and fought in numerous battles. After the war, he studied theology and was eventually ordained in November, 1785. He went on to become a minister in Rutland, Vermont, where he preached more than thirty years.

not convince white Americans that black people should be released from slavery. White people also had to believe general emancipation was in their self-interest and their Christian duty.

In the North, where all these forces operated and the economic stake in slave labor was relatively small, emancipation made steady progress. In the Chesapeake, where some of these forces operated, emancipationist sentiment grew, and many masters manumitted their slaves, but there was no serious threat to the slave system. In the low country of South Carolina and Georgia, where economic interest and white solidarity against large black populations outweighed intellectual and religious considerations, white commitment to black bondage remained absolute.

The movement among white people to abolish slavery began within the Society of Friends. This religious group, whose members were known as Quakers, had always emphasized conscience, human brotherhood, and nonviolence. Moreover, many leading Quaker families engaged in international business ventures that required educated, efficient, moral workers. This predisposed them against a system that forced workers to be uneducated, recalcitrant, and often ignorant of Christian religion.

During the 1730s Benjamin Lay, a former slaveholder who had moved from Barbados to the Quaker-dominated colony of Pennsylvania, began to exhort his fellow Friends to disassociate themselves from owning and buying slaves. A decade later, John Woolman, from southern New Jersey, urged northeastern and Chesapeake Quakers to emancipate their slaves. With assistance from British Quakers, Woolman and Anthony Benezet, a Philadelphia teacher, convinced the society's 1758 annual meeting to condemn slavery and the slave trade.

When the conflict with Great Britain made human rights a political as well as a religious issue, Woolman and Benezet carried their abolitionist message beyond the Society of Friends. They thereby merged their sectarian crusade with the rationalist efforts of northern white revolutionary leaders. Under Quaker leadership, antislavery societies organized in the North and the Chesapeake.

THE REVOLUTIONARY IMPACT

In calling for emancipation, the antislavery societies emphasized black service in the war against British rule and the religious and economic progress of northern African Americans. They also contended that emancipation would prevent black rebellions. As a result, by 1784 all the northern states except New Jersey and New York had undertaken either immediate or gradual abolition of slavery. Delaware, Maryland, and Virginia made manumission easier. Even the Deep South saw efforts to mitigate the most brutal excesses that slavery encouraged among masters. Many observers believed the Revolution had profoundly improved the prospects for African Americans.

In fact, the War for Independence dealt a heavy, although not mortal, blow to slavery (see Figure 4-1). While northern states prepared to abolish involuntary servitude, an estimated 100,000 slaves escaped from their masters in the South. Twenty thousand black people left with the British at the end of the war (see Map 4-2). Meanwhile, numerous escapees found their way to southern cities or to the North, where they joined an expanding free black class. In the Chesapeake, as well as in the North, individual slaves gained freedom either in return for service in the war or because their masters had embraced Enlightenment principles. Those Chesapeake slaves who did not become free also made gains during the Revolution because the war hastened the decline of tobacco raising. As planters switched to wheat and corn, they required fewer year-round, full-time workers. This encouraged them to free their excess labor force or to negotiate contracts that let slaves serve for a term of years rather than for life. Another alternative was for masters to allow slaves—primarily males—to practice skilled trades instead of doing fieldwork. Such slaves often **"hired their own time"** in return for giving their masters a large percentage of their wages.

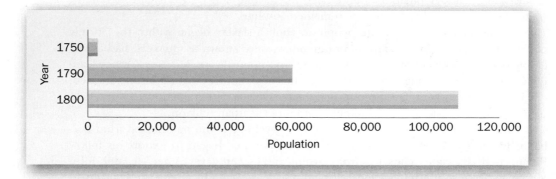

FIGURE 4-1 • The Free Black Population of the British North American Colonies in 1750, and of the United States in 1790 and 1800 The impact of revolutionary ideology and a changing economy led to a great increase in the free black population during the 1780s and 1790s.   *Source: A Century of Population Growth in the United States. 1790–1900 (1909), p. 80. Data for 1750 estimated.*

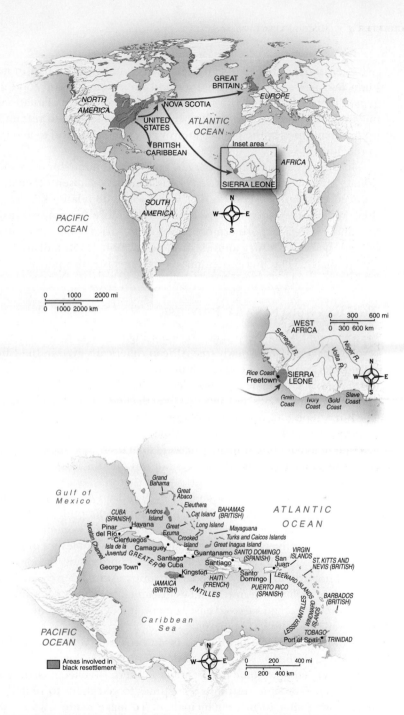

MAP 4-2 • The Resettlement of Black Loyalists after the American War for Independence Like their white Loyalist counterparts, many black Loyalists left with the British following the Patriot victory. Most of those who settled in Nova Scotia soon moved on to Great Britain or the British free black colony of Sierra Leone. Some black migrants to the British Caribbean were reenslaved. Adapted from *The Atlas of African-American History and Politics*, 1/e, by A. Smallwood and J. Elliot, © 1998, The McGraw-Hill Companies. Reproduced with permission of The McGraw-Hill Companies.

▶ *What does* the arrival of some black Loyalists in Sierra Leone indicate about Great Britain's changing attitudes toward slavery?

Even those slaves who remained agricultural workers had more time to garden, hunt, and fish to supply themselves and their families with food and income. They gained more freedom to visit relatives who lived on other plantations, attend religious meetings, and interact with white people. Masters tended to refrain from the barbaric punishments used in the past, to improve slave housing, and to allow slaves more access to religion.

In South Carolina and Georgia, greater autonomy for slaves during the revolutionary era took a different form. The war increased absenteeism among masters and reduced contacts between the black and white populations. The black majorities in these regions grew larger, more isolated, and more African in culture as South Carolina and Georgia imported more slaves from Africa. The constant arrival of Africans helped the region's African-American population retain a distinctive culture and the Gullah dialect. The increase in master absenteeism also permitted the task system of labor to expand.

THE REVOLUTIONARY PROMISE

Even though the northern states were moving toward general emancipation during the revolutionary era, most newly free African Americans lived in the Chesapeake. Free African Americans had, of course, always lived there, but before the Revolution they were few. Free black populations also grew in Delaware and Maryland, where—unlike Virginia—the number of slaves began a long decline.

But in South Carolina and Georgia, the free black class remained tiny. Most low-country free black people were the children of white slave owners. They tended to be less independent of their former masters than their Chesapeake counterparts and lighter complexioned because their freedom was often a result of a family relationship to their masters.

In the North and the Chesapeake, free African Americans frequently moved to cities. Boston, New York, Philadelphia, Baltimore, Richmond, and Norfolk gained substantial free black populations after the Revolution. Black women predominated in this migration because they could more easily find jobs as domestics in the cities than in rural areas. Cities also offered free black people opportunities for community development that did not exist in thinly settled farm country. Although African Americans often used their new mobility to reunite families disrupted by slavery, relocating to a city could disrupt families that had survived enslavement. It took about a generation for stable, urban, two-parent households to emerge.

Newly freed black people also faced economic difficulty, and their occupational status often declined. Frequently they emerged from slavery without the economic resources needed to become independent farmers, shopkeepers, or trades people. In the North such economic restraints sometimes forced them to remain with their former masters long after formal emancipation. To make matters worse, white artisans used legal and extralegal means to protect themselves from black competition.

Yet, in the North and Chesapeake, most African Americans refused to work for their old masters and left the site of their enslavement. Those who had escaped had to leave. For others, leaving indicated a desire to put the stigma of servitude behind and embrace the opportunities freedom offered despite the risks.

African-American Events	National Events
1750	
1750	**1754**
Crispus Attucks escapes from slavery	French and Indian War begins
1760	
1760	**1763**
Jupiter Hammon publishes a book of poetry	Expulsion of French power from North America
1761	**1764**
Phillis Wheatley arrives in Boston	Parliament passes Sugar Act
1765	
1765	**1765**
African Americans in Boston join protests against Stamp Act	Stamp Act Congress
1766	
Slaves in Charleston, South Carolina, demand "liberty"	
1770	
1770	**1770**
Crispus Attucks is killed during Boston Massacre	Boston Massacre
1773	**1773**
Phillis Wheatley publishes a book of poetry	Boston Tea Party
Black Bostonians petition for freedom	
1775	
1775	**1775**
Black Minutemen fight at Lexington and Concord	Battles of Lexington and Concord
1776	**1776**
Lord Dunmore recruits black soldiers in Virginia	Declaration of Independence
1777	**1777**
Emancipation begins in the North	British general John Burgoyne surrenders at Saratoga
1780	
1781–1783	**1781**
20,000 black Loyalists depart with the British troops	Cornwallis surrenders at Yorktown
	1783
	Britain recognizes U.S. independence

CONCLUSION

As the United States gained recognition of its independence, African Americans could claim they had helped secure it. As soldiers in the Continental Army or in Patriot state militias, many black men fought and died for the revolutionary cause. Others supported the British. African Americans, like white Americans, had been divided over the War for Independence. Yet both those black men and women who chose the Patriot side and those who became Loyalists had freedom as their goal.

This chapter has sought to place the African-American experience during the struggle for independence in the broad context of revolutionary ideology derived from the Enlightenment. Black men and women, such as Benjamin Banneker and Phillis Wheatley, exemplified the intellectually liberating impact of eighteenth-century rationalism and recognized its application to black freedom.

During the war, and with the assistance of white opponents of slavery, African Americans combined arguments for natural rights with action to gain freedom. The American Revolution seemed about to fulfill its promise of freedom to a minority of African Americans, and they were ready to embrace the opportunities it offered. By the war's end in 1783, slavery was dying in the North and seemed to be on the wane in the Chesapeake. The first steps toward forming free black communities were under way. Black leaders and intellectuals had emerged. Although most of their brothers and sisters remained in slavery, although the slave system began to expand again during the 1790s, and although free black people achieved *at best* second-class citizenship, they had made undeniable progress. Yet African Americans were also learning how difficult freedom could be despite the new republic's embrace of revolutionary ideals.

REVIEW QUESTIONS

1. How did the Enlightenment affect African Americans during the revolutionary era?

2. What was the relationship between the American Revolution and black freedom?

3. What was the role of African Americans in the War for Independence? How did their choices in this conflict affect how the war was fought?

4. How did the American Revolution encourage assimilation among African Americans? How did it discourage assimilation?

5. Why did a substantial class of free African Americans emerge from the revolutionary era?

PEARSON myhistorylab CONNECTIONS

Reinforce what you learned in this chapter by studying the many documents, images, maps, review tools, and videos available at **www.myhistorylab.com.**

READ AND REVIEW

✓●─Study and Review on **myhistorylab.com** STUDY PLAN FOR CHAPTER 4

📖●─Read the Document on **myhistorylab.com**

An Early Abolitionist Speaks Out against Slavery in 1757

A Free African American Petitions the Government for Emancipation of All Slaves (1777)

An American Patriot Tries to Stir Up the Soldiers of the American Revolution

Benjamin Banneker - Letter to Thomas Jefferson (1791)

Phillis Wheatley, Poems on Various Subjects, Religious and Moral (1772)

Proclamation of Lord Dunmore (November 14, 1775)

Report on Impending Ending of Slave Trade (1792)

Slave Petition to the Governor of Massachusetts (1774)

🔍─View the Map on **myhistorylab.com**

The American Revolution

Revolutionary War: Northern Theater, 1775-1780

European Claims in North America, 1750 and 1763

RESEARCH AND EXPLORE

mysearchlab

Consider these questions in a short research paper.

How did African Americans participate in the struggle for independence? What expectations did they have about the new nation they were helping create?

📖●─Read the Document on **myhistorylab.com**

Exploring America: Geography of the American Revolution

Exploring America: The Stamp Act

👁─Watch the Video on **myhistorylab.com**

The American Revolution as Different Americans Saw It

──────── ((•─Listen on **myhistorylab.com** ────────

Hear the audio files for Chapter 4 at
www.myhistorylab.com.

African Americans in
the New Nation • • *1783–1820*

((•─Listen on **myhistorylab.com**

Hear the audio files for Chapter 5 at **www.myhistorylab.com**.

FOCUS QUESTIONS

WHAT FORCES worked for black freedom in the first years after the revolution?

WHY DID slavery survive in the new United States?

WHAT were the characteristics of early free black communities?

HOW DID the War of 1812 affect African Americans?

WHAT IMPACT did the Missouri Compromise have on African Americans?

This recent photograph portrays one of several buildings used as slave quarters on Boone Hall Plantation, South Carolina. Built during the mid-seventeenth century, the small brick building housed two African-American families into the Civil War years.

I N THIS CHAPTER, we explore how a diverse group of African Americans helped shape the lives of black people during America's early years as an independent republic. We also examine how between 1783 and 1820 the forces for black liberty vied with the forces of slavery and inequality. The end of the War for Independence created great expectations among African Americans. But by 1820, when the Missouri Compromise confirmed the power of slaveholders in national affairs, black people in the North and the South had long known that the struggle for freedom was far from over.

FORCES FOR FREEDOM

After the War for Independence ended in 1783, a strong trend in the North and the Chesapeake favored emancipation. It had roots in economic change, evangelical Christianity, and a revolutionary ethos based on the natural rights doctrines of the Enlightenment. African Americans took advantage of these forces to escape from slavery, purchase the freedom of their families and themselves, sue for freedom in court, and petition state legislatures to grant them equal rights.

In the postrevolutionary North, slavery, although widespread, was not economically essential. Farmers could more efficiently hire hands during the labor-intensive seasons of planting and harvesting than they could maintain a year-round slave labor force. Northern slaveholders had wealth and influence, but they lacked the overwhelming authority of their southern counterparts. Moreover, transatlantic immigration brought to the North plenty of white laborers, who worked cheaply and resented slave competition. As the Great Awakening initiated a new religious morality, as natural rights doctrines flourished, and as a market economy based on wage labor emerged, northern slaveholders had difficulty defending perpetual black slavery.

NORTHERN EMANCIPATION

In comparison to other parts of the Atlantic world, emancipation in the northern portion of the United States began early. Its first stages preceded the revolt that had by 1804 ended slavery in Haiti, the first independent black republic. It preceded by a much greater margin the initiation in 1838 of peaceful, gradual abolition of slavery in the British Empire and the end in 1848 of slavery in the French colonies. Northern emancipation was exceptional in that it was not the result of force or outside intervention by an imperial power. Although free black communities were emerging throughout the Western Hemisphere, those in the North were distinctive because they included the bulk of the region's black population.

Emancipation in the North did not follow a single pattern. Instead the New England states of Massachusetts (which included Maine until it became a separate state in 1820), Connecticut, Rhode Island, New Hampshire, and Vermont moved more quickly than did the mid-Atlantic states of Pennsylvania, New York, and New Jersey (see Map 5-1).

Vermont and Massachusetts (certainly) and New Hampshire (probably) abolished slavery immediately during the 1770s and 1780s. Vermont, where there had never been more than a few slaves, prohibited slavery in the constitution it adopted in 1777. Massachusetts, in its constitution of 1780, declared "that all men are born free and equal; and that every subject is entitled to liberty." Although this constitution did not specifically

MAP 5-1 • **Emancipation and Slavery in the Early Republic** This map indicates the abolition policies adopted by the states of the Northeast between 1777 and 1804, the antislavery impact of the Northwest Ordinance of 1787, and the extent of slavery in the South during the early republic.

▶ **Why did** the states and territories shown in this map adopt different policies toward African Americans?

ban slavery, within a year Elizabeth Freeman and other slaves in Massachusetts sued under it for their freedom. Freeman, while serving as a waitress at her master's home in Sheffield, Massachusetts, overheard "gentlemen" discussing the "free and equal" clause of the new constitution. Shortly thereafter, she contacted a prominent local white lawyer, Theodore Sedgwick Sr., who agreed to represent her in court.

Meanwhile, another Massachusetts slave, Quok Walker, left his master and began living as a free person. In response, Walker's master sought a court order to force Walker to return to slavery. This case led in 1783 to a Massachusetts Supreme Court ruling that "slavery is … as effectively abolished as it can be by the granting of rights and privileges wholly incompatible and repugnant to its existence." Another judge used similar logic to grant Freeman her liberty. These decisions encouraged other Massachusetts slaves to sue for their freedom or to leave their masters because the courts had ruled unconstitutional the master's claim to his human chattel.

As a result, the first U.S. census in 1790 found no slaves in Massachusetts. Even before then, black men in the state had gained the right to vote. In 1780 Paul and John Cuffe, free black brothers who lived in the town of Dartmouth, protested with five other free black men to the state legislature that they were being taxed without representation. The courts finally decided in 1783 that African-American men who paid taxes in Massachusetts could vote there.

TABLE 5.1 Slave Populations in the Mid-Atlantic States, 1790–1860

	1790	1800	1810	1820	1830	1840	1850	1860
New York	21,324	20,343	15,017	10,888	75	4		
New Jersey	11,432	12,343	19,851	7,557	2,243	674	236	18
Pennsylvania	3,737	1,706	795	211	403	64		

Source: *Philip S. Foner*, History of Black Americans, from Africa to the Emergence of the Cotton Kingdom, vol. 1 (Westport, CT: Greenwood, 1975), 374.

New Hampshire's record on emancipation is less clear than that of Vermont and Massachusetts. In 1779 black residents petitioned the New Hampshire legislature for freedom. Evidence also indicates that court rulings based on New Hampshire's 1783 constitution, which was similar to that of Massachusetts, refused to recognize human property. Nevertheless, New Hampshire still had about 150 slaves in 1792 Slavery may have simply withered away there rather than having been abolished by the courts.

In Connecticut and Rhode Island, the state legislatures, rather than individual African Americans, took the initiative against slavery. In 1784 these states adopted gradual abolition plans, which left adult slaves in bondage but proposed to free their children over a period of years.

In New Jersey, New York, and Pennsylvania, the investment in slaves was much greater than in New England. After considerable debate, the Pennsylvania legislature in 1780 voted that the children of enslaved mothers would become free at age 28. Under this scheme, Pennsylvania still had 403 slaves in 1830 (see Table 5.1). But many African Americans in the state gained their freedom much earlier by lawsuits or by simply leaving their masters. Emancipation came even more slowly in New York and New Jersey. In 1785 their legislatures *defeated* proposals for gradual abolition. These states had relatively large slave populations, powerful slaveholders, and white workforces fearful of free black competition.

In 1799 the New York legislature finally agreed that male slaves born after July 4 of that year were to become free at age 28 and females at age 25. In 1804 New Jersey adopted a similar law that freed male slaves born after July 4 of that year when they reached age 25 and females when they reached age 21.

THE NORTHWEST ORDINANCE OF 1787

Nearly as significant as the actions of northern states against slavery was Congress's decision to limit slavery's expansion. Congress had jurisdiction over the region west of the Appalachian Mountains and east of the Mississippi River. During the War for Independence, increasing numbers of white Americans had migrated across the Appalachians into this huge region. The migrants—some of whom brought slaves with them—provoked hostilities with American Indian nations. Those who moved into the Old Northwest also faced British opposition, and those who moved into the Old Southwest contested against Spanish forces for control of that area. In response to these circumstances, Congress formulated policies to protect the migrants and provide for their effective government. The new nation's leaders also disparaged the westward expansion of slavery, and Thomas Jefferson sought to deal with both issues. First, he suggested that the western region be divided into separate territories and prepared for statehood. Second, he proposed that after 1800 slavery be banned from the entire region stretching from the Appalachians to the Mississippi River and from Spanish Florida (Spain had regained Florida in 1783) to British Canada.

In 1784 Jefferson's antislavery proposal failed by a single vote to pass Congress. Three years later, Congress adopted the **Northwest Ordinance.** This legislation applied the essence of Jefferson's plan to the region north of the Ohio River—what historians call the Old Northwest. The ordinance provided for the orderly sale of land, support for public education, territorial government, and the eventual formation of new states. Unlike Jefferson's plan, the ordinance banned slavery immediately. But, because it applied only to the Northwest Territory, the ordinance left the huge region south of the Ohio River open to slavery expansion.

Yet, by preventing slaveholders from taking slaves legally into areas north of the Ohio River, the ordinance set a precedent for excluding slavery from U.S. territories. Whether Congress had the power to do this became a contentious issue after President Jefferson annexed the huge Louisiana Territory in 1803 (see p. 104). The issue divided northern and southern politicians until the Civil War.

ANTISLAVERY SOCIETIES IN THE NORTH AND THE UPPER SOUTH

While African Americans helped destroy slavery in the northeastern states and Congress blocked its advance into the Old Northwest, a few white people organized to spread antislavery sentiment. In 1775 Quaker abolitionist Anthony Benezet organized the first antislavery society in the world. It became the **Pennsylvania Society for Promoting the Abolition of Slavery** in 1787, and Benjamin Franklin became its president. By 1800, there were abolition societies in New Jersey, Connecticut, and Virginia. By the end of the eighteenth century, there were abolition societies in New Jersey, Connecticut, and Virginia. Organized antislavery sentiment also arose in the new slave states of Kentucky and Tennessee. However, such societies never appeared in the Deep South.

From 1794 to 1832, antislavery societies cooperated within the loose framework of the **American Convention for Promoting the Abolition of Slavery and Improving the Condition of the African Race.** Only white people participated in these Quaker-dominated organizations, although members often cooperated with black leaders. As the northern states adopted abolition plans, the societies focused their attention on Delaware, Maryland, and Virginia. They aimed at gradual, compensated emancipation. They encouraged masters to free their slaves, attempted to protect free black people from reenslavement, and frequently advocated sending freed black people out of the country.

Experience with emancipation in the northern states encouraged the emphasis on gradual abolition. So did the reluctance of white abolitionists to challenge the property rights of masters. Abolitionists also feared that immediate emancipation might lead masters to abandon elderly slaves and assumed that African Americans would require long training before they could be free.

MANUMISSION AND SELF-PURCHASE

Another hopeful sign for African Americans was that after the Revolution most southern states liberalized their manumission laws. In general, masters could free individual slaves by deed or will. They no longer had to go to court or petition a state legislature to prove that an individual they desired to free had performed a "meritorious service."

As a result, hundreds of slaveholders in the Upper South began freeing slaves. Religious sentiment and natural rights principles motivated many of these masters. Even though most of them opposed general emancipation, they considered the slave system immoral. Yet noble motives were not always the most important. Masters often profited from self-purchase agreements they negotiated with their slaves. Slaves raised money by marketing farm produce or hiring themselves out for wages and then paid for their eventual freedom in installments. Masters liked the installments because they provided additional income in addition to what they otherwise received from a slave.

The title of this 1811 painting by German-American artist John Lewis Krimmel is *Pepper-Pot, a Scene in the Philadelphia Market*. Slavery still existed in Pennsylvania when Krimmel recorded this scene. It is likely, however, that the black woman who is selling pepper-pot (a type of stew) was free. 2001-196-1 Krimmel, John Lewis. Pepper Pot, A Scene in the Philadelphia Market. Philadelphia Museum of Art: Gift of Mr. and Mrs. Edward B. Leisenring, Jr. in honor of the 125th anniversary of the museum, 2001. Sumpter Priddy III, Inc.

Masters also sometimes manumitted slaves who were no longer profitable investments. A master might be switching from tobacco to wheat or corn—crops that did not need a year-round workforce. Or a master might manumit older slaves whose best years as workers were behind them. Frequently, however, slaves— usually young men— presented masters with the alternative of manumitting them after a term of years or having them escape immediately.

THE EMERGENCE OF A FREE BLACK CLASS IN THE SOUTH

As a result of manumission, self-purchase, and freedom suits, the free black population of the Upper South blossomed. Maryland and Virginia had the largest free black populations. However, most of the Upper South's black population remained in slavery while the North's was on the way to general emancipation. In the North, 83.9 percent of African Americans were free in 1820, compared with 10.6 percent of those in the Upper South.

In the Deep South (South Carolina, Georgia, Florida, Louisiana, Alabama, and Mississippi), both the percentage and the absolute numbers of free black people remained much smaller. During the eighteenth century, neither South Carolina nor Georgia restricted the right of masters to manumit their slaves, but far fewer masters in these states exercised this right after the Revolution than was the case in the Chesapeake. Manumission declined in Louisiana following its annexation to the United States in 1804. Generally, masters in the Deep South freed only their illegitimate slave children, other favorites, or those unable to work.

FORCES FOR SLAVERY

The forces for black freedom in the new republic rested on widespread African-American dissatisfaction with slavery, economic change, Christian morality, and revolutionary precepts. Most black northerners had achieved freedom by 1800, three-quarters were free by 1810, and by 1840 only 0.7 percent remained in slavery. Yet for the nation as a whole and for the mass of African Americans, the forces favoring slavery proved to be stronger. Abolition took place in the North where slavery was weak. In the South, where it was strong, slavery thrived and expanded.

THE U.S. CONSTITUTION

The U.S. Constitution, which went into effect in 1789, became a major force in favor of the continued enslavement of African Americans. During the War for Independence, the Continental Congress had provided a weak central government for the United States, as each of the thirteen states retained control over its own internal affairs. The Articles of Confederation, which served as the American constitution from 1781 to 1789, formalized this system of divided sovereignty.

However, by the mid-1780s, wealthy and powerful men perceived that the Confederation Congress was too weak to protect their interests. Democratic movements in the states threatened property rights. Congress's inability to regulate commerce led to trade disputes among the states, and its inability to tax prevented it from maintaining an army and navy. Congress could not control the western territories, and, most frightening to the wealthy, it could not help states suppress popular uprisings, such as that led by Daniel Shays in western Massachusetts in 1786.

The fears Shays's Rebellion caused led directly to the Constitutional Convention in Philadelphia that in 1787 produced the Constitution under which the United States is still governed. The new constitution gave the central government power to regulate commerce, to tax, and to have its laws enforced in the states. But the convention could not create a more powerful central government without first making important concessions to southern slaveholders.

Humanitarian opposition to the Atlantic slave trade had mounted during the revolutionary era. Under pressure from black activists—such as Prince Hall of Boston—and Quakers, northern state legislatures during the 1780s forbade their citizens to engage in the slave trade. Economic change in the Upper South also prompted opposition to the trade.

Yet convention delegates from South Carolina and Georgia maintained that their states had an acute labor shortage. They threatened that citizens of these states would not tolerate a central government that could stop them from importing slaves—at least not in the near future. Torn between these conflicting perspectives, the convention compromised by including a provision in the Constitution that prohibited Congress from abolishing the trade until 1808. During the 20 years prior to 1808, when Congress banned the trade, thousands of Africans were brought into the southern states. Overall, more slaves entered the United States between 1787 and 1808 than during any other 20-year period in American history. Such huge numbers helped fuel the westward expansion of the slave system.

Other proslavery clauses of the U.S. Constitution aimed to counteract slave rebellion and escape. The Constitution gave Congress power to put down "insurrections" and "domestic violence." It also provided that persons "held to service or labour in one State, escaping into another … shall be delivered up on claim of the party to whom such service or labour may be due." This clause was the basis for the **Fugitive Slave Act of 1793,** which allowed masters or their agents to pursue slaves across state lines, capture them, and take them before a magistrate. There, on presentation of satisfactory evidence, masters could regain legal custody of the person they claimed.

Finally, the Constitution strengthened the political power of slaveholders through the Three-Fifths Clause. This clause was also a compromise between northern and southern delegates at the Convention. Southern delegates wanted slaves to be counted toward representation in the national government but not counted for purposes of taxation. Northern delegates wanted just the opposite. The **Three-Fifths Clause** provided that a slave be counted as three-fifths of a free person in determining a state's representation in the House of Representatives and in the Electoral College. Slaves would be counted similarly if and when Congress instituted a per capita tax.

This gave southern slaveholders increased representation on the basis of the number of slaves they owned—slaves who, of course, had no vote or representation. The South gained enormous political advantage from it. If not for the Three-Fifths Clause, for example, northern nonslaveholder John Adams would have been reelected president in 1800 instead of losing the presidency to southern slaveholder Thomas Jefferson. For many years, this clause contributed to the domination of the U.S. government by slaveholding southerners, although the South's population steadily fell behind the North's.

Four other factors, however, were more important than constitutional provisions in fostering the continued enslavement of African Americans in the new republic: increased cultivation of cotton, the Louisiana Purchase, declining revolutionary fervor, and intensified white racism.

COTTON

The most obvious of the four developments was the increase in cotton production. By the late eighteenth century, Britain led the world in textile manufacturing. As mechanization made the spinning of cotton cloth more economical, Britain's demand for raw cotton increased dramatically. The United States led in filling that demand as a result of Eli Whitney's invention of the **cotton gin** in 1793. This simple machine provided an easy and quick way to remove the seeds from the type of cotton most commonly grown in the South.

Cotton reinvigorated the slave-labor system, which spread rapidly across Georgia and later into Alabama, Mississippi, Louisiana, and eastern Texas. Cotton cultivation also existed in South Carolina, North Carolina, Arkansas, and parts of Virginia and Tennessee. To make matters worse for African Americans, the westward expansion of cotton production encouraged an internal slave trade. Masters in the old tobacco-growing regions of Maryland, Virginia, and other states began to support themselves by selling their slaves to the new cotton-growing regions (see Figure 5-1).

THE LOUISIANA PURCHASE AND AFRICAN AMERICANS
IN THE LOWER MISSISSIPPI VALLEY

The Jefferson administration's purchase of Louisiana from France in 1803 accelerated the westward expansion of slavery and the **domestic slave trade**. The purchase nearly doubled the area of the United States. That slavery might extend over this vast region became an issue of great importance to African Americans. The purchase also brought under American sovereignty those black people, both free and slave, who lived in the portion of the territory that centered on the city of New Orleans. Although people of

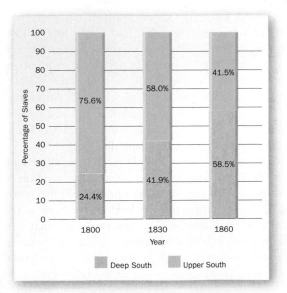

FIGURE 5-1 • Distribution of the Southern Slave Population, 1800–1860 The demand for slaves in the cotton-growing Deep South produced a major shift in the distribution of the slave population.

African descent were a majority of the city's population, they consisted of two distinct groups. First were the free people of color who called themselves Creoles. They were usually craftsmen and shopkeepers, spoke French, belonged to the Roman Catholic Church, and aspired to equal rights with other free inhabitants. The second black group consisted of slaves, most of whom had come directly from Africa and worked on Louisiana plantations. Spain had encouraged white Americans to settle in the lower Mississippi Valley. The Americans, in turn, demanded more strictly enforced slave codes and the expansion of the external slave trade. At first the slaves produced tobacco and indigo, but by the 1790s sugar and cotton had emerged as the crops of the future. As demand for these crops grew, conditions for slaves in Louisiana became increasingly harsh, especially after the region became part of the United States. The slaves' rural location, their predominantly African culture, and, eventually, their Protestant religion cut them off from free people of color. In 1770 the region that later became the state of Louisiana had a slave population of 5,600. By 1810 it had 34,660, and by 1820 the slave population numbered 149,654. This tremendous growth, involving an extremely harsh form of slavery in a huge region, constituted a warning to all opponents of that institution. With the termination of the external slave trade, the notorious slave markets of New Orleans became the dreaded destination of thousands of African Americans "sold south" by their masters in the domestic slave trade.

CONSERVATISM AND RACISM

By the 1790s white Americans had begun a long retreat from the egalitarianism of the revolutionary era. In the North and the Chesapeake, most white people became less willing to challenge the prerogatives of slaveholders and more willing to accept slavery as suitable for African Americans. Most Marylanders and Virginians came to think of emancipation as best left to the distant future. This outlook strengthened the slaveholders and their nonslaveholding white supporters in the Deep South who had never embraced the humanitarian precepts of the Enlightenment and Great Awakening.

Increasing proslavery sentiment among white Americans stemmed, in part, from revulsion against the radicalism of the French Revolution that had begun in 1789. Reports from France of class and religious warfare, disruption of the social order, and redistribution of property led most Americans to value property rights and order above equal rights. In addition, as cotton production spread westward and the value of slaves soared, rationalist and evangelical criticism of human bondage withered. Antislavery sentiment in the Upper South that had flourished among slaveholders, nonslaveholders, Deists, Methodists, and Baptists became increasingly confined to African Americans and Quakers. During the early 1800s, manumissions began a long decline.

Using race to justify slavery was an important component of this conservative trend. Unlike white people, the argument went, black people were unsuited for freedom or citizenship. The doctrines embodied in the Declaration of Independence, therefore, did not apply to them. A new scientific racism supported this outlook. As early as the 1770s, some American intellectuals challenged the Enlightenment theory that perceived racial differences were not essential or inherent but results of the different environments in which Africans and Europeans originated. Scholars instead proposed that God had created a great chain of being from lesser creatures to higher creatures.

In this chain, black people constituted a separate species as close to the great apes as to white people.

Such views became common among white northerners and white southerners. They also had practical results. During the 1790s Congress expressed its determination to exclude African Americans from the benefits of citizenship in "a white man's country." A 1790 law limited the granting of naturalized citizenship to "any alien, being a white person." In 1792 Congress limited enrollment in state militias to "each and every free, able-bodied white male citizen."

THE EMERGENCE OF FREE BLACK COMMUNITIES

The competing forces of slavery and racism, on one hand, and freedom and opportunity, on the other, shaped the growth of African-American communities in the early American republic. A distinctive black culture had existed since the early colonial period. But enslavement had limited black community life. The advent of large free black populations in the North and Upper South after the Revolution allowed African Americans to establish autonomous and dynamic communities. They appeared in Philadelphia, Baltimore, Newport (Rhode Island), Richmond, Norfolk (Virginia), New York, and Boston. Although smaller and less autonomous, there were also free black communities in such Deep South cities as Charleston, Savannah, and New Orleans. As free black people in these cities acquired a modicum of wealth and education, they established institutions that have shaped African-American life ever since.

A combination of factors encouraged African Americans to form these distinctive institutions. First, as they emerged from slavery, they realized they would have inferior status in white-dominated organizations or not be allowed to participate in them at all. Second, black people valued the African heritage they had preserved over generations in slavery. They wanted institutions that would perpetuate their heritage.

The earliest black community institutions were mutual aid societies. Patterned on similar white organizations, these societies were like modern insurance companies and benevolent organizations. They provided for their members' medical and burial expenses and helped support widows and children. African Americans in Newport, Rhode Island, organized the first black mutual aid society in 1780. Seven years later, Richard Allen and Absalom Jones established the more famous Free African Society in Philadelphia.

These ostensibly secular societies maintained a decidedly Christian moral character. They insisted that their members meet standards of middle-class propriety and, in effect, became self-improvement as well as mutual aid societies. Members had to pledge to refrain from fornication, adultery, drunkenness, and other "disreputable behavior." By the early 1800s, such societies also organized resistance to kidnappers who sought to recapture fugitive slaves or enslave free African Americans. Because the societies provided real benefits and reflected black middle-class aspirations, they spread to every black urban community.

Of particular importance were the black Freemasons because, unlike other free black organizations, the Masons united black men from several northern cities. Combining rationalism with secrecy and obscure ritual, Freemasonry was a major movement among European and American men during the late eighteenth and early nineteenth

Joshua Johnson

Joshua Johnson was born in Baltimore around 1763. He was the son of a white man, George Johnson, and an unknown black slave owned by a William Wheeler, Sr. When Joshua was a child, Wheeler sold him to George Johnson. Johnson acknowledged that Joshua was his son and freed him in 1782. We have no records of his training as an artist, but by 1796 he was listed in Baltimore city directories as a portrait painter, the first known African-American artist to earn his living in this way. There are a few tantalizing clues about his artistic development. Competition among portrait painters in Baltimore was stiff and Johnson could not afford to wait for customers to come to him. In a newspaper advertisement Johnson placed to attract new clients, he described himself as a "self-taught genius."

The available evidence suggests that Johnson lived in Maryland his whole life, earning his living as a painter in Baltimore for much of it. While the details of his life are sketchy, they do provide the historian with a window into the lives of free blacks in the Chesapeake in the decades after the Revolution. The decision by Johnson's father and master to acknowledge and free him was part of a larger trend towards manumission in the Chesapeake. Johnson's ability to find a space to develop his talents speaks to the complexity of evolving racial relationships and attitudes in early nineteenth-century Maryland.

Portrait of a Man, c. 1805–1810, ▲ oil on canvas.

◄ *Mrs. Thomas Everette and Her Children*, Joshua Johnson, 1818.

The Maryland Historical Society

Johnson's *Portrait of a Man* is one of the few confirmed works of his with an African-American subject. What does this portrait, and the fact that Johnson painted it, tell us about free black society in early nineteenth-century Maryland?

centuries. The most famous black Mason of his time was Prince Hall, the Revolutionary War veteran and abolitionist. During the 1770s he began in Boston what became known as the **Prince Hall Masons.** In several respects, Hall's relationship to Masonry epitomizes the free black predicament in America.

In 1775 the local white Masonic lodge in Boston rejected Hall's application for membership because of his black ancestry. Therefore, Hall, who was a Patriot, organized African Lodge No. 1 on the basis of a limited license he secured from a British Masonic lodge associated with the British Army that then occupied Boston. The irony of this situation compounded when, after the War for Independence, American Masonry refused to grant the African Lodge a full charter. Hall again had to turn to the British Masons, who approved his application in 1787.

This late eighteenth-century portrait of Prince Hall (1735?–1807) dressed as a gentleman places him among Masonic symbols. A former slave, a skilled craftsman and entrepreneur, an abolitionist, and an advocate of black education, Hall is best remembered as the founder of the African Lodge of North America, popularly known as the Prince Hall Masons.

THE ORIGINS OF INDEPENDENT BLACK CHURCHES

Although black churches emerged at least a decade later than black benevolent associations, the churches quickly became the core of African-American communities. Not only did these churches attend to the spiritual needs of free black people and—in some southern cities—slaves, their pastors also became the primary African-American leaders. Black church buildings housed schools, social organizations, and antislavery meetings.

During the late eighteenth century, as the egalitarian spirit of the Great Awakening waned among white Baptists, Methodists, and Episcopalians, separate, but not independent, black churches appeared in the South. The biracial churches the Awakening spawned had never embraced African Americans on an equal basis with white people. In response African Americans formed separate black congregations, usually headed by black ministers but subordinate to white church hierarchies. The first such congregations appeared during the 1770s in South Carolina and Georgia.

In contrast to these subordinate churches, a truly independent black church emerged gradually in Philadelphia between the 1780s and the early 1800s. The movement for such a church began within the city's white-controlled St. George's Methodist Church. Richard Allen and Absalom Jones who led the movement could rely for help on the Free African Society they established in 1787.

Allen in 1780 and Jones in 1783 had purchased their freedom. In 1786 Allen, a fervent Methodist since the 1770s, received permission from St. George's white leadership to use the church in the evenings to preach to black people. Jones joined Allen's congregation. Soon they and other black members of St. George's chafed under policies they considered un-Christian and insulting.

The break finally came in 1792 when St. George's white leaders grievously insulted the church's black members. An attempt by white trustees to prevent Jones from praying in what the trustees considered the white section of the church led black members to walk out. "We all went out of the church in a body," recalled Allen, "and they were no more plagued with us in the church."

Raphaelle Peale, the son of famous Philadelphia portraitist Charles Wilson Peale, completed this oil portrait of the Reverend Absalom Jones (1746–1818) in 1810. Reverend Jones is shown in his ecclesiastical robes holding a Bible in his hand.

St. George's white leaders fought hard and long to control the expanding and economically valuable black congregation. Yet other white Philadelphians, led by abolitionist Benjamin Rush, applauded the concept of an independent "African church." Rush and other sympathetic white people contributed to the new church's building fund. When construction began in 1793, Rush and at least one hundred other white people joined with African Americans at a banquet to celebrate the occasion.

However, the black congregation soon split. When the majority determined that the new church would be Episcopalian rather than Methodist, Allen and a few others refused to join. The result was *two* black churches in Philadelphia. St. Thomas's Episcopal Church, with Jones as priest, opened in July 1794 as an African-American congregation within the white-led national Episcopal Church. Then Allen's Mother Bethel congregation became the first truly independent black church. The white leaders of St. George's tried to control Mother Bethel until 1816. That year Mother Bethel became the birthplace of the **African Methodist Episcopal (AME) Church**. Allen became the first bishop of this organization, which quickly spread to other cities in the North and the South.

THE FIRST BLACK SCHOOLS

Schools for African-American children, slave and free, date to the early 1700s. But the first schools established by African Americans to instruct African-American children arose after the Revolution. The new black mutual aid societies and churches created and sustained them.

Schools for black people organized or taught by white people continued to flourish. But black people also founded their own schools because local white authorities regularly refused either to admit black children to public schools or to maintain adequate separate black schools. As early as 1790, Charleston's Brown Fellowship operated a school for its members' children. Free black people in Baltimore supported schools during the same decade, and during the early 1800s, similar schools opened in Washington, D.C. Such schools frequently employed white teachers. Not

This lithograph, c. 1887, portrays the New York African Free School, No. 2. The New York Manumission Society established the original school in 1787, at 137 Mulberry Street in New York City. Men who later became prominent black abolitionists, such as Henry Highland Garnet and James McCune Smith, attended the school during the 1820s.

VOICES

ABSALOM JONES PETITIONS CONGRESS ON BEHALF OF FUGITIVES FACING REENSLAVEMENT

Absalom Jones wrote his petition to Congress on behalf of four black men who had been manumitted in North Carolina. Because they were in danger of being reenslaved, they had taken refuge in Philadelphia. The men, under whose names the petition appears in the Annals of Congress, were Jupiter Nicholson, Jacob Nicholson, Joe Albert, and Thomas Pritchet. Jones provided brief accounts of their troubles. Here we include only the important general principles that Jones invoked. Southern representatives argued that accepting a petition from alleged slaves would set a dangerous precedent, and Congress refused to accept the petition.

To the President, Senate, and House of Representatives,

The Petition and Representation of the under-named Freemen, respectfully showeth:

That, being of African descent, the late inhabitants and natives of North Carolina, to you only, under God, can we apply with any hope of effect, for redress of our grievances, having been compelled to leave the State wherein we had a right of residence, as freemen liberated under the hand and seal of humane and conscientious masters, the validity of which act of justice in restoring us to our native right of freedom, was confirmed by judgment of the Superior Court of North Carolina ... yet, not long after this decision, a law of that State was enacted, under which men of cruel disposition, and void of just principle, received countenance and authority in violently seizing, imprisoning, and selling into slavery, such as had been so emancipated; whereby we were reduced to the necessity of separating from some of our nearest and most tender connections, and seeking refuge in such parts of the Union where more regard is paid to the public declaration in favor of liberty and the common right of man, several hundreds, under our circumstances, having, in consequence of the said law, been hunted day and night, like beasts of the forest, by armed men with dogs, and made a prey of as free and lawful plunder ...

until Philadelphia's Mother Bethel Church established the Augustine School in 1818 did a school entirely administered and taught by African Americans for black children exist.

These schools faced great difficulties. Many black families could not afford the fees, but rather than turn children away, the schools strained their meager resources by taking charity cases. Some black parents also believed education was pointless when African Americans often could not get skilled jobs. White people feared competition from skilled black workers, believed black schools attracted undesirable populations, and, particularly in the South, feared that educated free African Americans would encourage slaves to revolt. Threats of violence against black schools and efforts to suppress them were common. Nevertheless, similar schools continued to operate in the North and Upper South, producing a growing class of literate African Americans.

We beseech your impartial attention to our hard condition, not only with respect to our personal sufferings, as freemen, but as a class of that people who, distinguished by color, are therefore with a degrading partiality, considered by many, even of those in eminent stations, as unentitled to that public justice and protection which is the great object of Government.... .

If, notwithstanding all that has been publicly avowed as essential principles respecting the extent of human right to freedom; notwithstanding we have had that right restored to us, so far as was in the power of those by whom we were held as slaves, we cannot claim the privilege of representation in your councils, yet we trust we may address you as fellow-men, who, under God, the sovereign Ruler of the Universe, are intrusted with the distribution of justice, for the terror of evil-doers, the encouragement of protection of the innocent, not doubting that you are men of liberal minds, susceptible of benevolent feelings and clear conception of rectitude to a catholic extent, who can admit that black people ... have natural affections, social and domestic attachments and sensibilities; and that, therefore, we may hope for a share in your sympathetic attention while we represent that the unconstitutional bondage in which multitudes of our fellows in complexion are held, is to us a subject sorrowfully affecting; for we cannot conceive their condition (more especially those who have been emancipated and tasted the sweets of liberty, and again reduced to slavery by kidnappers and man-stealers) to be less afflicting or deplorable than the situation of citizens of the United States, captured and enslaved through the unrighteous policy prevalent in Algiers ... may we not be allowed to consider this stretch of power, morally and politically, a Governmental defect, if not a direct violation of the declared fundamental principles of the Constitution; and finally, is not some remedy for an evil of such magnitude highly worthy of the deep inquiry and unfeigned zeal of the supreme Legislative body of a free and enlightened people?

- On what principles does Jones believe the U.S. government is bound to act?

- What does Jones's petition indicate concerning the status of African Americans before the law?

SOURCE: *Annals of Congress*, 4 Cong., 2 sess. (January 23, 1797), 2015–18.

BLACK LEADERS AND CHOICES

By the 1790s an educated black elite existed in the North and the Chesapeake. It provided leadership for African Americans in religion, economic advancement, and racial politics. Experience had driven members of this elite to a contradictory perception of themselves and of America. On the one hand, they were acculturated, patriotic Americans who had achieved some personal well-being and security. On the other hand, they knew that American society had not lived up to its revolutionary principles. They lamented the continued enslavement of the mass of African Americans, and they had misgivings about the future.

Prominent among these leaders were members of the clergy. Two of the most important of them were Richard Allen and Absalom Jones. Besides organizing his church,

Allen opened a school in Philadelphia for black children, wrote against slavery and racial prejudice, and made his home a refuge for fugitive slaves. A year before his death in 1831, Allen presided over the first national black convention.

Jones, too, was an early abolitionist. In 1797 his concern for fugitives facing reenslavement led him to become the first African American to petition Congress. His petition anticipated later abolitionists in suggesting that slavery violated the spirit of the U.S. Constitution and that Congress could abolish it.

Vying with clergy for influence were African-American entrepreneurs. Prince Hall, for example, owned successful leather dressing and catering businesses in Boston, and Peter Williams, principal founder of New York's AME Zion Church, was a prosperous tobacco merchant. Another prominent black businessman was James Forten of Philadelphia, described as "probably the most noteworthy free African-American entrepreneur in the early nineteenth century."

American patriotism, religious conviction, organizational skill, intellectual inquisitiveness, and antislavery activism delineate the lives of most free black leaders in this era. Yet these leaders often were torn in their perceptions of what was best for African Americans. Some accommodated slavery and racial oppression maintaining that God would eventually end injustice. Others were more optimistic about the ability of African Americans to mold their own destiny in the United States. Such leaders believed that, despite setbacks, the egalitarian principles of the American Revolution would prevail if black people insisted on liberty. Forten never despaired that African Americans would be integrated into the larger American society on the basis of their individual talent and enterprise. Although he was often frustrated, Hall for four decades pursued a strategy based on the assumption that white authority would reward black protest and patriotism.

MIGRATION

African Americans, however, had another alternative: migration from the United States to establish their own society free from white prejudices. In 1787 British philanthropists, including Olaudah Equiano, had established Freetown in Sierra Leone on the West African coast as a refuge for former slaves. As we mentioned in Chapter 4, some African Americans who had been Loyalists during the American Revolution settled there. Other black and white Americans proposed that free black people should settle western North America or in the Caribbean islands. There were great practical obstacles to mass black migration to each of these regions. Migration was expensive, difficult to organize, and involved long, often fruitless, negotiations with foreign governments. But no black leader during the early national period was immune to the appeal of such proposals.

Aware of Freetown, Hall in 1787 petitioned the Massachusetts legislature to support efforts by black Bostonians to establish a colony in Africa. By the mid-1810s, a few influential white Americans had also decided there was no place in the United States for free African Americans. In 1816 they organized the **American Colonization Society**. In 1820, under its auspices, the first party of 86 African Americans sailed for the new colony of Liberia on the West African coast.

The major black advocate of migration to Africa during this period, however, was Paul Cuffe, the son of an Ashantee father and Wampanoag Indian mother. He became a prosperous New England sea captain and, by the early 1800s, cooperated with British humanitarians and entrepreneurs to promote migration. He saw African-American colonization in West Africa as a way to end the Atlantic slave trade, spread Christianity, create a refuge for free black people, and make profits. Before his death in 1817, Cuffe had influenced a number of important black leaders to consider colonization as a viable alternative for African Americans.

SLAVE UPRISINGS

While, after the Revolution, black northerners grew increasingly aware of the limits to their freedom, black southerners faced perpetual slavery. As cotton production expanded westward, as new slave states entered the Union, and as masters in such border slave states as Maryland and Virginia turned away from the revolutionary commitment to gradual emancipation, slaves faced several choices.

Some lowered their expectations and loyally served their masters. Most continued patterns of day-to-day resistance. Many escaped. A few risked their lives to join forceful revolutionary movements to destroy slavery violently. When just several hundred out of hundreds of thousands of slaves rallied behind Gabriel in 1800 near Richmond or Charles Deslondes in 1811 near New Orleans, they frightened white southerners and raised hopes for freedom among countless African Americans.

The egalitarian principles of the American and French revolutions influenced Gabriel and Deslondes. Unlike earlier slave rebels, they acted not to revenge personal grievances or to establish maroon communities but to destroy slavery because it denied natural human rights to its victims. The American Declaration of Independence and the legend of Haiti's Toussaint Louverture provided the intellectual foundations for their

Toussaint Louverture (1744–1803) led the black rebellion in the French colony of St. Domingue on the Caribbean island of Hispaniola that led to the creation of the independent black republic of Haiti in 1804. Louverture became an inspiration for black rebels in the United States.   Stock Montage, Inc./Historical Pictures Collection

efforts. Between 1791 and 1804, Louverture, against great odds, had led the enslaved black people of the French sugar colony of Saint Domingue—modern Haiti—to freedom and independence. Many white planters fled the island with their slaves to take refuge in Cuba, Jamaica, South Carolina, Virginia, and, somewhat later, Louisiana. The Haitian slaves carried the spirit of revolution with them to their new homes.

During the early 1790s, black unrest and rumors of pending revolt mounted in Virginia. In this revolutionary atmosphere, Gabriel, the human property of Thomas Prosser Sr., prepared to lead a massive slave insurrection. Gabriel was an acculturated and literate blacksmith well aware of the rationalist and revolutionary currents of his time.

While the ideology of the American Revolution shaped Gabriel's actions, he also perceived that white people were politically divided and distracted by an undeclared naval war with France. He enjoyed secret support from a few white people and hoped poor white people generally would rally to his cause as he and his associates planned to kill those who supported slavery and take control of central Virginia.

But on August 30, 1800—the day set for the uprising—two slaves revealed the plan to white authorities while a tremendous thunderstorm prevented Gabriel's followers from assaulting Richmond. Then Virginia governor—and future U.S. president—James Monroe quickly had suspects arrested. In October Gabriel and 26 others, convicted of "conspiracy and insurrection," were hanged. By demonstrating that slaves could organize for large-scale rebellion, they left a legacy of fear among slaveholders and hope for liberation among southern African Americans.

The far less famous Louisiana Rebellion took place under similar circumstances. By the early 1800s, refugees from Haiti had settled with their slaves in what was then known as Orleans Territory. As they arrived, rumors of slave insurrection spread across the territory. The rumors became reality on January 8, 1811, when Deslondes, a Haitian native and slave driver on a plantation north of New Orleans, initiated a massive revolt in cooperation with maroons.

Deslondes's force of at least 180 men and women marched south along the Mississippi River toward New Orleans, with leaders on horseback, and with flags and drums, but few guns. The revolutionaries plundered and burned plantations but killed only two white people and one recalcitrant slave. On January 10 a force of about 700 territorial militia, slaveholding vigilantes, and U.S. troops overwhelmed them. Well-armed white men slaughtered 66 of the rebels and captured 30. They tried the captives without benefit of counsel, found 22 (including Deslondes) guilty of rebellion, and shot them. Then they cut off the hands of the executed men and displayed them on pikes to warn other African Americans of the consequences of revolt.

THE WHITE SOUTHERN REACTION

Although Deslondes's uprising was one of the few major slave revolts in American history, Gabriel's conspiracy and events in Haiti left the more significant legacy. For generations, enslaved African Americans regarded Louverture as a black George Washington and recalled Gabriel's revolutionary message. The networks among slaves that Gabriel established survived his death and, as the domestic slave trade carried black Virginians southwestward, they carried his promise of liberation with them.

White southerners responded to these black revolutionary currents by rejecting the egalitarian values of the Enlightenment. Because white southerners feared race war and believed emancipation would encourage African Americans to begin such a war, most of them determined to make black bondage stronger, not weaker. Beginning with South Carolina in December 1800, southern states outlawed assemblies of slaves, placed curfews on slaves and free black people, and made manumissions more difficult.

THE WAR OF 1812

Many of the themes developed in this chapter—African-American patriotism, opportunities for freedom, migration sentiment, and influences pushing slaves toward revolutionary action—are reflected in the black experience during the U.S. war with Great Britain that began in 1812 and lasted until early 1815. The roots of this conflict lay in a massive military and economic struggle between Britain and France for mastery over the Atlantic world.

British military support for American Indian resistance in the Old Northwest, an American desire to annex Canada, and especially Britain's interference with American ships trading with Europe drew the United States into the Franco-British conflict and resulted in the War of 1812, which ended in a draw. Yet many Americans regarded the war as a second struggle for independence and, as had been the case during the American Revolution, black military service and white fear of slave revolt played important roles.

By 1812 prejudice and fear of revolt had nearly nullified positive white memories of black Patriot soldiers during the Revolution. When the war with Britain began, therefore, the southern states refused to enlist black men for fear they would use their guns to aid slave revolts. Meanwhile a lack of enthusiasm for the war among many northerners,

21 "We Have Met the Enemy and They Are Ours"

Perry's Famous Victory on Lake Erie in War of 1812, Erie, Pa.   99824

The Battle of Put-in Bay, fought on Lake Erie in September 1813, was a notable American victory during the War of 1812. This postcard suggests the prevalence of black sailors among American commandant Oliver Hazard Perry's crew.

combined with the absence of a British threat to their part of the country, kept northern states from mobilizing black troops in 1812 and 1813.

Southern fears of slave revolt mounted during the spring of 1813 when the British invaded the Chesapeake. As they had during the Revolution, British generals offered slaves freedom in Canada or the British West Indies in return for help. In response, African Americans joined the British army that burned Washington, D.C., in 1814 and attacked Baltimore.

The threat this British army posed to Philadelphia and New York led to the first active black involvement in the war on the American side. The New York state legislature authorized two black regiments, offered freedom to slaves who enlisted, and promised compensation to their masters. Meanwhile, African Americans in Philadelphia and New York City volunteered to help build fortifications. In Philadelphia, James Forten, Richard Allen, and Absalom Jones patriotically raised a "Black Brigade," which never saw action because the British halted when they failed to capture Baltimore. African-American men did fight, however, at two of the war's most important battles: the naval engagement at Put-in-Bay in September 1813 and at the Battle of New Orleans, fought in January 1815.

THE MISSOURI COMPROMISE

After 1815, as the United States emerged from a difficult war, sectional issues between the North and South, which constitutional compromises and the political climate had pushed into the background, revived. The nation's first political parties—Federalist and the Republican—had failed to confront slavery as a national issue. The northern wing of the modernizing Federalist Party had abolitionist tendencies. But during the 1790s when they controlled the national government, the Federalists did not raise the slavery issue. Then the victory of the state-rights-oriented Republican Party in the election of 1800 fatally weakened the Federalists as a national organization and brought a series of implicitly proslavery administrations to power in Washington.

It took innovations in transportation and production that began during the 1810s, as well as the rapid disappearance of slavery in the northern states, to transform the North into a region consciously at odds with the South's traditional culture and slave-labor economy. The first major expression of intensifying sectional differences over slavery and its expansion came in 1819 when the slaveholding Missouri Territory, which had been carved out of Louisiana Territory, applied for admission to the Union as a slave state. Northerners expressed deep reservations about the creation of a new slaveholding state. Many of them feared it would destroy the political balance between the sections and encourage the expansion of slavery elsewhere.

African American also appreciated the significance of the Missouri crisis. Black residents of Washington, D.C., crowded into the U.S. Senate gallery as that body debated the issue. Finally, Henry Clay of Kentucky, the slaveholding Speaker of the House of Representatives, directed an effort that produced in 1820 a compromise that temporarily quieted discord. This Missouri Compromise (see Map 5-2) permitted Missouri to become a slave state, maintained a sectional political balance by admitting Maine, which had been part of Massachusetts, as a free state, and banned slavery north of the 36° 309 line of latitude in the old Louisiana Territory. Yet sectional relations would never be the same, and a new era of black and white antislavery militancy soon confronted the South.

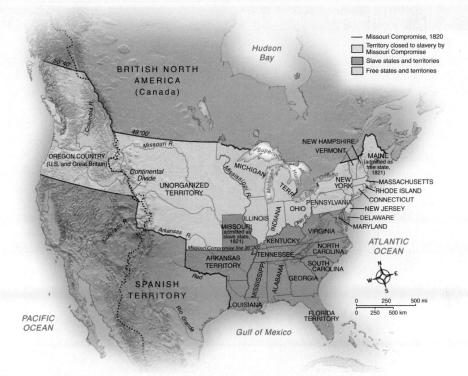

MAP 5-2 • The Missouri Compromise of 1820   Under the Missouri Compromise, Missouri entered the Union as a slave state, Maine entered as a free state, and Congress banned slavery in the huge unorganized portion of the old Louisiana Territory north of the 36° 30' line of latitude.

▶ *Which section of the United States did the Missouri Compromise favor?*

CONCLUSION

The period between the War for Independence and the Missouri Compromise was a time of transition for African Americans. On one hand, the legacy of the American Revolution brought emancipation in the North and a promise of equal opportunity with white Americans. On the other hand, by the 1790s slavery and racism had begun to grow stronger. Through a combination of antiblack prejudice among white people and African Americans' desire to preserve their own cultural traditions, black urban communities arose in the North, Upper South, and, occasionally—in Charleston and Savannah, for example—in the Deep South.

Spreading freedom in the North and the emergence of black communities North and South were heartening developments. There were new opportunities for education, spiritual expression, and economic growth. But the mass of African Americans remained in slavery. The forces for human bondage were growing stronger. Freedom for those who had gained it in the Upper South and North was marginal and precarious.

Gabriel's conspiracy in Virginia and Deslondes's rebellion in Louisiana indicated that revolutionary principles persisted among black southerners. But these rebellions

African-American Events	National Events

1775

| **1775**
First antislavery society formed
1777
Vermont bans slavery | **1776**
Declaration of Independence
1777
Battle of Saratoga |

1780

| **1780**
Pennsylvania begins gradual emancipation
1781
Elizabeth Freeman begins her legal suit for freedom
1782
Virginia repeals its ban on manumission
1783
Massachusetts bans slavery and black men gain the right to vote there
1784
Connecticut and Rhode Island begin gradual abolition | **1781**
Articles of Confederation ratified

1783
Great Britain recognizes independence of the United States |

1785

| **1785**
New Jersey and New York defeat gradual emancipation
1787
Northwest Ordinance bans slavery in the territory north of the Ohio River | **1786**
Shays's Rebellion

1787
Constitutional Convention

1789
Constitution ratified; George Washington becomes president |

1790

| **1793**
Congress passes Fugitive Slave Law

1794
Mother Bethel Church established in Philadelphia

New York adopts gradual abolition plan | |

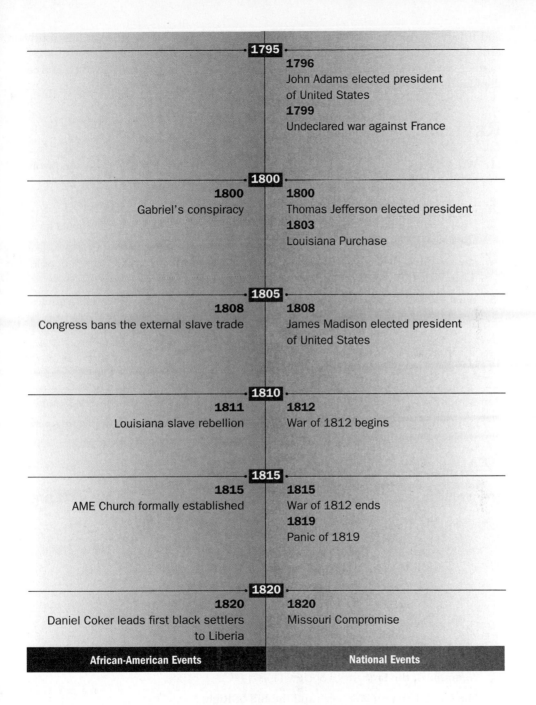

1795

1796
John Adams elected president
of United States
1799
Undeclared war against France

1800

1800
Gabriel's conspiracy

1800
Thomas Jefferson elected president
1803
Louisiana Purchase

1805

1808
Congress bans the external slave trade

1808
James Madison elected president
of United States

1810

1811
Louisiana slave rebellion

1812
War of 1812 begins

1815

1815
AME Church formally established

1815
War of 1812 ends
1819
Panic of 1819

1820

1820
Daniel Coker leads first black settlers
to Liberia

1820
Missouri Compromise

African-American Events   **National Events**

and British recruitment of slaves during the War of 1812 convinced most white south-erners that black bondage had to be permanent. Therefore, African Americans looked to the future with mixed emotions. A few determined that the only hope for real free-dom lay in migration from the United States.

REVIEW QUESTIONS

1. Which were stronger in the era of the early American republic, the forces in favor of black freedom or those in favor of continued enslavement?

2. How were African Americans able to achieve emancipation in the North?

3. How was the U.S. Constitution, as it was drafted in 1787, proslavery? How was it antislavery?

4. How important were separate institutions in shaping the lives of free black people during the late eighteenth and early nineteenth centuries?

5. What led Gabriel to believe he and his followers could abolish slavery in Virginia through armed uprising?

PEARSON myhistorylab CONNECTIONS

Reinforce what you learned in this chapter by studying the many documents, images, maps, review tools, and videos available at **www.myhistorylab.com**.

READD AND REVIEW

✔●▸ **Study** and **Review** on **myhistorylab.com** STUDY PLAN FOR CHAPTER 5

▢●▸ **Read** the **Document** on **myhistorylab.com**

Absalom Jones, Sermon on the Abolition of the International Slave Trade (1808)

An Architect Describes African-American Music and Instruments in 1818

Congress Prohibits Importation of Slaves (1807)

John Wesley, "Thoughts Upon Slavery" (1774)

Mathew Carey, "A Short Account of the Malignant Fever..." (1793)

Missouri Admitted to Statehood, Slavery at Issue (1820)

Preamble of the Free Africa Society (1787)

The United States *Constitution* and the Bill of Rights

Venture Smith Narrative (1798)

●▸ **View** the **Map** on **myhistorylab.com**

The Louisiana Purchase

The War of 1812

The Missouri Compromise of 1820

RESEARCH AND EXPLORE

mysearchlab

Consider this question in a short research paper.

How did the Missouri Compromise of 1820 shape the lives of African Americans?

▶ Read the **Document** on **myhistorylab.com**

Exploring America: Ratification of the Constitution

👁 Watch the **Video** on **myhistorylab.com**

Slavery and the Constitution

——————— ((•⌐ Listen on myhistorylab.com ———————

Hear the audio files for Chapter 5 at
www.myhistorylab.com.

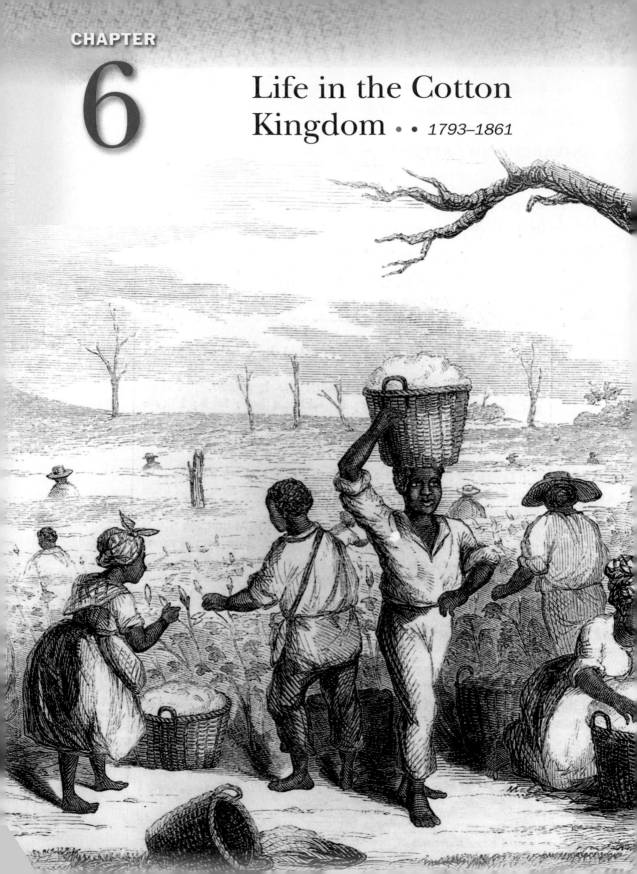

Life in the Cotton Kingdom •• *1793–1861*

Hear the audio files for Chapter 6 at **www.myhistorylab.com.**

FOCUS QUESTIONS

WHY DID slavery expand in the cotton kingdom?

WHAT TYPES of labor did slaves perform in the south?

WHAT WAS the domestic slave trade?

HOW DID African Americans adapt to life under slavery?

HOW HAVE historians evaluated slavery and slaves?

An illustration of cotton picking on a Georgia plantation taken from "The Illustrated London News" on September 27, 1856.

I n this chapter we describe the life of black people in the slave South from the rise of the Cotton Kingdom during the early 1800s to the eve of the Civil War in 1860. Between 1820 and 1861, slavery in the South was at its peak as a productive system and a means of white control over black southerners. We describe the extent of this slave system, how it varied across the South, and how it operated. We investigate the slave communities that African-American men, women, and children built.

THE EXPANSION OF SLAVERY

Eli Whitney's invention of the cotton gin in 1793 made the cultivation of cotton profitable on the North American mainland. It was the key to the rapid and extensive expansion of slavery from the Atlantic coast to Texas (see Map 6-1). In the process, enslaved black labor cleared forests and drained swamps to make these lands fit for cultivation.

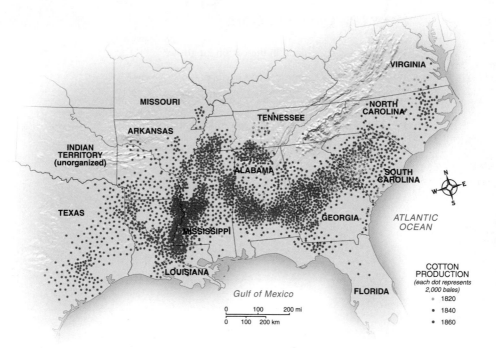

MAP 6-1 • Cotton Production in the South, 1820–1860 Cotton production expanded westward between 1820 and 1860 into Alabama, Mississippi, Louisiana, Texas, Arkansas, and western Tennessee.

Source: Sam Bowers Hilliard, Atlas of Antebellum Southern Agriculture *(Louisiana State University Press, 1984) pp. 67–71.*

▶ *Why did cotton production spread westward?*

The expansion of the cotton culture led to the removal of the American Indians—some of them slaveholders—who inhabited this vast region. During the 1830s and 1840s, the U.S. Army forced the Cherokee, Chickasaw, Choctaw, Creek, and most Seminole to leave their ancestral lands for Indian Territory in what is now Oklahoma. Many Indians died during this forced migration, and the Cherokee remember it as "The Trail of Tears." Yet the Cherokees created in Oklahoma an economy dependent on black slave labor. By 1860 there were 7,000 slaves there, 14 percent of the population. Far fewer slaves lived in the other western territories.

SLAVE POPULATION GROWTH

In the huge region stretching from the Atlantic coast to Texas, however, a tremendous increase in the number of African Americans in bondage accompanied territorial expansion. The slave population of the United States grew almost sixfold between 1790 and 1860, from 697,897 to 3,953,760 (see Table 6-1). But slaves were not equally distributed

TABLE 6.1 U.S. Slave Population, 1820 and 1860

	1820	1860
United States	1,538,125	3,953,760
North	19,108	64
South	1,519,017	3,953,696
Upper South	965,514	1,530,229
Delaware	4,509	1,798
Kentucky	127,732	225,483
Maryland	107,397	87,189
Missouri	10,222	114,931
North Carolina	205,017	331,059
Tennessee	80,107	275,719
Virginia	425,153	490,865
Washington, D.C.	6,377	3,185
Lower South	553,503	2,423,467
Alabama	41,879	435,080
Arkansas	1,617	111,115
Florida	*	61,745
Georgia	149,654	462,198
Louisiana	69,064	331,726
Mississippi	32,814	436,631
South Carolina	258,475	402,406
Texas	*	182,566

*Florida and Texas were not states in 1820.

Source: *Ira Berlin*, Slaves without Masters: The Free Negro in the Antebellum South *(New York: New Press, 1974), 396–97.*

across the region. Western North Carolina, eastern Tennessee, western Virginia, and most of Missouri never had many slaves. In contrast the slave populations in the newer cotton-producing states, such as Alabama and Mississippi, grew quickly. Virginia had the largest slave population throughout the period. But its growth rate slowed, while the rate greatly increased in the cotton producing states. By 1860 Mississippi had joined South Carolina as the only states that had more slaves than free inhabitants.

OWNERSHIP OF SLAVES IN THE OLD SOUTH

Slaveholders were as unevenly distributed as the slaves and, unlike slaves, were declining in number. In 1830, 1,314,272 white southerners (36 percent), out of a total white southern population of 3,650,758, owned slaves. In 1860 only 383,673 white southerners (4.7 percent), out of a total white southern population of 8,097,463, owned slaves. Even counting the immediate families of slaveholders, only 1,900,000 (or less than 25 percent of the South's white population) had a direct interest in slavery in 1860.

Almost half of the South's slaveholders owned fewer than five slaves, only 12 percent owned more than 20 slaves, and just 1 percent owned more than 50 slaves. Yet more than half the slaves belonged to masters who had 20 or more slaves. So although the typical slaveholder owned few slaves, the typical slave lived on a sizable plantation.

Since the time of Anthony Johnson in the mid-1600s, a few black people had been slaveholders, and this class continued to exist. Many of them became slaveholders to protect their families from sale and disruption. This was because, as the nineteenth century progressed, southern states made it more difficult for masters to manumit slaves and for slaves to purchase their freedom. The states also threatened to expel former slaves from their territory. In response to these circumstances, black men and women sometimes purchased relatives who were in danger of sale to traders and who—if legally free—might be forced by white authorities to leave a state.

Some African Americans, however, purchased slaves for financial reasons and passed those slaves on to their heirs. Most black people who became masters for financial reasons owned five or fewer slaves. But William Johnson, a wealthy free black barber of Natchez, Louisiana, owned many slaves whom he employed on a plantation he purchased. Some black women, such as Margaret Mitchell Harris of South Carolina and Betsy Somayrac of Natchitoches, Louisiana, also became slaveholders for economic reasons. Harris was a successful rice planter who inherited 21 slaves from her white father.

SLAVE LABOR IN AGRICULTURE

Agricultural laborers constituted 75 percent of the South's slave population. About 55 percent of the slaves cultivated cotton; 10 percent grew tobacco; and 10 percent produced sugar, rice, or hemp. About 15 percent were domestic servants, and the remaining 10 percent worked in trades and industries.

TOBACCO

Tobacco remained important in Virginia, Maryland, Kentucky, and parts of North Carolina and Missouri during the 1800s (see Map 6-2). A difficult crop to produce, tobacco required

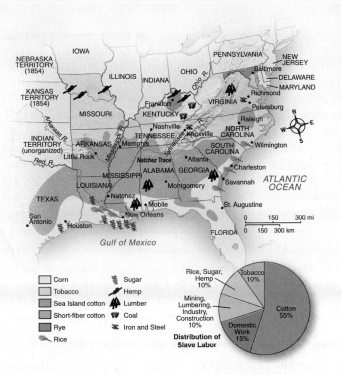

MAP 6-2 • Agriculture, Industry, and Slavery in the Old South, 1850 The experience of the African American in slavery varied according to their occupation and the region of the South in which they lived.

▶ *What does* this map suggest concerning slave labor?

a long growing season and careful cultivation. Robert Ellett, a former slave, recalled that when he was just eight years old he worked in Virginia "a-worming tobacco." He "examined tobacco leaves, pull[ed] off the worms, if there were any, and killed them." He claimed that if an overseer discovered that slaves had overlooked worms on the tobacco plants, the slaves were whipped or forced to eat the worms. Nancy Williams, another Virginia slave, recalled that sometimes as a punishment slaves had to inhale burning tobacco until they became nauseated.

RICE

Unlike the cultivation of tobacco, which spread westward and southward from Maryland and Virginia, rice production remained confined to the low country of South Carolina and Georgia. As they had since colonial times, slaves in these coastal regions worked according to task systems that allowed them considerable autonomy. Because rice fields needed to be flooded for the seeds to germinate, slaves maintained elaborate systems of dikes and ditches. Influenced by West African methods, they sowed, weeded, and harvested the rice crop.

Rice cultivation was labor intensive, and rice plantations needed large labor forces to grow and harvest the crop and maintain the fields. By 1860 twenty rice plantations had 300 to 500 slaves, and eight others had between 500 and 1,000. These vast plantations represented sizable capital investments, and masters or overseers carefully monitored slave productivity.

SUGAR

Another important crop that grew in a restricted region was sugar, which slaves cultivated on plantations along the Mississippi River in southern Louisiana. Commercial production of sugarcane did not begin in Louisiana until the 1790s. It required a consistently warm climate, a long growing season, and at least 60 inches of rain per year.

Raising sugarcane and refining sugar also required constant labor. Together with the great profitability of the sugar crop, these demands encouraged masters to work their slaves hard. Slave life on sugar plantations was extremely harsh, and African Americans across the South feared being sent to labor on them. Slaves did this work in hot and humid conditions, adding to the toll it took on their strength and health. Because cane could not be allowed to stand too long in the fields, harvest time was hectic. As one former slave recalled, "On cane plantations in sugar time, there is no distinction as to the days of the week. They [the slaves] worked on the Sabbath as if it were Monday or Thursday."

COTTON

Although tobacco, rice, and sugar were economically significant, cotton was by far the South's and the country's most important staple crop. By 1860 cotton exports amounted to more than 50 percent annually of the dollar value of all U.S. exports (see Figure 6-1).

Cotton as a crop did not require cultivation as intensive as that needed for tobacco, rice, or sugar. But the cotton culture was so extensive that cotton planters as a group employed the most slave labor. By 1860 out of the 2,500,000 slaves employed in agriculture in the United States, 1,815,000 produced cotton. Cotton drove the South's economy and its westward expansion.

Demand for cotton fiber in the textile mills of Britain and New England stimulated the westward spread of cotton cultivation. This demand increased by at least 5 percent per year between 1830 and 1860. In response—and with the essential aid of Whitney's cotton gin—American production of cotton rose from 10,000 bales in 1793 to 500,000 annually during the 1820s to 4,491,000 bales in 1860. The new states of Alabama, Louisiana, and Mississippi led this mounting production.

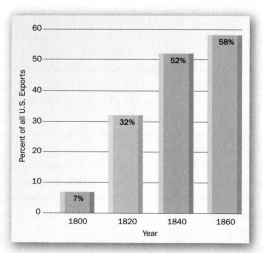

FIGURE 6-1 • Cotton Exports as a Percentage of all U.S. Exports, 1800–1860 Cotton rapidly emerged as the country's most important export crop after 1800 and key to its prosperity. Because slave labor produced the cotton, increasing exports strengthened the slave system itself.

Picturesque scenes of ripening cotton fields are part of the romantic image of the Old South that popular novels, songs, and movies have perpetuated for so long. Yet such scenes mask the backbreaking labor enslaved African Americans performed and the anxiety and fear they experienced.

During the early nineteenth century, potential profits drew white farmers to the rich Black Belt lands of Mississippi and Alabama. Rapid population growth allowed Mississippi to gain statehood in 1817 and Alabama in 1819. By 1860 these states had become the leading cotton producers. They also had the greatest concentration of plantations with one hundred or more slaves. Twenty-four of Mississippi's slaveholders each owned between 308 and 899 slaves.

As huge agricultural units drew in labor, the price of slaves increased. During the 1830s, a prime male field hand sold in the New Orleans slave market for $1,250 (more than 35,000 current dollars). By the 1850s, such slaves cost $1,800 (more than 50,000 current dollars). Young women usually sold for up to $500 less than young men. Elderly slaves, unless they were highly skilled, sold for far less.

The enslaved men and women who worked in the cotton fields rose before dawn when the master or overseer sounded the plantation bell or horn. They ate breakfast and then assembled in work gangs of 20 or 25 under the control of black slave drivers. They plowed and planted in the spring. They weeded with heavy hoes in the summer and harvested in the late fall. During harvest season, adult slaves picked about 200 pounds of cotton per day. Regardless of the season, the work was hard, and white overseers whipped those who seemed to be lagging. Slaves usually got a two-hour break at midday in the summer and an hour to an hour and a half in the winter. Then they returned to the fields until sunset, when they went back to their cabins for dinner and an early bedtime enforced by the master or overseer.

COTTON AND TECHNOLOGY

Agricultural technology in the Cotton Kingdom was primitive compared to that in the Old Northwest. Free northwestern farmers by the 1840s used a variety of complex machines drawn by teams of horses, to plant, cultivate, and harvest crops. In contrast southern slave workers relied on simple plows and harrows, drawn by a single mule—as well as hand-held shovels, rakes, and heavy hoes—to perform similar work. Masters did not trust slaves with expensive machinery. They also preferred to invest in slaves and land rather than labor-saving devices. And the nature of the South's major crop had an essential impact. Because cotton ripened unevenly, nineteenth-century mechanical harvesters could not discern which plants were ready for harvest. Therefore, three times each harvest season, enslaved men, women, and children picked cotton bolls by hand.

Nineteenth-century technology nevertheless impacted slaves' lives. After 1811 the Mississippi River teamed with steamboats. Railroads helped open the Old Southwest to cotton production, which encouraged the growth of the domestic slave trade and the disruption of black families.

In some instances technology improved plantation conditions. Early in the nineteenth century, cotton gins became much larger and more efficient that the ones Eli Whitney designed during the 1790s. Enslaved men operated gins powered by mules. Once bolls had been cleaned of their seeds, slaves used presses, driven by either man or mule power, to form bales. Slaves packaged the bales in cloth bagging and took them by wagon to river steamboat landings for shipment to market.

By the early nineteenth century many slaves in Delaware, Maryland, and Virginia were cultivating wheat rather than tobacco. This 1831 lithograph portrays a demonstration of Cyrus McCormick's automatic reaper. It indicates the adaptability of slave labor to new technology. Neg.# ICHi-00013/Chicago History Museum

The technology available to enslaved women on cotton plantations was less sophisticated. They used heavy cast iron kettles for cooking food and washing clothes. Washing involved boiling garments in soapy water, beating them with "battling sticks" on "battling blocks," and returning them for another boiling before hanging them out to dry.

OTHER CROPS

Besides cotton, sugar, tobacco, and rice, slaves in the Old South produced other crops, including hemp, corn, wheat, oats, rye, white potatoes, and sweet potatoes. They also raised cattle, hogs, sheep, and horses. The hogs, and corn and other grains, were mainly for consumption on the plantations. But all the hemp, and much of the other livestock and wheat, were raised for the market. In fact, wheat replaced tobacco as the main cash crop in much of Maryland and Virginia. The transition to wheat encouraged many planters to substitute free labor for slave labor, but slaves grew wheat in the South until the Civil War.

Kentucky was the center of the hemp industry. Before the Civil War, planters used hemp, which is closely related to marijuana, to make rope and bagging for cotton bales. This tied Kentucky economically to the Deep South. But, because hemp required much less labor than rice, sugar, or cotton, Kentucky developed a distinctive slave system. Three slaves could tend 50 acres of hemp, so slave labor forces were much smaller than elsewhere.

HOUSE SERVANTS AND SKILLED SLAVES

About 75 percent of the slave workforce in the nineteenth century consisted of field hands. But because masters wanted to make their plantations as self-sufficient as possible, they also employed some slaves as house servants and skilled craftsmen. Slaves who did not have to do field labor were an elite and considered themselves privileged. However, they were also suspended between two different worlds.

House slaves worked as cooks, maids, butlers, nurses, and gardeners. Their work was less physically demanding than fieldwork, and they often received better food and clothing. But house servants' jobs were also more stressful than field hands' jobs because the servants were under closer white supervision.

In addition, house servants were by necessity cut off from the slave community centered in the slave quarters. Yet, house servants rarely sought to become field hands. Conversely, field hands had little desire to be exposed to the constant surveillance house servants had to tolerate.

Skilled slaves tended to be even more of a slave elite than house servants. Slave carpenters, blacksmiths, and millwrights built and maintained plantation houses, slave quarters, and machinery. Because they might need to travel to get tools or spare parts, such skilled slaves gained a more cosmopolitan outlook than field hands or house servants. They got a taste of freedom, which from the masters' point of view was dangerous.

As plantation slavery declined in the Chesapeake, skilled slaves could leave their master's estate to "hire their time." In effect, these slaves worked for money. Although masters often kept all or most of what they earned, some of these skilled slaves merely paid their master a set rate and lived as independent contractors.

URBAN AND INDUSTRIAL SLAVERY

Most skilled slaves who hired their time lived in the South's towns and cities, where they interacted with free black communities. Many of them resided in Baltimore and New Orleans, which were major ports and the Old South's largest cities.

Slave populations in southern cities were often large, although they tended to decline between 1800 and 1860. In 1840 slaves were a majority of Charleston's population of 29,000. They nearly equaled white residents in Memphis and Augusta, which had total populations of 14,700 and 6,000, respectively. Slaves were almost one-quarter of New Orleans's population of 145,000.

Urban slaves served as domestics, washwomen, waiters, artisans, stevedores, drayers, hack drivers, and general laborers. In general, they did the urban work that foreign immigrants undertook in northern cities. If urban slaves purchased their freedom, they usually continued in the same line of work they had done as slaves. Particularly in border cities like Baltimore, Louisville, and Washington, urban slaves increasingly relied on their free black neighbors—and sympathetic white people—to escape north. Urban masters often let slaves purchase their freedom over a term of years to keep them from leaving. In Baltimore, during the early nineteenth century, this sort of **"term slavery"** was gradually replacing slavery for life.

Industrial slavery overlapped with urban slavery, but southern industries that employed slaves were often in rural areas. By 1860 about 5 percent of southern slaves—approximately 200,000 people—worked in industry. Enslaved men, women, and children worked in textile mills in South Carolina and Georgia, sometimes beside white people.

The bulk of the 16,000 people who worked in the South's lumber industry in 1860 were slaves. Slaves also did most of the work in the naval stores industry of North Carolina and Georgia. In western Virginia, they labored in the salt works of the Great Kanawha

River Valley, producing the salt used to preserve meat. During the 1820s many workers in the Maryland Chemical Works in Baltimore, which manufactured industrial chemicals, pigments, and medicines, were slaves. Most southern industrialists did not purchase slaves. Instead they hired slaves from their masters. The industrial work slaves performed was often dangerous and tiring. But, like urban slaves, industrial slaves had more opportunities to advance themselves, enjoyed more autonomy, and often received cash incentives. Industrial labor, like urban labor, was a path to freedom for some.

PUNISHMENT

Those who used slave labor, whether on plantations, small farms, in urban areas, or industry, frequently offered incentives to induce slaves to perform well. Yet slave labor by definition is forced labor based on the threat of physical punishment. Masters denied that this brutal aspect detracted from what they claimed was the essentially benign and paternalistic character of the South's "peculiar institution." After all, Christian masters found support in the Bible for using corporal punishment to chastise servants.

While fear of the lash drove slaves to work, it also encouraged them to cooperate among themselves for mutual protection. Parents and older relatives taught slave children how to avoid punishment and still resist masters and overseers. They worked slowly—but not too slowly—and feigned illness to maintain their strength. They broke tools and injured mules, oxen, and horses to tacitly protest their condition. This pattern of covert resistance and physical punishment caused anxiety for both masters and slaves. Resistance (described in more detail in Chapter 3) often forced masters to reduce work hours and improve conditions. Yet few slaves escaped being whipped at least once during their lives in bondage.

THE DOMESTIC SLAVE TRADE

The expansion of the Cotton Kingdom south and west combined with the decline of slavery in the Chesapeake to stimulate the domestic slave trade. As masters in Delaware, Maryland, Virginia, North Carolina, and Kentucky trimmed excess slaves from their workforces—or switched entirely from slave to wage labor—they sold men, women, and children to slave traders. The traders in turn shipped these unfortunate people to the slave markets of New Orleans and other cities for resale. Masters also sold slaves as punishment, and fear of being "sold down river" led many slaves in the Chesapeake to escape.

The number of people traded was huge and, considering that many of them were ripped away from their families, tragic. Starting in the 1820s, about 150,000 slaves per decade moved toward the southwest either with their masters or traders. Between 1820 and 1860, an estimated 50 percent of the slaves of the Upper South moved involuntarily into the Southwest.

Traders operated compounds called slave prisons or slave pens in Baltimore, Maryland; Washington, D.C.; Alexandria and Richmond, Virginia; Lexington, Kentucky; Charleston, South Carolina; and in smaller cities. Most of the victims of the trade moved on foot in groups called **coffles,** chained or roped together. There was also a considerable coastal trade in slaves from Chesapeake ports to New Orleans and, by the 1840s, some slave traders were carrying their human cargoes in railroad cars.

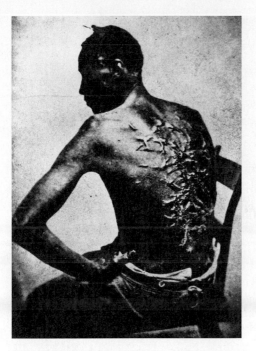

In this 1863 photograph a former Louisiana slave displays the scars that resulted from repeated whippings. Although this degree of scarring is exceptional, few slaves were able to avoid being whipped at least once in their lives.
National Archives and Records Administration

The domestic slave trade demonstrated the falseness of slaveholders' claims that slavery was a benign institution. Driven by economic necessity, profit, or a desire to frustrate escape plans, masters in the Upper South irrevocably separated husbands and wives, mothers and children, brothers and sisters. Traders sometimes tore babies from their mothers' arms. A few slaves who had been sold south managed to keep in touch with those they had left behind through letters and travelers. But most could not, and after the abolition of slavery in 1865, many African Americans used their new freedom to travel across the South looking for relatives from whom they had been separated long before.

SLAVE FAMILIES

The families that enslaved African Americans sought to preserve had been developing in America since the seventeenth century. However, such families had no legal standing. Most enslaved men and women could choose their own mates, although masters sometimes arranged such things.

Families were the core of the African-American community in slavery. Even though no legal sanctions supported slave marriages and the domestic slave trade could sunder them, many such marriages endured. Before they wed, some couples engaged in courting rituals while others rejected "such foolishness." Similarly, slave weddings ranged from simply "taking up" and living together to religious ceremonies replete with food and frolics.

Slave couples usually lived together in cabins on their master's property. They had little privacy because nineteenth-century slave cabins were rude, small, one-room dwellings that two families might have to share. But couples who shared cabins were generally better off than husbands and wives who were the property of different masters and

This woodcut of a black father being sold away from his family appeared in *The Child's Anti Slavery Book* in 1860. Family ruptures, like the one shown, were among the more common and tragic aspects to slavery, especially in the upper South, where masters claimed slavery was "mild."
Courtesy of the Library of Congress

lived on different plantations. In these cases, children lived with their mother, and their father visited when he could in the evenings.

CHILDREN

Despite these difficulties, slave parents were able to instruct their children in family history, religion, and the skills required to survive in slavery. In particular, parents impressed on children the importance of extended family relationships. The ability to rely on grandparents, aunts and uncles, cousins, and honorary relatives was a hedge against the family disruption that the domestic slave trade might inflict. The extended black family also provided slaves with the independent resources they needed to avoid complete physical, intellectual, cultural, and moral subjugation to their masters.

Infant mortality rates for black southerners were higher than they were for white people. There were several reasons for this. Enslaved black women usually had to do field labor up to the time they delivered a child, and their diets lacked necessary nutrients. Consequently, they tended to have babies whose weights at birth were less than normal. Enslaved infants were also more likely to be subject to postpartum maladies than were other children. More than 50 percent of slave children died before the age of five.

Slaveholders contributed to high infant mortality rates probably more from ignorance than malevolence. It was, after all, in the master's economic self-interest to have slave mothers produce healthy children. Masters often allowed mothers a month to recuperate after giving birth and several months thereafter off from fieldwork to nurse their babies. Although this reduced the mother's productivity, the loss might be made up by the children's labor when they entered the plantation workforce. Unfortunately, many infants needed more than a few months of breast-feeding to survive.

Slave childhood was short. Early on, parents and others taught youngsters about the realities of plantation life, and—as early as age six—they undertook so-called light chores. Work became more taxing as the children grew older, until, between the ages of eight and twelve, they performed adult fieldwork. Sale away from their families, particularly in the Upper South, also accelerated progress to adulthood.

VOICES

A SLAVEHOLDER DESCRIBES A NEW PURCHASE

In this letter to her mother, a white Louisiana woman, Tryphena Blanche Holder Fox, describes her husband's purchase of a slave woman and her children. Several things are apparent in the letter—that investing in slaves was expensive, that the white woman's only concern for the slave woman and her children was their economic value, that it was up to the white woman to supervise the new slaves, and that the slave woman showed her displeasure with her situation.

Hygiene [Jesuit Bend, Louisiana]
Sunday, Dec. 27th 1857

Dear Mother,

We are obliged to save every dollar he can "rake & scrape" to pay for a negro woman . . . She has two likely children . . . and is soon to have another, and he only pays fourteen hundred for the three. She is considered an excellent bargain . . . he would not sell her and the children for less than $2,000. She came & worked two days, so we could see what she was capable of. . . . She was sold by a Frenchman. . . . He has a family of ten & she had all the work to do besides getting her own wood & water from the river. She was not used to do this, and gave them a great deal of trouble. . . . How much trouble she will give me, I don't know, but I think I can get along with her, passable well any how. Of course it increased my cares, for having invested so much in one purchase, it will be to my interest to see that the children are well taken care of & clothed and fed. All of them give more or less trouble. . . .

■ What does Tryphena reveal about the management of slaves?
■ What does she indicate about the ability of slaves to force concessions from their masters?

SOURCE: Tryphena Blanche Holder Fox to Anna Rose Holder, December 27, 1857, Mississippi Department of Archives and History, Jackson, Mississippi.

SEXUAL EXPLOITATION

As with forced separations, masters' sexual exploitation of black women disrupted enslaved families. Abuse of black women began during the Middle Passage and continued after the abolition of slavery in the United States in 1865. Long-term relationships between masters and enslaved women were common in the nineteenth-century South. The relationship between Thomas Jefferson and his slave Sally Hemings is the most infamous of these. It began in 1787 when Hemings served as caretaker to one of Jefferson's daughters at his household in Paris, where he was U.S. ambassador to France. At that time Jefferson was 44 and Hemings was about fourteen. By modern standards, their relationship began with statutory rape, and Hemings's unfree status and that of her children limited her ability to resist sexual advances.

Even more common than relationships like that of Jefferson and Hemings were instances in which masters, overseers, and their sons forced slave women to have sex against their will. This routine rape caused great distress. Former slave Harriet Jacobs wrote in her autobiography, "I cannot tell how much I suffered in the presence of these wrongs, nor how I am still pained by the retrospect."

White southerners justified sexual abuse of black women in several ways. They maintained that black women were naturally promiscuous and seduced white men. Some proslavery apologists argued that the sexual exploitation of black women by white men reduced prostitution and promoted purity among white women.

DIET

The slaves' diet hardly raised the moral issues associated with the sexual exploitation of black women by white men. The typical plantation's weekly ration was enough to maintain an adult's body weight and, therefore, appeared to be adequate. But even when black men and women added vegetables, eggs, and poultry that they raised or fish and small game that they caught, this diet was (according to modern medical science) deficient in calcium, vitamin C, riboflavin, protein, and iron and other minerals. Because these vitamins and nutrients are essential to the health of people who perform hard labor in a hot climate, slaves frequently suffered from chronic illnesses. Yet masters and white southerners generally consumed the same sort of food that slaves ate and, in comparison to people in other parts of the Atlantic world, enslaved African Americans were not undernourished.

African-American cooks, primarily women, developed a distinctive cuisine based on African culinary traditions. The availability in the South of such African foods as okra, yams, collard greens, benne seeds, and peanuts strengthened their culinary ties to that continent. Cooking also gave black women the ability to control part of their lives and to demonstrate their creativity.

CLOTHING

Enslaved men and women had less control over what they and their children wore than how they cooked. The clothing worn by slaves was usually made of homespun cotton or wool. Some slaves also received hand-me-downs from masters and overseers. Slaves usually received clothing allotments twice a year. At the fall distribution, slave men received two outfits for the cold weather along with a jacket and a wool cap. At the spring distribution, they received two cotton outfits. Slave women received at each distribution two simply cut dresses of calico or homespun.

Because masters gave priority to clothing adult workers, small children often went naked during the warm months. Depending on their ages and the season, children received garments called *shirts* if worn by boys and *shifts* if worn by girls.

HEALTH

Low birth weight, diet, and clothing all affected the health of slaves. Before the 1830s various diseases were endemic among them, and death could come quickly. Much of this ill health resulted from overwork in the South's hot, humid summers, exposure to cold during the winter, and poor hygiene. Slave quarters, for example, rarely had privies, human waste could contaminate drinking water, and food was prepared under unsanitary conditions.

The South's warm climate encouraged mosquito-borne diseases like yellow fever and malaria, the growth of bacteria, and the spread of viruses. Interaction between

Freed African Americans sit outside old slave headquarters at Fort George Island in Florida. "Remains of Slave Quarters, Fort George Island, Florida," ca. 1865, Stereograph. © Collection of The New-York Historical Society, Negative no. 48163.

people of African and European descent increased the types of illnesses. Smallpox, measles, and gonorrhea were European diseases. Malaria, hookworm, and yellow fever came from Africa. The sickle-cell blood trait protected people of African descent from malaria but could cause sickle-cell anemia, a painful, debilitating, and fatal disease.

African Americans were also more susceptible to other afflictions than were persons of European descent. They suffered from lactose intolerance, which greatly limited the amount of calcium they could absorb from dairy products, and from a limited ability to acquire enough vitamin D from the sunlight in temperate regions. Because many slaves lost calcium through perspiration while working, these characteristics led to a high incidence of debilitating diseases.

However, black southerners constituted the only New World slave population that grew by natural reproduction. Although the death rate among slaves was higher than among white southerners, it was similar to that of Europeans. Slave health also improved after 1830 when their rising economic value persuaded masters to improve slave quarters, provide warmer winter clothing, reduce overwork, and hire physicians to care for bond people. During the 1840s and 1850s, slaves were more likely than white southerners to be cared for by a physician, although there was often little that nineteenth-century doctors could do to combat disease.

Enslaved African Americans also used traditional remedies—derived from Africa and passed down by generations of women—to treat the sick. Nineteenth-century medical knowledge was so limited that some of these folk remedies were more effective than those prescribed by white physicians.

African-American Spirituals

Enslaved African Americans drew strength to endure their difficult lives from community, tradition, religion, and music. Combining all of these was the African-American spiritual. In these religious songs, enslaved African Americans merged African musical traditions with biblical stories and Protestant hymns to create a unique form of music. Spirituals were rarely sung the same way twice, and their original versions were never recorded. Still, many of the songs survive in some form.

▲ Music was an important part of life on the plantation.

Excerpt from "Go Down Moses"

When Israel was in Egypt's Land,
Let my people go,
Opressed so hard they could not stand,
Let my people go.

Chorus
Go down, Moses,
Way down in Egypt's Land.
Tell ol' Pharaoh,
Let my people go.

Thus saith the Lord, bold Moses said,
Let my people go,
If not, I'll smite your first-born dead,
Let my people go.

Chorus
Go down, Moses,
Way down in Egypt's Land.
Tell ol' Pharaoh,
Let my people go.

No more shall they in bondage toil,
Let my people go,
Let them come out with Egypt's spoil,
Let my people go.

Chorus
Go down, Moses,
Way down in Egypt's Land.
Tell ol' Pharaoh,
Let my people go.

In what way did African-American spirituals combine African and European influences to create something new?

THE SOCIALIZATION OF SLAVES

African Americans had to acquire the skills needed to protect themselves and their loved ones from a brutal slave system. Folk tales often derived from Africa, but on occasion from American Indians, helped pass such skills from generation to generation.

The heroes of the tales are animal tricksters with human personalities. Most famous is Brer Rabbit, who in his weakness and cleverness represents African Americans in slavery. Although the tales portray Brer Rabbit as far from perfect, he uses his wits to overcome threats from strong and vicious antagonists, principally Brer Fox, who represents slaveholders. By hearing these stories and rooting for Brer Rabbit, slave children learned how to conduct themselves in a difficult environment.

They learned to watch what they said to white people, not to talk back, to withhold information about other African Americans, to dissemble. In particular, they refrained from making antislavery statements and camouflaged their awareness of how masters exploited them. Masters tended to miss the subtlety of the divided consciousness of their bond people. When slaves refused to do simple tasks correctly, masters saw it as black stupidity rather than resistance.

RELIGION

Along with family and socialization, religion helped African Americans cope with slavery. Some masters denied their slaves access to Christianity, and some slaves ignored the religion. But by the mid-nineteenth century, most American slaves practiced a Protestantism similar, but not identical, to that of most white southerners.

Many masters during the nineteenth century sponsored plantation churches for slaves, and white missionary organizations also supported such churches. These churches, white ministers told their black congregations that Christian slaves must obey their earthly masters as they did God. This was not what slaves wanted to hear.

Instead of services sponsored by masters, slaves preferred a semisecret black church they conducted themselves under the leadership of self-called, often illiterate black preachers. They emphasized Moses and deliverance from bondage rather than consistent theology or Christian meekness.

THE CHARACTER OF SLAVERY AND SLAVES

For over a century, historians have debated the character of the Old South's slave system and the people it held in bondage. During the 1910s southern historian Ulrich B. Phillips portrayed slavery as a benign, paternalistic institution in which Christian slaveholders cared for largely content slaves. With different emphasis, historian Eugene D. Genovese has, since the 1960s, also placed paternalism at the heart of southern plantation slavery.

Other historians, however, deny that paternalism had much to do with a system that rested on force. Since the 1950s they have contended that slaveholders exploited their bondpeople in a selfish quest for profits. Many masters never met their slaves face to face. Most slaves suffered whippings at some point in their lives, and over half the slaves caught up in the domestic slave trade were separated from their families.

Scholars have also compared slavery in the American South with its counterpart in Latin America. Historians note that slaves in Latin American countries influenced by Roman law and the Roman Catholic Church enjoyed more protection from abusive masters than did slaves in the United States, where English law and Protestant Christianity dominated. Routes to freedom, through self-purchase and manumission, were more available in Latin America than in the Old South. There was more interracial marriage and therefore, some historians maintain, less racism in Latin America than in the United States. But other historians have established that protections offered by law and religion to slaves in Latin America were more theoretical than practical. They argue that racism there merely took a different form than it did in the United States.

Another debate has centered on the character of enslaved African Americans. Historians such as Phillips, who were persuaded by the slaveholders' justifications of the "peculiar institution," argued that African Americans were genetically predisposed to being slaves and were therefore content in their status. In 1959 Stanley M. Elkins changed the debate by arguing that black people were not inherently inferior or submissive, but that concentration-camp-like conditions on plantations made them into childlike "Sambos" as dependent on their masters as inmates in Nazi extermination camps were on their guards.

A scholarly reaction to Elkins's study led to current understandings of the character of African Americans in slavery. Since the 1960s historians have argued that rather than dehumanizing black people, slavery led them to create institutions that allowed them some control over their lives. Slaves built families, churches, and communities. According to these historians, African-American resistance forced masters to accept African work patterns and black autonomy in the slave quarters. Although these historians may idealize the strength of slave communities within a brutal plantation context, they have enriched our understanding of slave life.

CONCLUSION

African-American life in slavery during the time of the Cotton Kingdom is a vast subject. As slavery expanded westward before 1860, it varied from region to region and according to the crops slaves cultivated. Although cotton became the South's most important product, many African-American slaves continued to produce tobacco, rice, sugar, and hemp. In the Chesapeake, slaves grew wheat. Others tended livestock or worked in cities and industry. Meanwhile, enslaved African Americans continued to build the community institutions that allowed them to maintain their cultural autonomy and persevere within a brutal system.

The story of African Americans in southern slavery is one of labor, perseverance, and resistance. Black labor was responsible for the growth of a southern economy that helped produce prosperity throughout the United States. Black men and women preserved and expanded an African-American cultural heritage that included African, European, and American Indian roots. They resisted determined efforts to dehumanize them. They developed family relationships, communities, churches, and traditions that helped them preserve their character as a people.

African-American Events	National Events
1810	
	1812
	Louisiana becomes a state
1815	
1816	**1817**
William Ellison purchases his freedom	Mississippi becomes a state
1818	**1819**
Suppression of Charleston's AME Church	Alabama becomes a state
1819	
Frederick Douglass born in Maryland	
1820	
1822	**1820**
Denmark Vesey Conspiracy, Charleston, S.C.	Missouri Compromise
	1821
	Missouri becomes a state
	1824
	John Quincy Adams elected president
1825	
	1828
	Andrew Jackson elected president
1830	
1831	
Nat Turner's revolt	
1832	
Virginia legislature defeats gradual abolition	
1835	
1838	**1836**
Frederick Douglass apprenticed in Baltimore	Cherokee Trail of Tears
1839	
Amistad slave revolt	
1840	
1841	
Solomon Northup kidnapped	

African-American Events	National Events
1845	
1845	**1845**
Betsy Somayrac's will	Texas annexed as a slave state
	1846
	War against Mexico begins
	1848
	Annexation of New Mexico and California
1850	
1852	**1850**
Frederick Law Olmsted's first tour of southern states	Compromise of 1850
1853	**1854**
Solomon Northup publishes *Twelve Years a Slave*	Kansas-Nebraska Act
1855	
1855	**1856**
Celia's trial and execution for killing her master	Republican Party's first presidential election
1857	
Supreme Court issues *Dred Scott* decision	
1860	
	1860
	The secession movement begins

REVIEW QUESTIONS

1. How did the domestic slave trade and the exploitation of black women by white males affect slave families?

2. Were black slaveholders significant in the history of slavery?

3. How did urban and industrial slavery differ from plantation slavery in the Old South?

4. What impact did housing, nutrition, and disease have on the lives of slaves between 1820 and 1860?

5. How did black Christianity differ from white Christianity in the Old South? How did black Christianity in the South differ from black Christianity in the North?

myhistorylab CONNECTIONS

Reinforce what you learned in this chapter by studying the many documents, images, maps, review tools, and videos available at **www.myhistorylab.com.**

READ AND REVIEW

✔•**Study** and **Review** on **myhistorylab.com** STUDY PLAN FOR CHAPTER 6

Read the **Document** on **myhistorylab.com**

A Muslim Slave Speaks Out (1831)

A Slave Girl Tells of Her Life (1861)

A Slave Tells of His Sale at Auction (1848)

Charles C. Jones, The Religious Instruction of Negroes in the United States (1842)

E. S. Abdy, Description of a Washington, D.C. Slave Pen (1835)

Farm Journal Reports on the Care and Feeding of Slaves (1836)

Frederick Douglass, excerpt from Narrative of the Life (1845)

Georgia Slave Codes (1848)

Southern Novel Depicts Slavery (1832)

State Laws Govern Slavery (1824)

View the **Map** on **myhistorylab.com**

Agriculture, Industry, and Slavery in the Old South 1850

RESEARCH AND EXPLORE

mysearchlab

Consider these questions in a short research paper.

How did blacks resist the oppression of the slave system? What steps did whites take to eliminate resistance?

((•**Listen** on **myhistorylab.com**

"Go Down Moses" sung by Bill McAdoo

——————— ((•**Listen** on **myhistorylab.com** ———————

Hear the audio files for Chapter 6 at
www.myhistorylab.com.

FOCUS QUESTIONS

WHAT WERE the demographics of black freedom?

HOW DID the policies of the Jacksonian democrats favor slaveholders?

HOW WAS black freedom limited in the north?

WHAT WERE the characteristics of northern black communities?

WHAT INSTITUTIONS did African Americans rely on most?

HOW DID free African Americans live in the south and in the west?

This lithograph, published in 1818 by antislavery author Jesse Torrey Jun, depicts a free black man still in handcuffs and leg irons after an attempt to kidnap him into slavery. He is relating details of his experience to a sympathetic white man. The sparsely furnished attic room reflects the living conditions of many free African Americans of the time.

During the 40 years before the Civil War, pervasive white prejudice limited the lives of black people. Such prejudice was nearly as common in the North as in the South. While southern legislatures considered expelling free black people from their states, northern legislatures—particularly in the Old Northwest—restricted black people's ability to move into their states. White workers North and South, fearing competition for jobs, sponsored legislation that limited most free African Americans to menial employment. White people also required most black people to live in segregated areas of cities. Yet such ghettoized African-American communities cultivated a dynamic cultural legacy and built enduring institutions. This chapter picks up the story of free black communities begun in Chapter 5 to provide a portrait of free African Americans between 1820 and the start of the Civil War.

DEMOGRAPHICS OF FREEDOM

In 1820 there were 233,504 free African Americans living in the United States. In comparison there were 1,538,125 slaves and 7,861,931 white people. Of the free African Americans, 99,281 lived in the North, 114,070 in the Upper South, and only 20,153 in the Deep South (see Map 7-1). Free people of color accounted for 2.4 percent of the American population and 3 percent of the southern population.

By 1860 the free African-American population had reached 488,070 (see Figures 7-1 and 7-2). In that year 226,152 free black people lived in the North, 224,963 lived in the Upper South, and 36,955 lived in the Deep South. A few thousand free black people also lived in the west beyond Missouri, Arkansas, and Texas. Meanwhile slaves had increased

MAP 7-1 • The Slave, Free Black, and White Population of the United States in 1830 This map does not distinguish the slave from the free black population of the free states, although the process of gradual emancipation in several northeastern states was still under way and some black northerners remained enslaved. Note: Figures for free states are rounded to the nearest thousand.
Source: For slave states, Ira Berlin, *Slaves without Masters: The Free Negro in the Antebellum South* (New York: New Press, 1971); for free states, *Historical Statistics of the United States* (Washington: GPO, 1960).

▶ *Which states* had the largest and the smallest free black populations in 1830?

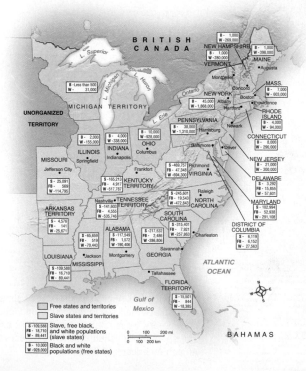

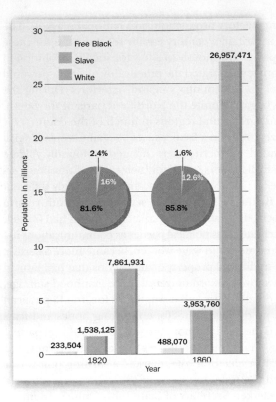

FIGURE 7-1 • The Free Black, Slave, and White Population of the United States in 1820 and 1860 The bar graph shows the relationship among free African-American, slave, and white populations in the United States in the years 1820 and 1860. The superimposed pie charts illustrate the percentages of these groups in the population in the same years.

to just under four million, and massive immigration had tripled the white population to 26,957,471. The proportion of free African Americans had dropped to just 1.6 percent of the total American population and to 2.1 percent of the southern population when the Civil War began in 1861.

Free African Americans accounted for a significantly larger percentage of the population of large cities than they did of the total American population. In Baltimore free black people represented 12 percent of the 212,418 residents. There, as well as in Richmond, Norfolk, and other smaller cities of the Upper South, free African Americans interacted with enslaved populations to create communities embracing both groups. The largest black urban population in the North was in Philadelphia, where 22,185 African Americans made up 4.2 percent of approximately 533,000 residents.

THE JACKSONIAN ERA

After the War of 1812, free African Americans—like other Americans of the time—witnessed rapid economic, social, and political change. Between 1800 and 1860, a **market revolution** transformed the North into a modern industrial society. An economy based on subsistence farming, goods produced by skilled artisans, and local markets grew

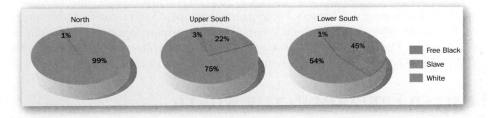

FIGURE 7-2 • The Free Black, Slave, and White Population by Region, 1860 These pie charts compare the free black, slave, and white populations of the North, Upper South, and lower South in 1860. Note the near balance of the races in the lower South.

into one marked by commercial farming, factory production, and national markets. The Industrial Revolution that had begun in Britain a century earlier set the stage for these changes. But transportation had to improve enormously to allow for such a revolution in America. After 1807 when Robert Fulton demonstrated the practicality of steam-powered river vessels, steamboats speeded travel on the country's inland waterways. During the 1820s a system of turnpikes and canals began to unite the North and parts of the South. By the 1830s railroads linked urban and agricultural regions in much of the country.

As faster transportation revolutionized trade, as a factory system began to replace small shops run by artisans, and as cities expanded, northern society changed profoundly. A large urban working class arose. Artisans and small farmers feared for their future. Entrepreneurs began to replace the traditional social elite. The North also became increasingly different from a still largely premodern South. By the 1820s northern states bristled with reform movements designed to deal with the social dislocations the market revolution had caused.

The market revolution also helped create mass political parties as communications improved, populations became more concentrated, and wage workers became more assertive. By 1810 states had begun dropping the traditional property qualifications that had limited citizens' right to vote. One by one, they moved toward universal white manhood suffrage. This trend doomed the openly elitist Federalist Party and disrupted its foe, the Republican Party. As the market revolution picked up during the 1820s, unleashing hopes and fears among Americans, politicians recognized the need for more broadly based political parties.

The 1824 presidential election in which four candidates ran as Republicans, but none received a majority of the popular or electoral vote, marked a turning point. War hero Andrew Jackson of Tennessee led the field, but in early 1825 Congress—exercising its duty to decide such elections—elected Secretary of State John Quincy Adams of Massachusetts. Adams, along with his secretary of state, Henry Clay, hoped to promote industrialization through a national program of federal government aid. Led by Martin Van Buren of New York, Jackson's supporters organized a new Democratic Party to counter the Adams-Clay program. By appealing to slaveholders—who believed economic nationalism favored the North over the South—and to "the common man" throughout the country, the Democrats elected Jackson in 1828.

Jackson was a strong but controversial president. During the **Nullification Crisis** of 1832–1833 he acted as a nationalist in facing down South Carolina's attempt to nullify—to block—the collection of the U.S. tariff (tax) on imports within the state. Otherwise, Jackson, who owned many slaves, promoted states' rights, economic localism, and the territorial expansion of slavery. In opposition to Jackson, Henry Clay, a Kentucky slaveholder, and others formed the Whig Party during the early 1830s.

In contrast to Democratic politicians who increasingly made racist appeals to antiblack prejudices among white voters, Whigs generally adopted a more conciliatory tone on race. By the late 1830s, a few northern Whigs claimed their party opposed slavery and racial oppression. They were, however, exaggerating. The Whigs often nominated slaveholders for the presidency, and few Whig politicians defended the rights of African Americans.

LIMITED FREEDOM IN THE NORTH

Addressing an interracial audience in Boston, white abolitionist Joseph C. Lovejoy in 1846 described the North as a land "partially free." Lovejoy was especially concerned that the Fugitive Slave Law of 1793 extended into the northern states the power of southern masters to enslave African Americans. But white northerners also limited black freedom by enacting **black laws**, by rarely allowing black men to vote, by advocating segregated housing, schools, and transportation, and by limiting African Americans' employment opportunities.

The Fugitive Slave Law endangered the freedom of northern black men, women, and children. Those who had escaped from slavery, of course, lived in fear that as long as they stayed in the United States they might be seized and returned to their erstwhile masters. But any black northerner could be kidnapped, taken to a southern state, and enslaved under the aegis of this law. Throughout the antebellum period, vigilance against kidnapping was an important part of northern African-American life.

BLACK LAWS

As indicated in previous chapters, the racially egalitarian impulse of the revolutionary era had by the 1790s begun to wane among white Americans. Meanwhile, the dawning Romantic Age—characterized by a sentimental fascination with uniqueness—encouraged a general belief that each ethnic and racial group had its own inherent spirit that set it apart from others. As white Americans began to perceive self-reliance, intellectual curiosity, the capacity for self-government, military valor, and an energetic work ethic as inherently "Anglo-Saxon" characteristics, they began to believe other racial groups lacked these virtues.

Most white northerners wanted nothing to do with African Americans. They paradoxically dismissed black people as incapable of honest work and feared black competition for jobs. Contact with African Americans, they believed, had degraded white southerners and would also corrupt white northerners if permitted. Therefore, as historian Leon Litwack puts it, "Nearly every northern state considered, and many adopted, measures to prohibit or restrict the further immigration of Negroes."

Between 1804 and 1849, Ohio's "black laws" required that African Americans entering the state produce legal evidence that they were free, register with a county clerk, and post a $500 bond "to pay for their support in case of want." State and local authorities rarely enforced these provisions, and when the Ohio Free Soil Party brought about their repeal in 1849, about 25,000 African Americans lived in the state. But these rules made black people insecure. Moreover, other provisions of Ohio's black laws were rigorously enforced, including those that prohibited black testimony against white people, black service on juries, and black enlistment in the state militia.

In 1813 Illinois Territory threatened that African Americans who tried to settle within its borders would be repeatedly whipped until they left. Indiana citizens ratified a state constitution in 1851 that explicitly banned all African Americans from the state, and Michigan, Iowa, and Wisconsin followed Indiana's example. Yet, as in Ohio, these states rarely enforced such restrictive laws. As long as they did not feel threatened, white Northerners were usually willing to tolerate a few black people (see Table 7-1).

DISFRANCHISEMENT

The disfranchisement of black voters was, except in most of New England, common throughout the North during the antebellum decades. The same white antipathy to African Americans that led to exclusionary legislation supported the movement to deny the right to vote to black men (no women could vote anywhere in the United States during most of the nineteenth century). Because northern antiblack sentiment was so strong in the Old Northwest, before the Civil War no black men were ever allowed to vote in

TABLE 7.1 Black Population in the States of the Old Northwest, 1800–1840

	1800	1810	1820	1830	1840
Ohio	337	1,899	4,723	9,574	17,345
Michigan		144	174	293	707
Illinois		781	1,374	2,384	3,929
Indiana	298	630	1,420	3,632	7,168
Iowa					188

SOURCE: *James Oliver Horton and Lois E. Horton,* In Hope of Liberty: Culture, Community, and Protest among Northern Free Blacks, 1700–1860 (*Oxford University Press, 1997*), 104.

Ohio, Indiana, Illinois, Michigan, Wisconsin, and Iowa. But the older northern states had allowed black male suffrage, and efforts to curtail it were by-products of Jacksonian democracy.

During the eighteenth and early nineteenth centuries, the dominant elite in the northeastern states had used property qualifications to prevent poor black and poor white men from voting. Because black people were generally poorer than white people, these property qualifications gave most white men the right to vote and denied it to most black men. It was the egalitarian movement to remove property qualifications that led to the outright disfranchisement of most black voters in the Northeast.

Both advocates and opponents of universal white male suffrage opposed allowing all black men to vote. They alleged that in cer-

Masters often posted monetary offers for the return of runaway slaves.

tain places black men would be elected to office, morally suspect African Americans would corrupt the political process, black people would be encouraged to try to mix socially with white people, and justifiably angry white people would react violently. Therefore, the movement for universal white manhood suffrage transformed a class issue into a racial one.

New Jersey stopped allowing black men to vote in 1807 and in 1844 adopted a white-only suffrage provision in its state constitution. In 1818 Connecticut determined that, although black men who had voted before that date could continue to vote, no new black voters would be allowed. At the other extreme, Maine, New Hampshire, Vermont, and Massachusetts—none of which had a significant African-American minority—made no effort to deprive black men of the vote. In the middle were Rhode Island, New York, and Pennsylvania, which had protracted struggles over the issue.

In 1822 Rhode Island denied that black men were eligible to vote in its elections, but in 1842 a popular uprising against the state's conservative government extended the franchise to all men, black and white. In New York an 1821 state constitutional convention defeated an attempt to disfranchise all black men. Instead, it raised the property qualification for black voters while eliminating it for white voters. This provision denied the right to vote to nearly all of the 10,000 black men who had previously voted in the state. African Americans nevertheless remained active in New York politics. As supporters of the Liberty Party in 1844, the Whig Party in 1846, and of the **Free-Soil Party** in 1848, they fought unsuccessfully to regain equal access to the polls.

Developments in Pennsylvania resulted in a more absolute elimination of black suffrage. In 1838, delegates to a convention to draft a new state constitution voted to enfranchise all white men and disfranchise all black men. Although African-American leaders organized to prevent the new constitution from being adopted, Pennsylvanians ratified it by a narrow margin.

SEGREGATION

Exclusionary legislation was confined to the Old Northwest, and not all northern states disfranchised black men. But no black northerner could avoid being victimized by a pervasive determination among white people to segregate society.

Northern hotels, taverns, and resorts turned black people away unless they were the servants of white guests. African Americans were either banned from public lecture halls, art exhibits, and religious revivals or could attend only at certain times. When they were allowed in churches and theaters, they had to sit in segregated sections.

African Americans faced special difficulty trying to use public transportation. They could ride in stagecoaches only if there were no white passengers. As rail travel became more common during the late 1830s, companies set aside special cars for African Americans. In Massachusetts in 1841, a railroad first used the term **Jim Crow**, which derived from a blackface minstrel act, to describe these cars. Later the term came to define other forms of racial segregation as well. In cities, many omnibus and streetcar companies barred African Americans entirely, even though urban black people had little choice but to try to use these means of transportation. Steamboats refused to rent cabins to African Americans, forcing them to remain on deck at night and during storms. All African Americans, regardless of their wealth or social standing, endured such treatment.

In this atmosphere, African Americans learned to distrust white people. Even when African Americans interacted with white people on an ostensibly equal basis, there were underlying tensions. James Forten's wealthy granddaughter Charlotte Forten, who attended an integrated school in Boston, wrote in her diary, "It is hard to go through life meeting contempt with contempt, hatred with hatred, fearing with too good reason, to love and trust hardly any one whose skin is white—however lovable, attractive, and congenial."

African Americans moving to northern cities were not surprised to find segregated black neighborhoods. There were "Nigger Hill" in Boston, "Little Africa" in Cincinnati, "Hayti" in Pittsburgh, and Philadelphia's "Southside." Conditions in these ghettoes were often dreadful, but they provided a refuge from constant insult and a place where black institutions could develop.

Because African Americans representing all social and economic classes lived in segregated neighborhoods, the quality of housing in them varied. But, at its worst, such housing was bleak and dangerous. One visitor called the black section of New York City's Five Points "the worst hell of America," and other black urban neighborhoods were just as bad. Southern visitors to northern cities blamed the victims, insisting that the plight of many urban black northerners proved that African Americans were better off in slavery.

TABLE 7.2 Free Black Population of Selected Cities, 1800–1850

City	1800	1850
Baltimore	2,771	25,442
Boston	1,174	1,999
Charleston	951	3,441
New Orleans	800 (estimated)	9,905
New York	3,499	13,815
Philadelphia	4,210	10,736
Washington	123	8,158

SOURCE: *Leonard P. Curry,* The Free Black in Urban America, 1800–1850: The Shadow of the Dream *(Chicago: University of Chicago Press, 1981), 250.*

BLACK COMMUNITIES IN THE URBAN NORTH

Northern African Americans lived in both rural and urban areas during the antebellum decades, but it was urban neighborhoods with their more concentrated black populations that nurtured black community life (see Table 7-2). African-American urban communities of the antebellum period developed from the free black communities that had emerged from slavery in the North during the late eighteenth century. The communities varied from city to city and from region to region, yet they had much in common and interacted with each other. Resilient families, poverty, class divisions, active church congregations, the continued development of voluntary organizations, and concern for education characterized them.

THE BLACK FAMILY

As they became free, northern African Americans left their masters and established their own households. Some left more quickly than others, and in states such as New York and New Jersey, where gradual emancipation extended into the nineteenth century, the process continued into the 1820s. By then the average black family in northern cities had two parents and between two and four children. However, in both the Northeast and Old Northwest, single-parent black families, usually headed by women, became increasingly common during the antebellum period. The difficulty black men had gaining employment may have influenced this trend. It certainly was a function of a high mortality rate among black men, which made many black women widows during their forties.

Both financial need and African-American culture encouraged black northerners to take in boarders and create extended families. Economic considerations determined such arrangements, but friendship and family relationships also played a part. Sometimes entire nuclear families boarded, but most boarders were young, single, and male.

THE STRUGGLE FOR EMPLOYMENT

The rising tide of immigration from Europe hurt northern African Americans economically. Before 1820 black craftsmen had been in demand but, given the choice, white people referred to employ other white people, and black people suffered. To make matters worse for African Americans, white workers excluded young black men from apprentice-ships, refused to work with black people, and used violence to prevent employers from hiring black workers when white workers were unemployed. By the 1830s these practices had driven African Americans from the skilled trades. By the 1850s black men were losing to Irish immigrants unskilled work as longshoremen, drayers, railroad workers, hod-carriers, porters, and shoe-shiners and positions in such skilled trades as barbering.

By 1847 in Philadelphia, 80 percent of employed black men did unskilled labor. Barbers and shoemakers predominated among those black workers with skills. Only .5 percent held factory jobs. Among employed black women, 80 percent either washed clothes or worked as domestic servants. By the 1850s black women, too, were losing work to Irish immigrants.

Unskilled black men often could not find work. When they did work, they received low wages. To escape such conditions in Philadelphia and other port cities, they became sailors. By 1850 about 50 percent of the crewmen on American merchant and whaling vessels were black.

THE NORTHERN BLACK ELITE

Despite the poor prospects of most northern African Americans, a northern black elite emerged during the first six decades of the nineteenth century. Membership in this elite could be achieved through talent, wealth, occupation, family connections, complexion, and education. The elite led in the development of black institutions and culture, in the antislavery movement, and in the struggle for racial justice. It was also the bridge between the black community and sympathetic white people.

Although few African Americans achieved financial security during the antebellum decades, black people could become rich in many ways. Segregated neighborhoods gave rise to a black professional class of physicians, lawyers, ministers, and undertakers who served an exclusively black clientele. Black merchants could gain wealth selling to black communities. Other relatively well-off African Americans included skilled tradesmen, such as carpenters, barbers, waiters, and coachmen, who generally found employment among white people.

Although less so than in the South, complexion also influenced social standing among African Americans in the North, especially in cities like Cincinnati that were close to the South. White people often preferred to hire people of mixed race, successful black men often chose light-complexioned brides, and African Americans generally accepted white notions of human beauty.

By the 1820s the black elite had become better educated and more socially polished than its less wealthy black neighbors, yet it could never disassociate itself from them. Segrega-tion and discriminatory legislation in the North applied to all African Americans regardless of class and complexion, and all African Americans shared a common culture and history.

Conspicuous among the black elite were entrepreneurs who, against considerable odds, gained wealth and influence in the antebellum North. As we noted in Chapter 5, James Forten was one of the first of them, and several other examples indicate the char-acter of such people. John Remond—who as a child migrated from Curacao, a Dutch-ruled island in the Caribbean, to Salem, Massachusetts—and his wife, Nancy Lenox Remond, became prosperous restaurateurs, caterers, and retailers. Louis Hayden, who escaped from slavery in Kentucky in 1845, had by 1849 become a successful haberdasher and an abolitionist in Boston. Perhaps most successful were Stephen Smith and his part-ner William Whipper, who had extensive business interests in southeastern Pennsylvania.

INVENTORS

In some cases, members of the black elite owed their success to technological innovations. In 1834 Henry Blair of Maryland became the first African American to patent an invention—a horse-drawn mechanized corn seed planter. In 1836 he patented a similar cotton seed planter. Another black inventor was Henry Boyd. Born in Kentucky in 1802, Boyd purchased his freedom in 1826 and moved to Cincinnati. In 1835, as that city's leading bed manufacturer, he patented the "Boyd Bedstead."

Lewis Temple was another prominent black inventor of the period. Born free in Richmond, Virginia, Temple moved to the whaling port of New Bedford, Massachusetts. In 1845 Temple devised the toggle harpoon. Set with a wooden pin, the barbed toggle secured a whale to a harpooner's line on impact. At the same time Temple devised his harpoon, Joseph Hawkins of West Windsor, New Jersey, patented "a gridiron used to broil meat," which preserved juices as the meat cooked.

PROFESSIONALS

The northern black elite also included physicians and lawyers. Among the physicians, some, such as James McCune Smith and John S. Rock, received medical degrees. Either because they had been forced out of medical school or they chose not to go, other prominent black physicians practiced medicine without having earned a degree. (This was legal in the nineteenth century.)

Prominent black attorneys included Macon B. Allen, who gained admission to the Maine bar in 1844, and Robert Morris, who qualified to practice law in Massachusetts in 1847. Both Allen and Morris apprenticed with white attorneys, and Morris had a particularly successful and lucrative practice. Yet white residents thwarted his attempt to purchase a mansion in a Boston suburb.

ARTISTS AND MUSICIANS

Although they rarely achieved great wealth and have not become famous, black artists and musicians were also part of the northern African-American elite. Among the best-known artists were Robert S. Duncanson, Robert Douglass, Patrick Reason, and Edmonia Lewis. Several of them supported the antislavery movement through their artistic work.

Douglass, a painter who studied in England before establishing himself in Philadelphia, and Reason, an engraver, created portraits of abolitionists during

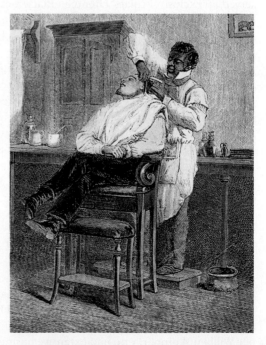

Barbering was one of the skilled trades open to black men during the antebellum years. Several wealthy African Americans began their careers as barbers. The Granger Collection, New York.

the 1830s. Reason also etched illustrations of the sufferings of slaves. Duncanson, who was born in Cincinnati and worked in Europe between 1843 and 1854, painted landscapes and portraits. Lewis, the daughter of a black man and a Chippewa woman, enrolled with abolitionist help at Oberlin College in Ohio and studied sculpture in Rome. Her works, which emphasized African-American themes, came into wide demand after the Civil War.

The reputations of black professional musicians of the antebellum period have suffered in comparison with the great tradition of black folk music epitomized by spirituals. But in Philadelphia a circle of black musicians wrote and performed a wide variety of music for orchestra, voice, and solo instruments. Similar circles existed in New Orleans, Boston, Cleveland, New York, Baltimore, and St. Louis.

AUTHORS

The antebellum era was a golden age of African-American literature. Driven by suffering in slavery and limited freedom in the North, black authors portrayed an America that had not lived up to its revolutionary ideals. Black autobiography recounted life in bondage and dramatic escapes. The best known narrative of this type is Frederick Douglass's *Narrative of the Life of Frederick Douglass,* an American Slave, published in 1845.

African Americans also wrote history, novels, and poetry. In 1855 William C. Nell published *The Colored Patriots of the American Revolution,* which reminded its readers that black men had fought for freedom. William Wells Brown, who had escaped from slavery in Kentucky, became the first African-American novelist. His *Clotel, or the President's Daughter,* published in 1853, used the affair between Thomas Jefferson and Sally Hemings to explore in fiction the moral ramifications of slaveholders who fathered children with their bondwomen. Another black novelist of the antebellum years was Martin R. Delany. His *Blake, or the Huts of America,* a story of emerging revolutionary consciousness among southern slaves, ran as a serial in the *Weekly Anglo-African* during 1859. Black poets included George M. Horton, a slave living in North Carolina, who in 1829 published *The Hope of Liberty,* and James W. Whitfield of Buffalo.

African-American women who published fiction during the period included Frances Ellen Watkins Harper and Harriet E. Wilson. Harper was born free in Baltimore in 1825. Associated with the antislavery cause in Pennsylvania and Maine, she published poems that depicted the sufferings of slaves. Wilson published *Our Nig: Or, Sketches from the Life of a Free Black, in a Two-Story White House, North* in 1859. This was the first novel published by a black woman in the United States. In the genre of autobiographical fiction, it compared the lives of black domestic workers in the North with those of southern slaves.

At about the same time that Wilson wrote *Our Nig,* Hanna Crafts, who had recently escaped from slavery in North Carolina, wrote *The Bondwoman's Narrative.* Unpublished until 2002, this melodramatic autobiographical novel tells the story of a house slave and her escape to freedom.

AFRICAN-AMERICAN INSTITUTIONS

In the antebellum decades, the black institutions that had appeared during the revolutionary era in urban areas of the North, Upper South, and—to a lesser extent—the Deep South grew in strength, numbers, and variety. This was the result of growing black populations, the exertions of the African-American elite, and the persistence

VOICES

MARIA W. STEWART ON THE CONDITION OF BLACK WORKERS

Maria W. Stewart (1803–1879) was the first black female public speaker in the United States. She was strong willed and spoke without qualification what she believed to be the truth. At times she angered both black and white people. In the following speech, which she delivered in Boston in September 1831, Stewart criticized the treatment accorded to black workers—especially black female workers—in the North.

Tell us no more of southern slavery; for with few exceptions, although I may be very erroneous in my opinion, yet I consider our condition but little better than that.... After all, methinks there are no chains so galling as those that bind the soul, and exclude it from the vast field of useful and scientific knowledge....

I have asked several [white] individuals of my sex, who transact business for themselves, if providing our girls were to give them the most satisfactory references, they would not be willing to grant them an equal opportunity with others? Their reply has been—for their own part, they had no objection; but as it was not the custom, were they to take them into their employ, they would be in danger of losing the public patronage.

And such is the powerful force of prejudice. Let our girls possess whatever amiable qualities of soul they may; let their characters be fair and spotless as innocence itself; let their natural taste and ingenuity be what they may; it is impossible for scarce an individual of them to rise above the condition of servants....

I observed a piece ... respecting us, asserting that we were lazy and idle. I confute them on that point. Take us generally as a people, we are neither lazy nor idle: and considering how little we have to excite or stimulate us, I am almost astonished that there are so many industrious and ambitious ones to be found....

Again it was asserted that we were "a ragged set, crying for liberty." I reply to it, the whites have so long and so loudly proclaimed the theme of equal rights and privileges, that our souls have caught the flame also, ragged as we are. As far as our merit deserves, we feel a common desire to rise above the condition of servants and drudges. I have learnt, by bitter experience, that the continual hard labor deadens the energies of the soul, and benumbs the faculties of the mind; the ideas become confined, the mind barren, and, like the scorching sands of Arabia, produces nothing: or like the uncultivated soil, brings forth thorns and thistles....

Most of our color have dragged out a miserable existence of servitude from the cradle to the grave.... Do you [women] ask, why are you wretched and miserable? I reply, look at many of the most worthy and most interesting of us doomed to spend our lives in gentlemen's kitchens. Look at our young men, smart, active, and energetic, with souls filled with ambitious fire; if they look forward, alas! What are their prospects? They can be nothing but the humblest laborers, on account of their dark complexions; hence many of them lose their ambition, and become worthless....

■ Is Stewart correct in assuming that conditions for black northerners were little better than those for slaves?

■ According to Stewart, what was the impact of northern white prejudice on black workers?

SOURCE: Maria W. Stewart, "Lecture Delivered at the Franklin Hall, Boston, September 21, 1831," as quoted in Roy Finkenbine, *Sources of the African-American Past: Primary Sources in American History* (New York: Longman, 1997), 30–32.

John S. Rock, portrayed in an 1860 *Harper's Weekly* illustration, was born free in Salem, New Jersey in 1825. He earned a medical degree in 1852 and practiced law beginning in 1861.

of racial exclusion and segregation. Black institutions of the time included schools, mutual aid organizations, benevolent and fraternal societies, self-improvement and temperance associations, literary groups, newspapers and journals, and theaters. But, aside from families, the most important black community institution remained the church.

CHURCHES

Black church buildings were community centers. They housed schools and meeting places for other organizations. Antislavery societies often met in churches, and the churches harbored fugitive slaves. All of this went hand in hand with the community leadership black ministers provided. They began schools and various voluntary associations. They spoke against slavery, racial oppression, and what they considered weaknesses among African Americans. However, black ministers never spoke with one voice. Throughout the antebellum decades, many followed Jupiter Hammon in admonishing their congregations that preparing one's soul for heaven was more important than gaining equal rights on earth.

By 1846 the independent African Methodist Episcopal (AME) Church had 296 congregations in the United States and Canada with 17,375 members. Most black Baptist, Presbyterian, Congregationalist, Episcopal, and Roman Catholic congregations remained affiliated with white denominations, although they were rarely represented in regional and national church councils.

Many northern African Americans continued to attend white churches. To do so, they had to submit to second-class status. Throughout the antebellum years, northern white churches required their black members to sit in special sections during services, provided separate Sunday schools for black children, and insisted that black people take communion after white people.

During the 1830s and 1840s, some black leaders criticized the existence of separate black congregations and denominations. Frederick Douglass called them "negro pews, on a higher and larger scale." Growing numbers of African Americans, nevertheless, regarded such churches as sources of spiritual integrity and legitimate alternatives to second-class status among white Christians.

SCHOOLS

Education, like religion, was racially segregated in the North between 1820 and 1860. Some public schools, such as those in Cleveland, Ohio, during the 1850s, were racially

Edmonia Lewis

The life of Edmonia Lewis (1843–1911?) defied all expectations. When Lewis was about nine years old, her parents–a black man and a Chippewa woman–died. She and her brother Samuel were sent to live with her mother's sisters. At this point her options seemed limited, as mid-nineteenth-century America offered few choices to orphaned girls of mixed race. However, her situation changed dramatically when her brother, twelve years Edmonia's senior, went west to make his fortune and, against all odds, succeeded. Now in a position to support Edmonia, Samuel arranged for her to attend a series of schools, including Oberlin College. After college, Edmonia moved to Boston in 1863 to continue the study of sculpture she had begun in school. The sale of the sculptures she produced there, along with additional financial help from her brother, allowed her to fulfill her dream of studying and working in Italy. There she would stay for most of her adult life, producing work that found a ready audience in the United States. Her studio in Rome became a required stop for American travelers in Italy.

▲ *Hagar*, 1875. Many artists used the biblical figure Hagar as a symbol of slavery. Carved marble, 52 5/8 × 15 1/4 × 17 in.

Art Resource/Smithsonian American Art Museum

▲ Edmonia Lewis.

▲ Bust of American poet Henry Wadsworth Longfellow, 1872. Carved marble. 65.5 cm × 41 cm × 22 cm.

What themes connect the works pictured here? To what groups might Lewis's work have appealed?

integrated. But usually, as soon as 20 or more African-American children appeared in a school district, white parents demanded that black children attend separate schools.

How to educate African-American children who were not allowed to attend school with white children became a persistent issue in the North. Until 1848 Ohio and the other states of the Old Northwest simply excluded black children from public schools and refused to allocate tax revenues to support separate facilities. The northeastern states were more willing to undertake such expenditures. But across the North, white people were reluctant to use tax dollars to fund education for African Americans. As a result, appropriations for black public schools lagged far behind those for public schools white children attended.

Woefully inadequate public funding resulted in poor education or none at all for most black children across the North. The few black schools were dilapidated and overcrowded. White teachers who taught in them received lower pay than those who taught in white schools, and black teachers received even less, so teaching was generally poor.

Some black leaders defended segregated schools as better for black children than integrated ones. They probably feared that the real choice was between separate black schools or none at all. But, by the 1830s, most northern African Americans favored racially integrated public education, and during the 1840s Frederick Douglass became a leading advocate for such a policy. Douglass, other black leaders, and their white abolitionist allies made the most progress in Massachusetts, where by 1845 all public schools, except for those in Boston, had been integrated. After a ten-year struggle, the Massachusetts legislature finally ended segregated schools in that city too. By 1860 integration had advanced among the region's smaller school districts. But, except for those in Boston, urban schools remained segregated on the eve of the Civil War.

In fact, the black elite had more su ccess gaining admission to northern colleges during the antebellum period than most Africa n-American children had in gaining an adequate primary education. Some colleges served African Americans exclusively. Ashmum Institute in Oxford, Pennsylvania, was founded in 1854 to prepare black missionaries who would go to Africa. Ashmum, later renamed Lincoln University, was the first black institution of higher learning in the United States. Earlier some northern colleges had begun to admit a few black students. By 1860 many northern colleges, law schools, medical schools, and seminaries admitted black applicants, although not on an equal basis with white applicants.

VOLUNTARY ASSOCIATIONS

The African-American mutual aid, benevolent, self-improvement, and fraternal organizations that originated during the late eighteenth century proliferated during the antebellum decades. So did black literary and temperance associations.

Mutual aid societies became very attractive to black women. Among black benevolent societies, African Dorcas Associations were especially prevalent. Begun in 1828 in New York City by black women, these societies distributed used clothing to the poor, especially poor schoolchildren. During the early 1830s, black women also began New York City's Association for the Benefit of Colored Orphans.

Meanwhile, the Prince Hall Masons created new lodges in the cities of the Northeast and the Chesapeake. Beginning during the 1840s, Black Odd Fellows lodges also became common. But more prevalent were self-improvement, library, literary, and temperance organizations. These were manifestations of the reform spirit that swept the North and much of the Upper South during the antebellum decades. Closely linked to evangelical

Protestantism, reformers maintained that the moral regeneration of individuals was essential to perfecting society. African Americans shared this belief and formed myriad organizations to put it into practice.

Among the more prestigious of the societies for black men were the Phoenix Literary Society established in New York City, the Philadelphia Library Company of Colored Persons Pittsburgh's Theban Literary Society, and Boston's Adelphi Union for the Promotion of Literature and Science. Black women had the Female Literary Society of Philadelphia, New York City's Ladies Literary Society, the Ladies Literary Society of Buffalo, and Boston's Afric-American Female Intelligence Society. All of these societies were founded in the 1830s.

Black temperance societies were even more widespread than literary and benevolent organizations, although they also tended to be more short-lived. Like their white counterparts, black temperance advocates were middle-class activists who sought to stop those lower on the social ladder from abusing alcoholic beverages.

FREE AFRICAN AMERICANS IN THE UPPER SOUTH

The free black people of the Upper South had much in common with their northern counterparts. In particular, African Americans in the Chesapeake cities of Baltimore, Washington, Richmond, and Norfolk had ties to black northerners, ranging from family and church affiliations to business connections and membership in fraternal organizations. But significant differences that resulted from the South's agricultural economy and slavery set free people of color in the Upper South apart. Although nearly half the free black population in the North lived in cities, only one-third did so in the Upper South, hampering the development of black communities there.

A more important difference was the impact of slavery on the lives of free African Americans in the Upper South. Unlike black northerners, free black people in the

This lithograph depicts the bishops of the AME church and suggests both the church's humble origins and its remarkable growth during the antebellum years. Founder Richard Allen is portrayed at the center.

Upper South lived alongside slaves. Many had family ties to slaves and were more directly involved than black northerners in the slaves' suffering. They did so in several capacities, including efforts to prevent the sale south of relatives and friends, reimbursing masters for manumissions, and funding for freedom suits. Southern white politicians and journalists used the close connection between free black southerners and slaves to justify limiting the freedom of the former group.

Free black people of the Upper South were also more at risk of *being* enslaved than were black northerners. Except for Louisiana, with its French and Spanish heritage, all southern states assumed African Americans were slaves unless they could prove otherwise. Free black people had to carry **free papers**, which they had to renew periodically. They could be enslaved if their papers were lost or stolen, and sheriffs routinely arrested free black people on the grounds that they might be fugitive slaves. Free African Americans who got into debt in the South risked being sold into slavery to pay off their creditors.

As the antebellum period progressed, the distinction between free and enslaved African Americans narrowed in the Upper South. Although a few northern states allowed black men to vote, no southern state did after 1835. Free black people of the Upper South also had more difficulty traveling, owning firearms, congregating in groups, and being out after dark than did black northerners. Although residential segregation was less pronounced in southern cities than in the North, African Americans of the Upper South faced a more thorough exclusion from hotels, taverns, trains and coaches, parks, theaters, and hospitals.

Free black people in the Upper South also experienced various degrees of hardship in earning a living, although, during the nineteenth century, their employment expanded as slavery declined in Maryland and northern Virginia. Free persons of color in rural areas were generally tenant farmers. Some of them had to sign labor contracts that reduced them to semislavery. But others owned land and a few owned slaves. Rural free African Americans also worked as miners, lumberjacks, and teamsters. In Upper South urban areas, most free black men were unskilled day laborers, waiters, whitewashers, and stevedores. Free black women worked as laundresses and domestic servants. As in the North, the most successful African Americans were barbers, butchers, tailors, caterers, merchants, and those teamsters and hack drivers who owned their own horses and vehicles. Before 1850 free black people in the Upper South had less competition from European immigrants for jobs than was the case in northern cities. Therefore, although the Upper South had fewer factories than the North, more free black men worked in them. This changed during the 1850s when Irish and German immigrants competed against free black people in the Upper South just as they did in the North for all types of employment. As was the case in the North, immigrants often used violence to drive African Americans out of skilled trades.

These circumstances made it more difficult for free black people in the Upper South to maintain community institutions. In addition, the measures white authorities adopted to prevent slave revolt greatly limited free black autonomy, and such measures became pervasive after the revolt Nat Turner led in southern Virginia in 1831. Many black churches and schools had to close or curtail their activities. Yet free black southerners persevered. During the late 1830s, new black churches organized in Louisville and Lexington, Kentucky, and in St. Louis, Missouri. By 1860 Baltimore had 15 black churches. Louisville had nine, and Nashville, St. Louis, and Norfolk had four each.

Black schools and voluntary associations also survived white efforts to suppress them, although the schools faced great challenges. Racially integrated schools and public funding for segregated black schools were out of the question in the South. Most black children received no formal education. Black churches, a few white churches, and a scattering of black and white individuals maintained what educational facilities the Upper South had for black children.

Elizabeth Clovis Lange, who was of Haitian descent, established the Oblate Sisters of Providence, the first black Roman Catholic religious order in the United States in Baltimore in 1829 to provide a free education to the children of French-speaking black refugees from the Haitian Revolution. John F. Cook, who was an AME and Presbyterian minister, taught black children at his Union Seminary from 1834 until his death in 1854. Both the sisters and Cook confronted persecution and inadequate funding. Cook had to flee Washington temporarily in 1835 to avoid being killed. Nevertheless he passed his school on to his son, who kept it going through the Civil War years. Meanwhile, the Oblate Sisters had become influential in the black community.

Black voluntary associations, particularly in urban areas of the Upper South, fared better than black schools. By 1838 Baltimore had at least 40 such organizations. As in the North, black women organized their own voluntary associations.

FREE AFRICAN AMERICANS IN THE DEEP SOUTH

More than half the South's free black population lived in Maryland, Delaware, and Virginia. To the west and south of these states, the number of free people of color declined sharply. The smaller free black populations in Kentucky, Tennessee, Missouri, and North Carolina had much in common with that in the Chesapeake states. But free African Americans who lived in the Deep South were different in several respects from their counterparts in other southern regions.

Neither the natural rights ideology of the revolutionary era nor changing economic circumstances led to many manumissions in the Deep South. Free black people there were not only far fewer than in either the Upper South or the North, they were also "largely the product of illicit sexual relations between black slave women and white men." Slaveholder fathers either manumitted their mixed-race children or let them buy their freedom. However, some free black people of the Deep South traced their ancestry to free mixed-race refugees from Haiti, who sought during the 1790s to avoid that island nation's bloody revolutionary struggle by fleeing to such Deep South cities as Charleston, Savannah, and New Orleans.

A three-caste system similar to that in Latin America developed in the antebellum Deep South during the antebellum period. It included white people, free black people, and slaves. Most free African Americans in the region identified more closely with their former masters than with slaves. To ensure the loyalty of such free people of color, powerful white people provided them with employment, loans, protection, and such special privileges as the ability to vote and to testify against white people. Some states and municipalities formalized this relationship by requiring free African Americans to have white guardians—often their blood relatives.

The relationship between free African Americans of the Deep South and their former masters was also evident in religion. An AME church existed in Charleston until 1818, when the city authorities suppressed it, fearing it would become a center of sedition. African Baptist churches existed in Savannah during the 1850s. In 1842 New Orleans's

Sisters of the Holy Family became the second Roman Catholic religious order for black women in the United States. But free black people in the region were more likely than those farther north to remain in white churches largely because they identified with the white elite.

In the Deep South, free African Americans—over half of whom lived in cities—were more concentrated in urban areas than were their counterparts in the North and Upper South. Although Deep South cities restricted their employment opportunities, free black people in Charleston, Savannah, Mobile, and New Orleans maintained stronger positions in the skilled trades than free black people in the Upper South or the North. Free African Americans made up only 15 percent of Charleston's male population. Yet they constituted 25 percent of its carpenters, 40 percent of its tailors, and 75 percent of its millwrights. The close ties between free black people and the upper-class white people who did business with them explain much of this success.

Despite these ties, free black communities comparable to those in the Upper South and North arose in the cities of the Deep South. Although they usually lacked separate black churches as community centers, free African Americans in the region created other institutions. In Charleston the Brown Fellowship Society survived throughout the antebellum period. Charleston also had a chapter of the Prince Hall Masons, and free black men and women in the city maintained other fraternal and benevolent associations. In addition to similar sorts of organizations, the free black elite in New Orleans published literary journals and supported an opera house. Because black churches were rare, wealthy African Americans and fraternal organizations organized private schools for black children in the cities of the Deep South.

In all, free people of color in the Deep South differed substantially from those in the Upper South and the North. Their ties to the white slaveholding class gave them tangible advantages. However, they were not without sympathy for those who remained in slavery, and white authorities were never certain of their loyalty to the slave regime. In particular, white people feared contact between free African Americans in the port cities of the Deep South and black northerners—especially black sailors. As a new round of slave unrest began in the South and a more militant northern antislavery movement got under way during the 1820s, free black people in the Deep South faced difficult circumstances.

Mother Mary Elizabeth Clovis Lange, O.S.P.
(c. 1784–1882), was born in Haiti. She organized the Oblate Sisters of Providence in Baltimore in 1828. This Roman Catholic order helped black refugees from Haiti and operated a school for the refugees' children.

FREE AFRICAN AMERICANS IN THE FAR WEST

Free black communities in the North, Upper South, and Deep South each had unique features, but all of them had existed for decades by the antebellum period. In the huge region stretching from the Great Plains to the Pacific coast, which had become part of the United States by the late 1840s, free black people were rare. Black communities there were just emerging in a few isolated localities. The prevalence of discriminatory "black laws" in the region's states and territories partially explains the small number of free black westerners. Like similar laws in the states of the Old Northwest, these laws either banned free African Americans entirely or restricted the activities of those who were allowed to settle. Nevertheless, a few black families sought economic opportunities in the West. During the 1840s they joined white Americans in settling Oregon. The California gold rush of 1849 had by 1852 attracted about 2,000 African Americans, most whom were men, among hundreds of thousands of white Americans.

Usually black Californians lived and worked in multicultural communities that also included people of Chinese, Jamaican, Latin American, and white American descent. But in a few localities, African Americans predominated. Some black Californians were prosperous gold prospectors. Others worked as steamship stewards, cooks, barbers, laundresses, mechanics, saloonkeepers, whitewashers, porters, and domestics. By the early 1850s, there were black communities centered on churches in San Francisco, Sacramento, and Los Angeles. As was the case in the East, these black communities organized a variety of benevolent and self-help societies. Although most African Americans who went west were men, black women sometimes accompanied their husbands and families. The better off of them raised funds for AME churches and voluntary associations. Others worked as cooks, laundresses, and prostitutes. (For more on free African Americans in California, see Chapter 10.)

CONCLUSION

During the antebellum period, free African-American communities that had emerged during the revolutionary era grew and fostered black institutions. Particularly in the urban North, life in these segregated communities foreshadowed the pattern of black life from the end of the Civil War into the twentieth century. Although the black elite could gain education, professional expertise, and wealth despite white prejudices, most northern people of color were poor. Extended families, churches, segregation, political marginality, and limited educational opportunities still influence African-American life today.

Life for free black people in the Upper South and Deep South was even more difficult. Presumed to be slaves if they could not prove otherwise, black people confronted more danger of enslavement and restrictive legislation than in the North. But energetic black communities existed in the Upper South throughout the antebellum period. In the Deep South, the small free black population was better off economically than were free black people in other regions, but it depended on the region's white slaveholders, who were unreliable allies as sectional controversy mounted. The antislavery movement, secession, and the Civil War would have a more profound impact on the free black communities in the South than in the North. Although it is not wise to generalize about free black people in the trans-Mississippi West, their presence on the Pacific coast in particular demonstrates their involvement in the westward expansion that characterized the United States during the antebellum years. Their West Coast communities indicate the adaptability of black institutions to new circumstances.

African-American Events	National Events

1800

1804	**1803**
Ohio enacts black laws	Louisiana Purchase

1805

1807	**1807**
New Jersey disfranchises black men	Robert Fulton's steamboat is launched in New York harbor

1810

1812	**1812**
African School becomes part of Boston public school system	War of 1812 begins
	1815
	War of 1812 ends

1815

1818	**1819**
Connecticut bars new black voters	Panic of 1819 begins

1820

1821	
New York retains property qualification for black voters	
1822	
Rhode Island disfranchises black voters	
1824	
Massachusetts defeats attempt to ban black migration to that state	

1825

1827	**1825**
Freedom's Journal begins publication	John Quincy Adams becomes president
1828	
African Dorcas Association is established	Erie Canal opens
1829	**1827**
Cincinnati expels black residents	Massachusetts pioneers compulsory public education
	1828
	Andrew Jackson is elected president

1830

1831
Maria W. Stewart criticizes treatment of black workers

1834
African Free Schools become part of New York City public school system

1832
Surge in European immigration begins

1832–1833
Nullification Crisis

1835

1838
Pennsylvania disfranchises black voters

1837
Panic of 1837 begins gold discovered in California

1840

1842
Rhode Island revives black male voting

1843
Edmonia Lewis born

1845

1845
Narrative of the Life of Frederick Douglass is published

1849
Ohio black laws repealed

1846–1848
War against Mexico

1850

1850
Compromise of 1850

African-American Events   **National Events**

REVIEW QUESTIONS

1. How was black freedom in the North limited in the antebellum decades?

2. How did northern African Americans deal with these limits?

3. What was the relationship of the African-American elite to urban black communities?

4. How did African-American institutions fare between 1820 and 1861?

5. Compare black life in the North to free black life in the Upper South, Deep South, and California.

myhistorylab CONNECTIONS

Reinforce what you learned in this chapter by studying the many documents, images, maps, review tools, and videos available at **www.myhistorylab.com.**

READ AND REVIEW

✔️ **Study** and **Review** on **myhistorylab.com** STUDY PLAN FOR CHAPTER 7

📖 **Read** the **Document** on **myhistorylab.com**

"Reflections, Occasioned by the Late Disturbances in Charleston" (1830)

An African-American Novel Critiques Racism in the North (1859)

Maria Stewart, "The Miseries We Tasted" (1835)

North Carolina Codes (1855)

Richard Allen, "Address to the Free People of Colour of these United States" (1830)

Sarah Mapps Douglass, Letter to William Basset (1837)

Senator Sees Slavery as a "Positive Good" (1837)

South Carolina's Ordinance of Nullification (1832)

Thomas R. Dew's Defense of Slavery (1832)

🔍 **View** the **Map** on **myhistorylab.com**

The Slave, Free Black, and White Population of the United States in 1830

RESEARCH AND REVIEW

mysearchlab

Consider these questions in a short research paper.

Compare and contrast the lives of free blacks in the North and the South. What key differences do you note?

((•—**Listen** on **myhistorylab.com** —

Hear the audio files for Chapter 7 at
www.myhistorylab.com.

Hear the audio files for Chapter 8 at **www.myhistorylab.com**.

FOCUS QUESTIONS

WHY AND how did abolitionism begin in America?

HOW DID the revolts of Gabriel, Denmark Vesey, and Nat Turner affect African Americans?

WHAT WERE the goals of the American colonization society?

WHAT ROLE did black women play in the abolition movement?

WHY WAS Walker's *Appeal* important?

This drawing, known as "Nat Turner Preaches Religion," portrays Turner telling "friends and brothers" in August 1831 that God has chosen them to lead a violent "struggle for freedom"

THIS CHAPTER EXPLORES the emergence, during the eighteenth century, of abolitionism in America, its transformation during the early nineteenth century, and the beginning of a more radical antislavery movement by the late 1820s. Slave revolt conspiracies; political, social, and religious turmoil, and wide-ranging reform shaped this process. Black leaders, including David Walker, Denmark Vesey, and Nat Turner, were major contributors. So was white abolitionist William Lloyd Garrison.

ABOLITIONISM BEGINS IN AMERICA

The antislavery movement in its broadest context reflected economic, intellectual, and moral changes that affected the Atlantic world during the Age of Revolution that began during the 1760s. In the United States, that age forged two antislavery movements that survived until the end of the Civil War. Although separate, the two movements influenced each other. The first movement arose in the South among slaves with the help of free African Americans and a few sympathetic white people. As we mentioned in earlier chapters, enslaved African Americans, sought their freedom from the seventeenth century onward. Before the revolutionary era, however, they only wanted to free themselves. They did not seek to destroy slavery as a social system.

The second antislavery movement consisted of black and white abolitionists in the North, with outposts in the Upper South. In the North, white people controlled the larger antislavery organizations, although African Americans led in direct action against slavery and its influences in the North. In the Upper South, African Americans could not openly establish or participate in antislavery organizations, but they cooperated covertly and informally with white abolitionists.

This second and essentially northern movement began during the 1730s when white Quakers in New Jersey and Pennsylvania realized slaveholding contradicted their belief in spiritual equality. As members of a denomination that emphasized nonviolence, Quakers generally worked for the peaceful and gradual abolition of slavery.

Quakers remained prominent in the northern antislavery movement for the next 130 years. But the American Revolution, together with the French Revolution that began in 1789 and the Haitian struggle for independence between 1791 and 1804, revitalized the northern and southern antislavery movements and changed their nature. The revolutionary doctrine that all men had natural rights led other northerners besides Quakers and African Americans to endorse the antislavery cause.

In 1775 Philadelphia Quakers organized the first antislavery society in the world. But their organization lapsed during the War for Independence. When they regrouped in 1784, they attracted non-Quakers, including Benjamin Rush and Benjamin Franklin, both of whom embraced natural rights doctrines. Revolutionary principles also influenced Alexander Hamilton and John Jay, who helped organize New York's first antislavery society. Similarly Prince Hall, the most prominent black abolitionist of his time, based his effort to abolish slavery in Massachusetts on universal rights.

Black and white abolitionists were instrumental in abolishing slavery in the North. However, the early northern antislavery movement had several limiting features. First, black and white abolitionists had similar goals but worked in separate organizations. Second, except in parts of New England, abolition in the North proceeded gradually to protect the economic interests of slaveholders. Third, despite natural rights rhetoric, white abolitionists did not advocate equal rights for black people. In most northern states, laws kept black

TO THE PEOPLE,
Who wish to do Right!

There are thousands of persons in Kentucky who conscientiously believe, that

Slavery is injurious to the prosperity of our beloved State:—
Inconsistent with the fundamental principles of free government:—
Contrary to the natural rights of mankind:—
Adverse to a pure state of morals:—
A great hindrance to the establishment of Free Schools:—
That it depresses the energies of the laboring white man:—
And in many other ways, is

A CURSE TO THE COUNTRY.

Many of the persons who so believe, have formed themselves into a party,

OPPOSED TO THE PERPETUATION OF SLAVERY IN KENTUCKY,

Composed of such men as Henry Clay and Dr. R. J. Breckinridge, of Fayette; Judge Nicholas, Wm. L. Breckinridge and Hon. Wm. P. Thomasson, of Louisville; C. M. Clay, of Madison; Judge Monroe, of Franklin; Dr. J. C. Young, of Boyle; J. McClung, of Mason; Judge Ballinger, of Mercer; J. R. Thornton, of Bourbon, and thousands of other persons of both parties; hard-working, honest, industrious, virtuous Mechanics, Manufacturers, Laborers, Farmers and Slaveholders of the Commonwealth, who for *Talent, Education, Virtue, Uprightness of Character* and *Intelligence*, can't be beat in any State in the Union!

These men object to the Perpetuation of Slavery by the Constitution of the State, and so *ought* every other GOOD REPUBLICAN who loves the prosperity of his home. The *way* and the *time* to do this, belongs to the CONVENTION TO CHANGE THE CONSTITUTION, which will assemble in Frankfort in October.

This party has adopted and published a PLATFORM OF THEIR PRINCIPLES, so that every body may see that their *design is a good one*, and the manner in which they wish to do this, is a **Peaceable, Quiet and Lawful one.** For which purpose, they are going to run candidates in the various counties in the State, favorable to the two following objects, and no matter how their *enemies may misrepresent them*, this is

THEIR PLATFORM.

1st. "The absolute prohibition of the importation of any more slaves into Kentucky."
2d. "The complete power in the People of Kentucky to enforce and perfect *in* or *under* the new Constitution, a system of gradual prospective Emancipation of Slaves."

We believe that a majority of the people of this State, are *in favor of the principles* laid down in this Platform; and that if left alone to vote their *real sentiments*, uninfluenced by Democratic and Whig *party demagogues*, they will give a tremendous vote in their favor. But cunning, long-headed demagogues, wire-workers and politicians of both political parties, will try to convince you that we are Abolitionists. If a man tells you so, set him down forthwith as a person *who is trying to mislead and deceive you.*

We are *opposed to any more Slaves being brought into Kentucky, and wish* TO RESERVE THE RIGHT AND POWER TO THE PEOPLE, *whenever they please,* if it is tomorrow, or next week, or next year, or within five years, or ten years, or fifty years, or *for any unnamed length of time, and at all times,* when they shall find that SLAVERY IS NOT A BLESSING, but the reverse, to say so; and that the *Constitution shall be left open for THE PEOPLE to say so!*

What more do you want? Are we not right?

Lay your hands on your hearts, and you will answer YES!

You will no doubt, find some persons who will curse and damn this party; but are *you* willing to curse and damn them, because these men tell you to do so; and before you have heard the arguments? As sensible and good men, we know you ought not, you will not.

If you are willing *to do what is right;* if you are willing to be *guided* by TRUTH and JUSTICE; if you are willing to listen to *Reason* and *Argument;* if you are *not* willing to be bound up in the horrid shackles and fetters of PARTY *names* and PARTY *preferences,* come

Next Saturday, the 12th of May,

At 2 o'clock in the afternoon, to the COURT-HOUSE in Lexington, and listen to Mr. CLAY, Dr. BRECKINRIDGE, Mr. SHY, and others who may address you on that occasion.

Come with your aprons on! Come any way! Drop your work for one afternoon, and bring all your hands, and you will hear splendid speeches,

FULL OF TRUTH AND ARGUMENT.

Whilst "the whole world is vocal with the shouts of men made free," add your voice; lend your shout; peal out your loudest hosannas in unison with the HYMN OF LIBERTY which has just commenced to be sung throughout the length and breadth of *this great, this beautiful, this noble State,* and remember

"Where the SPIRIT of the LORD is, THERE IS LIBERTY."

Leaflet appealing to citizens to attend a meeting to hear a platform against slavery, published in Lexington, 1850.

people from enjoying full freedom after their emancipation. Fourth, early northern abolitionists did little to bring about abolition in the South, where most slaves lived.

All this indicates that neither Quaker piety nor natural rights principles created a truly egalitarian or sectionally aggressive northern abolitionism. Rather major antislavery efforts carried out by black southerners, widespread religious revivalism, demands for reform, and the growth of northern black institutions established a framework for a more biracial and wide-ranging antislavery movement.

FROM GABRIEL TO DENMARK VESEY

Gabriel's abortive slave revolt conspiracy of 1800 (discussed in Chapter 5) owed as much to revolutionary ideology as did the northern antislavery movement. The arrival of Haitian refugees in Virginia led to slave unrest throughout the 1790s, and Gabriel

MAP 8–1 • Slave Conspiracies and Uprisings, 1800–1831 Major slave conspiracies and revolts were rare between 1800 and 1860. This was in part because those that took place frightened masters and led them to adopt policies aimed at preventing recurrences.

hoped to attract French revolutionary support. Although his uprising failed, the revolutionary spirit and insurrectionary network he established lived on (see Map 8-1). Virginia authorities suppressed another slave conspiracy in 1802, and sporadic minor revolts erupted there for years.

Gabriel's conspiracy had two other consequences. The first involved the Quaker-led antislavery societies of the Chesapeake. These organizations had always been small and weak compared with antislavery societies in the North, and the revelation of Gabriel's plot worsened conditions for these organizations. State and local governments suppressed them, or they withered under negative public opinion. The chance all but vanished that Maryland, Virginia, and North Carolina would follow the northeastern states' example in abolishing slavery gradually and peacefully.

The second consequence was that white southerners and many white northerners became convinced that, free African Americans instigated slave resistance and revolt. Free African Americans were, slavery's defenders contended, a dangerous, criminal, and potentially revolutionary class that had to be regulated, subdued, and ultimately expelled from the country to prevent a race war like the one in Haiti. No system of emancipation that would increase the number of free black people in the United States could be tolerated. Without the restrictions slavery placed on African Americans, southern politicians and journalists argued, they would become economic competitors to white workers, a perpetual criminal class, and a revolutionary threat to white rule.

Events in and about Charleston, South Carolina, in 1822 appeared to confirm the threat. In that year black informants revealed that Denmark Vesey, a free black carpenter, had organized a massive slave revolt conspiracy. Like Gabriel before him, Vesey could read and was aware of the revolutions that had shaken the Atlantic world. Vesey—a former sailor—had been to Haiti and hoped for Haitian aid for an antislavery revolution in the South Carolina low country. He understood the significance of the storming of the Bastille (a fortress-prison in Paris) on July 14, 1789 that marked the start of the French Revolution and planned to start his revolution on July 14, 1822.

While revolution inspired both conspiracies, religion had a more prominent role in Vesey's plot than in Gabriel's. Vesey, a Bible-quoting Methodist, resented white authorities' attempts in 1818 to suppress Charleston's AME Church. Vesey believed passages in the Bible about the enslavement of the Hebrews in Egypt and their deliverance promised freedom for African Americans. But Vesey also relied on aspects of African religion that had survived among low-country slaves to promote his revolutionary efforts. To reach slaves whose Christian convictions blended in with West African spiritualism, he relied on Jack Pritchard—known as Gullah Jack. A "conjure-man" born in East Africa, Pritchard distributed charms and cast spells he claimed would make black revolutionaries invincible.

Vesey and his associates planned to capture arms and ammunition and seize control of Charleston. About a month before the revolt was to begin, however, the arrest of one of Vesey's lieutenants put authorities on guard. On June 14, a house servant told his master about the plot, the local government called in the state militia, and arrests followed. Over several weeks, law officers rounded up 131 suspects. The accused received public trials, and juries convicted 71 of them. Thirty-five, including Vesey and Gullah Jack, were hanged.

After the executions, Charleston's city government destroyed what remained of the local AME church, and white churches assumed responsibility for supervising other black congregations. Meanwhile, white South Carolinians sought to make slave patrols more efficient. The state legislature outlawed assemblages of slaves and banned teaching slaves to read. Local authorities jailed black seamen whose ships docked in Charleston until the ships were ready to sail. Assuming that free black and white abolitionists inspired slave unrest, white South Carolinians became more suspicious of local free African Americans and of white Yankees who visited their state.

A COUNTRY IN TURMOIL

The United States in the first half of the nineteenth century was a country in economic, political, and social turmoil. By the late 1820s, southern slaveholders and their slaves had pushed into what was then the Mexican province of Texas. Meanwhile, the states of the Old Northwest passed from frontier conditions to commercial farming. By 1825 the Erie Canal had linked this region economically to the Northeast. Later, railroads carried the Old Northwest's agricultural products to East Coast cities. An enormous amount of grain and meat also flowed down the Ohio and Mississippi rivers, encouraging the growth of such cities as Pittsburgh, Cincinnati, Louisville, St. Louis, Memphis, and New Orleans. As steamboats became common and networks of turnpikes, canals, and railroads spread, travel time diminished. Americans became more mobile, families scattered, and ties to local communities weakened. For African Americans, subject to the domestic slave trade, mobility came with a high price.

The factory system, which arose in urban areas of the Northeast and spread to parts of the Old Northwest and Upper South, was also distruptive. Cities grew, and increased immigration from Europe meant native black and white people had to compete for employment with foreign-born workers. Farmers became more dependent on urban markets for their crops. The money economy expanded, banks became essential, and private fortunes influenced public policy. Many Americans believed forces beyond their control threatened their way of life and the nation's republican values. They distrusted change and wanted someone to blame for the uncertainties they faced. This outlook encouraged American politics to become paranoid—dominated by fear of hostile conspiracies.

POLITICAL PARANOIA

Charges that John Quincy Adams and Henry Clay had cheated Andrew Jackson out of the presidency in early 1825 reflected this fear of conspiracies. What Jackson's supporters called "the corrupt bargain" and claims that Adams favored a wealthy and intellectual elite at the expense of the common white man led to the organization of the Democratic Party and the election of Jackson to the presidency in 1828. The Democrats claimed to stand for the natural rights and economic well-being of American workers and farmers against what they called the "money power," a conspiratorial alliance of bankers and businessmen.

Yet, from its start, the Democratic Party also represented the interests of the South's slaveholding elite. Democratic politicians, North and South, favored a state rights doctrine that protected slavery from interference by the national government. They sought through legislation, judicial decisions, and diplomacy to make the right to hold human property inviolate. They became the most ardent supporters of expanding slavery into new regions. Most Democratic politicians also openly advocated white male supremacy.

Democratic politicians led in demanding the removal of Indians to the area west of the Mississippi River, which led to the Cherokee "Trail of Tears" in 1838. Democrats also supported patriarchy, meaning a subservient role for women in family life and the church, and their exclusion from the public sphere. And almost all Democratic leaders believed God and nature had designed African Americans to be slaves.

By the mid-1830s, those Americans who favored a more enlightened political program turned—often reluctantly—to the Whig Party, which opposed Jackson and the Democrats. Politicians such as Henry Clay, Daniel Webster, William H. Seward, and John Quincy Adams, who identified with the Whig Party, emphasized Christian morality and an active national government more than the Democrats did. They regarded themselves as conservatives, did not seek to end slavery in the South, and included many wealthy slaveholders within their ranks. But in the North, the party's moral orientation and its opposition to territorial expansion by the United States made it attractive to slavery's opponents.

The Whig Party also served as the channel through which evangelical Christianity influenced politics. In the North, Whig politicians appealed to evangelical voters. Often evangelicals themselves, some Whig politicians and journalists defended the human

This 1844 lithograph by Peter S. Duval, derived from a painting by Alfred Hoffy, portrays Julianne Jane Tillman. Tillman was an AME preacher and one of the few women of her time to be employed in such a capacity.

rights of African Americans and American Indians. When and where they could, black men voted for Whig candidates.

THE SECOND GREAT AWAKENING

Under the influence of a wave of religious revivalism, evangelicals carried Christian morality into politics during the 1830s. During the 1730s and 1740s, the revival known as the Great Awakening had encouraged men and women to embrace Jesus and reform their lives. During this period, American churches converted black people, and African Americans in turn helped shape the revival. At the end of the eighteenth century, a new, emotional revivalism began. Known as the Second Great Awakening, it lasted through the 1830s. It led laymen to replace established clergy as leaders and seek to impose moral order on a turbulent society.

The Second Great Awakening influenced Richard Allen and Absalom Jones's efforts to establish separate black churches in Philadelphia during the 1790s. It helped shape the character of other black churches that emerged during the 1800s and 1810s. These black churches became an essential part of the antislavery movement. However, the Second Great Awakening did not reach its peak until the 1820s. During that decade, Charles G. Finney, a white Presbyterian, and other revivalists helped democratize religion in America. At days-long camp meetings, revivalists preached that all men and women—not just a few—could become faithful Christians and save their souls. The Second Great Awakening revolutionized the nation's spiritual life and—especially in the Northeast and Old Northwest—led many Americans, black and white, to join reform movements.

THE BENEVOLENT EMPIRE

Evangelicals emphasized "practical Christianity." Those who were truly among the saved, they maintained, had actively to oppose sin and save others. Black evangelicals, in particular, called for "a *liberating* faith" applied in ways that would advance material and spiritual well-being. This emphasis on action led during the 1810s and 1820s to what became known as the **Benevolent Empire,** a network of church-related organizations designed to fight sin and rescue souls. The Benevolent Empire launched what is now known as antebellum or Jacksonian reform.

Centered in the Northeast, this social movement flourished through the 1850s. Voluntary associations organized on behalf of a host of causes. Among them were public education, self-improvement, limiting or abolishing alcohol consumption and sales (the temperance movement), prison reform, and aid to the mentally and physically challenged. Other associations distributed Bibles and religious tracts, funded missionary activities, and discouraged prostitution. Still others sought to improve health through diet and medical fads, alleviate shipboard conditions for sailors, and—by the 1840s—gain equal rights for women. The self-improvement, temperance, and missionary associations that free black people—and sometimes slaves—formed in urban areas in conjunction with their churches were part of this movement.

The most important of these reform associations, were those that addressed the problem of African-American bondage. Called societies for promoting the abolition of slavery during the eighteenth and early nineteenth centuries, by the 1830s they became known as antislavery sociieties. Whatever they called themselves, their members were abolitionists, people who favored abolishing slavery in their respective states and throughout the country.

COLONIZATION

The most significant antislavery organization of the 1810s and 1820s was the American Colonization Society (ACS). But whether its aim was abolition is debatable. In late 1816 concerned white leaders met in Washington, D.C., to form this organization, formally named the American Society for Colonizing Free People of Colour of the United States.

The ACS had a twofold program. First, it proposed to abolish slavery gradually in the United States, perhaps giving slaveholders financial compensation for freeing their human property. Second, it proposed to send emancipated slaves and free black people to Liberia. The founders of the ACS believed that masters would never emancipate their slaves if they thought that would increase the size of what they regarded as a shiftless and dangerous free black class. Despite this agenda, the ACS became an integral part of the Benevolent Empire and commanded widespread support among many who regarded themselves as friends of humanity. At first black and white abolitionists did not perceive the moral and practical objections to the ACS program.

Although the ACS always had its greatest strength in the Upper South and enjoyed the support of slaveholders, by the 1820s it had branches in every northern state. Such northern white abolitionists as Arthur and Lewis Tappan, Gerrit Smith, and William Lloyd Garrison initially supported colonization.

BLACK NATIONALISM AND COLONIZATION

Prominent black abolitionists initially shared this positive assessment of the ACS. They were part of a black nationalist tradition dating back at least to Prince Hall that, disappointed with repeated rebuffs from white people, endorsed black American migration to Africa. During the early 1800s, the most prominent advocate of this point of view was Paul Cuffe of Massachusetts. In 1811, six years before the ACS organized, Cuffe, a

Quaker of African and American Indian ancestry, addressed Congress on the subject of African-American Christian colonies in Africa.

The colonization argument that appealed to Cuffe and many other African Americans was that white prejudice would never allow black people to enjoy full citizenship, equal protection under the law, and economic success in the United States. Black people born in America, this argument held, could enjoy equal rights only in the land of their ancestors. The spirit of American evangelicalism also led many African Americans to embrace the prospect of bringing Christianity to African nations.

In 1815 Cuffe, who owned and commanded a ship, took 34 African-American settlers to the British free black colony of Sierra Leone, located just north of what became Liberia. Cuffe's American-Indian wife's reluctance to leave her native land and his death in 1817 prevented him from transporting more settlers to West Africa. Therefore it was former AME bishop Daniel Coker who in 1820 led the first 86 African-American colonists to Liberia. By 1838 approximately 2,500 colonists had made the journey. They lived less than harmoniously with Liberia's 28,000 indigenous inhabitants.

In 1847 Liberia became an independent republic. But despite the efforts of such **black nationalist** advocates as Henry Highland Garnet and Alexander Crummell, only about 10,000 African-American immigrants had gone there by 1860. Well before 1860 it was clear that African colonization would never fulfill the dreams of its black or white advocates.

BLACK OPPOSITION TO COLONIZATION

Some African Americans had always opposed overseas colonization. By the mid-1820s, many black abolitionists in East Coast cities from Richmond to Boston had criticized colonization in general and the ACS in particular.

Among them was Samuel Cornish, who in New York City in 1827 began publishing *Freedom's Journal,* the first African-American newspaper. Cornish, a young Presbyterian minister and fierce opponent of the ACS, called for independent black action against slavery. The *Journal*—reflecting the values of antebellum reform—also encouraged northern self-improvement, education, civil rights, and sympathy for slaves. However John Russwurm—the *Journal's* co-founder—was less opposed than Cornish to the ACS. This disagreement contributed to the suspension of the newspaper in 1829. That same year Russwurm moved to Liberia.

People like Cornish, however, wanted to improve their condition in the United States. They considered Liberia to be foreign and unhealthy. They also feared that ACS proposals for voluntary colonization were misleading because nearly every southern state required the expulsion of slaves individually freed by their masters. The Maryland and Virginia legislatures were considering legislation designed to require all free black people to leave those states or be enslaved. These efforts had little practical impact, but African Americans feared colonization would be forced on them.

By the mid-1820s most black abolitionists had concluded that the ACS was part of a proslavery effort to drive free African Americans from the United States. America, they argued, was their native land. They knew nothing of Africa. Efforts to force them to go there were based on a racist assumption that they were not entitled to live in freedom in the land of their birth. "Do they think to drive us from our country and homes, after having enriched it with our blood and tears?" asked David Walker.

VOICES

WILLIAM WATKINS OPPOSES COLONIZATION

In response to a white clergyman who argued that migration to Africa would help alleviate the plight of African Americans, William Watkins stressed black unity, education, and self-improvement in this country.

The Reverend Mr. Hewitt says "Let us unite into select societies for the purpose of digesting a plan for raising funds to be appropriated to this grand object" [African colonization]. This we cannot do; we intend to let the burden of this work rest upon the shoulders of those who wish us out of the country. We will, however, compromise the matter with our friend. We are willing and anxious to "unite into select societies for the purpose of digesting a plan": for the improvement of our people in science, morals, domestic economy, &c. We are willing and anxious to form union societies . . . that shall discountenance and destroy, as far as possible, those unhappy schisms which have too long divided us, though we are brethren. We are willing to unite . . . in the formation of temperance societies . . . that will enable us to exhibit to the world an amount of moral power that would give new impetus to our friends and "strike alarm" into the breasts of our enemies, if not wholly disarm them of the weapons they are hurling against us.

- According to Watkins, how will black self-improvement societies help counter colonization?

- What difficulties does Watkins believe African Americans must overcome to make themselves stronger in the United States?

SOURCE: "A Colored American [Watkins] to Editors," n.d., in *Genius of Universal Emancipation*, December 18, 1829.

BLACK ABOLITIONIST WOMEN

Black women joined black men in opposing slavery. In considering their role, it is important to understand that the United States in the early nineteenth century had a rigid gender hierarchy. Law and custom proscribed women from engaging in politics, the professions, and most businesses. Those women deemed respectable by black and white Americans—the women of wealthy families—were expected to devote themselves exclusively to domestic concerns and to remain socially aloof. Church and benevolent activities constituted their only opportunities for public action. Even in these arenas, custom relegated them to work in auxiliaries to men's organizations.

This was true of the first *formal* abolitionist groups of black women. Among the leaders were Charlotte Forten, the wife of James Forten, and Maria W. Stewart, the widow of a well-to-do Boston ship outfitter. In 1833 Charlotte and her daughters Sarah, Margaretta, and Harriet joined with other black and white women to found the **Philadelphia Female Anti-Slavery Society**. A year earlier, other black women had established in Salem, Massachusetts, the first women's antislavery society.

Freedom's Journal

Founded in 1827, *Freedom's Journal* was America's first black-owned and operated newspaper. A complete newspaper, It served as a forum for discussion and debate of the great questions of the day. The newspaper also carried birth, marriage, death announcements, and covered news from around the world. It printed biographies of famous African Americans and ran advertisements for schools, housing, and jobs.

We wish to plead our own cause. Too long have others spoken for us. . . . It is our earnest wish to make our Journal a medium of intercourse between our brethren in the different states of this great confederacy; that through its columns an expression of our sentiments, on many interesting subjects which concern us, may be offered to the publick; that plans which apparently are beneficial may be candidly discussed and properly weighed; if worthy receive our cordial support; if not our marked disapprobation.
—Freedom's Journal, Volume 1, Number 1, March 16, 1826

▲ John Brown Russwurm (1799–1851) served as the newspaper's editor along with Samuel Cornish. After Cornish resigned in September 1827, Russwurm began to use *Freedom's Journal* to promote colonization. This shift in editorial policy resulted in a significant loss of readership. In 1829 Russwurm emigrated to Liberia where he became governor of the Maryland colony.
The Granger Collection

▲ The back page of *Freedom's Journal* carried advertisements of interest to the black community, like these from Volume 2, Number 52, March 28, 1829, advertising lodging, shoemaking, and employment.

◀ Samuel Cornish (1795–1858) was a leader in the abolition movement and was a cofounder of the American Anti-Slavery Society (1835). After training for the ministry, he served as a missionary to slaves on Maryland's Eastern Shore.

Why did the editors think their newspaper was necessary? What did they hope to achieve? What does the sample page suggest about the black community and its needs in the late 1820s?

Many African-American women (and white women), however, did not fit the early-nineteenth-century criteria for respectability that applied to the Fortens, Stewart, and others among African-American elite. Most black women were poor and uneducated. They had to work outside their homes. Particularly in the Upper South, these women were *practical* abolitionists. From the revolutionary era onward, count-less anonymous black women, both slave and free, living in such southern border cities as Baltimore, Louisville, and Washington, risked everything to harbor fugitive slaves. Others saved their meager earnings to purchase freedom for themselves and their loved ones.

THE BALTIMORE ALLIANCE

Among the stronger black abolitionist opponents of the ACS were William Watkins, Jacob Greener, and Hezekiah Grice. All three were associates in Baltimore of Benjamin Lundy, a white Quaker abolitionist who published an antislavery newspaper named the *Genius of Universal Emancipation*. In 1829 Watkins, Greener, and Grice profoundly influenced a young white abolitionist and temperance advocate named William Lloyd Garrison, who later became the most influential of all the American antislavery leaders. Lundy had convinced Garrison to leave his native Massachusetts to come to Baltimore as the associate editor of the *Genius*. Garrison, a deeply religious product of the Sec-ond Great Awakening and a well-schooled journalist, had decided before he came to Baltimore that *gradual* abolition was neither practical nor moral. Gradualism was im-practical, he said, because it continually put off the date of general emancipation. It was immoral because it encouraged slaveholders to continue sinfully and criminally oppress-ing African Americans.

Garrison, however, tolerated the ACS until he came under the influence of Watkins, Greener, and Grice. They set him on a course that transformed the abolitionist move-ment in the United States during the early 1830s. They also initiated a bond between African Americans and Garrison that—although strained at times—shaped the rest of his antislavery career. That bond intensified in 1830 when Garrison served 49 days in Baltimore Jail on charges he had libeled a slave trader. While in jail, Garrison met im-prisoned fugitive slaves and denounced—to their faces—masters who came to retrieve the slaves.

In 1831 when he began publishing his abolitionist newspaper, *The Liberator,* in Boston, Garrison led the antislavery movement in a radical direction. It was radical not so much because Garrison rejected gradual abolition and called for immedi-ate emancipation. He had earlier rejected **gradualism** and was not the first to en-dorse **immediatism.** What made his brand of abolitionism revolutionary was the insight he gained from his association with African Americans in Baltimore: that immediate emancipation must be combined with a commitment to racial justice in the United States. Watkins and Greener convinced Garrison that African Americans must have equal rights in America and not be sent to Africa after their emancipation. Immediate emancipation without compensating slaveholders and without expatriat-ing African Americans became the core of Garrison's program for the rest of his long antislavery career.

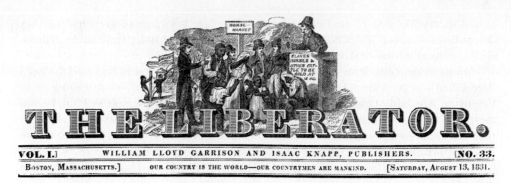

This is the masthead of William Lloyd Garrison's abolitionist newspaper, the *Liberator*, as it appeared in August 1831. It portrays a slave auction in Washington, D.C., taking place in sight of the U.S. Capitol Building, where the flag of "Liberty" flies.

DAVID WALKER AND NAT TURNER

Two other black abolitionists, David Walker and Nat Turner, helped shape Garrison's brand of abolitionism. They were from the South—Walker from North Carolina and Turner from Virginia—and they were deeply religious. They also advocated employing violent means against slavery and had an impact on both the white South and abolitionists. Otherwise their circumstances differed, as did the form of their antislavery efforts.

In his *Appeal . . . to the Colored Citizens of the World*, which he published in 1829, Walker furiously attacked slavery and white racism, suggesting that slaves use violence to secure their liberty.

The *Appeal* shaped the struggle over slavery in three ways. First, although Garrison was committed to peaceful means, Walker's aggressive writing style influenced the tone of Garrison and other advocates of immediate abolition. Second, Walker's desperate effort to instill hope and pride in an oppressed people inspired an increasingly militant black abolitionism. Third, his pamphlet and his ability to have it circulated among free African Americans in the South contributed to white southern fear of encirclement from without and subversion from within. This fear encouraged the section's leaders to make demands on the North that helped bring on the Civil War.

In this last respect, Nat Turner's contribution was even more important than Walker's. In 1831 Turner, a privileged slave from eastern Virginia, became the first African American to initiate a large-scale slave uprising since Charles Deslondes revolt in Louisiana in 1811.

During the late 1820s and early 1830s, unrest among slaves in Virginia had increased. Walker's *Appeal*, may have contributed to this. Divisions among white Virginians may have also encouraged slaves to seek advantages for themselves. In anticipation of a state constitutional convention in 1829, white people in western Virginia, where there were few slaveholders, called for emancipation. Poorer white men demanded an end to the property qualifications that denied them the vote. As the convention approached, a "spirit of dissatisfaction and insubordination" became manifest among slaves. Some armed themselves and escaped northward. As proslavery Virginians grew fearful, they demanded additional restrictions on the ability of local free black people and northern abolitionists to influence slaves.

Yet no evidence indicates that Nat Turner or any of his associates had read Walker's *Appeal*, had contact with northern abolitionists, or were aware of divisions among white Virginians. Also, although Turner knew about the successful slave revolt in Haiti, he was more of a religious visionary than a political revolutionary. Born in 1800, he learned to read as a child. As a young man, he spent much of his time studying and memorizing the Bible. He became a lay preacher and a leader among local slaves. By the late 1820s, he had begun to have visions that convinced him God intended him to lead his people to freedom through violence.

After considerable planning, Turner began his uprising on the evening of August 21, 1831. His band, which numbered between 60 and 70, killed 57 white men, women, and children before militia put down the revolt the following morning. In November, Turner and 17 others were found guilty of insurrection and treason and were hanged. Meanwhile, panicked white people in nearby parts of Virginia and North Carolina killed more than 100 African Americans whom they suspected of being in league with the rebels.

Turner, like Walker and Garrison, shaped a new era in American abolitionism. The bloodshed in Virginia inspired general revulsion. White southerners—and some northerners—accused Garrison and other abolitionists of inspiring the revolt. In response, northern abolitionists of both races asserted their commitment to a peaceful struggle against slavery. Yet both black and white abolitionists respected and admired Turner. This tension between lip service to peaceful means and admiration for violence against slavery characterized the antislavery movement for the next 30 years.

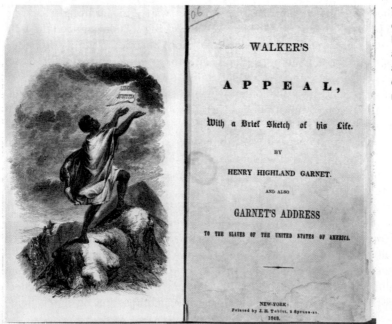

The frontispiece of the Appeal of David Walker with an illustration of a mystic below a cloudy sky on a mountain peak.

African-American Events	National and World Events
	• 1790 •
	1791 Haitian Revolution begins
	1795
1796 or 1797 David Walker born	**1796** John Adams Elected President
	1798 Unelclared Franco-American Naval War
	• 1800 •
1800 Gabriel's conspiracy is exposed	**1800** Thomas Jefferson elected president
1803 Maria W. Stewart born	**1803–1806** Lewis and Clark Expedition
	• 1805 •
1805 William Lloyd Garrison born	**1807** Britain Bans Atlantic Slave Trade
	1808 United States Bans Atlantic Slave Trade
	• 1810 •
1811 Louisiana Slave Revolt	**1812** War of 1812 begins
	• 1815 •
1815 Paul Cuffe leads African Americans to Sierra Leone	**1815** War of 1812 ends
1816 American Colonization Society is formed	**1816** James Madison elected president
	• 1820 •
1822 Denmark Vesey's conspiracy exposed	**1820** Missouri Compromise passed
1824 Benjamin Lundy comes to Baltimore	**1824** John Quincy Adams elected president
	• 1825 •
1827 *Freedom's Journal* begins publication	**1828** Andrew Jackson elected president
1829 William Lloyd Garrison Comes To Baltimore; David Walkers's Appeal	

African-American Events	National Events
1831 Nat Turner's Revolt is suppressed	**1830** Indian Removal Act Passed by Congress **1832** Great increase in migration to United States begins

1830

CONCLUSION

This chapter has focused on the two principal antislavery movements in the United States before 1833. One movement existed in the South among slaves. The other centered in the North and the Chesapeake among free African American and white abolitionists. Both movements had roots in the age of revolution and gained vitality from evangelical Christianity. The Second Great Awakening and the reforming spirit of the Benevolent Empire shaped the northern antislavery effort. The black church, the Bible, and elements of African religion helped inspire slave revolutionaries.

Gabriel, Denmark Vesey, and Nat Turner had to rely on violence to fight slavery. Northern abolitionists used peaceful means, such as newspapers, books, petitions, and speeches to spread their message. But the two movements had similarities and influenced each other. David Walker's life in Charleston at the time of Denmark Vesey's conspiracy shaped his beliefs. In turn, his *Appeal* may have influenced slaves. Turner's revolt helped determine the course of northern abolitionism after 1831. During the subsequent decades, the efforts of slaves to resist their masters, to rebel, and to escape influenced radical black and white abolitionists in the North.

The antislavery movement that existed in the North and portions of the Upper South was always biracial. During the 1810s and for much of the 1820s, many black abolitionists embraced a form of nationalism that encouraged them to cooperate with the conservative white people who led the ACS. As the racist and proslavery nature of that organization became clear, northern black and white abolitionists called for immediate, uncompensated general emancipation that would not force former slaves to leave the United States.

REVIEW QUESTIONS

1. What did the program of the ACS mean for African Americans? How did they respond to this program?

2. Analyze the role abolitionism played (1) by Christianity and (2) by the revolutionary tradition in the Atlantic world. Which was more important in shaping the views of black and white abolitionists?

3. Evaluate the interaction of black and white abolitionists during the early nineteenth century. How did their motives for becoming abolitionists differ?

4. How did Gabriel, Denmark Vesey, and Nat Turner influence the northern abolitionist movement?

5. What risks did Maria W. Stewart take when she called publicly for antislavery action?

myhistörylab CONNECTIONS

Reinforce what you learned in this chapter by studying the many documents, images, maps, review tools, and videos available at **www.myhistorylab.com**.

READ AND REVIEW

✔•⌐ **Study** and **Review** on **myhistorylab.com** STUDY PLAN FOR CHAPTER 8

⌐•⌐ **Read** the **Document** on **myhistorylab.com**

A Black Feminist Speaks Out in 1851

Abolitionist Demands Immediate End to Slavery (1831)

An African American Advocates Radical Action in 1829

Angelina E. Grimké, Appeal to the Christian Women of the South (1836)

Confession of Solomon (1800)

Southern Belle Denounces Slavery (1838)

The Confessions of Nat Turner (1831)

⌐ **View** the **Map** on **myhistorylab.com**

Slave Conspiracies and Uprisings, 1800–1831

RESEARCH AND EXPLORE

mysearchlab

Consider these questions in a short research paper.

What forces and events fueled the antislavery movement? What role did antislavery advocates see free blacks playing in America after slavery was abolished?

((•⌐ **Listen** on **myhistorylab.com**

"What if I am a Woman" speech by Maria W. Stewart; read by Ruby Dee The Liberator

—————— ((•⌐ **Listen** on **myhistorylab.com** ——————

Hear the audio files for Chapter 8 at
www.myhistorylab.com.

Let Your Motto Be Resistance • • *1833–1850*

Hear the audio files for Chapter 9 at **www.myhistorylab.com.**

FOCUS QUESTIONS

HOW DID THE RACISM and violence of the 1830s and 1840s affect the antislavery movement?

WHAT ROLES DID BLACK institutions and moral suasion play in the antislavery movement?

HOW DID abolitionism become more aggressive during the 1840s and 1850s?

HOW DID the views of Frederick Douglass differ from those of Henry Highland Garnet?

In this 1867 oil painting by Theo Kaufman, a group of women and children prepare to ford a river as they escape from slavery. Most escapees were young men, but people of both sexes and all age-groups undertook to reach freedom in the North or Canada.
Theodor Kaufmann (1814–1896), "On to Liberty,' 1867, Oil on canvas, 36 3 56 in (91.4 3 142.2 cm). The Metropolitan Museum of Art. Gift of Erving and Joyce Wolf, 1982 (1982.443.3) Photograph ©The Metropolitan Museum of Art./Art Resource, NY.

A growing militancy among black and white abolitionists that shaped the antislavery movement during the two decades before the Civil War. This chapter investigates the causes of that militancy and explores the role of African Americans in the antislavery movement from the establishment of the American Anti-Slavery Society in 1833 to the **Compromise of 1850.** Largely in response to changes in American culture, unrest among slaves, and sectional conflict between North and South, the biracial northern antislavery movement during this period became splintered and diverse, but more powerful.

A RISING TIDE OF RACISM AND VIOLENCE

Militancy among abolitionists reflected increasing American racism and violence from the 1830s through the Civil War. White Americans' embrace of an exuberant nationalism called **Manifest Destiny** contributed to this trend. This doctrine, which defined political and economic progress in racial terms, held that God intended the United States to expand its territory, by war if necessary.

Another factor was that American ethnologists—scientists who studied racial diversity—rejected the eighteenth-century idea that the physical and mental characteristics of the world's peoples are the product of environment. Instead, they argued that what they perceived to be racial differences are intrinsic and permanent. White people—particularly white Americans—they maintained, were a superior race culturally, physically, economically, politically, and intellectually.

As Manifest Destiny gave divine sanction to imperialism, scientific racism provided white Americans with a justification for the continued enslavement of African Americans and extermination of American Indians, because they deemed these groups to be inferior. Prejudice against European immigrants to the United States also increased. By the late 1840s, a movement known as *nativism* pitted native-born Protestants against foreign-born Roman Catholics, whom the natives saw as competitors for jobs and as cultural subversives.

A wave of racially motivated violence, committed by the federal and state governments as well as white vigilantes, accompanied these intellectual and demographic developments. Starting in the 1790s, the U.S. Army waged a systematic campaign to remove American Indians from the states and relocate them west of the Mississippi River. This campaign affected several southeastern Indian nations. But it is epitomized by the Trail of Tears, when in 1838 the army forced 16,000 Cherokees from Georgia to what is now Oklahoma. Many Cherokees died along the way. During the same decade, antiblack riots became common in northern cities. Starting in 1829, white mobs attacked abolitionist newspaper presses and wreaked havoc in African-American neighborhoods. Wealthy "gentlemen of property and standing," who believed they defended the social order, led the rioters.

ANTIBLACK AND ANTIABOLITIONIST RIOTS

Antiblack riots coincided with the start of immediate abolitionism during the late 1820s. The riots became more common as abolitionism gained strength during the 1830s and 1840s (see Figure 9-1 and Map 9-1).

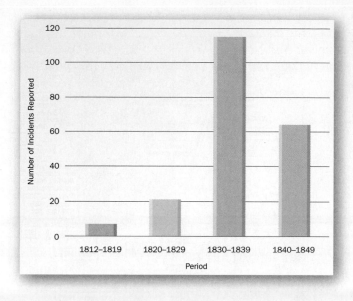

FIGURE 9-1 • Mob Violence in the United States, 1812–1849 This graph illustrates the rise of mob violence in the North in reaction to abolitionist activity. Attacks on abolitionists peaked during the 1830s and then declined as antislavery sentiment spread in the North.

In 1829 a three-day riot instigated by local politicians led many black Cincinnatians to flee to Canada. In 1836 and 1841 mob attacks on the *Philanthropist*, Cincinnati's white-run abolitionist newspaper, expanded into attacks on African-American homes and businesses. During each riot, black residents defended their property with guns. In 1831 white sailors led a mob in Providence, Rhode Island that literally tore that city's black neighborhood to pieces. In New York City in 1834, a mob destroyed twelve houses owned by black residents, a black church, a black school, and the home of white abolitionist Lewis Tappan.

No city had more or worse race riots than Philadelphia—the City of Brotherly Love. In 1820, 1829, 1834, 1835, 1838, 1842, and 1849, antiblack rampages broke out there. The ugliest riot came in 1842 when Irish immigrants led a mob that assaulted members of a black temperance society, who were commemorating the abolition of slavery in the British colony of Jamaica. When African Americans defended themselves with muskets, the mob looted and burned Philadelphia's principal black neighborhood.

TEXAS AND THE WAR AGAINST MEXICO

Not only northern cities experienced violence. Under President James K. Polk, the United States adopted a belligerent foreign policy, culminating in a war against the Republic of Mexico, which lasted from 1846 to 1848. Mexico had gained its independence from Spain in 1822 and in 1829 had abolished slavery within its borders. Meanwhile slaveholding Americans began settling in the Mexican province of Texas. At the time, the gigantic regions then known as California and New Mexico (and now comprising the states of California, Arizona, New Mexico, Utah, and part of Colorado) also belonged to Mexico. In 1836 Texas won independence from Mexico, and—as an independent slaveholding republic—applied for annexation to the United States as a slave state. Democratic and Whig Party leaders, who realized that adding a large new slave state to the Union would divide the country along North–South lines, rebuffed the application. But the desire for new territory, encouraged by Manifest Destiny and an expanding slave-labor economy, could not be denied. In 1844 Polk, the Democratic presidential candidate, called for the annexation of Texas and Oregon, a huge territory in the Pacific Northwest that the United States and Great Britain had been jointly administering. When Polk defeated the Whig candidate Henry Clay, who favored delaying annexation, Congress in early 1845 annexed Texas by joint resolution.

MAP 9-1 • Antiabolitionist and Antiblack Riots during the Antebellum Period

African Americans faced violent conditions in both the North and South during the antebellum years. Fear among whites of growing free black communities and white antipathy toward spreading abolitionism sparked numerous antiblack and antiabolitionist riots.

▶ *Why did* *most of these riots occur in the Northeast?*

This vastly expanded the area within the United States open to slavery.

In early 1846 Polk backed away from a confrontation with Great Britain over Oregon. A few months later, he provoked the war against Mexico that by 1848 forced that country to recognize American sovereignty over Texas and to cede New Mexico and California (see Map 10-1 on page 212). Immediately, the major political question in the United States became would slavery expand into these southwestern territories? Many northerners suspected slaveholders would create slave states out of the new territories, dominate the federal government, and enact policies detrimental to white workers and farmers.

As these sentiments spread across the North, slaveholders feared they would be excluded from the western lands they had helped wrest from Mexico. The resulting Compromise of 1850 (see Chapter 10) attempted to satisfy both sections. But it subjected African Americans to additional violence as part of the Compromise met slaveholders' demands for a stronger fugitive slave law. This law provided federal aid for masters in recapturing bond people who had escaped to the North. It also encouraged attempts to kidnap free black northerners into slavery.

THE RESPONSE OF THE ANTISLAVERY MOVEMENT

The increase in race-related violence caused difficulties for the antislavery movement. Even though African Americans found loyal white allies within the movement, interracial understanding did not come easily. As white abolitionists assumed they should set policy, their black colleagues became resentful. Meanwhile abolitionist commitment to nonviolence weakened. Rejection of force seemed to many to limit abolitionist options in a violent environment. By the end of the 1830s, greater autonomy for black abolitionists and peaceful versus violent means became contentious issues within the movement.

THE AMERICAN ANTI-SLAVERY SOCIETY

Before the era of Manifest Destiny, the American Anti-Slavery Society (AASS)—the most significant abolitionist organization of the 1830s—emerged from a major turning point in the abolitionist cause. This was William Lloyd Garrison's decision in 1831 to create a movement dedicated to immediate, uncompensated emancipation and to equal rights for African Americans in the United States. To reach these goals, abolitionists organized the AASS in December 1833 at Philadelphia's Adelphi Hall.

No white American worked harder than Garrison to bridge racial differences. He spoke to black groups, stayed in the homes of African Americans when he traveled, and welcomed them to his home. Black abolitionists responded with affection and loyalty. They provided financial support for his newspaper, *The Liberator*, worked as subscription agents, paid for his speaking tour in England in 1833, and served as his bodyguards. But Garrison, like most other white abolitionists, remained stiff and condescending in conversation with his black colleagues, and the black experience in the AASS reflected this.

On one hand, it is remarkable that the AASS allowed black men to participate in its meetings without formal restrictions. At the time, no other American organization did so. On the other hand, that black participation was paltry. Throughout its history, black people rarely held positions of authority in the AASS.

As state and local auxiliaries of the AASS organized across the North during the early 1830s, these patterns repeated themselves. Black men participated but did not lead, although a few held prominent offices. Black and white women—with some exceptions—could observe the proceedings of these organizations but not participate in them. It took a three-year struggle between 1837 and 1840 over "the woman question" before an AASS annual meeting elected a woman to a leadership position, and that victory helped split the organization.

BLACK AND WOMEN'S ANTISLAVERY SOCIETIES

In these circumstances, black men, black women, and white women formed auxiliaries to the AASS. Often African Americans belonged to all-black *and* to integrated, predominantly white organizations. Black men's auxiliaries to the AASS formed across the North during the mid-1830s. As mentioned in Chapter 8, the earliest black women's abolitionist organization appeared in Salem, Massachusetts, in 1832, a year before the AASS formed. The black organizations arose because of racial discord in the predominantly white organizations and because of a black desire for racial solidarity. But despite their differences, black and white abolitionists belonged to a single movement.

All of the women's antislavery societies concentrated on fund-raising. They held bake sales, organized antislavery fairs and bazaars, and sold antislavery memorabilia. The proceeds went to the AASS or to antislavery newspapers. But the separate women's societies also inspired the birth of feminism by creating an awareness that women had rights and interests that a male-dominated society had to recognize. By writing essays and poems on political subjects and making public speeches, black and white abolitionist women challenged a culture that relegated *respectable* women to domestic duties.

MORAL SUASION

During the 1830s the AASS adopted a reform strategy based on **moral suasion**—what we would call moral *persuasion* today. This was an appeal to Americans to support abolition and racial justice on the basis of their Christian consciences. Slaveholding, the AASS argued, was a sin and a crime that deprived African Americans of the freedom of conscience they needed to save their souls. Abolitionists also argued that, slavery was an inefficient labor system that enriched a few masters while impoverishing black and white southerners and hurting the American economy.

Abolitionists did not just criticize white southerners. They noted that northern industries thrived by manufacturing cloth from cotton produced by slave labor. They pointed out that the U.S. government protected the interests of slaveholders in the District of Columbia, in the territories, in the interstate slave trade, and through the Fugitive Slave Act of 1793. Northerners who profited from slave labor and supported the national government with their votes and taxes bore their share of guilt for slavery and faced divine punishment.

The AASS sought to use these arguments to convince masters to free their slaves and to persuade northerners and nonslaveholding white southerners to put moral pressure on slaveholders. To reach a southern audience, the AASS in 1835 launched the Great Postal Campaign, designed to send antislavery literature to southern post offices and individual slaveholders. At about the same time, the AASS also organized a petitioning campaign aimed to agitate the slavery issue in Congress. Antislavery women led in circulating and signing the petitions. In 1836 over 30,000 of the petitions reached Washington.

In the North, AASS agents gave public lectures against slavery and distributed antislavery literature. Often a pair of agents—one black and one white—traveled together. Ideally, the black agent would be a former slave, so he could attack the brutality and immorality of slavery from personal experience.

The reaction to these efforts in the North and the South was not what the leaders of the AASS anticipated. As the story in the nearby *Voices* box on Frederick Douglas relates, by speaking of racial justice and exemplifying interracial cooperation, the abolitionists trod new ground. This created awkward situations that are—in retrospect—humorous. But their audiences often reacted violently. Southern postmasters burned antislavery literature when it arrived at their offices, and southern states censored the mail. Vigilantes drove off white southerners who openly advocated abolition. Black abolitionists, of course, did not attempt openly to denounce slavery while in the South.

Wealthy black abolitionist Robert Purvis is at the very center of this undated photograph of the Philadelphia Anti-Slavery Society. The famous Quaker abolitionist Lucretia Mott and her husband James Mott are seated to Purvis's left. As significant as Purvis's central location in the photograph, is that he is the *only* African American pictured.

VOICES

FREDERICK DOUGLASS DESCRIBES AN AWKWARD SITUATION

rederick Douglass wrote this passage during the mid-1850s. It is from My Bondage and My Freedom, the second of his three autobiographies. It relates with humor, not only the racial barriers that black and white abolitionists had to break, but the primitive conditions they took for granted.

In the summer of 1843, I was traveling and lecturing in company with William A. White, Esq., through the state of Indiana. Anti-slavery friends were not very abundant in Indiana ... and beds were not more plentiful than friends.... At the close of one of our meetings, we were invited home with a kindly-disposed old farmer, who, in the generous enthusiasm of the moment, seemed to have forgotten that he had but one spare bed, and that his guests were an ill-matched pair.... White is remarkably fine looking, and very evidently a born gentleman; the idea of putting us in the same bed was hardly to be tolerated; and yet there we were, and but the one bed for us, and that, by the way, was in the same room occupied by the other members of the family.... After witnessing the confusion as long as I liked, I relieved the kindly-disposed family by playfully saying, "Friend White, having got entirely rid of my prejudice against color, I think, as proof of it, I must allow you to sleep with me to-night." White kept up the joke, by seeming to esteem himself the favored party, and thus the difficulty was removed.

What does this passage reveal about American life during the 1840s?

What does Douglass reveal about his own character?

SOURCE: Michael Meyer, ed., *Frederick Douglass: The Narrative and Selected Writings* (New York: Modern Library, 1984), 170–71.

In 1836 southern representatives and their northern allies in Congress passed the Gag Rule forbidding petitions related to slavery from being introduced in the House of Representatives. In response, the AASS sent 415,000 petitions in 1838, and Congressman (and former President) John Quincy Adams began his struggle against the Gag. Technically not an abolitionist but a defender of the First Amendment right to petition Congress, Adams succeeded in having the Gag repealed in 1844.

Meanwhile northern mobs continued to assault abolitionist agents, disrupt their meetings, destroy their newspaper presses, and attack black neighborhoods. In 1837 a proslavery mob killed white abolitionist journalist Elijah P. Lovejoy as he defended his printing press in Alton, Illinois. On another occasion, as Douglass, White, and older white abolitionist George Bradburn held an antislavery meeting in the small town of Pendleton, Indiana, an enraged mob attempted to kill Douglass.

BLACK COMMUNITY INSTITUTIONS

A maturing African-American community undergirded the antislavery movement and helped it survive violent opposition. The free black population of the United States grew from 59,000 in 1790 to 319,000 in 1830 and 434,449 in 1850. The concentration of this growing population in such cities as New York, Philadelphia, Baltimore, Boston, and Cincinnati strengthened it. These cities had enough African Americans to support the independent churches, schools, benevolent organizations, and printing presses that self-conscious communities required. These communities became bedrocks of abolitionism.

THE BLACK CONVENTION MOVEMENT

The dozens of local, state, and national black conventions held in the North between 1830 and 1864 manifested the antebellum American reform impulse. Their agenda transcended the antislavery cause. They nevertheless provided a forum for the more prominent black abolitionist men, such as Henry H. Garnet, Frederick Douglass and Martin R. Delany. They provided a setting in which abolitionism could grow and change its tactics to meet the demands of a sectionally polarized and violent time.

Hezekiah Grice, a young black man who had worked with Benjamin Lundy and William Lloyd Garrison in Baltimore during the 1820s (see chapter 8), organized the first Black National Convention. It met on September 24, 1830, at the Bethel Church in Philadelphia with the venerable churchman Richard Allen presiding. The national convention became an annual event for the next five years. During the same period, many state and local black conventions met across the North. All the conventions were small and informal—particularly those at the local level—and had no strict guidelines for choosing delegates. They were nevertheless attractive venues for discussing and publicizing black concerns. They called for the abolition of slavery and improving conditions for northern African Americans. Among other reforms, the conventions advocated integrated public schools and the rights of black men to vote, serve on juries, and testify against white people in court.

The conventions also stressed black self-help through temperance, sexual morality, education, and thrift. These causes remained important parts of the black agenda throughout the antebellum years. But by the mid-1830s the national convention movement faltered as black abolitionists placed their hopes in the AASS.

In an effort to stir antiabolitionist feelings, this broadside announces an upcoming abolitionist lecture at a local New York church.

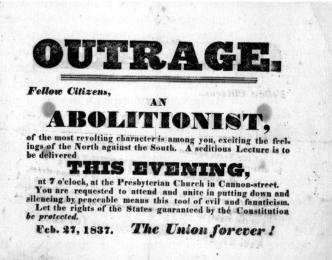

OUTRAGE.

Fellow Citizens,

AN

ABOLITIONIST,

of the most revolting character is among you, exciting the feelings of the North against the South. A seditious Lecture is to be delivered

THIS EVENING,

at 7 o'clock, at the Presbyterian Church in Cannon-street. You are requested to attend and unite in putting down and silencing by peaceable means this tool of evil and fanaticism. Let the rights of the States guaranteed by the Constitution be protected.

Feb. 27, 1837.   *The Union forever!*

BLACK CHURCHES IN THE ANTISLAVERY CAUSE

Black churches were even more important than black conventions in the antislavery movement. With a few major exceptions, the leading black abolitionists were ministers. These clergy used their pulpits to attack slavery, racial discrimination, proslavery white churches, and the American Colonization Society (ACS). Having covered most of these topics in a sermon to a white congregation in 1839, Daniel Payne, who had grown up free in South Carolina, declared, "Awake! AWAKE! to the battle, and hurl the hottest thunders of divine truth at the head of this cruel monster, until he shall fall to rise no more; and the groans of the enslaved are converted into the songs of the free!" Black churches also provided forums for abolitionist speakers, such as Frederick Douglass and Garrison, and meeting places for predominantly white antislavery organizations, which frequently could not meet in white churches.

BLACK NEWSPAPERS

Although less influential than black churches, black antislavery newspapers had an important role in the antislavery movement, particularly by the 1840s. Like their white counterparts, they almost always faced financial difficulties, and few survived for long. This was because reform, as opposed to commercial, newspapers were a luxury many subscribers, black and white, could not afford. Black newspapers faced added difficulties finding readers because most African Americans were poor, and many were illiterate. An additional, self-imposed, burden was that publishers eager to get their message out almost never required subscribers to pay in advance.

Nevertheless several influential black abolitionist newspapers existed between the late 1820s and the Civil War. The first black newspaper, *Freedom's Journal*, owned and edited by Samuel Cornish and John B. Russwurm, lasted only from 1827 to 1829. It showed that African Americans could produce interesting and competent journalism and attract black and white subscribers. The *Journal* also established a framework for black journalism during the antebellum period by emphasizing antislavery, racial justice, and Christian and democratic values.

The most ubiquitous black journalist of the period was Philip A. Bell. Bell was either publisher or copublisher of the *New York Weekly Advocate* in 1837, the **Colored American** from 1837 to 1842, and, during the 1860s, two San Francisco newspapers, the *Pacific Appeal* and the *Elevator.* However, Frederick Douglass's **North Star** and its successor *Frederick Douglass' Paper* were the most influential black antislavery newspapers of the late 1840s and the 1850s. Heavily subsidized by Gerrit Smith, a wealthy white abolitionist, and attracting more white than black subscribers, Douglass's weeklies gained the support of many black abolitionist organizations.

THE AMERICAN AND FOREIGN ANTI-SLAVERY SOCIETY AND THE LIBERTY PARTY

In 1840 the AASS splintered. Most of its members left to establish the **American and Foreign Anti-Slavery Society** (AFASS) and the **Liberty Party,** the first antislavery political party. In part the split resulted from long-standing disagreements about the role of women in abolitionism and William Lloyd Garrison's broadening radicalism. By declaring that slavery had irrevocably corrupted the existing American society, by denouncing organized religion, by becoming a feminist, and by embracing a form of Christian anarchy that precluded formal involvement in politics, Garrison seemed to have lost sight of abolitionism's main concern. But the failure of moral suasion to make progress against slavery—particularly in the South—and the question of how abolitionists should respond to increasing signs of slave unrest also helped fracture the AASS.

Garrison and a minority of New-England-centered abolitionists who agreed with his radical critique of America retained control of the AASS, which became known as the "Old Organization." By 1842 they had de-emphasized moral suasion and had begun calling for disunion—the separation of the North from the South—as the only means of ending northern support for slavery. The U.S. Constitution, Garrison declared, was a thoroughly proslavery document that had to be replaced before African Americans could gain their freedom.

Those who withdrew from the AASS took a more traditional stand on the role of women, believed the country's churches could be converted to abolitionism, and asserted that the Constitution could be used on behalf of abolitionism. Under the leadership of Lewis Tappan, a wealthy white New York City businessman, some of them formed the church-oriented AFASS. Others created the Liberty Party and nominated James G. Birney, a slaveholder-turned-abolitionist, as their candidate in the 1840 presidential election.

Most black abolitionists joined the AFASS. The Liberty Party also attracted black support, although few black men could vote. Particularly appealing to black abolitionists was the platform of the radical New York wing of the party led by Gerrit Smith. Of all the antislavery organizations, the New York party advocated the most aggressive action against slavery in the South and became most directly involved in helping slaves escape.

A MORE AGGRESSIVE ABOLITIONISM

The New York Liberty Party maintained that the U.S. Constitution, interpreted in the light of the Bible and natural law, outlawed slavery throughout the country. Therefore, the party's supporters argued, since masters had no legal right to own human beings, slaves who escaped and those who aided them acted within the law.

This position, which dated to the late 1830s, reflected northern abolitionist empathy with slaves as they struggled for freedom. At that time, the domestic slave trade in the Border South states of Maryland, Virginia, Kentucky, and Missouri tore black families apart to feed the demand for labor in new cotton-producing areas farther south. As some slaves responded by escaping or staging minor rebellions, the radical wing of the Liberty Party supported them. It encouraged black and white northerners to go south to help escapees.

THE *AMISTAD* AND THE *CREOLE*

In particular, two maritime slave revolts encouraged northern abolitionist militancy. The first of these revolts, however, did not involve enslaved Americans. In June 1839 54 African captives, under the leadership of Joseph Cinque, seized control of the Spanish schooner *Amistad* (meaning "friendship"). After a U.S. warship captured them off the coast of Long Island, New York, the Africans were imprisoned in New Haven, Connecticut. There they gained the assistance of Lewis Tappan and other abolitionists. As a result of that aid, and arguments presented by Congressman John Quincy Adams, the Supreme Court in November 1841 freed Cinque and the others.

Later that month, Madison Washington led a revolt aboard the brig *Creole,* as it transported 135 American slaves from Richmond, Virginia, to New Orleans. Washington had earlier escaped from Virginia to Canada. When he returned to rescue his wife, he was captured, reenslaved, and shipped aboard the *Creole.* At sea, Washington and about a dozen other black men seized control of the vessel and sailed it to the Bahamas, a British colony where slavery had been abolished. There local black fishermen surrounded the *Creole* with their boats to protect it, and most of the people on board immediately gained their freedom under British law. A few days later, so did Washington and the other rebels. Although Washington soon vanished from the public eye, the *Creole* revolt made him a hero among abolitionists and a symbol of black bravery.

The Underground Railroad

The famous **underground railroad** must be placed within the context of increasing southern white violence against black families, slave resistance, and aggressive northern abolitionism. Because the underground railroad had to be secret, few details of how it operated are known. Slaves, since colonial times, escaped from their masters, and free black people and some white people had always assisted them. But the organized escape of slaves from the Chesapeake, Kentucky, and Missouri along predetermined routes to Canada became common only after the mid-1830s (see Map 9-2).

The best documented underground railroad organizations centered in Washington, D.C., and Ripley, Ohio. In Washington Charles T. Torrey, a white Liberty Party abolitionist from Albany, New York, and Thomas Smallwood, a free black resident of Washington, began in 1842 to help slaves escape along a northward route. Between March and November of that year, they sent at least 150 enslaved men, women, and children to Philadelphia. From there, a local black vigilance committee provided the fugitives with transportation to Albany, New York, where a local, predominantly white, vigilance group helped them get to Canada. In southern Ohio and Indiana some residents, black and white, had since the 1810s helped fugitive slaves as they headed north from the slaveholding state of Kentucky. Ripley, located on the north shore of the Ohio River, was the center of much of this activity."

Mutiny, **painted by Hale Woodruff** in 1939, provides a dramatic and stylized portrayal of the successful uprising of African slaves on board the Spanish schooner *Amistad* in 1839. Savery Library Archives, Talladega College, Talledega, Alabama.

The escapees were by no means passive "passengers" in the underground railroad network. They raised money to pay for their transportation northward, recruited and helped other escapees, and sometimes became underground railroad agents themselves. During the mid-1850s, Arrah Weems of Rockville, Maryland, whose freedom black and white abolitionists had recently purchased and whose daughter Ann Maria had been rescued by underground railroad agents, became an agent. She brought an enslaved infant from Washington through Philadelphia to Rochester, New York, where she met Frederick Douglass.

This was not an easy journey, and the underground railroad work was risky. In 1843 Smallwood had to flee to Canada as Washington police closed in on his home. In 1846 Torrey died of tuberculosis in a Maryland prison while serving a six-year sentence for helping slaves escape. At Ripley one black underground railroad agent recalled "real warfare" with slaveholders from Kentucky. "I never thought of going uptown without a pistol in my pocket, a knife in my belt, and a blackjack handy," he later recalled.

During the early 1850s, Harriet Tubman, a fugitive slave, became the most active worker on the eastern branch of the underground railroad. Born in 1820 on a Maryland plantation, she suffered years of abuse at the hands of her master. When in 1849 he threatened to sell her and her family south, she escaped to the North. Then she returned about thirteen times to Maryland to help others flee. She had the help of Thomas Garrett, a white Quaker abolitionist who lived in Wilmington, Delaware, and William Still, the black leader of the Philadelphia Vigilance Association. During the 1850s, Still, who as a child had been a fugitive slave, coordinated the work of many black and white underground agents between Washington and Canada.

MAP 9-2 • The Underground Railroad

This maps illustrates *approximate* routes traveled by escaping slaves through the North to Canada. Although some slaves escaped from the Deep South, most who utilized the underground railroad network came from the border slave states.

▶ *By what means did escaping slaves travel the routes shown on this map?*

TECHNOLOGY AND THE UNDERGROUND RAILROAD

Steam engines were the great technological innovation of the nineteenth century. These engines, whether used to power locomotives or vessels, promoted northward escapes. By the early 1840s, police in Border South cities patrolled steamboat wharves to prevent fugitive slaves from boarding. In Washington, D.C. in 1842, Torrey and Smallwood often helped escapees get on steamboats. As rail lines spread, masters in Maryland and Virginia, despaired of recapturing slaves who crossed the Mason-Dixon Line.

Railroads and steamboats were essential in two famous escapes of the late 1840s. In December 1848, Ellen and William Craft (see Chapter 10) used both means of transportation to reach Philadelphia from Macon, Georgia. A few months later, Henry Brown traveled by train from Richmond to the Potomac River "where the tracks ended," then by steamer to Washington, and once again by train to freedom in Philadelphia. Improving transportation technology posed a threat to slavery.

CANADA WEST

The ultimate destination for many African Americans on the underground railroad was Canada West (present-day Ontario) between Buffalo and Detroit on the northern shore of Lake Erie. Black Americans began to settle in Canada West as early as the 1820s and, because slavery was illegal in the British Empire after 1833, fugitive slaves were safe there. The stronger fugitive slave law that Congress passed as part of the Compromise of 1850 (see Chapter 10) made Canada an even more important refuge for African Americans.

Mary Ann Shadd Cary was the chief advocate of black migration to Canada West, and she was the only advocate of migration who also supported racial integration. Between 1854 and 1858, she edited the *Provincial Freeman,* an abolitionist paper published in Toronto, and lectured in northern cities promoting emigration to Canada. Carry knew, however, that by the 1850s black people faced the same sort of segregation and discrimination in Canada that existed in the northern United States.

Harriet Tubman, standing at the left, is shown in this undated photograph with a group of people she helped escape from slavery. Because she worked in secret during the 1850s, she was known only to others engaged in the underground railroad, the people she helped, and a few other abolitionists.

BLACK MILITANCY

During the 1840s growing numbers of northern black abolitionists advocated forceful action against slavery. This resolve accompanied a trend toward separate black antislavery action. The black convention movement revived during the 1840s, and there were well-attended meetings in Buffalo in 1843, in Troy, New York, in 1844, and in Cleveland in 1848. Meanwhile more newspapers owned and edited by black abolitionists appeared.

The rise in black militancy had several causes. The breakup of the AASS weakened abolitionist loyalty to the national antislavery organizations. All abolitionists, black and white, explored new antislavery tactics. Many black abolitionists came to believe that most white abolitionists enjoyed antislavery debate and theory more than action.

Influenced by the examples of Cinque, Madison Washington, and other rebellious slaves, many black abolitionists during the 1840s and 1850s wanted to do more to encourage slaves to resist and escape. Henry Highland Garnet, in his "Address to the Slaves" of 1843, suggested that slaves might have to resort to violence against their masters. However, black abolitionists, like white abolitionists, approached violence and slave rebellion with caution. As late as 1857, Garnet and Frederick Douglass described slave revolt as "inexpedient."

The black abolitionist desire to go beyond rhetoric found its best outlet in the local vigilance organizations. Such associations appeared during the mid-1830s and often had white as well as black members. As the 1840s progressed, African Americans formed more of them and led those that already existed. In this they reacted against a facet of the growing violence in the United States: "slave catchers" use of force in northern cities to recapture fugitive slaves.

Black militancy also encouraged charges that white abolitionists did not live up to their words in favor of racial justice. Black abolitionists charged that white abolitionists failed to employ African Americans in their businesses and excluded African Americans from positions in antislavery organizations.

FREDERICK DOUGLASS

The career of Frederick Douglass illustrates the impact of the failure of white abolitionists to live up to their egalitarian ideals. Douglass was born a slave in Maryland in 1818. Brilliant, ambitious, and charming, he resisted brutalization, learned to read, and acquired a trade before escaping to New England in 1838. By 1841 he had, with Garrison's encouragement, become an antislavery lecturer.

But as time passed, Douglass, who had remained loyal to Garrison during the 1840s when most other black abolitionists had left the AASS, suspected that his white colleagues wanted him to continue in the role of a fugitive slave when he was becoming one of the premier American orators.

Finally, Douglass decided he had to free himself from the AASS. In 1847 he asserted his independence by leaving Massachusetts for Rochester, New York, where he began publishing the *North Star*. This decision angered Garrison and his associates but enabled Douglass to chart his course as a black leader. Although Douglass continued to work closely with white abolitionists, especially Gerrit Smith, he could now do it on his own terms and be more active in the black convention movement, which he considered essential to gaining general emancipation and racial justice. In 1851 he completed his break with the AASS by endorsing the constitutional arguments and tactics of the New York Liberty Party as better designed than Garrison's disunionism to achieve emancipation.

VOICES

MARTIN R. DELANY DESCRIBES HIS VISION OF A BLACK NATION

This excerpt comes from the appendix of Martin R. Delany's The Condition, Elevation, Emigration and Destiny of the Colored People of the United States, Politically Considered, *which he published in 1852. It embodies Delany's black nationalist vision.*

Every people should be the originators of their own designs, the projectors of their own schemes, and creators of the events that lead to their destiny—the consummation of their desires.

Situated as we are in the United States, many, and almost insurmountable obstacles present themselves. We are four-and-a-half millions in numbers, free and bond; six hundred thousand free, and three-and-a-half millions bond.

We have native hearts and virtues, just as other nations; which in their pristine purity are noble, potent, and worthy of example. We are a nation within a nation. . . .

But we have been, by our oppressors, despoiled of our purity, and corrupted in our native characteristics, so that we have inherited their vices, and but few of their virtues, leaving us in character, really a broken people.

Being distinguished by complexion, we are still singled out—although having merged in the habits and customs of our oppressors—as a distinct nation of people. . . . The claims of no people, according to established policy and usage, are respected by any nation, until they are presented in a national capacity.

To accomplish so great and desirable an end, there should be held, a great representative gathering of the colored people of the United States; not what is termed a National Convention, representing en masse, such as have been, for the last few years, held at various times and places; but a true representation of the intelligence and wisdom of the colored freemen. . . . A Confidential Council. . . .

By this Council to be appointed, a Board of Commissioners . . . to go on an expedition to the EASTERN COAST OF AFRICA, to make researches for a suitable location on that section of the coast, for the settlement of colored adventurers from the United States, and elsewhere.

The whole continent is rich in minerals, and the most precious metals, as but a superficial notice of the topographical and geological reports from that country, plainly show. . . . The land is ours—there it lies with inexhaustible resources; let us go and possess it. In Eastern Africa must rise up a nation, to whom all the world must pay commercial tribute.

- What elements of black nationalism appear in this document?

- How does Delany perceive Africa?

SOURCE: Herbert Aptheker, ed., *A Documentary History of the Negro People in the United States*, 5th ed. (New York: Citadel, 1968), 1: 327–28.

REVIVAL OF BLACK NATIONALISM

Douglass always believed that black people were part of a larger American nation and that their best prospects for political and economic success lay in the United States. He was, despite his differences with some white abolitionists, an ardent integrationist. He opposed separate black churches and predicted that African Americans would eventually merge into a greater American identity. Most black abolitionists did not go that far, but they believed racial oppression in all its forms could be defeated in the United States.

Martin Delany and Black Nationalism

The life and writings of Martin Delany (1812–1885) demonstrate the deep roots of black nationalism in African-American culture. His 1852 pamphlet, *The Condition, Elevation, Emigration and Destiny of the Colored People of the United States,* was the first major statement of black nationalism. His 1858 novel, *Blake,* explored themes of black rebellion and revolution. In 1879, Delany published *Principia of Ethnology,* an exploration of the origins of the races that made the argument that Egypt should be considered a "black" civilization. Long before Delany was born, African Americans debated whether or not black freedom was truly possible in white society. Delany's work serves to remind us that the fight over slavery was not just a two-sided argument about the legal right of white people to own black people. It was a multifaceted debate about the very nature of race and its role in American society and culture. Slavery ended with the conclusion of the Civil War, but the debate over race Martin Delany participated in continues to this day.

> In our own country, the United States, there are *three million five hundred thousand slaves;* and we, the nominally free colored people, are *six hundred thousand* in number; estimating one-sixth to be men, we have *one hundred thousand* able bodied freemen, which will make a powerful auxiliary in any country to which we may become adopted—an ally not to be despised by any power on earth. We love our country, dearly love her, but she don't love us—she despises us, and bids us begone, driving us from her embraces; but we shall not go where she desires us; but when we do go, whatever love we have for her, we shall love the country none the less that receives us as her adopted children.

... To compete now with the mighty odds of wealth, social and religious preferences, and political influences of this country, at this advanced stage of its national existence, we never may expect. A new country, and new beginning, is the only true, rational, politic remedy for our disadvantageous position ... .

... A child born under oppression, has all the elements of servility in its constitution; who when born under favorable circumstances, has to the contrary, all the elements of freedom and independence of feeling. Our children then, may not be expected, to maintain that position and manly bearing; born under the unfavorable circumstances with which we are surrounded in this country; that we so much desire. To use the language of the talented Mr. Whipper, "they cannot be raised in this country, without being stoop shouldered." Heaven's pathway stands unobstructed, which will lead us into a Paradise of bliss. Let us go on and possess the land, and the God of Israel will be our God.

The lessons of every school book, the pages of every history, and columns of every newspaper, are so replete with stimuli to nerve us on to manly aspirations, that those of our young people, who will now refuse to enter upon this great theatre of Polynesian adventure, and take their position on the stage of Central and South America, where a brilliant engagement, of certain and most triumphant success, in the drama of human equality awaits them; then, with the blood of *slaves*, write upon the lintel of every door in sterling Capitals, to be gazed and hissed at by every passer by—
Doomed by the Creator
To servility and degradation;

The SERVANT of the *white man*,
And despised of every nation!

—*From the Conclusion* of *The Condition, Elevation, Emigration and Destiny of the Colored People of the United States* (1852)

◀ In this photograph Delany wears the uniform he wore as a major in the Union Army.

Why does Delany think emigration is the only solution to the problems of African Americans? What does Delany's argument in favor of emigration suggest about his views on the relative importance of inheritance and environment in economic and cultural achievement?

African-American Events	National Events
1830	
1831 Publication of *Liberator* begun by William Lloyd Garrison	**1832** Andrew Jackson reelected president
1833 Formation of AASS	**1833** End of Nullification Controversy
1835	
1835 Abolitionist postal campaign	**1836** Martin Van Buren elected president; Texas independence from Mexico
1839 *Amistad* mutiny	
1840	
1840 Breakup of AASS	**1840** William H. Harrison elected president
1841 *Creole* revolt	**1844** James K. Polk elected president
1843 Henry Highland Garnet's "Address to the Slaves"	
1845	
1847 Publication of the *North Star* begun by Frederick Douglass	**1845** Annexation of Texas
1849 Harriet Tubman's career begins	**1846** War against Mexico begins
	1848 Annexation of Mexico's California and New Mexico provinces
1850	
1851 Start of resistance to the Fugitive Slave Act of 1850 Black migration advocated by Martin Delany	**1850** Compromise of 1850
1855	
African-American Events	National Events

During the 1840s and 1850s, however, an influential minority of black leaders disagreed with this point of view. Prominent among them were Garnet and Douglass's sometime colleague on the *North Star* Martin R. Delany.

Since the postrevolutionary days of Prince Hall and Paul Cuffe, some black leaders had believed African Americans could thrive only as a separate nation. They suggested sites in Africa, Latin America, and the American West as possible places to pursue this goal. But it took the rising tide of racism and violence emphasized in this chapter to induce a respectable minority of black abolitionists to consider migration again.

Douglass and most black abolitionists rejected migration, insisting the aim must be freedom in the United States. Nevertheless, emigration plans developed by Garnet and Delany during the 1850s became a significant part of African-American reform culture. Delany, a physician and novelist, was born free in western Virginia in 1812. He grew up in Pennsylvania and by the late 1840s championed black self-reliance. To further this cause, he promoted mass black migration to Latin America or Africa.

In contrast, Garnet welcomed white assistance for his plan to foster Christianity and economic development in Africa by encouraging *some*—not all—African Americans to migrate there under the patronage of his African Civilization Society.

Little came of these nationalist visions, largely because of the successes of the antislavery movement. Black and white abolitionists, although not perfect allies, awoke many in the North to the brutalities of slavery. They helped convince most white northerners that the slave-labor system and slaveholder control of the national government threatened their economic and political interests. At the same time, abolitionist aid to escaping slaves and their defense of fugitive slaves from recapture pushed southern leaders to adopt policies that led to secession and the Civil War. The northern victory in the war, general emancipation, and constitutional protection for black rights made most African Americans—for a time—optimistic about their future in the United States.

CONCLUSION

This chapter has focused on the radical movement for the immediate abolition of slavery. The movement flourished in the United States from 1831, when William Lloyd Garrison began publishing the *Liberator,* through the Civil War. Garrison hoped slavery could be abolished peacefully. But during the 1840s abolitionists adjusted their antislavery tactics to deal with increasing racism and antiblack violence, both of which were related to the existence of slavery. Slave resistance also inspired a more confrontational brand of abolitionism. Many black abolitionists and their white colleagues concluded that the tactic of moral suasion, typical of abolitionism during the 1830s, could not by itself achieve their goals or prevent violence against free and enslaved black people. Most black abolitionists came to believe they needed a combination of moral suasion, political involvement, and direct action to end slavery and improve the lives of African Americans in the United States. By the late 1840s, a minority of black abolitionists contended they had to establish an independent nation beyond the borders of the United States to promote African-American rights, interests, and identity.

REVIEW QUESTIONS

1. What was the historical significance of Henry Highland Garnet's "Address to the Slaves"? How did Garnet's attitude toward slavery differ from that of William Lloyd Garrison?
2. Evaluate Frederick Douglass's career as an abolitionist. How was he consistent? How was he inconsistent?
3. Discuss the contribution of black women to the antislavery movement. How did participation in this movement alter their lives?

4. Compare and contrast the integrationist views of Frederick Douglass with the nationalist views of Martin Delany and Henry Highland Garnet.
5. Why did black abolitionists leave the AASS in 1840?

myhistorylab CONNECTIONS

Reinforce what you learned in this chapter by studying the many documents, images, maps, review tools, and videos available at **www.myhistorylab.com.**

READ AND REVIEW

✓•⌐**Study** and **Review** on **myhistorylab.com** STUDY PLAN FOR CHAPTER 9

📖•⌐**Read** the **Document** on **myhistorylab.com**

> A Call for Women to Become Abolitionists
>
> An Abolitionist Lecturer's Instructions
>
> Frederick Douglass, Independence Day Speech (1852)
>
> Garnet's "Call to Rebellion" (1843)
>
> Levi Coffin's Underground Railroad Station (1826–1827)
>
> The American Anti-Slavery Society Declares Its Sentiments (1833)

🔍⌐**View** the **Map** on **myhistorylab.com**

> The Underground Railroad

RESEARCH AND EXPLORE

mysearchlab

> Consider these questions in a short research paper.
> *Compare and contrast the attitudes of black and white antislavery activists. What tensions existed within the antislavery movement?*

📖•⌐**Read** the **Document** on **myhistorylab.com**

> Exploring America: Angelina Grimké

((•⌐**Listen** on **myhistorylab.com**

> "If There is No Struggle, There is No Progress" excerpt; speech by Frederick Douglass, read by Ossie Davis
>
> "The Rebirth of Sojourner Truth" read by Jean Brannon

👁⌐**Watch** the **Video** on **myhistorylab.com**

> The Underground Railroad

———————— ((•⌐**Listen** on **myhistorylab.com** ————————

Hear the audio files for Chapter 9 at
www.myhistorylab.com.

Hear the audio files for Chapter 10 at **www.myhistorylab.com.**

FOCUS QUESTIONS

WHY WAS the expansion of slavery such a divisive issue?

WHAT DID "free labor" mean to nineteenth-century Americans?

HOW DID African Americans react to the passage of the fugitive slave law of 1850?

WHY WAS the Supreme Court decision in the *Dred Scott* case so controversial?

WHAT WAS the impact of John Brown's raid on Harpers Ferry?

HOW DID African Americans and white southerners react to the election of Abraham Lincoln in 1860?

In January 1856, Margaret Garner, her husband Robert, and their four children escaped from Kentucky to Ohio across the frozen Ohio River. They were pursed to the home of a black man by slave owners as well as deputy marshals. The Garners fiercely resisted. Robert Garner shot and wounded one of the deputies. But when it became clear that they were about to be captured, Margaret killed her daughter rather than have the child returned to slavery.

BY THE END of the 1840s in the United States, no issue was as controversial as slavery. Slavery, or more accurately its expansion, deeply divided the American people and led to the bloodiest war in American history. Try as they might from 1845 to 1860, political leaders could not solve, evade, or escape slavery and agree on whether to allow it to expand into the nation's western territories.

Caught in this monumental dispute were the South's nearly four million enslaved men, women, and children. Their future, as well as the fate of the country, was at stake. More than 620,000 Americans—northern and southern, black and white—would die before a divided nation would be reunified and slavery would be abolished.

THE LURE OF THE WEST

In 1846–1847 U.S. troops fought an eighteen-month conflict that resulted in the acquisition of more than half of Mexico and was a major step toward the fulfillment of Manifest Destiny. Even before the war with Mexico, hundreds of Americans made the long journey west, drawn by the opportunity to settle the fertile valleys of California and the Oregon Territory, which included what is today the states of Oregon and Washington. African Americans shared these hopes and dreams. In 1844 a black Missouri farmer with the improbable name of George Washington Bush caught "Oregon fever" and set out with his wife, six children, and four other families on the 1,800-mile trek by wagon train to Oregon. Bush settled north of the Columbia River in what later became the Washington Territory because Oregon's territorial constitution forbade black settlement. Although the law was rarely enforced, black residents were legally subject to whipping every six months until they departed. The statute remained Oregon state law until the 1920s.

FREE LABOR VERSUS SLAVE LABOR

Westward expansion revived the issue of slavery's future in the territories. Should slavery be legal or prohibited in western lands? Most white Americans held thoroughly ingrained racist beliefs that people of African descent were not and could never be their intellectual, political, or social equals. Yet those same white Americans disagreed vehemently on where those unfree African Americans should be permitted to work and reside.

Most northern white people adamantly opposed allowing southern slaveholders to take their slaves into the former Mexican territories and detested the prospect of slavery spreading westward and limiting their opportunities to settle and farm those lands. Except for the increasing number of militant abolitionists, white Northerners detested both slavery as a labor system and the black people who were enslaved.

By the mid-nineteenth century, northern black and white people embraced the system of **free labor**—that is, free men and women who worked for compensation to earn a living and improve their lives. If southern slave owners managed to gain a foothold for their unfree labor on the western plains, in the Rocky Mountains, or on the Pacific coast, then the future for free white laborers would be severely restricted, if not destroyed.

THE WILMOT PROVISO

In 1846, during the Mexican War, a Democratic congressman from Pennsylvania, David Wilmot, introduced a measure in Congress, the so-called Wilmot Proviso, to prohibit slavery in any lands acquired from Mexico. Wilmot later explained that he wanted neither slavery nor black people to taint territory that should be reserved exclusively for whites.

The Wilmot Proviso failed to become law. But white Southerners were enraged, and they saw the proviso as a blatant attempt to prevent them from moving west and enjoying the prosperity and way of life that an expanding slave-labor system would create. They considered any attempt to limit the growth of slavery to be the first step toward eliminating it.

White southerners had convinced themselves that black people were a childlike and irresponsible race wholly incapable of surviving as a free people if they were emancipated and compelled to compete with white Americans. Most white people believed the black race would decline and disappear if it were freed. Thus southern white people considered slavery "a positive good"—in the words of Senator John C. Calhoun of South Carolina—that benefited both races and resulted in a society vastly superior to that of the North.

To prevent slavery's expansion, the Free-Soil Party was formed in 1848. It was composed mainly of white people who vigorously opposed slavery's expansion and the supposed desecration that the presence of black men and women might bring to the new western lands. But some black and white abolitionists also supported the Free-Soilers as a way to oppose slavery. They reasoned that even though many Free-Soil supporters were hostile to black people, the party still represented a serious challenge to slavery and its expansion. Frederick Douglass felt comfortable enough with the Free-Soil Party to attend its convention in 1848.

AFRICAN AMERICANS AND THE GOLD RUSH

The discovery of gold in California in 1848 sent thousands of Americans hurrying west in 1849. The **Forty-Niners,** as these migrants were called, were almost exclusively male, and most were white Americans. But the desire to get rich had universal appeal, and the gold rush attracted Europeans, Asians (mostly Chinese), and African Americans. By 1850 nearly 900 black men (and fewer than 100 black women) were living in California, including people of African descent from Mexico, Peru, Chile, and Jamaica.

Most of the Forty-Niners—whatever their race or nationality—were placer miners. Using the most basic technology–little more than a pan, a pick, and a shovel–they sought the chips and flakes of gold deposited in the streams that flowed down the western slopes of the Sierra Nevada Mountains. Few of these placer miners struck it rich. But many of them made a modest living from the gold they recovered.

The richer gold veins were deeper underground and required more sophisticated technology and expensive equipment to mine it. Hydraulic mining used high pressure hoses to wash away sand and soil, revealing the rock, stone, and sometimes gold embedded below. A black man known only as Smith worked his mining claim in Amador County with hydraulic equipment. He earned a respectable five to six dollars a day.

Quartz mining involved heavy and costly machinery that crushed huge quantities of rock and bolders. Only larger corporations, not individual miners, had the financial resources to buy and install the machinery and hire the workers to operate it. Moses L. Rodgers was an ex-slave from Missouri who became knowledgable and successful in quartz mining operations in the late 1860s. He was both an investor and superintendent of several California gold mines in the 1870s. Most of the laborers under Rodgers' supervision were Chinese immigrants.

CALIFORNIA AND THE COMPROMISE OF 1850

As California's population soared to more than 100,000, its new residents applied for admission to the Union as a free state. White Southerners were aghast at the prospect of California prohibiting slavery, and they refused to consider its admission unless slavery was lawful there. Most Northerners would not accept this.

Into the dispute stepped Whig senator Henry Clay, who had assisted with the Missouri Compromise 30 years earlier. In 1850 the aging Clay put together an elaborate piece of legislation, **the Compromise of 1850,** designed not only to settle the controversy over California, but also to resolve the issue of slavery's expansion once and for all. To placate Northerners, he proposed admitting California as a free state and eliminating the slave trade (but not slavery) in the District of Columbia. To satisfy white Southerners, he offered a stronger fugitive slave law to make it easier for slave owners to apprehend runaway slaves and return them to slavery. New Mexico and Utah would be organized as territories with no mention of slavery (see Map 10-1).

Clay's measures were hammered into a single bill and produced one of the most remarkable debates in the history of the Senate, but it did not pass. Southern opponents like Senator John C. Calhoun of South Carolina could not tolerate the admission of California

Free states and territories
Slave states
Slave status unresolved

MAP 10–1 • The Compromise of 1850 As a result of the war against Mexico, the United States acquired the regions shown on this map as California, Utah Territory, New Mexico Territory, and the portions of Texas not included in the Province of Texas.

▶ **With the** Compromise of 1850, California entered the Union as a free state. In which remaining western lands would slavery be accepted or rejected?

without slavery. Northern opponents like Senator William Seward of New York could not tolerate a tougher fugitive slave law. President Zachary Taylor shocked his fellow Southerners and insisted that California should be admitted as a free state, and that Clay's compromise was unnecessary. Taylor promised to veto the compromise if Congress passed it.

Clay's effort failed—or so it seemed. But in the summer of 1850, Taylor died unexpectedly and was succeeded by Millard Fillmore, who was willing to accept the compromise. Senator Stephen Douglas, an ambitious Democrat from Illinois, guided Clay's compromise through Congress by breaking it into separate bills. California entered the Union as a free state, and a stronger fugitive slave law entered the federal legal code.

FUGITIVE SLAVE LAWS

Those who may have hoped the compromise would resolve the dispute over slavery forever were mistaken. The **Fugitive Slave Law of 1850** created bitter resentment among black and white abolitionists and made slavery a more emotional and personal issue for many white people who had previously considered slavery a remote southern institution.

Had runaway slaves not been an increasingly frustrating problem for slave owners, the federal fugitive slave law would not have needed to be strengthened in 1850. The U.S. Constitution and the fugitive slave law passed in 1793 would seem to have provided ample authority for slave owners to recover runaway slaves.

But by the 1830s and 1840s, hundreds if not thousands of slaves had escaped to freedom by way of the underground railroad, and white Southerners increasingly found the 1793 law too weak to overcome the resistance of northern communities to the return of escapees. Northern states had enacted personal liberty laws that made it illegal for state law enforcement officials to help capture runaways. Not only did many Northerners refuse to cooperate in returning fugitives to slavery under the 1793 law, but they also encouraged and assisted the fleeing slaves. The local black vigilance committees that were created in many northern communities and discussed in Chapter 9—among them the League of Freedom in Boston and the Liberty Association in Chicago—were especially effective in these efforts. These actions infuriated white Southerners and prompted their demand for a stricter fugitive slave law.

The Fugitive Slave Law of 1850 was one of the toughest and harshest measures the U.S. Congress ever passed. Anyone apprehended under the law was almost certain to be sent back to slavery. The law required U.S. marshals, their deputies, and even ordinary citizens to help seize suspected runaways. Those who refused to help apprehend fugitives or who helped the runaway could be fined or imprisoned. The law made it nearly impossible for black people to prove they were free. Slave owners and their agents only had to provide legal documentation from their home state or the testimony of white witnesses before a federal commissioner that the captive was a runaway slave. The federal commissioners were paid $10 for captives returned to bondage but only $5 for those declared free. Supporters of the law claimed the extra paperwork involved in returning a fugitive to slavery necessitated the higher fee. Opponents of the law saw it as a bribe to encourage federal authorities to return men and women to bondage. While the law was in effect, 332 captives were returned to the South and slavery, and only 11 were released as free people.

VOICES

AFRICAN AMERICANS RESPOND TO THE FUGITIVE SLAVE LAW

These two passages reflect the outrage the Fugitive Slave Law of 1850 provoked among black Americans. In the first, John Jacobs, a fugitive slave from South Carolina, urges black people to take up arms to oppose the law. In the second, from a speech he delivered a few days after the passage of the law, Martin Delany defies authorities to search his home for runaway slaves.

My colored brethren, if you have not swords, I say to you, sell your garments and buy one. . . . They said that they cannot take us back to the South; but I say, under the present law they can; and now they say unto you; let them take only dead bodies. . . . I would, my friends, advise you to show a front to our tyrants and arm yourselves . . . and I would advise the women to have their knives too.

SOURCE: William F. Cheek, *Black Resistance before the Civil War* (Beverly Hills: Glencoe Press, 1970), 148–49.

Sir, my house is my castle; in that castle are none but my wife and my children, as free as the angels of heaven, and whose liberty is as sacred as the pillars of God. If any man approaches that house in search of a slave—I care not who he may be, whether the constable, or sheriff, magistrate or even judge of the Supreme Court—nay, let it be he who sanctioned this act to become law [President Millard Fillmore] surrounded by his cabinet as his bodyguard, with the Declaration of Independence waving above his head as his banner, and the constitution of this country upon his breast as his shield—if he crosses the threshold of my door, and I do not lay him a lifeless corpse at my feet, I hope the grave may refuse my body a resting place, and righteous. Heaven my spirit a home, O, no! He cannot enter that house and we both live.

■ How and why did these two black men justify the use of violence against those who were enforcing a law passed by Congress?

■ Under what circumstances is it permissible to violate the law or threaten to kill another human being?

SOURCE: Victor Ullman, *Martin R. Delany: The Beginnings of Black Nationalism* (Boston: Beacon Press, 1971).

The new fugitive slave law outraged many black and white Northerners. An angry Frederick Douglass insisted in October 1850 that "the only way to make the Fugitive Slave Law a dead letter is to make a half dozen or more dead kidnappers." White abolitionist Wendell Phillips exhorted his listeners to disobey the law. "We must trample this law under our feet."

FUGITIVE SLAVES

The fugitive slave law did more than anger black and white Northerners. It exposed them to cruel and heart-wrenching scenes as southern slave owners and slave catchers took advantage of the new law and—with the vigorous assistance of federal authorities—relentlessly pursued runaway slaves. Many white people and virtually all black people felt revulsion over this crackdown on those who had fled from slavery to freedom.

Even California was not immune to the furor over fugitive slaves. Although the new state prohibited slavery, several hundred black people were held illegally there as slaves in the 1850s. Nevertheless, some slaves ran away to the far West rather than the north. Black abolitionist Mary Ellen Pleasant hid fugitive Archy Lee in San Francisco in 1858. Other black Californians provided security for runaways from as far east as Maryland.

WILLIAM AND ELLEN CRAFT

Black and white abolitionists had organized vigilance committees to resist the fugitive slave law and to prevent—by force if necessary—the return of fugitives to slavery. In October 1850 slave catchers arrived in Boston prepared to capture and return William and Ellen Craft to slavery in Georgia. In 1848 the Crafts had devised an ingenious escape. Ellen's fair complexion enabled her to disguise herself as a sickly young white man who, accompanied by "his" slave, was traveling north for medical treatment. They journeyed to Boston by railroad and ship and thus escaped from slavery—or so they thought.

Slave catchers vowed to return the Crafts to servitude no matter how long it took. While white abolitionists protected Ellen and black abolitionists hid William, the vigilance committee plastered posters around Boston describing the slave catchers, calling them "man-stealers," and threatening their safety. Within days the Southerners left without the Crafts. Soon thereafter, the Crafts sailed to security in England.

SHADRACH MINKINS

Black and white abolitionists were prepared to use force against the U.S. government and the slave owners and their agents. Sometimes the abolitionists succeeded, sometimes they did not. In early 1851, a few months after the Crafts left Boston, federal marshals apprehended a black waiter there who had escaped from slavery and given himself the name Shadrach Minkins. But a well-organized band of black men led by Lewis Hayden invaded the courthouse and spirited Minkins to safety in Canada on the underground railroad. Federal authorities brought charges against four black men and four white men who were then indicted by a grand jury for helping Minkins, but local juries refused to convict them.

THE BATTLE AT CHRISTIANA

In September 1851 a battle erupted in the little town of Christiana, in southern Pennsylvania, when a Maryland slave owner, Edward Gorsuch, arrived to recover two runaway slaves. Accompanied by family members and three deputy U.S. marshals, he confronted a well-armed crowd of at least 25 black men and several white men. Black leader William Parker told Gorsuch to give up any plans to take the runaway slaves. Gorsuch refused, and a battle ensued. Gorsuch was killed and several black and white men were hurt. The runaway slaves escaped to Canada.

President Fillmore sent U.S. Marines to Pennsylvania, and they helped round up the alleged perpetrators of the violence. Thirty-six black men and five white men were arrested and indicted for treason by a federal grand jury. But after the first trial ended in acquittal, the remaining cases were dropped.

ANTHONY BURNS

Of all the fugitive slave cases, none elicited more support or sorrow than that of Anthony Burns. In 1854 Burns escaped from slavery in Virginia by stowing away on a ship to Boston. After gaining work in a clothing store, he unwisely sent a letter to his brother who was still a slave. The letter was confiscated, and Burns's former owner set out to capture him. Burns was arrested by a deputy marshal who, recalling Shadrach Minkins's escape, placed him under guard in chains in the federal courthouse. Efforts by black and white abolitionists to break into the courthouse with axes, guns, and a battering ram failed, although a deputy U.S. marshal was killed during the assault.

President Franklin Pierce, a northern Democrat who had been elected with southern support in 1852, sent U.S. troops to Boston, including Marines, cavalry, and artillery, to uphold the law and return Burns to Virginia. Black minister Leonard A. Grimes and the vigilance committee tried to purchase Burns's freedom, but the U.S. attorney refused. In June 1854, with church bells tolling and buildings draped in black, thousands of Bostonians watched silently—many in tears—as Anthony Burns was marched through the streets to a ship that would take him to Virginia.

The spectacle of a lone black man, escorted by hundreds of armed troops, trudging from freedom to slavery moved even people who had shown no special interest in nor sympathy for fugitives or slaves. One staunchly conservative white man remarked, "When it was all over, and I was left alone in my office, I put my face in my hands and I wept. I could do nothing less." William Lloyd Garrison burned a copy of the Constitution on the Fourth of July as thousands looked on with approval.

Yet the government was unrelenting. A federal grand jury indicted seven black men and white men for riot and inciting a riot in their attempt to free Burns. One indictment was set aside on a technicality, and the other charges were then dropped because no Boston jury would convict the accused. Several months later, black Bostonians led by the Rev. Grimes purchased Burns for $1,300. He settled in St. Catherine's, Ontario, in Canada where he died in 1862.

MARGARET GARNER

If the Burns case was the most moving, then Margaret Garner's was one of the most tragic examples of the lengths to which slaves might go to gain freedom for themselves and their children. In the winter of 1856, Margaret Garner and seven other slaves escaped from Kentucky across the Ohio River to freedom in Cincinnati. But their owner, Archibald Grimes, pursued them. Grimes, accompanied by a U.S. deputy marshal and several other people, attempted to arrest the fugitives at a small house where they had hidden. Refusing to surrender, the slaves were overpowered and subdued.

Before the fugitives were captured, Garner slit the throat of her daughter with a butcher knife rather than see the child returned to slavery. Before she could kill her two sons, she was disarmed. Ohio authorities charged her with murder, but by that time she had been returned to Kentucky and then sent with her surviving children to Arkansas to be sold. On the trip down the river, her youngest child and 24 other people drowned in a shipwreck, thereby cruelly fulfilling her wish that the child not grow up to be a slave. Margaret Garner was later sold at a slave market in New Orleans.

The "trial" and subsequent return of Anthony Burns to slavery in 1854 resulted in the publication of a popular pamphlet in Boston. Documents like this generated increased support—and funds—for the abolitionist cause.

THE ROCHESTER CONVENTION, 1853

In 1853, while northern communities grappled with the consequences of the fugitive slave law, African-American leaders gathered for a national convention in Rochester, New York. The **Rochester Convention** warned that black Americans were not prepared to submit quietly to a government more concerned about the interests of slave owners than people seeking to free themselves from bondage. The delegates looked past the grim conditions of the times to call for greater unity among black people and to find ways to improve their economic prospects. They asserted their claims to the rights of citizenship and equal protection before the law, and they worried that the wave of European immigrants entering the country would deprive poor black Northerners of the menial and unskilled jobs on which they depended.

NATIVISM AND THE KNOW-NOTHINGS

Not only did many white Americans look with disfavor and often outright disgust at African Americans, they were also distressed by and opposed to the increasing numbers of white immigrants coming to the United States. Hundreds of thousands of Europeans—mostly Germans and Irish—arrived in the 1840s and 1850s. In one year—1854—430,000 people arrived on American shores.

The mass starvation that accompanied the potato famine of the 1840s in Ireland drove thousands of Irish people to the United States, where they often encountered intense hostility. Native-born, Protestant, white Americans considered the Catholic Irish crude, ignorant drunks. Irish immigrants also competed with Americans for low-paying unskilled jobs. Anti-Catholic propaganda warned that the influence of the Vatican would weaken American institutions. Some even charged there was a Roman Catholic conspiracy to take over the United States. Mobs attacked Catholic churches and convents.

These anti-immigrant, anti-Catholic, anti-alcohol sentiments helped foster in 1854 the rise of a nativist third political party, the American Party—better known as the **"Know-Nothing Party."** The Know-Nothings attracted considerable support. Feeding on resentment and prejudice, the party grew to one million strong. Most Know-Nothings were in New England, and they even for a short time took control of Massachusetts, where many of the Irish had settled. But the party was also strong in Kentucky, Texas, and elsewhere.

Resistance

Before 1850, many white northerners assumed that slavery was not their problem. When a new Fugitive Slave Law forced them to participate in the slave system, they resisted. In several northern cities, crowds tried to rescue fugitive slaves from their captors. The free black community also took action. The law meant that no African American could feel safe. Through urban networks known as "Vigilance Committees," and through antislavery newspapers, African Americans remained in constant communication. The committees looked out for slave hunters and helped fugitives avoid capture. In his paper, the *North Star*, Frederick Douglass printed the names of "every slave-hunter who meets a bloody death. . . ."

▲ Abolitionists used engravings such as this one of slave owners firing upon four escaping slaves to dramatize the impact of the Fugitive Slave Law.

A reward poster ▶ for the capture and return of one slave.

$100 REWARD!

RANAWAY

From the undersigned, living on Current River, about twelve miles above Doniphan, in Ripley County, Mo., on 3d of March, 1860, ... about 30 years old, weighs about 160 pounds; high forehead, with a scar on it; had on brown pants and coat very much worn, and an old black wool hat; shoes size No. 11.

The above reward will be given to any person who may apprehend this ...

APOS TUCKER.

A MAN KIDNAPPED!

A PUBLIC MEETING AT

FANEUIL HALL!

WILL BE HELD

THIS FRIDAY EVEN'G,

May 26th, at 7 o'clock,

To secure justice for A MAN CLAIMED AS A SLAVE by a

VIRGINIA KIDNAPPER!

And NOW IMPRISONED IN BOSTON COURT HOUSE, in defiance of the Laws of Massachusetts. Shall he be plunged into the Hell of Virginia Slavery by a Massachusetts Judge of Probate?

BOSTON, May 26th, 1854.

▲ A Boston poster (May 25, 1854) announces a meeting to discuss the arrest and forthcoming trial of fugitive slave Anthony Burns. His arrest and trial touched off riots and protests by abolitionists and citizens of Boston in the spring of 1854.

▲ **Fugitive slaves** aim guns at slave-catchers in an attempt to preserve their freedom.

Examine the political cartoon of fugitive slaves. What does this image tell us about the way abolitionists portrayed the evils of the Fugitive Slave Law? Read the handbills about Anthony Burns's capture and the runaway slave reward. Why was the Fugitive Slave Law seen as such a threat to the free black community of the city?

"Border ruffians" were armed men from Missouri who crossed the border to support pro-slavery forces in the Kansas territory. They sought the legalization of slavery in Kansas. They—as well as the opponents of slavery—were willing to resort to violence to achieve their aims.

Although Know-Nothings opposed immigrants and Catholics, they disagreed among themselves over slavery and its expansion. As a result the party soon split into northern and southern factions and collapsed.

UNCLE TOM'S CABIN

No one contributed more to the growing opposition to slavery among white Northerners than Harriet Beecher Stowe. Raised in a religious environment—her father, brothers, and husband were ministers—Stowe developed a hatred of slavery that she converted into a melodramatic, but moving, novel about slaves and their lives.

Uncle Tom's Cabin moved Northerners to tears and made slavery more emotional to readers who had previously considered it only a distant system of labor that exploited black people. In stage versions of the book that were later produced across the North, Uncle Tom was transformed from a dignified man into a pitiful and fawning figure eager to please white people—hence the emergence of the derogatory term, Uncle Tom.

THE KANSAS-NEBRASKA ACT

After the Compromise of 1850, the disagreement over slavery's expansion intensified and became violent. In 1854 Senator Stephen Douglas introduced a bill in Congress to organize the Kansas and Nebraska Territories that soon provoked white settlers in Kansas to kill each other over slavery. Douglas's primary concern was to secure the Kansas and Nebraska region for the construction of a transcontinental railroad. Until 1853 it had been part of the Indian Territory the federal government had promised would not be open to white settlement. To win the support of southern Democrats, who wanted slavery in at least one of the two new territories, Douglas's bill would permit Kansas residents to decide for themselves whether to allow slavery (see Map 10-2).

This proposal—known as **"popular sovereignty"**—angered many Northerners because it created the possibility that slavery might expand to areas where it had been prohibited. The Missouri Compromise banned slavery north of the 36° 30 N latitude. Douglas's **Kansas-Nebraska Act** would repeal that limitation and allow settlers in Kansas,

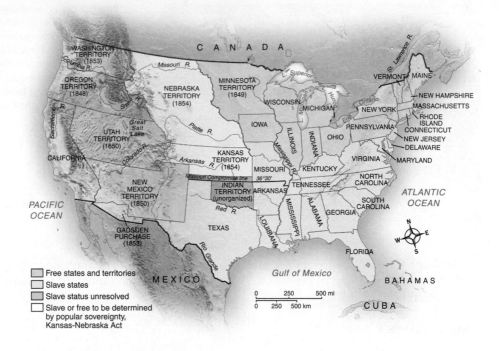

MAP 10-2 • The Kansas-Nebraska Act This measure guided through Congress by Democratic senator Steven A. Douglas opened up the Great Plains to settlement and to railroad development. It also deeply divided the nation by repealing the 1820 Missouri Compromise Line of 36° 309 and permitting—through popular sovereignty—the people in Kansas to determine slavery's fate in that territory. Eastern Kansas became a bloody battleground between proslavery and antislavery forces.

▶ *Where exactly could slavery conceivably exist where it had previously been prohibited?*

which was north of that line, to vote on slavery there. Thus, if enough proslavery people moved to Kansas and voted for slavery, slaves and their owners would be legally permitted to dwell on land that had been closed to them for more than 30 years.

Douglas managed to muster enough votes in Congress to pass the bill, but its enactment destroyed an already divided Whig Party and drove a wedge between the North and South. The Whig Party disintegrated. Northern Whigs joined supporters of the Free-Soil Party to form the Republican Party, which was organized expressly to oppose the expansion of slavery. Southern Whigs drifted, often without enthusiasm, to the Democrats or Know-Nothings.

Violence soon erupted in Kansas between proslavery and antislavery forces. **"Border ruffians"** from Missouri invaded Kansas to attack antislavery settlers and to vote illegally in Kansas elections. The New England Emigrant Aid Society dispatched people to the territory and the Rev. Henry Ward Beecher encouraged them to pack "Beecher's Bibles," which were firearms and not the Word of the Lord. By 1856 Kansas had 8,500 settlers, including 245 slaves, and two rival territorial governments. Civil war had erupted—prompting the press to label the territory "Bleeding Kansas." More than 200 people died in the escalating violence. Among those participating in the mayhem was abolitionist John Brown.

PRESTON BROOKS ATTACKS CHARLES SUMNER

The violence in Kansas spread to Congress. In May 1856 Massachusetts Senator Charles Sumner delivered a tirade in the Senate denouncing the proslavery settlers in Kansas and the Southerners who supported them. Speaking of "The Crime against Kansas," Sumner accused South Carolina Senator Andrew P. Butler of keeping slavery as his lover. Butler "has chosen a mistress to whom he has made his vows, and who . . . though polluted in the sight of the world, is chaste in his sight—I mean the harlot slavery." Butler was not present for the speech, but his distant cousin, South Carolina Congressman Preston Brooks, was in the chamber.

Two days later, Brooks exacted his revenge. Waiting until the Senate adjourned, Brooks strode to the desk where Sumner was seated and attacked him with a rattan cane. The blows rained down until the cane shattered and Sumner tumbled to the floor, bloody and semiconscious. Sumner suffered lingering physical and emotional effects from the beating and did not return to the Senate for almost four years. Brooks resigned from the House of Representatives, paid a $300 fine, and went home to South Carolina a hero. He was easily reelected to his seat.

In the 1856 presidential election, the Democrats—although divided over the debacle in Kansas—nominated James Buchanan of Pennsylvania, another northern Democrat who was acceptable to the South. The Republicans supported a handsome army officer, John C. Fremont. Their slogan was "Free Soil, Free Speech, Free Men, and Fremont." But the Republicans were exclusively a northern party, and with the demise of the Whigs, the South had become largely a one-party region. Almost no white southerners would support the Republicans, a party whose very existence was based on its opposition to slavery's expansion.

Buchanan won the presidency with nearly solid southern support and enough northern votes to carry him to victory, but the Republicans gained enough support and confidence to give them hope for the 1860 election.

THE *DRED SCOTT* DECISION

Dred Scott was born in Virginia, but by the 1830s he belonged to John Emerson, an army doctor in Missouri. Emerson took Scott to military posts in Illinois and Fort Snelling in what is now Minnesota. While at Fort Snelling, Scott married Harriet, a slave woman,

The *Dred Scott* case was front page news on *Frank Leslie's Illustrated Newspaper* in 1857. Harriet and Dred with their two daughters are depicted sympathetically as members of the middle class rather than as abused and mistreated slaves.

and they had a daughter, Eliza, before Emerson returned with the three of them to St. Louis. In 1846, after Emerson's death, and with the support of white friends, Scott and his wife filed separate suits for their freedom. By agreement, her suit was set aside pending the outcome of her husband's litigation. Scott and his lawyers contended that because Scott had been taken to territory where slavery was illegal, he had become a free man.

Scott lost his first suit, won his second, but lost again on appeal to the Missouri Supreme Court. His lawyers then appealed to the federal courts where they lost again. The final appeal in ***Dred Scott v. Sanford*** was to the U.S. Supreme Court. Although 79-year-old Chief Justice Roger Taney of Maryland had freed his own slaves, he was an unabashed advocate of the southern way of life. Moreover, Taney, a majority of the other justices, and President Buchanan were convinced that the prestige of the Court would enable it to render a decision about slavery that might be controversial but would still be accepted as the law of the land.

QUESTIONS FOR THE COURT

Taney framed two questions for the Court to decide in the Scott case: Could Scott, a black man, sue in a federal court? And was Scott free because he had been taken to a state and a territory where slavery was prohibited? In response to the first question, the Court, led by Taney, ruled that Scott—and every other black American—could not sue in a federal court because black people were not citizens. Speaking for the majority (two of the nine justices dissented), Taney emphatically stated that black people had no rights.

Taney was wrong. Although not treated as equals, free black people in many states had enjoyed rights associated with citizenship since the ratification of the Constitution in 1788. Black men had entered into contracts, held title to property, sued in the courts, and voted at one time in five of the original thirteen states.

A majority of the Court also answered no to the second question. Scott was not a free man, although he had lived in places where slavery was illegal. Scott, Taney maintained, again speaking for the Court, was slave property—and the slave owner's property rights took precedence. To the astonishment of those who opposed slavery's expansion, the Court also ruled that Congress could not pass measures—including the Missouri Compromise or the Kansas-Nebraska Act—that might prevent slave owners from taking their property into any territory.

REACTION TO THE *DRED SCOTT* DECISION

The Court had spoken. Would the nation listen? White Southerners were delighted with Taney's decision. Republicans were horrified. But instead of earning the acceptance—let alone the approval—of most Americans, the case further inflamed the controversy over slavery. But if white Americans were divided in their reaction to the *Dred Scott* decision, black Americans were discouraged, disgusted, and defiant. Taney's decision delivered another setback to a people—already held in forced labor—who believed their toil, sweat, and contributions over the previous 250 years to what had become the United States gave them a legitimate role in American society. Now the Supreme Court said they had no rights. They knew better.

At rallies across the North, black people condemned the decision. Black writer, abolitionist, and women's rights advocate Frances Ellen Watkins Harper heaped scorn on the U.S. government as "the arch traitor to liberty, as shown by the Fugitive Slave Law and the *Dred Scott* decision."

WHITE NORTHERNERS AND BLACK AMERICANS

Many white Northerners were genuinely concerned by the struggles of fugitive slaves, moved by *Uncle Tom's Cabin,* and disturbed by the *Dred Scott* decision. Yet as sensitive and sympathetic as some of them were to the plight of black people, most white Americans—including Northerners—remained indifferent to, fearful of, or hostile to people of color.

The same white Northerners who opposed the expansion of slavery to California or Kansas also opposed the migration of free black people to northern states and communities. In 1851 Indiana and Iowa outlawed the emigration to their territory of black people, slave or free. Illinois did likewise in 1853. White male voters in Michigan in 1850 voted overwhelmingly—32,000 to 12,000—against permitting black men to vote. Only Ohio was an exception. In 1849 it repealed legislation excluding black people from the state.

Foreign observers were struck by northern racism. Alexis de Tocqueville, a French aristocrat, toured America in 1831 and wrote a perceptive analysis of American society. He considered Northerners more antagonistic toward black people than Southerners. "The prejudice of race appears to be stronger in the states that have abolished slavery than in those where it still exists; and nowhere is it so intolerant as in those states where servitude has never been known."

THE LINCOLN-DOUGLAS DEBATES

In 1858 Senator Stephen Douglas of Illinois, a Democrat, ran for reelection to the Senate against Republican Abraham Lincoln. The main issues in the campaign were slavery and race, which the two candidates addressed in debates around the state. In carefully reasoned speeches and responses, these experienced and articulate lawyers focused almost exclusively on slavery's expansion and its future in the Union. At Freeport, Illinois, Lincoln, a former Whig congressman, attempted to trap Douglas by asking him if slavery could expand now that the *Dred Scott* decision had ruled slaves were property whom their owners could take into any federal territory. In reply, Douglas who wanted to be president and had no desire to offend northern or southern voters, cleverly defended "popular sovereignty" and the *Dred Scott* decision. He insisted that slave owners could indeed take their slaves where they pleased. But, he contended, if the people of a territory failed to enact slave codes to protect and control slave property, slave owners were not likely to settle there with their slaves.

ABRAHAM LINCOLN AND BLACK PEOPLE

But the **Lincoln-Douglas debates** did not always turn on the fine points of constitutional law or the fate of slavery in the territories. Thanks mainly to Douglas, who accused Lincoln and the Republicans of promoting the interests of black people over those of white people, the debates sometimes degenerated into crude exchanges about which candidate favored white people more and black people less. Douglas proudly advocated white supremacy. He later charged that Lincoln and the Republicans wanted black and white equality.

Lincoln did not believe in racial equality, and he made that plain. In exasperation, he explained that merely because he opposed slavery did not mean he believed in equality. "I do not understand that because I do not want a negro woman for a slave I must necessarily have her for a wife." But without repudiating these views, Lincoln later tried to transcend this blatant racism. "Let us discard all this quibbling about this man and the other man— this race and that race and the other race being inferior." Instead, he added, let us "unite as one people throughout this land, until we shall once more stand up declaring that all men are created equal." Lincoln stated unequivocally that race had nothing to do with whether a man had the right to be paid for his labor. He pointed out that the black man, "in the right to eat the bread, without leave of anybody else, which his own hand earns, he is my equal and the equal of Judge Douglas, and the equal of every living man."

Lincoln may have won the debate in the minds of many, but Douglas won the election. Lincoln, however, made a name for himself that would work to his political advantage in the near future, and Douglas, despite his best efforts, had thoroughly offended many Southerners by suggesting that slave owners would not risk taking their human property to a territory that lacked a slave code. Douglas also antagonized white Southerners when he opposed the proslavery Kansas Lecompton constitution that he and many others believed had been fraudulently adopted. In two years, these disagreements over slavery would contribute to a decisive split in the Democratic Party.

JOHN BROWN AND THE RAID ON HARPERS FERRY

While Lincoln and Douglas were debating, John Brown was plotting. Following his participation in the violence that followed the passage of the Kansas–Nebraska Act, Brown began to plan the overthrow of slavery in the South itself. In May 1858, accompanied by eleven white followers, he met 34 black people led by Martin Delany in Canada and appealed for their support. Brown hoped to attract legions of slaves as his "army" moved down the Appalachian Mountains into the heart of the plantation system.

PLANNING THE RAID

Only one man at the Canadian gathering agreed to join the raid. Brown returned to the United States and garnered financial support from prosperous white abolitionists.

Brown also asked Frederick Douglass and Harriet Tubman to join him. They declined. By the summer of 1859, at a farm in rural Maryland, Brown had assembled an "army" consisting of 17 white men (including three of his adult sons) and five black men. The black men who enlisted were Osborne Anderson, Sheridan Leary, Leary's nephew John A. Copeland, and two escaped slaves, Shields Green and Dangerfield Newby.

THE RAID

Brown's invasion began on Sunday night October 16, 1859, with a raid on Harpers Ferry, Virginia, and the federal arsenal there. Brown hoped to secure weapons and then advance south, but the operation went awry from the start. The dedication and devotion of Brown and his men were not matched by their strategy or his leadership. The first person Brown's band killed was ironically a free black man, Heyward Shepard, who was a baggage handler at the train station. The alarm went out, and opposition gathered.

Although they had lost the initiative, Brown and his men neither advanced nor retreated. Instead they remained in Harpers Ferry while Virginia and Maryland militia converged on them. Fighting began, and two townspeople, the mayor, and eight of

Brown's men, including Sheridan Leary, Dangerfield Newby, and two of Brown's sons, were killed. But Brown managed to seize hostages, including Lewis W. Washington, the great grandnephew of George Washington.

By Tuesday morning, Brown, with his hostages and what remained of his "army," was holed up in an engine house. U.S. Marines under the command of Robert E. Lee arrived, surrounded the building, and demanded Brown's surrender. He refused. The Marines broke in. Brown was wounded and captured.

About 150 adult slaved lived near the vicinity of Harpers Ferry. Most of them were aware of the raid, and many of them joined the insurrection. Osborne Anderson provided pikcs to slaves. Some of them acquired firearms. Several slaves managed to flee to freedom in the North. Perhaps a dozen black men—in addition to those who accompanied Brown—died during and after the raid.

There was no massive slave uprising. Shields Green and John A. Copeland fled but were caught. Osborne Anderson eluded capture and later fought in the Civil War. Virginia tried Brown, Green, and Copeland for treason. They were found guilty and sentenced to hang. But the violence did not end. In the weeks that followed, the barn of every juror who convicted Brown was burned. Many horses and cattle died. They were apparently poisoned.

THE REACTION

John Brown's raid had not proceeded as planned. But Brown and his men succeeded in intensifying the deep emotions of those who supported and those who opposed slavery. At first regarded as crazed zealots and insane fanatics, they showed they were willing—even eager—to die for the antislavery cause. The dignity and assurance that Brown, Green, and Copeland displayed as they awaited the gallows impressed many black and white Northerners.

For many Northerners, the day Brown was executed, December 2, 1859, was a day of mourning. Church bells tolled, and people bowed their heads in prayer. One unnamed black man later solemnly declared, "The memory of John Brown shall be indelibly written upon the tablets of our hearts, and when tyrants cease to oppress the enslaved, we will teach our children to revive his name, and transmit it to the latest posterity, as being the greatest man in the 19th century."

White Southerners were traumatized by the

JOHN BROWN AT HARPER'S FERRY.

John Brown was captured in the Engine House at Harpers Ferry on October 18, 1859. He was quickly tried for treason and convicted. On December 2, 1859, he was hanged. Although his raid failed to free a single slave, it helped catapult the nation toward civil war.

raid and outraged that Northerners made Brown a hero and a martyr. A wave of hysteria and paranoia swept the South as incredulous white people wondered how Northerners could admire a man who sought to kill slave owners and free their slaves.

Brown's raid and the reaction to it further divided a nation already badly split over slavery. Although neither he nor anyone else realized it at the time, Brown and his "army" had propelled the South toward secession from the Union—and thereby moved the nation closer to his goal of destroying slavery.

THE ELECTION OF ABRAHAM LINCOLN

With the country fracturing over slavery, four candidates ran for president in the election of 1860. The Democrats split into a northern faction, which nominated Stephen Douglas, and a southern faction, which nominated John C. Breckenridge of Kentucky. The Constitutional Union Party, a new party formed by former Whigs, nominated John Bell of Tennessee. The breakup of the Democratic Party assured victory for the Republican candidate, Abraham Lincoln (see Map 10-3).

Lincoln's name was not even on the ballot in most southern states, because his candidacy was based on the Republican Party's adamant opposition to the expansion of slavery into any western territory. Although Lincoln took pains to reassure white Southerners that slavery would continue in states where it already existed, they were not persuaded.

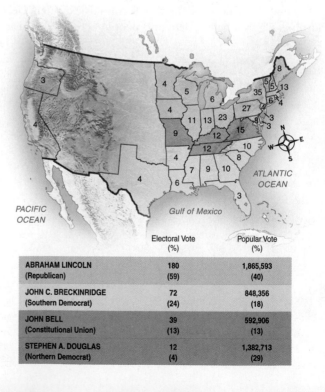

MAP 10-3 • The Election of 1860
The results reflect the sectional schism over slavery. Lincoln carried the election although he won only in northern states. His name did not even appear on the ballot in most southern states.

▶ *How was Lincoln able to win without getting any electoral votes from the South?*

	Electoral Vote (%)	Popular Vote (%)
ABRAHAM LINCOLN (Republican)	180 (59)	1,865,593 (40)
JOHN C. BRECKINRIDGE (Southern Democrat)	72 (24)	848,356 (18)
JOHN BELL (Constitutional Union)	39 (13)	592,906 (13)
STEPHEN A. DOUGLAS (Northern Democrat)	12 (4)	1,382,713 (29)

BLACK PEOPLE RESPOND TO LINCOLN'S ELECTION

Although they were less opposed to Lincoln than white Southerners, black Northerners and white abolitionists were not eager to see Abraham Lincoln become president. Dismayed by his contradictions and racism, many black people refused to support him or did so reluctantly. The New York *Anglo-African* opposed both Republicans and Democrats in the 1860 election, telling its readers to depend on each other. "We have no hope from either [of the] political parties. We must rely on ourselves, the righteousness of our cause, and the advance of just sentiments among the great masses of the . . . people."

After Lincoln's election, black leaders almost welcomed the secession of southern states. H. Ford Douglas urged the southern states to leave the Union. "Stand not upon the order of your going, but go at once. . . . There is no union of ideas and interests in this country, and there can be no union between freedom and slavery." Frederick Douglass was convinced that there were men prepared to follow in the footsteps of John Brown's "army" to destroy slavery. "I am for dissolution of the Union—decidedly for a dissolution of the Union! . . . In case of such a dissolution, I believe that men could be found . . . who would venture into those states and raise the standard of liberty there."

DISUNION

When South Carolina seceded on December 20, 1860, it began a procession of southern states out of the Union. By February 1861 seven states—South Carolina, Mississippi, Alabama, Florida, Louisiana, Georgia, and Texas—had seceded and formed the Confederate States of America in Montgomery, Alabama. Before there could be the kind of undertaking against slavery that Douglass had proposed, Abraham Lincoln tried to persuade the seceding states to reconsider. In his inaugural address of March 4, 1861, Lincoln attempted to calm the fears of white Southerners but informed them he would not tolerate their withdrawal from the Union. Lincoln repeated his assurance that he would not tamper with slavery in the states where it was already legal.

Lincoln added that the "only" dispute between the North and South was over the expansion of slavery. He emphatically warned, however, that he would enforce the Constitution and not permit secession. He pleaded with white Southerners to contemplate their actions patiently and thoughtfully, actions that might provoke a civil conflict.

Southern whites did not heed him. Slavery was too essential to give up merely to preserve the Union. Barely a month after Lincoln's inauguration, Confederate leaders demanded that U.S. Army major Robert Anderson surrender Fort Sumter in the harbor of Charleston, South Carolina. Anderson refused, and on April 12, 1861, Confederate artillery fired on the fort. In the aftermath, Virginia, North Carolina, Tennessee, and Arkansas joined the Confederacy. The Civil War had begun.

CONCLUSION

Virtually every event and episode of major or minor consequence in the United States between 1846 and 1861 involved black people and the expansion of slavery. From the Wilmot Proviso and the Compromise of 1850 to the *Dred Scott* decision and John Brown's raid, white Americans were increasingly perplexed about how the nation could remain half slave and half free. They were unable to resolve the problem of slavery's expansion.

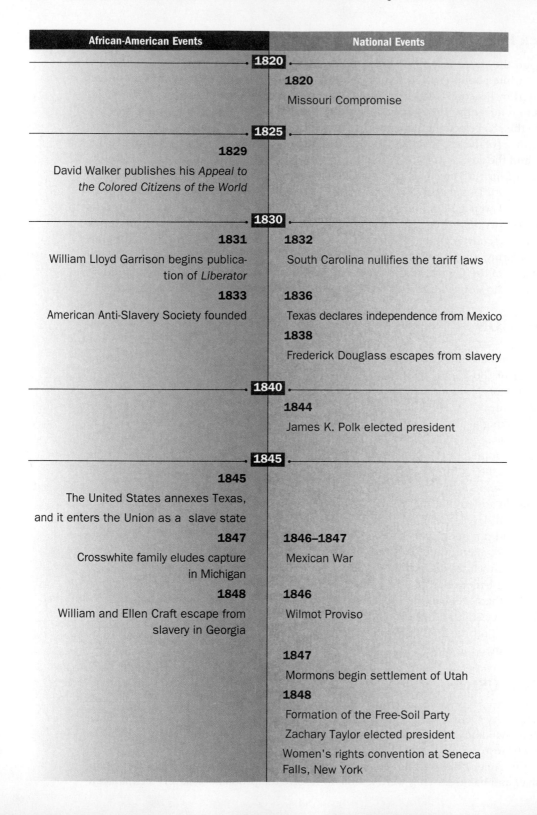

African-American Events	National Events

1820

1820
Missouri Compromise

1825

1829
David Walker publishes his *Appeal to the Colored Citizens of the World*

1830

1831
William Lloyd Garrison begins publication of *Liberator*

1832
South Carolina nullifies the tariff laws

1833
American Anti-Slavery Society founded

1836
Texas declares independence from Mexico

1838
Frederick Douglass escapes from slavery

1840

1844
James K. Polk elected president

1845

1845
The United States annexes Texas, and it enters the Union as a slave state

1847
Crosswhite family eludes capture in Michigan

1846–1847
Mexican War

1848
William and Ellen Craft escape from slavery in Georgia

1846
Wilmot Proviso

1847
Mormons begin settlement of Utah

1848
Formation of the Free-Soil Party

Zachary Taylor elected president

Women's rights convention at Seneca Falls, New York

1850

African-American Events	National Events
1850	**1850**
Fugitive Slave Act	Compromise of 1850
1850–1860	**1852**
Fugitive slaves captured	Publication of *Uncle Tom's Cabin*
	Franklin Pierce elected president
1851	**1854**
Shadrach Minkins eludes capture in Boston	Kansas-Nebraska Act
Thomas Sims returned to slavery "Battle" at Christiana	
1853	
Black convention at Rochester, New York	
1854	
Anthony Bums returned to slavery in Boston	

1855

1856	**1855–1856**
Margaret Garner kills her daughter in unsuccessful escape	"Bleeding" Kansas
1857	**1856**
The *Dred Scott* decision	James Buchanan elected president
	Congressman Preston Brooks assaults Senator Charles Sumner
1859	**1858**
John Brown's raid on Harpers Ferry	The Lincoln-Douglas debates

1860

1861	**1860**
Free black men in Charleston offer their support to South Carolina	Abraham Lincoln elected president
	South Carolina secedes from the Union
	1861
	Six more southern states secede and from the Confederacy; Civil War begins after firing on Fort Sumter in April; four more southern states join the Confederacy

| **African-American Events** | **National Events** |

Without the presence of black people in America, neither secession nor civil war would have occurred. Yet the Civil War began because white Americans had developed contradictory visions of the future. White Southerners contemplated a future that inextricably linked their security and prosperity to slavery. The South, they believed, could neither advance nor endure without slavery.

Northern white people believed their future rested on the opportunities for white men and their families to flourish as independent, self-sufficient farmers, shopkeepers, and skilled artisans. For their future to prevail, they insisted the new lands in the American West should exclude the slave system that white Southerners considered so vital. Neither northern nor southern white people—except for some abolitionists—ever believed people of color should fully participate as free people in American society or in the future of the American nation.

REVIEW QUESTIONS

1. How and why did southern and northern white people differ over slavery? On what did white people of both regions agree and disagree about race and slavery?

2. If you were a northern African American in the 1850s, how would you have responded to the policies of the U.S. government?

3. If you were a white Southerner in the 1850s, would you have been encouraged or discouraged by U.S. government policies?

4. Why did seven southern states secede from the Union within three months after Abraham Lincoln was elected president in 1860?

5. If you were a black person—either a slave or free—would you have welcomed the secession of the southern states? How might secession affect the future of your people?

myhistorylab CONNECTIONS

Reinforce what you learned in this chapter by studying the many documents, images, maps, review tools, and videos available at **www.myhistorylab.com.**

READ AND REVIEW

✔•─Study and Review on **myhistorylab.com** STUDY PLAN FOR CHAPTER 10

▶•─Read the Document on **myhistorylab.com**

A Senatorial Candidate Addresses the Question of Slavery in 1858

A Slave Sues for Freedom in 1857

An Abolitionist is Given the Death Sentence in 1859

Letter from Anthony Burns to the Baptist Church, 1855

New England Writer Portrays Slavery in 1852

Northern State Defies Fugitive Slave Act, (1855)

The Compromise of 1850

The Lincoln-Douglas Debates of 1858

Vilet Lester Letter to Miss Patsey Patterson, August 19th 1857

View the **Map** on **myhistorylab.com**

The Compromise of 1850

The Compromise of 1850 and the Kansas-Nebraska Act

Slave Population Patterns, 1790 and 1860

RESEARCH AND EXPLORE

mysearchlab

Consider these questions in a short research paper.

Why did the conflict over slavery intensify in the 1840s and 1850s? What efforts were made to resolve the conflict?

Read the **Document** on **myhistorylab.com**

Exploring America: Anthony Burns

Listen on **myhistorylab.com**

John Brown: An Address by Frederick Douglass; pamphlet excerpt

Remembering Slavery, #1; newly-released recordings of former slaves talking about slavery

Watch the **Video** on **myhistorylab.com**

Dred Scott and the Crises that Led to the Civil War

Harriet Beecher Stowe and the Making of *Uncle Tom''s Cabin*

Trials of Racial Identity in Nineteenth-Century America

——————— **Listen** on **myhistorylab.com** ———————

Hear the audio files for Chapter 10 at
www.myhistorylab.com.

Liberation: African Americans and the Civil War •• *1861–1865*

Hear the audio files for Chapter 11 at **www.myhistorylab.com.**

FOCUS QUESTIONS

WHEN THE civil war began, what was Abraham Lincoln's primary objective?

HOW DID African Americans respond to the outbreak of the Civil War?

HOW DID Lincoln's policies on slavery change as the Civil War continued?

WHY DID Lincoln issue the Emancipation Proclamation?

HOW DID black and white people react to the Emancipation Proclamation?

HOW DID African Americans affect the outcome of the Civil War?

Company E of the Fourth United States Colored Infantry at Fort Lincoln in the District of Columbia in 1865.

SLAVERY CAUSED THE CIVIL WAR. Yet when the war began in 1861, neither the Union nor the Confederacy entered the conflict with any intention or desire to change the status of black Americans. It was supposed to be a white man's war. White Southerners would wage war to make the Confederacy a separate and independent nation free to promote slavery. White Northerners took up arms to maintain the Union but not to free a single slave. African Americans who wanted to enlist in 1861 were rejected. The Union might be disrupted, but slavery was not going to be disturbed.

Both North and South expected a quick victory. No one anticipated that 48 months of brutal war would rip the nation apart. When the Civil War ended in April 1865, almost 620,000 Americans were dead—including nearly 40,000 black men. The Union was preserved. Four million people had been freed. Nothing in American history compares with it.

LINCOLN'S AIMS

Throughout the war, President Lincoln's unwavering objective was to preserve the Union. Any policies that helped or hindered black people were subordinate to that goal. Following the attack on Fort Sumter in April 1861 and Lincoln's call for state militias to help suppress the rebellion, four more slave states—North Carolina, Virginia, Tennessee, and Arkansas—seceded from the Union and joined the Confederacy. For most of 1861, Lincoln was determined to do nothing that would drive the four remaining slave states—Delaware, Maryland, Kentucky, and Missouri—into the Confederacy. Lincoln feared that if he did or said anything that could be interpreted as interfering with slavery, those four states would leave the Union too.

Meanwhile, Lincoln called for 75,000 men to enlist in the military for 90 days of service to the national government. Thousands of black and white men, far more than 75,000, responded. White men were accepted. Black men were rejected. Spurned by federal and state authorities, black men remained determined to aid the cause.

BLACK MEN VOLUNTEER AND ARE REJECTED

Black people recognized long before most white Northerners that the fate of the Union was inextricably tied to the issue of slavery and the future of slavery was tied to the outcome of the war. "Talk as we may," insisted the *Anglo-African*, a black New York newspaper, "we are concerned in this fight and our fate hangs upon its issues."

Black men in New York formed their own military companies and began to drill. In Boston, they drew up a resolution modeled on the Declaration of Independence and appealed for permission to go to war. Black men in Philadelphia volunteered to infiltrate the South to incite slave revolts but were turned down. In Washington D.C., Jacob Dodson, a black employee of the Senate, wrote to Secretary of War Simon Cameron shortly after the fall of Fort Sumter volunteering the services of local black men. "I desire to inform you that I know of some 300 reliable colored free citizens of this city who desire to enter the service for the defense of the city." Cameron curtly rejected Dodson, "This Department has no intention at the present to call into the service of the government any colored soldiers."

UNION POLICIES TOWARD CONFEDERATE SLAVES

Slaves started to liberate themselves as soon as the war began, but Union leaders had no coherent policy for dealing with them. To the deep disappointment of black Northerners and white abolitionists, Union military commanders showed more concern for the interests of Confederate slave owners than for the people in bondage. General Henry Halleck ordered slaves who escaped in the Ohio Valley returned to their owners. In Tennessee in early 1862, General Ulysses S. Grant returned runaway slaves to their owners if the owners supported the Union cause, but put them to work on fortifications if their owners favored secession.

"CONTRABAND"

Not all Union commanders were so callous. A month after the war began, three bondmen working on Confederate fortifications in Virginia escaped to the Union's Fortress Monroe on the coast. Their owner, a Confederate colonel, appeared at the fortress the next day under a flag of truce and demanded the return of his slaves under the 1850 Fugitive Slave Act. The incredulous Union commander, General Benjamin Butler, informed him that because Virginia had seceded from the Union, the law was no longer in force. Butler did not free the three slaves, but he did not reenslave them either. He declared them **"contraband"**—enemy property—and put them to work for the Union. Soon, over a thousand slaves fled to Fortress Monroe.

On August 6, 1861, Congress clarified the status of runaway slaves when it passed the First Confiscation Act. Federal forces could seize any property that belonged to Confederates used in the war effort. Any slaves their masters used to benefit the Confederacy—and only those slaves—would be freed. Almost immediately, Union General John C. Fremont (the 1856 Republican presidential candidate) exceeded the strict limits of the act by freeing all the slaves belonging to Confederates in Missouri.

These African-American troops served as teamsters for the Union Army in Virginia. Most Northern white people—including political leaders—believed that black men lacked the courage and fortitude for combat. They expected black men would do little more as soldiers than haul freight, erect fortifications, serve guard duty, and prepare food.

President Lincoln countermanded the order and told Fremont that only slaves actively used to aid the Confederate war effort were to be freed. Lincoln worried that Fremont's decision would drive Missouri or Kentucky into the Confederacy.

Black leaders were—to put it mildly—displeased with Lincoln and with federal policies that both prohibited the enlistment of black troops and ignored the plight of the enslaved. To fight a war against the South without fighting against slavery, the institution on which the South was so dependent, seemed absurd.

Joseph R. Hawley, a white Connecticut Republican, thought Lincoln was foolish to worry about whether the border states might leave the Union. "Permit me to say damn the border states. . . . A thousand Lincolns cannot stop the people from fighting slavery." In the New York *Anglo-African*, a letter writer who identified himself as "Ivanhoe" urged northern black men to decline any request to serve in Union military forces until the slaves were freed and black Northerners received treatment equal to that of white people.

Lincoln was unmoved. Union military forces occupied an enclave on South Carolina's southern coast and the Sea Islands in late 1861, and on May 9, 1862, General David Hunter ordered slavery abolished in South Carolina, Georgia, and Florida. Lincoln revoked Hunter's order and reprimanded him. Nevertheless, thousands of slaves along the South Carolina and Georgia coast threw off their shackles and welcomed Union troops as plantation owners fled to the interior.

LINCOLN'S INITIAL POSITION

For more than a year, Lincoln remained reluctant to strike decisively against slavery. He believed the long-term solution to slavery and the race problem in the United States was the compensated emancipation of slaves followed by their colonization outside the country. That is, slave owners would be paid for their slaves. The slaves would be freed but forced to settle in the Caribbean, Latin America, or West Africa.

In 1861 he tried—but failed—to persuade the Delaware legislature to support compensated emancipation. Then in April 1862, at Lincoln's urging, Republicans in Congress (against almost unanimous Democratic opposition) voted to provide funds to "any state which may adopt gradual abolishment of slavery." Lincoln wanted to eliminate slavery from the border states with the approval of slave owners there and thus diminish the likelihood that those states would join the Confederacy.

But leaders in the border states rejected the proposal. Lincoln brought it up again in July. This time he warned congressmen and senators from the border states that if their states opposed compensated emancipation they might have to accept uncompensated emancipation. They ignored his advice and denounced compensated emancipation as a "radical change in our social system" and an intrusion by the federal government into a state issue.

To many white Americans, Lincoln's support for compensated emancipation and colonization was a misguided attempt to link the war to the issue of slavery. But to black Americans, abolitionists, and an increasing number of Republicans, Lincoln's refusal to abolish slavery immediately was tragic. Antislavery advocates regarded Lincoln's willingness to purchase the freedom of slaves as an admission that he considered those human beings to be property. They deplored his seeming inability to realize the Union would not win the war unless slaves were liberated.

LINCOLN MOVES TOWARD EMANCIPATION

However, by the summer of 1862, after the border states rejected compensated emancipation, Lincoln concluded that victory and the future of the Union were tied directly to the issue of slavery. Slavery became the instrument Lincoln would use to hasten the end of the war and restore the Union.

In cabinet meetings in July 1862, Lincoln discussed abolishing slavery. Secretary of State William H. Seward supported abolition but advised Lincoln not to issue a proclamation until the Union Army won a major victory. Otherwise emancipation might look like the desperate gesture of the leader of a losing cause. Lincoln accepted Seward's advice and postponed emancipation.

LINCOLN DELAYS EMANCIPATION

Nevertheless, word circulated that Lincoln intended to abolish slavery. But weeks passed, and slavery did not end. Frustrated abolitionists and Republicans attacked Lincoln. Frederick Douglass was exasperated with a president who had shown inexcusable deference to white Southerners who had rebelled against the Union and accused him of playing "lawyer for the benefit of the rebels."

In his *Prayer of Twenty Millions*, Horace Greeley, editor of the New York *Tribune*, expressed his disappointment that the president had not moved promptly against slavery, the issue that had led the southern states to leave the Union and go to war: "We ask you to consider that Slavery [is the] inciting cause and sustaining base of treason." Greeley insisted that Lincoln should have long ago warned white Southerners that secession would endanger slavery.

On August 22, 1862, Lincoln replied to Greeley and explained his priorities. Placing the preservation of the Union before freedom for the enslaved, Lincoln declared, "My paramount object in this struggle is to save the Union, and is not either to save or destroy slavery. If I could save the Union without freeing any slave I would do it; and if I could save it by freeing all the slaves, I would do it; and if I could do it by freeing some and leaving others alone, I would also do that."

BLACK PEOPLE REJECT COLONIZATION

Lincoln's policy on emancipation had shifted dramatically, but he remained committed to colonization. On August 14, 1862, Lincoln invited black leaders to the White House and appealed for their support for colonization. After condemning slavery as "the greatest wrong inflicted on any people," he explained that white racism made it unwise for black people to remain in the United States. "There is an unwillingness on the part of our people, harsh as it may be, for you free colored people to remain among us. . . . I do not mean to discuss this, but to propose it as a fact with which we have to deal. I cannot alter it if I would." Lincoln asked the black leaders to begin enlisting volunteers for a colonization project in Central America.

Most black people were unimpressed by Lincoln's words and unmoved by his advice. A black leader from Philadelphia condemned the president. "This is our country as much as it is yours, and we will not leave it." Frederick Douglass accused Lincoln of hypocrisy and claimed that support for colonization would lead white men "to commit all kinds of violence and outrage upon the colored people." Lincoln, however, would not retreat from his support for colonization, and pushed forward with attempts to put compensated emancipation and colonization into effect.

THE PRELIMINARY EMANCIPATION PROCLAMATION

Finally on September 22, 1862—more than two months after Lincoln first seriously considered freedom for the enslaved—the president issued the Preliminary Emancipation Proclamation. It came five days after General George B. McClellan's Army of the Potomac turned back an invasion of Maryland at Antietam by General Robert E. Lee's Army of Northern Virginia. This bloody but indecisive victory allowed Lincoln to justify emancipation. But this first proclamation freed no people that September—or during the rest of 1862. Instead, it stipulated that anyone in bondage in states or parts of states still in rebellion on January 1, 1863, would be "thenceforward, and forever free." Lincoln's announcement gave the Confederate states one hundred days to return to the Union. If any or all of those states rejoined the Union, the slaves there would remain in bondage. The Union would be preserved, and slavery would be maintained.

NORTHERN REACTION TO EMANCIPATION

In the Union, the Preliminary Emancipation Proclamation was greeted with little enthusiasm. Most black people and abolitionists, of course, were gratified that Lincoln had finally issued the proclamation. Frederick Douglass was ecstatic. "We shout for joy that we live to record this righteous decree." In *The Liberator*, William Lloyd Garrison wrote that it was "an act of immense historical consequence." But they also worried that—however remote the possibility—some slave states would return to the Union by January 1, denying freedom to those enslaved.

Many white Northerners resented emancipation. Even before the announcement of emancipation, antiblack riots flared in the North. In Cincinnati in the summer of 1862, Irish dock workers invaded black neighborhoods after black men had replaced the striking wharf hands along the city's river front. In Brooklyn, New York, Irish Americans burned a tobacco factory that employed black women and children.

POLITICAL OPPOSITION TO EMANCIPATION

Northern Democrats almost unanimously opposed emancipation. They accused Lincoln and the Republicans of "fanaticism" and regretted that emancipation would liberate "two or three million semi savages" who would "overrun the North" and compete with white working people. The Democratic-controlled lower houses of the legislatures in Indiana and Illinois condemned the Proclamation as "wicked, inhuman, and unholy."

And as some Republicans had predicted and feared, the Democrats capitalized on dissatisfaction with the war's progress and with Republican support for emancipation to make gains in the fall elections.

THE EMANCIPATION PROCLAMATION

On January 1, 1863, Abraham Lincoln issued the **Emancipation Proclamation**. It was not the first step toward freedom. Since 1861 several thousand slaves had already freed themselves, but it was the first significant effort by Union authorities to assure freedom to nearly four million people of African descent who, with their ancestors, had been enslaved for 250 years in North America. The Civil War was now a war to make people free.

Elizabeth Keckley

In 1868 Elizabeth Keckley (1818–1907) published *Behind the Scenes: Or Thirty Years a Slave and Four Years in the White House.* The book told the story of her life: the abuse she suffered as a slave, her struggle to buy her freedom, and the challenges that she faced as she tried to turn her talent for dressmaking into a successful business. It also told the story of Keckley's friendship with Mary Todd Lincoln. The response to her book sheds light on the rigidity of the unwritten social and racial rules of Victorian America. Much of her book fit into a well-established genre, the slave narrative. Her descriptions of Mrs. Lincoln were positive and intended to help defend Mrs. Lincoln against the false accusations of her many critics. However, in describing the private life of a white lady and her own place in it, Keckley broke the social and racial rules of her times. Her work was met with outrage. An anonymous racist parody was written that portrayed Keckley as illiterate and used racial epithets to describe her. Keckley's defense of the book and her intentions in writing it were to no avail. In time, the uproar over her memoir died down, but the damage had been done and the book was a financial failure.

The publishers of Keckley's memoirs tried to boost ▶ sales by suggesting that it contained dramatic revelations.

Elizabeth Keckley. ▲

BEHIND THE SCENES.

BY
ELIZABETH KECKLEY,
FORMERLY A SLAVE, BUT MORE RECENTLY MODISTE, AND FRIEND TO MRS.
ABRAHAM LINCOLN.

OR,

THIRTY YEARS A SLAVE, AND FOUR YEARS IN
THE WHITE HOUSE.

NEW YORK:
G. W. Carleton & Co., Publishers.
M DCCC LXVIII.

What does Keckley's experience tell us about the limits of friendship between black and white women in Victorian America?

Black communities and many white people across the North celebrated. Church bells pealed. Poems were written, and prayers of thanksgiving were offered. Many considered it the most momentous day in American history since July 4, 1776. Frederick Douglass had difficulty describing the emotions of people in Boston when word reached the city late on the night of December 31 that Lincoln would issue the Proclamation the next day. "The effect of this announcement was startling beyond description, and the scene was wild and grand. Joy and gladness exhausted all forms of expression, from shouts of praise to sobs and tears."

LIMITS OF THE PROCLAMATION

Despite this excitement, the language of the Emancipation Proclamation was uninspired and unmoving. Moreover, by limiting emancipation to those states and areas still in rebellion, Lincoln did not include enslaved people in the four border states still in the Union or in areas of Confederate states that Union forces had already occupied (see Map 11-1). Thus hundreds of thousands of people would remain in bondage despite the proclamation. The immediate practical effect of the Proclamation was negligible. Yet the Emancipation Proclamation remains one of the most important documents in American history. It made the Civil War a war to free people, as well as to preserve the Union, and it gave the Union cause moral authority. And as many black people had freed themselves before the Proclamation, many more would liberate themselves after.

EFFECTS OF THE PROCLAMATION ON THE SOUTH

The Emancipation Proclamation destroyed any chance that Britain or France would offer diplomatic recognition to the Confederate government. Diplomatic recognition would have meant accepting the Confederacy as a legitimate state equal in international law to the Union, and it would almost surely have led to financial and military assistance for the South. British leaders, who had considered recognizing the Confederacy, now declined to support a "nation" that relied on slavery while its opponent moved to abolish it.

MAP 11-1 • Effects of the Emancipation Proclamation When Abraham Lincoln issued the Emancipation Proclamation on January 1, 1863, it applied only to slaves in those portions of the Confederacy not under Union authority. No southern slave owners freed their slaves at Lincoln's command. But many black people already had freed themselves as well as family and friends in the aftermath of Lincoln's order. The Emancipation Proclamation was of extreme importance. It helped the Union win the war. It meant that at long last the U.S. government had joined the abolitionist movement.

▶ *Where, according to the map, did slaves reside who were to be freed under the terms of the Proclamation?*

Even more important, it undermined slavery in the South and contributed directly to the Confederacy's defeat. Black people—aware a Union victory in the war meant freedom—were far less likely to labor for their owners or for the Confederacy. More slaves ran away, especially as Union troops approached. Slave resistance became more likely. The institution of slavery cracked, crumbled, and collapsed after January 1, 1863.

Without emancipation, the United States would not have survived as a unified nation. Abraham Lincoln, after first failing to make the connection between eliminating slavery and preserving the Union, came to understand it fully and grasped what freedom meant to both black and white people. In his annual message to Congress in December 1862, one month before the Proclamation, Lincoln described the importance of emancipation with a passion and feelings that were absent in the Proclamation itself. "We know how to save the Union. The world knows we do know how to save it. We—even we here—hold the power, and bear the responsibility. In giving freedom to the slave, we assure freedom to the free—honorable alike in what we give, and what we preserve."

BLACK MEN FIGHT FOR THE UNION

The Emancipation Proclamation not only marked the beginning of the end of slavery, it also authorized the enlistment of black troops in the Union Army. Just as white leaders in the North came to realize the preservation of the Union necessitated the abolition of slavery, they also began to understand that black men were needed for the military effort if the Union was to triumph in the Civil War.

Like the decision to free the slaves, the decision to employ black troops proceeded neither smoothly nor logically. The commitment to the Civil War as a white man's war was entrenched, and many white Northerners opposed the initial attempts to enlist black

troops. As with emancipation, Lincoln moved slowly from outright opposition to cautious acceptance to enthusiastic support for enlisting black men in the Union Army.

THE FIRST SOUTH CAROLINA VOLUNTEERS

Some Union officers recruited black men long before emancipation was proclaimed and before most white Northerners were prepared to accept, much less welcome, black troops. In May 1862 General David Hunter began recruiting former slaves along the South Carolina

The Emancipation Proclamation was essentially a military directive and not a ringing declaration of liberation. Nevertheless its uninspiring words would free more than three million people from bondage by 1865. Decorative copies such as this circulated for many decades after the Civil War.

coast and the Sea Islands, an area Union forces had captured in late 1861. But some black men did not want to enlist, and Hunter used white troops to force black men to "volunteer" for military service. He managed to organize a 500 man regiment—the **First South Carolina Volunteers.**

Through the summer of 1862, Hunter trained and drilled the regiment while awaiting official authorization and funds to pay them. When Congress balked, Hunter disbanded all but one company of the regiment that August. The surviving company was sent to St. Simon's Island off the Georgia coast to protect former slaves.

Although Congress failed to support Hunter, it did pass the Second Confiscation Act and the Militia Act of 1862, which authorized President Lincoln to enlist black men. In Louisiana that fall, two regiments of free black men, the Native Guards, were accepted for federal service, and General Benjamin Butler organized them into the Corps d'Afrique. General Rufus Saxton gained the approval of Secretary of War Edwin Stanton to revive Hunter's dispersed regiment and to recall the company that had been sent to St. Simon's Island.

As commander, Saxton appointed Thomas Wentworth Higginson. Higginson was an ardent white abolitionist. Higginson was determined not merely to end slavery but to prove that black people were equal to white people. On Emancipation Day, January 1, 1863, near Beaufort, South Carolina, the First South Carolina Volunteer Regiment was inducted into the U.S. Army.

THE 54TH MASSACHUSETTS REGIMENT

While ex-slaves joined the Union ranks in South Carolina, free black men in the North enlisted in what would become the most famous black unit, **the 54th Massachusetts Regiment.** In January 1863 Governor John A. Andrew received permission from Secretary of War Stanton to raise a black regiment, but because few black men lived in Massachusetts, Andrew asked prominent black men across the North for help. The Black Committee—as it became known—included Frederick Douglass, Martin Delany, Charles Remond, and Henry Highland Garnet.

These black leaders were convinced that by serving in the military, black men would prove they deserved to be treated as equals and had earned the right to be citizens. Frederick Douglass put it succinctly: "Once let the black man get upon his person the brass letters, U.S.; let him get an eagle on his button, and a musket on his shoulder and bullets in his pocket, and there is no power on earth which can deny that he has earned the right to citizenship." Douglass's sons, Charles and Lewis, joined the 54th.

Governor Andrew selected 25-year-old Robert Gould Shaw to command the 54th Massachusetts Regiment. Shaw was a Harvard graduate from a prominent Massachusetts family, and he had already been wounded at the battle at Antietam. Although not an active abolitionist, he opposed slavery and was determined to prove that black men would fight well. The men the Black Committee recruited came from most of the northern states. Their average age was around 25 and virtually all of them were literate. They were farmers, seamen, butchers, blacksmiths, and teamsters. Only one of them had grown up in a slave state.

On May 28, 1863, the 54th paraded through Boston to board a ship for the trip to South Carolina and the war. Thousands turned out to see the black men in blue uniforms. As they passed the home of fiery abolitionist William Lloyd Garrison, he stood erect with a bust of John Brown. As they passed the customhouse where Crispus Attucks and four others had been killed in the Boston Massacre in 1770, the regiment sang "John Brown's Body." The departure of the 54th from the city was perhaps the most emotional event Boston had witnessed since Anthony Burns was forcibly returned to slavery in 1854.

Poised with their rifles, these African-American soldiers were members of the Twenty-first U.S. Colored Infantry at the battle of Dutch Gap in Virginia in August, 1864. Corbis/Bettmann

BLACK SOLDIERS CONFRONT DISCRIMINATION

But the enthusiastic departure could not disguise the discrimination and hostility that black troops faced during the war. Many white Northerners would accept neither the presence of black troops nor the idea that black men could endure combat. Many white people tolerated black troops only because they preferred that a black man die rather than a white man. A white Union soldier wrote that a "Negro can fall from a rebel shot as well as me or my friends, and better them than us." That black troops would serve in separate, all-black units was taken for granted.

Almost all black troops had white officers. Yet many white officers, convinced such service would taint their military record, refused to command black troops. Others believed black men could not be trained for combat. Even those white officers who were willing to command black troops sometimes regarded their men as "niggers" suited only for work or fatigue duty.

Black soldiers were paid less than white soldiers. Based on the assumption that black troops would be used almost exclusively for construction, transportation, cooking, and burial details, and not for fighting, the War Department authorized a lower pay scale for them. A white private earned $13 per month, a black private $10 per month. This demoralized black soldiers, particularly after they had shown they were more than capable of fighting.

The 54th Massachusetts Regiment refused to accept their pay until they received equal pay. To take no compensation was an enormous sacrifice for men who had wives, children, and families to support. For some, it was more than a monetary loss. Sergeant William Walker insisted—despite orders—that the men in his company take no pay until they received equal pay. He was charged with mutiny, convicted, and shot. In Texas, a soldier in a black artillery unit from Rhode Island threatened a white officer in the dispute over pay. The white lieutenant shot and killed him, and the regiment's commander declined to press charges.

BLACK MEN IN COMBAT

Once black men put on the Union uniform, they took part in almost every battle that was fought during the rest of the Civil War. Black troops not only faced an enemy dedicated to the belief that the proper place of black people was in slavery, but they also confronted doubts about their fighting abilities among white Northerners. Yet by war's end, black units had suffered disproportionately more casualties than white units.

THE ASSAULT ON BATTERY WAGNER

Since 1861 and the Confederate capture of Fort Sumter in Charleston harbor, Union leaders had been determined to retake the fort and occupy nearby Charleston—the heart of secession. In 1863 Union commanders began a land and sea offensive to seize the fort. But **Battery Wagner,** a fortified installation on the northern tip of Morris Island, guarded the entrance to the harbor.

Frustrated in their efforts to enter the harbor, Major General Quincy A. Gilmore and Rear Admiral John Dahlgren decided on a full-scale assault on Wagner. After an unsuccessful attack by white troops, Colonel Shaw volunteered to lead the 54th in a second attack on the battery.

To improve the Union's chances, artillery fired more than 9,000 shells on Wagner on July 18, 1863. Everyone but the fort's Confederate defenders was convinced that no one could survive the bombardment. In fact, it had killed only 8 of the 1,620 defenders.

At sunset, 650 men of the first brigade of the 54th prepared to lead more than 5,000 Union troops in storming the battery. The regiment was tired and hungry but eager for the assault. Colonel Shaw told his troops: "Now I want you to prove yourselves men."

At 7:45 p.m., the 54th charged and was met by heavy rifle and artillery fire. Within minutes, the sand was littered with injured and dying men. Sergeant Major Lewis Douglass (the son of Frederick Douglass) was among those who took part. The 54th reached the walls only to be thrown back in hand-to-hand combat. Shaw was killed.

Sergeant Major William H. Carney, although wounded four times, saved the regiment's flags. In May 1900, he was awarded the Congressional Medal of Honor for his gallantry that night.

Although white troops supported the 54th, the attack could not be sustained, and the battle was over by 1 a.m. But within days, the courage of the 54th was known across the North, putting to rest—for a time—the myth that black men lacked the nerve to fight.

THE CRATER

But as impressive as black troops often were in battle, northern commanders sometimes hesitated to commit them to combat. In 1864, after Union troops laid siege to Petersburg, Virginia, white soldiers of the 48th Pennsylvania, who had been coal miners before the

On the evening of July 18, 1863, more than six hundred black men led by their white commander, Colonel Robert Gould Shaw, attacked the heavily fortified Battery Wagner on Morris Island near the southern approach to Charleston harbor. They made a frontal assault through withering fire and managed to breach the battery before Confederate forces threw them back. Shaw was killed and the 54th suffered heavy losses. It was a defining moment of the Civil War, demonstrating to skeptical white people the valor and determination of black troops.

war, offered to dig a tunnel and set off an explosion under Confederate lines. General Ambrose Burnside assigned black troops to be prepared to lead the attack after the blast.

Four tons of powder were placed in the tunnel, but only hours before the blast was set to go off, Burnside's superior, General George Meade, replaced the black troops with inadequately trained white soldiers commanded by an alcoholic. Meade either lacked confidence in the black unit or was worried he would be blamed for using black men as shields for white soldiers if the attack failed.

On July 30, 1864, at 4:45 a.m., what was perhaps the largest man-made explosion in history up to that time buried a Confederate regiment and an artillery battery and created a crater 170 feet long, 60 feet wide, and 30 feet deep. But the white Union troops rushed down into the crater instead of fanning out around it in pursuit of the stunned enemy. While the Union soldiers marveled at the destruction, the Confederates counterattacked and threw back the Union troops, including the black troops that were finally brought forward. Some black men were murdered after they surrendered. More than 4,000 Union troops, many of them black, were killed or wounded.

THE CONFEDERATE REACTION TO BLACK SOLDIERS

On June 7, 1863, Confederate forces attempting to relieve the Union siege of Vicksburg attacked black Union troops at Milliken's Bend on the Mississippi River. Although armed with outdated muskets and not fully trained, the defenders fought off the Confederate attack. Assistant Secretary of War Charles A. Dana claimed that their valor would change the attitudes of white people toward the use of black troops. "The bravery of the blacks completely revolutionized the sentiment of the army with regard to the employment of negro troops. I heard prominent officers who formerly in private sneered at the idea of negroes fighting express themselves after that as heartily in favor of it."

The southern soldiers who lost at Milliken's Bend, however, felt differently. Enraged by having to fight black troops, they executed several black men prisoners and sold others into slavery.

THE ABUSE AND MURDER OF BLACK TROOPS

Confederate leaders and troops refused to recognize black men as legitimate soldiers. Captured black soldiers were abused and even murdered, rather than treated as prisoners of war. Confederate Secretary of War James A. Seddon ordered that captured black soldiers be executed. "We ought never to be inconvenienced with such prisoners . . . summary execution must therefore be inflicted on those taken."

Protests erupted across the North after Confederate authorities decided to treat 80 men of the 54th Massachusetts Regiment who had been captured in the attack on Battery Wagner not as prisoners of war, but as rebellious slaves. Frederick Douglass refused to recruit any more black men and held Abraham Lincoln personally responsible for tolerating the mistreatment of black prisoners.

Lincoln issued General Order 11, threatening to execute southern troops or confine them to hard labor. "For every soldier of the United States killed in violation of the laws of war a rebel soldier shall be executed, and for every one enslaved by the enemy or sold into slavery a rebel soldier shall be placed at hard labor on the public works, and continued at such labor until the other shall be released and receive the treatment due to a prisoner of war."

Lincoln's order did not prevent the Confederates from sending the men of the 54th to trial by the state of South Carolina. The state regarded the black soldiers as either rebellious slaves or free black men inciting rebellion. Four black soldiers went on trial in Charleston police court, but the court declared it lacked jurisdiction. The black prisoners were eventually sent to prisoner of war camps.

THE FORT PILLOW MASSACRE

The war's worst atrocity against black troops occurred at **Fort Pillow** in Tennessee on April 12, 1864. Confederates under the command of Nathan Bedford Forrest slaughtered 300 black troops and their white commander, William F. Bradford, after many of them had surrendered. (After the Civil War, Forrest gained notoriety as a founder of the Ku Klux Klan. Before the war he had been a slave trader.) The Fort Pillow Massacre became the subject of an intense debate in Lincoln's cabinet. But rather than retaliate indiscriminately—as General Order 11 required—the cabinet decided to punish only those responsible for the killings, if and when they were apprehended. But no one was punished during or after the war. Instead, black troops exacted revenge themselves. In fighting around Petersburg later that year, black soldiers shouting, "Remember Fort Pillow!" reportedly murdered several Confederate prisoners.

On their own, Union commanders in the field also retaliated for the Confederate treatment of captured black troops. When captured black men were virtually enslaved and forced to work at Richmond and Charleston on Confederate fortifications that were under Union attack, Union officers put Confederate prisoners to work on Union installations that were under fire. Aware they were not likely to be treated as well as white soldiers if they were captured, black men often fought desperately.

In April 1864 fifteen hundred Confederate forces under General Nathan Bedford Forrest attacked and captured Fort Pillow, a Union installation on the Mississippi River forty miles north of Memphis, Tennessee, that was defended by 550 black and white troops. After the Union forces surrendered, Confederate troops executed some of the black soldiers. Forrest and his men denied the atrocity, but there is little doubt it occurred.

VOICES

A BLACK NURSE ON THE HORRORS OF WAR AND THE SACRIFICE OF BLACK SOLDIERS

Susie King Taylor was born a slave on a Georgia Sea Island and learned to read and write in Savannah. She escaped to Union forces in 1862 and served as a nurse and laundress with the First South Carolina Volunteers. In these passages, written years later, she recalls her service with the black men who went into combat and pays tribute to them.

It seems strange how our aversion to seeing suffering is overcome in war,—how we are able to see the most sickening sights, such as men with their limbs blown off and mangled by the deadly shells, without a shudder; and instead of turning away, how we hurry to assist in alleviating their pain, bind up their wounds, and press the cool water to their parched lips, with feelings only of sympathy and pity. . . .

I look around now and see the comforts that our younger generation enjoy, and think of the blood that was shed to make these comforts possible for them, and see how little some of them appreciate the old soldiers. My heart burns within me at this want of appreciation. There are only a few of them left now, so let us all, as the ranks close, take a deeper interest in them. Let the younger generation take an interest also, and remember that it was through the efforts of these veterans that we older ones enjoy our liberty today.

■ How does Taylor describe what men in combat endure?

■ Who is the object of Taylor's criticism, and why does she offer that criticism?

SOURCE: Susie King Taylor, *Reminiscences of My Life in Camp*, 1902, pp. 31–32, 51–52.

BLACK MEN IN THE UNION NAVY

Black men had a tradition of serving at sea and had been in the U.S. Navy almost continuously since its creation in the 1790s. In the early nineteenth century, there were so many black sailors that some white people tried to ban black men from the navy. Nor did black sailors serve in segregated units. Naval crews were integrated.

Nonetheless, black sailors encountered rampant discrimination and exploitation during the Civil War. They were paid less than white sailors. They were assigned the hardest and filthiest tasks. Many were stewards who waited on white officers. White officers and sailors often treated black sailors with contempt.

But some white men admired the black sailors. One observed, "We never were betrayed when we trusted one of them, they were always our friends and were ready, if necessary, to lay down their lives for us." (He did not say whether white men were willing to lay down their lives for black men.) About 10,000 or 8% of the men who served in the Union Navy during the war were black sailors.

Robert Smalls was born a slave in Beaufort, South Carolina, in 1839. In May 1862 while still a slave and working as a pilot in Charleston on a 150-foot Confederate vessel, *The Planter,* Smalls devised an audacious plan to seize the ship. With the ship's white officers enjoying a night on the town. Smalls sailed *The Planter* with family and friends aboard to the Union Navy outside the harbor. Smalls' exploits created a sensation in the North. He went on to become a successful Republican politician in South Carolina in the decades following the Civil War.

LIBERATORS, SPIES, AND GUIDES

Besides serving as soldiers and sailors, black men and women aided themselves and the Union cause as liberators, spies, guides, and messengers. At about 3 a.m. on May 13, 1862, Robert Smalls, a 23-year-old slave, fired the boiler on *The Planter*, a Confederate supply ship moored in Charleston harbor. With the aid of seven black crewmen, Smalls sailed *The Planter* past Confederate fortifications, including Fort Sumter, to the Union fleet outside the harbor and to freedom. Smalls liberated himself and 15 other slaves, including the families of several crewmen and his own wife, daughter, and son.

Smalls managed the daring escape because he knew the South Carolina coast and was familiar with Confederate navigation signals and regulations. He became an overnight hero in the North, a slave who wanted freedom and had possessed the leadership, knowledge, and tenacity to liberate 16 people.

In 1863 Harriet Tubman organized a spy ring in the South Carolina low country, and in cooperation with the all-black Second South Carolina Volunteer Regiment, she helped organize an expedition that destroyed plantations and freed nearly 800 slaves, many of whom joined the Union Army.

In Richmond in 1864, slaves helped more than one hundred escaped Union prisoners of war. Other slaves drew sketches and maps of Confederate fortifications and warned Union forces about troop movements. A black couple near Fredericksburg, Virginia, cleverly transmitted military intelligence to Union general Joseph Hooker. The woman washed laundry for a Confederate officer and hung shirts and blankets in patterns that conveyed information to her husband, who was a cook and groom for Union troops and relayed the information to Union officers.

Mary Elizabeth Bowser was a former slave who worked as a servant at the Confederate White House in Richmond. She overheard conversations by President Jefferson Davis and his subordinates, and—because she was literate—she covertly examined Confederate correspondence. She relayed the information to Union agents until the Confederates became suspicious. Bowser and slave Jim Pemberton fled after trying to burn down the mansion to distract their pursuers.

VIOLENT OPPOSITION TO BLACK PEOPLE

No matter how well black men fought, no matter how much individual black women contributed, and no matter how many people—black and white—died "to make men free," many white Northerners, both civilian and military, remained bitter and often violently hostile to black people. They used intimidation, threats, and terror to injure and kill people of color.

The New York City Draft Riot

Irish Catholic Americans, themselves held in contempt by prosperous white Protestants, indulged in an orgy of violence in New York City in July 1863. The New York draft riot arose from racial, religious, and class antagonisms. Democrats, including New York Governor Horatio Seymour, convinced poor, unskilled Irish workers and other white Northerners that the war had become a crusade to benefit black people.

The violence began when federal officials prepared to select the first men to be drafted by the Union for military service. An enraged mob of mostly Irish men attacked the draft offices and any black people who were around. Many of the Irish men were angry because black men had replaced striking Irish stevedores on the city's wharves the month before and because rich white Northerners could purchase an exemption from the draft.

The riot went on for four days. The city police could not control it. The violence and destruction did not end until the army arrived. Soldiers who had been fighting Confederates at Gettysburg two weeks earlier found themselves firing on New York rioters.

Visualizing the Past NY Draft Riots Union Troops and Slaves

White Union troops who brutalized southern freedmen sometimes exceeded the savagery of northern civilians. In November 1861 men from the 47th New York Regiment raped an eight-year-old black girl. On Sherman's march through Georgia in 1864, a drunken Irish soldier from an Ohio regiment shot into a crowd of black children, wounding one youngster. He was tried and convicted but released on a technicality and returned to the army.

However, some Union soldiers wanted to fight for the liberation of black people. One Wisconsin private wrote, "I have no heart in this war if the slaves cannot be free." The desire of slaves for freedom moved many. Several Union soldiers wept when they witnessed a daughter reunited with her mother ten years after a slave sale had separated them.

Refugees

Throughout the war, black people freed themselves. It was not easy. Confederate authorities did not hesitate to reenslave or even execute black people who sought freedom.

As Union armies plunged deep into the Confederacy in 1863 and 1864, thousands of black people liberated themselves and became refugees. When General William Tecumseh Sherman's army of 60,000 troops laid waste to Georgia in 1864, an estimated 10,000 former slaves followed his troops to Savannah, although they lacked adequate food, clothing, and housing. As one elderly black couple prepared to leave a plantation, Union soldiers as well as their master urged them to remain. They declined. "We must go, freedom is as sweet to us as it is to you."

Black People and the Confederacy

The Confederacy was based on the defense of slavery, and it benefited from the usually coerced, but sometimes willing, labor of black people. Slaves toiled in southern fields and factories during the Civil War. The greater the burden of work the slaves took on, the more white men there were who could become soldiers. When the war began, southern whites believed their disadvantage in manpower would be partly offset by the slaves whose presence would free a disproportionately large number of white Southerners to go to war. While slaves would tend cotton, corn, and cattle, white southern men would fight.

SKILLED AND UNSKILLED SLAVES IN SOUTHERN INDUSTRY

Slave labor helped sustain the Confederate war effort. More than 800 slaves and several hundred free black people, for example, worked at the South's largest industrial complex, the Tredegar Iron Works in Richmond, Virginia. Tredegar produced canons, iron plate, boilers, and nails.

As white men departed for military service, the Tredegar operators relied increasingly on slaves for skilled and unskilled labor. By 1864, slaves represented half of the work force at Tredegar. They toiled in the machine shop, rolling mill, foundry, and as blacksmiths. Ed Taylor, who was one of the blacksmiths, performed the highly specialized task of hammering out iron bands that were fixed on artillery pieces to strengthen them. The company paid Taylor's owner the extraordinary sum of $1000 a year for his technical expertise. Unfortunately for Tredegar and the Confederacy, but fortunately for its slave laborers, many of them escaped as Union military forces closed in on Richmond in 1864. Other black men across the South loaded and unloaded ships, worked on the railroads, and labored in salt mines.

THE IMPRESSMENT OF BLACK PEOPLE

As the war went on, the Confederacy needed more troops and laborers. Slave owners were first asked and then compelled to contribute their slave laborers to the war effort. In July 1861, the Confederate Congress required free black people to register and enroll for military labor. In the summer of 1862 the Virginia legislature authorized the impressment of 10,000 slaves between the ages of 18 and 45 for up to 60 days.

In South Carolina in 1863, Confederate officials appealed to slave owners for 2,500 slaves to help fortify Charleston. The owners offered fewer than 1,000. During the Union bombardment of Fort Sumter, 500 slaves were did the difficult, dirty, and dangerous work of building and rebuilding the fort. Slaves were even forced into combat.

Although many slave owners resisted the impressment of their bondmen, other white Southerners who did not own slaves were infuriated when the Confederate conscription law in 1862 exempted men who owned 20 or more slaves from military service. One Mississippi soldier deserted the Confederate Army, claiming he "did not propose to fight for the rich men while they were home having a good time." Although the law was widely criticized, planters—always a small percentage of the white southern population—dominated the Confederate government and would not permit the repeal of the exemption.

CONFEDERATES ENSLAVE FREE BLACK PEOPLE

After Lincoln's Emancipation Proclamation, Confederate President Jefferson Davis issued a counterproclamation in February 1863 declaring that free people would be enslaved. This directive was not widely enforced. Davis, however, also ordered Confederate armies that invaded Union states to capture free black people in the North and enslave them.

·This was done. Several hundred northern black people were taken south after Confederate forces invaded Pennsylvania in 1863 and fought at Gettysburg. Robert E.

Lee's Army of Northern Virginia at Greensburg, Pennsylvania, captured at least 50 black people. A southern victory in the Civil War could have led to the enslavement of more than 132,000 free black residents of the Confederate States.

BLACK CONFEDERATES

Most of the labor black people did for the Confederacy was involuntary, but a few free black men and women offered their services to the southern cause. In Lynchburg, Virginia, in the spring of 1861, 70 free black people volunteered "to act in whatever capacity may be assigned them." In Memphis in the fall, several hundred black residents cheered for Jefferson Davis and sang patriotic songs. These demonstrations of black support were made early in the conflict when the outcome was in doubt and long before the war became a crusade against slavery.

The status of many free black Southerners remained precarious. In Virginia in 1861, impressment laws, like those applying to slaves, compelled free black men to work on Confederate defenses around Richmond and Petersburg. Months before the war, South Carolina considered forcing its free black population to choose between enslavement and exile. The legislature rejected the proposal, but it terrified the state's free black people. Many people of color there had been free for generations. Fair in complexion, they had education, skills, homes, and businesses. Some even owned slaves. When the war came, many were willing to demonstrate their devotion to the South in a desperate attempt to gain white acceptance before they lost their freedom and property.

White southern leaders generally ignored offers of free black support unless it was for menial labor. But when Charleston was under siege between 1863 and 1865, black and white residents were grateful that volunteer fire brigades composed of free black men turned out to fight fires caused by Union artillery.

BLACK MEN FIGHTING FOR THE SOUTH

Approximately 144,000 black men from the southern states fought with the Union Army. Most had been slaves. Although it was technically not legal until almost the end of the war, a much smaller number of black men also fought for the Confederacy. White New York troops claimed to have encountered about 700 armed black men in late 1861 near Newport News, Virginia. In 1862 a black Confederate sharpshooter positioned himself in a chimney and shot several Union soldiers before he was killed. Fifty black men served as pickets for the Confederates along the Rappahannock River in Virginia in 1863.

John Wilson Buckner, a free black man with a light complexion, enlisted in the First South Carolina Artillery. As a member of the well-regarded free black Ellison family of Stateburg, South Carolina, Buckner was considered an "honorary white man." He fought for the Confederacy in the defense of Charleston at Battery Wagner in July 1863 and was wounded just before the 54th Massachusetts Regiment assaulted the fort.

Some black civilians supported the war effort and stood to profit if the South won. Buckner's uncles grew corn, sweet potatoes, peas, sorghum, and beans on the Ellison family plantation to feed Confederate troops. By hiring out horses, mules, and slaves they owned, the Ellisons had earned nearly $1,000 by 1863. By 1865 they had paid almost $5,000 in taxes to the Confederacy, nearly one-fifth of their total income. They also patriotically invested almost $7,000 in Confederate bonds and notes. Like prosperous white families, the Ellisons lost most of this investment with the defeat of the Confederacy.

At war's end, the bonds were as worthless as Confederate cash, and the 80 slaves the Ellisons owned—worth approximately $100,000—were free people (see Chapter 6).

White Southerners praised the few black people who actively supported the South. Several states awarded pensions to black men who served in the war and survived. Henry Clay Lightfoot, a slave in Culpeper, Virginia, went to war as a body servant of Captain William Holcomb. After the war, he bought a house, raised a family, and was elected to the Culpeper town council. He collected a pension from Virginia, and when he died in 1931, the United Daughters of the Confederacy draped his coffin in a Confederate flag.

BLACK OPPOSITION TO THE CONFEDERACY

Although many white Southerners and some Northerners believed most slaves would support their masters, in fact most slaves did not. When a slave named Tom was asked if slaves would fight for their masters, he replied, "I know they say dese tings, but dey lies. Our masters may talk now all dey choose; but one ting's sartin,—dey don't dare to try us. Jess put de guns in our hans, and you'll soon see dat we not only knows how to shoot, but who, to shoot. My master wouldn't be wuff much ef I was a soldier."

THE CONFEDERATE DEBATE ON BLACK TROOPS

By late 1863 and 1864, prospects for the Confederacy had become grim. The Union naval blockade had become increasingly effective, and the likelihood of British aid had all but vanished. Confederate armies suffered crushing defeats at Vicksburg and Gettysburg in 1863 and absorbed terrible losses in Tennessee, Georgia, and Virginia in 1864.

As defeat loomed, white Southerners began to discuss the possibility of arming black men. Several newspapers advocated it. In September 1863 the Montgomery (Alabama) *Weekly Mail* admitted it would have been preposterous to contemplate the need for black troops earlier in the war, but it had now become necessary to save the white South.

In early 1864 General Patrick Cleburne recommended enlisting slaves and promising them their freedom if they remained loyal to the Confederacy. Cleburne argued that this policy would gain recognition and aid from Britain and would disrupt Union military efforts to recruit black Southerners. Yet the prospect of arming slaves and free black men appalled most white Southerners. Jefferson Davis ordered military officers, including Cleburne, to cease discussing it.

Most white Southerners were convinced that to arm slaves and put black men in gray uniforms defied the assumptions on which southern society was based. Black people were inferior, and their proper status was to be slaves. The Richmond *Whig* declared in 1864 that "servitude is a divinely appointed condition for the highest good of the slave." It was absurd to contemplate black people as soldiers and as free people. Georgia politician Howell Cobb explained that slaves could not be armed. "If slaves will make good soldiers our whole theory of slavery is wrong."

The Civil War for white Southerners was a war to prevent the abolition of slavery. Now white southern voices were proposing abolition to preserve the southern nation. North Carolina Senator Robert M. T. Hunter opposed any attempt to enlist slaves and free them. "If we are right in passing this measure we were wrong in denying to the old government the right to interfere with the institution of slavery and to emancipate slaves. Besides, if we offer slaves their freedom . . . we confess that we were insincere, were hypocritical, in asserting that slavery was the best state for the negroes themselves."

Nevertheless, as the military situation deteriorated, the South moved toward employing black troops. In February 1865, Jefferson Davis and the Confederate cabinet conceded, "We are reduced to choosing whether the negroes shall fight for us or against us."

The opinion of General Robert E. Lee was critical to determining whether the Confederacy would decide to arm black men. No Southerner was more revered and respected. With his army struggling to survive a desperate winter around Petersburg and Richmond, Lee announced in February 1865 that he favored both enrolling and emancipating black troops. "My own opinion is that we should employ them without delay." Their service as slaves would make them capable soldiers. "They possess the physical qualities in an eminent degree. Long habits of obedience and subordination, coupled with moral influence which in our country the white man possesses over the black, furnish an excellent foundation for that discipline which is the best guarantee of military efficiency."

Less than a month later in March 1865, although many white Southerners still opposed it, the Confederate Congress voted to enlist 300,000 black men between the ages of 18 and 45. They would receive the same pay, equipment, and supplies as white soldiers. But those who were slaves would not be freed unless their owner consented and the state where they served agreed to their emancipation.

It was a desperate measure by a nearly defeated government and did not affect the outcome of the conflict. Before the war ended in April, authorities in Virginia managed to recruit some black men and send a few into combat. By the end of March, one company of 35 black men—12 free black men and 23 slaves—was organized. On April 4, 1865, Union troops attacked Confederate supply wagons that the black troops were guarding in Amelia County. Less than a week later, Lee surrendered to Grant at Appomattox Court House, and the Civil War ended.

African-American Events	National Events
1860	
	November 1860 Abraham Lincoln elected president
	December 1860 South Carolina secedes from the Union
1861	
April–May 1861 Black men volunteer for military service and are rejected	**February 1861** The Confederate States of America is formed
August 1861 First Confiscation Act	**March 1861** Lincoln inaugurated
	April 1861 The firing on Fort Sumter begins the Civil War
	November 1861 Union forces capture the Sea Islands and coastal areas of South Carolina and Georgia
1862	
May 1862 Robert Smalls escapes with the *Planter* and 16 slaves	**September 1862** Battle of Antietam

May–August 1862
The First South Carolina Volunteers, an all-black regiment, forms

September 1862
Lincoln announces the Preliminary Emancipation Proclamation

October 1862
Black troops see combat for the first time in Missouri

1863

African-American Events	National Events
January 1, 1863 Lincoln issues the Emancipation Proclamation	**March 1863** The U.S. government enacts a Conscription Act
January–March 1863 Troops recruited for the 54th and the 55th Massachusetts Regiments	**July 1863** Battles of Vicksburg and Gettysburg
June 1863 Battle of Milliken's Bend	
July 1863 Assault on Battery Wagner; New York City draft riots	

1864

African-American Events	National Events
February 1864 Battle at Olustee	**November 1864** Lincoln is reelected
April 1864 Fort Pillow Massacre	**November–December 1864** Sherman's march to the sea

1865

African-American Events	National Events
February 1865 Black troops lead the occupation of Charleston	**February 1865** Charleston falls
March 1865 Confederate Congress approves the enlistment of black men	**March 1865** Richmond falls
December 1865 Thirteenth Amendment ratified	**April 1865** Lee surrenders at Appomatox; Lincoln is assassinated

African-American Events   **National Events**

CONCLUSION

The Civil War ended with the decisive defeat of the Confederacy. The Union was preserved. The ordeal of slavery for millions of people of African descent was over. Slavery—having thrived in America for nearly 250 years—was finally abolished by an amendment to the Constitution. Congress passed the Thirteenth Amendment on January 31, 1865. It was ratified by 27 states and declared in effect on December 18, 1865.

Were it not for the presence and labors of more than four million black people, there would have been no Civil War. Had it not been for the presence and contributions of more than 185,000 black soldiers and sailors, the Union would not have won. Almost 40,000 of those black men died in combat and of disease during the war. Twenty-one black men were awarded the Medal of Honor for heroism.

Abraham Lincoln represents the dramatic shift in attitudes and policies toward African Americans during the Civil War. When the war began, Lincoln insisted it was a white man's conflict to suppress rebellious white Southerners. Black people, Lincoln remained convinced, would be better off outside the United States. But the war went on, and thousands of white men died. Lincoln issued the Emancipation Proclamation and welcomed the enlistment of black troops. The president came to appreciate the achievements and devotion of black troops and condemned the mean-spiritedness of white Northerners who opposed the war. Lincoln wrote in 1863, "And then there will be some black men who can remember that, with silent tongue, and clenched teeth, and steady eye, and well-poised bayonet, they have helped mankind on to this great consummation; while, I fear, there will be some white ones, unable to forget that, with malignant heart, and deceitful speech, they have strove to hinder it."

REVIEW QUESTIONS

1. How did the Union's purposes in the Civil War change between 1861 and 1865? What accounts for those changes?
2. How did policies of the Confederate government toward slaves change during the Civil War? What were those changes, and when and why did they occur?
3. When the Civil War began, why did northern black men volunteer to serve in the Union army if the war had not yet become a war to end slavery?
4. To what extent did Abraham Lincoln's policies and attitudes toward black people change during the Civil War? Does Lincoln deserve credit as "the Great Emancipator"? Why or why not?
5. What was the purpose of the Emancipation Proclamation? Why was it issued? Exactly what did it accomplish?
6. What did black men and women contribute to the Union war effort? Was it in their interests to participate in the Civil War? Why or why not?
7. Why did at least some black people support the southern states and the Confederacy during the Civil War?
8. Was the result of the Civil War worth the loss of 620,000 lives?

PEARSON myhistorylab CONNECTIONS

Reinforce what you learned in this chapter by studying the many documents, images, maps, review tools, and videos available at **www.myhistorylab.com.**

READ AND REVIEW

✔—[Study and Review on **myhistorylab.com** STUDY PLAN FOR CHAPTER 11

[◉—[Read the Document on **myhistorylab.com**

Abraham Lincoln, The Gettysburg Address, (1863)

Abraham Lincoln, The Emancipation Proclamation, (1863)

Elizabeth Keckley, *Thirty Years a Slave, and Four Years in the White House* (1868)

James Henry Gooding, Letter to President Lincoln (1863)

Letter from H. Ford Douglas to Frederick Douglass's Monthly (1863)

President Lincoln Responds to the Working Men of Manchester on the Subject of Slavery (1863)

The Working Men of Manchester, England Write to President Lincoln on the Question of Slavery (1862)

"I Hope to Fall with My Face to the Foe": Lewis Douglass Describes the Battle of Fort Wagner (1863)

"If It Were Not for My Trust in Christ I Do Not Know How I Could Have Endured It": Testimony from Victims of New York's Draft Riots (1863)

View the **Map** on **myhistorylab.com**

Effects of the Emancipation Proclamation

The Civil War Part I 1861-1862

The Civil War Part II 1863-1865

RESEARCH AND REVIEW

mysearchlab

Consider these questions in a short research paper.

Why were African Americans who wanted to enlist rejected in 1861? What role did African Americans play in gaining their own freedom, and how did their struggle affect the lives of ordinary people?

Read the **Document** on **myhistorylab.com**

Exploring America: Fort Pillow Massacre

A Nation Divided: The Civil War

Listen on **myhistorylab.com**

Free At Last

Harriet Tubman; read by Jean Brannon

When This Cruel War Is Over

Watch the **Video** on **myhistorylab.com**

The Meaning of the Civil War for Americans

—————— **Listen** on **myhistorylab.com** ——————

Hear the audio files for Chapter 11 at

www.myhistorylab.com.

((•—Listen on **myhistorylab.com**

Hear the audio files for Chapter 12 at **www.myhistorylab.com.**

FOCUS QUESTIONS

WHAT DID freedom mean to nearly four million people who had been slaves?

HOW SUCCESSFUL were former slaves in acquiring land of their own?

WHAT WAS the Freedmen's Bureau and how effective was it?

WHY WAS education so important to African Americans?

WHAT WAS the purpose of the Fourteenth Amendment?

HOW DID African American men gain the right to vote?

Students assembled in front of James Plantation School in North Carolina shortly after the Civil War ended in 1865. Compared to many such schools, this one was exceptionally well constructed. Notice the students' clothes and lack of shoes.

WHAT DID FREEDOM mean to a people who had endured and survived 250 years of enslavement in America? What did the future hold for nearly four million African Americans in 1865? Freedom meant many things to many people. But to most former slaves, it meant that families would stay together. Freedom meant that women would no longer be sexually exploited. Freedom meant learning to read and write. Freedom meant organizing churches. Freedom meant moving around without having to obtain permission. Freedom meant that labor would produce income for the laborer and not the master. Freedom meant working without the whip. Freedom meant land to own, cultivate, and live on. Freedom meant a trial before a jury if charged with a crime. Freedom meant voting. Freedom meant citizenship and having the same rights as white people.

Years after slavery ended, a former Texas slave, Margrett Nillin, was asked if she preferred slavery or freedom. She answered unequivocally, "Well, it's dis way, in slavery I owns nothin' and never owns nothin'. In freedom I's own de home and raise de family. All dat causes me worryment and in slavery I has no worryment, but I takes freedom."

THE END OF SLAVERY

With the collapse of slavery, many black people were quick to inform white people that whatever loyalty, devotion, and cooperation they might have shown as slaves had never reflected of their inner feelings and attitudes. Near Opelousas, Louisiana, a Union officer asked a young black man why he did not love his master, and the youth responded sharply. "When my master begins to lub me, den it'll be time enough for me to lub him. What I wants is to get away. I want to take me off from dis plantation, where I can be free."

Emancipation was traumatic for many former masters. One former slave, Robert Falls, recalled that his master assembled the slaves to inform them they were free. "I hates to do it, but I must. You all ain't my niggers no more. You is free. Just as free as I am. Here I have raised you all to work for me, and now you are going to leave me. I am an old man, and I can't get along without you. I don't know what I am going to do." In less than a year, he was dead. Falls attributed his master's death to the end of slavery. "It killed him."

DIFFERING REACTIONS OF FORMER SLAVES

Other slaves bluntly displayed their reaction to years of bondage. Aunt Delia, a cook with a North Carolina family, revealed that she secretly had been gaining retribution for the indignity of servitude. "How many times I spit in the biscuits and peed in the coffee just to get back at them mean white folks."

In contrast, some slaves, especially elderly ones, were apprehensive about freedom. On a South Carolina plantation, an older black woman refused to accept emancipation. "I ain' no free nigger! I is got a marster and mistiss! Dee right dar in de great house. Ef you don' b'lieve me, you go dar an' see."

REUNITING BLACK FAMILIES

As slavery ended, the most urgent need for many freed people was finding family members who had been sold away from them. Slavery had not destroyed the black family. Husbands, wives, and children went to great lengths to reassemble their families after the Civil War. For years and even decades after the end of slavery, advertisements in black newspapers appealed for information about missing kinfolk.

In North Carolina a northern journalist met a middle aged black man "plodding along, staff in hand, and apparently very footsore and tired." The nearly exhausted freedman explained that he had walked almost 600 miles looking for his wife and children who had been sold four years earlier.

There were emotional reunions as family members found each other after years of separation. Ben and Betty Dodson had been apart for 20 years when Ben found her in a refugee camp after the war. "Glory! glory! hallelujah," he shouted as he hugged his wife. "Dis is my Betty, shuah. I foun' you at las'. I's hunted and hunted till I track you up here. I's boun' to hunt till I fin' you if you's alive."

Other searches had more heart-wrenching results. Husbands and wives sometimes learned that their spouses had remarried during the separation. Believing his wife had died, the husband of Laura Spicer remarried—only to learn after the war that Laura was still alive. Sadly, he wrote to her but refused to meet: "I would come and see you but I know I could not bear it. I want to see you and I don't want to see you. I love you just as well as I did the last day I saw you, and it will not do for you and I to meet."

Tormented, he wrote again pledging his love: "Laura I do not think that I have change any at all since I saw you last—I thinks of you and my children every day of my life. Laura I do love you the same. My love to you never have failed. Laura, truly, I have got another wife, and I am very sorry that I am. You feels and seems to me as much like my dear loving wife, as you ever did Laura."

One freedman testified to the close ties that bound many slave families when he replied bitterly to the claim that he had had a kind master who had fed him and never used the whip: "Kind! yes, he gib men corn enough, and he gib me pork enough, and he neber gib me one lick wid de whip, but whar's my wife?—whar's my chill'en? Take away de pork, I say; take away de corn, I can work and raise dese for myself, but gib me back de wife of my bosom, and gib me back my poor chill'en as was sold away."

LAND

As people embraced freedom and left their masters, they wanted land. Former slaves believed their future as a free people was tied to the possession of land. But just as it had been impossible to abolish slavery without federal intervention, it would not be possible to procure land without the assistance of the U.S. government. At first, federal authorities seemed determined to make land available to freedmen.

SPECIAL FIELD ORDER #15

On January 16, 1865, Union General William T. Sherman issued **Special Field Order #15.** This military directive set aside a 30-mile-wide tract of land along the Atlantic coast from Charleston, South Carolina, 245 miles south to Jacksonville, Florida. White owners had abandoned the land, and Sherman reserved it for black families. The head of each family would receive "possessory title" to 40 acres of land. Sherman also gave the freedmen the use of army mules, thus giving rise to the slogan, "Forty acres and a mule." Within six months, 40,000 freed people were working 400,000 acres in the South Carolina and Georgia low country and on the Sea Islands.

THE PORT ROYAL EXPERIMENT

Meanwhile, hundreds of former slaves had been cultivating land for three years. In late 1861 Union military forces carved out an enclave around Beaufort and Port Royal, South Carolina, that remained under federal authority for the rest of the war. White planters fled to the interior, leaving their slaves behind. Under the supervision of U.S. Treasury officials and northern reformers and missionaries who hurried south in 1862, ex-slaves began to work the land in what came to be known as the **"Port Royal Experiment."** When Treasury agents auctioned off portions of the land for nonpayment of taxes, freedmen purchased some of it. But northern businessmen bought most of the real estate and then hired black people to raise cotton.

White owners sometimes returned to their former lands only to find that black families had taken charge. Black farmers told one former owner, "We own this land now, put it out of your head that it will ever be yours again." And on one South Carolina Sea Island, white men were turned back by armed black men.

THE FREEDMEN'S BUREAU

As the war ended in early 1865, Congress created the Bureau of Refugees, Freedmen, and Abandoned Lands—commonly called the **Freedmen's Bureau.** Created as a temporary agency to assist freedmen to make the transition to freedom, the bureau was placed under the control of the U.S. Army and, General Oliver O. Howard was put in command. Howard, a devout Christian who had lost an arm in the war, was eager to aid the freedmen.

The bureau was given enormous responsibilities. It was to help freedmen obtain land, gain an education, negotiate labor contracts with white planters, settle legal and criminal disputes involving black and white people, and provide food, medical care, and transportation for black and white people left destitute by the war. However, Congress never provided sufficient funds or personnel to carry out these tasks.

The need for assistance was desperate as thousands of black and white southerners endured extreme privation in the months after the war ended. The bureau established camps for the homeless, fed the hungry, and cared for orphans and the sick as best it could.

In July 1865 the bureau took a first step toward distributing land when General Howard issued Circular 13 ordering agents to "set aside" 40 acre plots for freedmen. But the allocation had hardly begun when the order was revoked, and it was announced that land already distributed under Sherman's Special Field Order #15 was to be returned to its white owners.

The reason for this reversal was that Andrew Johnson, who had become president after Lincoln's assassination in April 1865, began to pardon hundreds and then thousands of former Confederates and restore their lands to them. General Howard had to tell black people that they had to relinquish the land they thought they had acquired. Speaking to some 2,000 freedmen on South Carolina's Edisto Island in October 1865, Howard pleaded with them to "lay aside their bitter feelings, and to become reconciled to their old masters."

A committee rejected Howard's appeal for reconciliation and forgiveness and insisted the government provide land. These appeals moved Howard. He returned to

OFFICE OF THE FREEDMEN'S BUREAU, MEMPHIS, TENNESSEE.
[SEE PAGE 316.]

Freedmen's Bureau agents often found themselves in the middle of angry disputes over land and labor that erupted between black and white southerners. Too often the Bureau officers sided with the white landowners in these disagreements with former slaves.   *Harper's Weekly*, July 25, 1868

Washington and attempted to persuade Congress provide land. Congress refused, and President Johnson was determined that white people would get their lands back.

SOUTHERN HOMESTEAD ACT

In early 1866 Congress attempted to provide land for freedmen with the passage of the **Southern Homestead Act.** More than three million acres of public land were set aside for black people and white southerners who had remained loyal to the Union. Much of this land, however, consisted of swampy wetlands or unfertile pinewoods unsuitable for farming. More than 4,000 black families—three-quarters of them in Florida—did claim some of this land, but many lacked the financial resources to cultivate it. Eventually timber companies acquired much of it, and the Southern Homestead Act largely failed.

SHARECROPPING

To make matters worse, by 1866 bureau officials tried to force freedmen to sign labor contracts with white landowners—returning black people to white authority. Black men who refused to sign contracts could be arrested. Theoretically, these contracts were legal agreements between two equals: landowner and laborer. But they were seldom freely

VOICES

A FREEDMEN'S BUREAU COMMISSIONER TELLS FREED PEOPLE WHAT FREEDOM MEANS

In June 1865 Charles Soule, the commissioner of contracts for the Freedmen's Bureau, told freedmen in Orangeburg, South Carolina, what to expect and how to behave in the coming year:

You are now free, but you must know that the only difference you can feel yet, between slavery and freedom, is that neither you nor your children can be bought or sold. You may have a harder time this year than you have ever had before; it will be the price you pay for your freedom. You will have to work hard, and get very little to eat, and very few clothes to wear. If you get through this year alive and well, you should be thankful. . . . You cannot be paid in money, for there is no good money in the District, nothing but Confederate paper. Then, what can you be paid with? Why, with food, with clothes, with the free use of your little houses and plots. You do not own a cent's worth except yourselves.

You do not understand why some of the white people who used to own you do not have to work in the field. It is because they are rich. If every man were poor, and worked in his own field, there would be no big farms, and very little cotton or corn raised to sell; there would be no money, and nothing to buy. Some people must be rich, to pay the others, and they have the right to do no work except to look out after their property.

Remember that all of your working time belongs to the man who hires you: therefore you must not leave work without his leave not even to nurse a child, or to go and visit a wife or husband. When you wish to go off the place, get a pass as you used to, and then you will run no danger of being taken up by our soldiers.

In short, do just about as the good men among you have always done. Remember that even if you are badly off, no one can buy and sell you: remember that if you help yourselves, GOD will help you, and trust hopefully that next year and the year after will bring some new blessing to you.

- According to Soule, what is the difference between slavery and freedom?
- Does freedom mean that freed people will have economic opportunities equal to those of white people?
- How should freed people have responded to Soule's advice?

SOURCE: Ira Berlin et al., "The Terrain of Freedom: The Struggle over the Meaning of Free Labor in the U.S. South," *History Workshop* 22 (Autumn 1986): 108–30.

---

concluded. Bureau agents usually sided with the landowner and pressured freedmen to accept unequal terms.

Occasionally, the landowner would pay wages to the laborer. But because most landowners lacked cash to pay wages, they agreed to provide the laborer with part of the crop. The laborer, often grudgingly, agreed to work under the supervision of the landowner. The contracts required labor for a full year. The laborer could neither quit nor strike. Landowners demanded that the laborers work the fields in gangs. Freedmen resisted this system. They sometimes insisted on making decisions involving planting, fertilizing, and harvesting as they sought to exercise independence (see Map 12-1).

Freed women washing laundry along a creek near Circleville, Texas, ca. 1866.

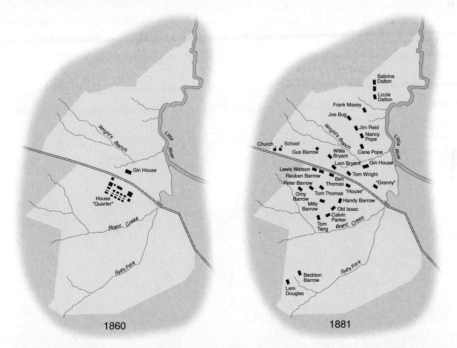

MAP 12-1 • The Effect of Sharecropping on the Southern Plantation: The Barrow Plantation, Oglethorpe County, Georgia. With the end of slavery and the advent of sharecropping, black people would no longer agree to work in fields as gangs. They preferred to have each family cultivate separate plots of land, thereby distancing themselves as much as possible from slavery and white supervision.

▶ *Although many* freed people worked the same land that they had as slaves, how does this map suggest the changes experienced by black people in family life, religion, education, and their relationships with white people?

Thus it took time for a new form of agricultural labor to develop. But by the 1870s, the system of **sharecropping** dominated most of the South. There were no wages. Freedmen worked land as families—not in gangs—and not under direct white supervision. When the landowner provided seed, tools, fertilizer, and work animals (mules, horses, oxen), the black family received one-third of the crop. There were many variations on these arrangements, and black families were often cheated out of their fair share of the crop.

THE BLACK CHURCH

In the years after slavery, the church became the most important institution among African Americans other than the family. It filled deep spiritual and inspirational needs, it offered enriching music, provided charity and compassion to those in need, developed community and political leaders, and was free of white supervision. Before slavery's demise, free black people and slaves often attended white churches where they participated in religious services conducted by white clergymen and where they were treated as second-class Christians. Once liberated, black men and women organized their own churches with their own ministers.

Church members struggled, scrimped, and saved to buy land and build churches. Most former slaves founded Baptist and Methodist churches. These denominations tended to be more autonomous and less subject to outside control. Their doctrine was usually simple and direct without complex theology. Of the Methodist churches, the African Methodist Episcopal (AME) church made giant strides in the South after the Civil War.

Hundreds of black churches were founded across the South following the Civil War, and they grew spectacularly in the decades that followed. This illustration shows a congregation crowded into Richmond's First African Baptist Church in 1874.

White Methodists initially encouraged cooperation with black Methodists and helped establish the Colored (now Christian) Methodist Episcopal church (CME). But the white Methodists lost some of their fervor after they failed to persuade the black Methodists to keep political issues out of the CME church and to dwell solely on spiritual concerns.

The Presbyterian, Congregational, and Episcopal churches appealed to the more prosperous members of the black community. Their services tended to be more formal and solemn. Black people who had been free before the Civil War were usually affiliated with these congregations and remained so after the conflict. Well-to-do free black people in Charleston organized St. Mark's Protestant Episcopal Church when they separated from the white Episcopal church. But they retained their white minister Joseph Seabrook as rector.

The Roman Catholic Church made modest in-roads among black southerners. There were all-black parishes in St. Augustine, Savannah, Charleston, and Louisville after the Civil War. For generations before the conflict, many well-to-do free people of color in New Orleans had been practicing Catholics, and their descendants remained faithful to the church.

Religious differences not withstanding, the black churches, their parishioners, and clergymen would play a vital role in Reconstruction politics. More than one hundred black ministers were elected to political office after the Civil War.

EDUCATION

Freedom and education were inseparable. To remain illiterate after emancipation was to remain enslaved. Almost every freed black person—young or old—desperately wanted to learn. Elderly people were especially eager to read the Bible. During the war and before slavery ended, black people began to establish schools. In 1861 Mary Peake, a free black woman, opened a school in Hampton, Virginia. On South Carolina's Sea Islands, a black cabinetmaker began teaching openly after having covertly operated a school for years. In 1862 northern missionaries arrived on the Sea Islands to begin teaching. Laura Towne and Ellen Murray, two white women, and Charlotte Forten, a black woman, opened Penn school on St. Helena's Island as part of the Port Royal Experiment. They enrolled 138 children and 58 adults. By 1863 there were 1,700 students and 45 teachers at 30 schools in the South Carolina low country.

With the end of the Civil War, northern religious organizations in cooperation with the Freedmen's Bureau organized hundreds of schools. Classes were held in stables, homes, former slave cabins, taverns, churches, and even—in Savannah and New Orleans—in the old slave markets. Former slaves spent hours in the fields and then trudged to a makeshift school to learn the alphabet and arithmetic. In 1865 black ministers created the Savannah Educational Association, raised $1,000, employed 15 black teachers, and enrolled 600 students.

In 1866 the Freedmen's Bureau set aside $500,000 for education. The bureau furnished the buildings while former slaves hired, housed, and fed the teachers. By 1869 the Freedmen's Bureau was involved with 3,000 schools and 150,000 students. Even more impressive, by 1870 black people had contributed $1 million to educate their people.

Charlotte Forten and "Life on the Sea Islands"

Charlotte Forten (1837–1914) was born into prominent black family in Philadelphia. Forten spent her early years acquiring the education she would need to take her place among the black elite of Philadelphia. As a teenager at Salem Normal School, she studied literature and teaching, both thoroughly appropriate subjects for a respectable young lady. In the mid-nineteenth century, reform work was also expected of people of her background. Her family had been involved in the abolitionist movement for generations. Forten followed in their footsteps, joining the Salem Anti-Slavery Society and playing an active role in organization and fund-raising. In time, she became a teacher and began to write poetry, much of which dealt with abolition and social issues. In 1862 she got an opportunity to combine her interests in education and reform. When, under pressure from Union troops, white planters fled the Sea Islands off the coast of South Carolina, they left their slaves behind. Government officials, missionaries, and northern reformers went south to help build a new community, a project that came to be known as the Port Royal Experiment. Charlotte Forten was the first black teacher to join the project. Her essay, "Life in the Sea Islands," was drawn from her diaries and was published in the *Atlantic Monthly* in 1864. For many in the North, it offered a glimpse of the postwar future, a future in which activists from the North would be called upon to rebuild the South.

▲ Charlotte Forten—shown here in an 1866 photograph—taught on the South Carolina Sea Islands from 1862 to 1864.

"I never before saw children so eager to learn, although I had several years' experience in New-England schools. Coming to school is a constant delight and recreation to them. They come here as other children come to play. The older ones, during the summer, work in the fields from early morning to eleven or twelve o'clock, and then come into school, after their hard toil in the hot sun, as bright and as anxious to learn as ever. . . . It is wonderful how a people who have been so long crushed to the earth, so imbruted as these have been— and they are said to be among the most degraded negroes of the South—can have so great a desire for knowledge, and such a capacity for attaining it."

"After the lessons, we used to talk freely to the children, often giving them slight sketches of the great and good men. Before teaching them the 'John Brown' song, which they learned to sing with great spirits, Miss T. told them of the story of the brave old man who died for them. I told them about Toussaint, thinking it well they should know what one of their own color had done for his race."

"Daily the long-oppressed people of these islands are demonstrating their capacity for improvement in learning and labor. What they have accomplished in one short year exceeds our utmost expectations. Still the sky is dark; but through the darkness we can discern a brighter future. We cannot but feel that the day of final and entire deliverance, so long and so hopelessly prayed for, has at length begun to dawn upon this much-enduring race. An old freedman said to me one day, 'De Lord makes me suffer long time, Miss. 'Peared like we nebber was gwine to git troo. But now we's free. He brings us all out right at las'.' In their darkest hours they have clung to Him, and we know He will not forsake them."

What did Forten want to teach the inhabitants of the Sea Islands? Did her ambitions go beyond teaching basic literacy? What lessons did Forten want readers to draw from her essay?

BLACK TEACHERS

Although freedmen appreciated the dedication of the white teachers affiliated with the missionary societies, they usually preferred black teachers. The Rev. Richard H. Cain, an AME minister who came south from Brooklyn, New York, said that black people needed to learn to control their own futures. "We must take into our own hands the education of our race. . . . Honest, dignified whites may teach ever so well, but it has not the effect to exalt the black man's opinion of his own race, because they have always been in the habit of seeing white men in honored positions, and respected."

Black men and women responded to the call to teach. Virginia C. Green, a northern black woman, felt compelled to go to Mississippi. "Though I have never known servitude they are . . . my people. Born as far north as the lakes I have felt no freer because so many were less fortunate. . . . I look forward with impatience to the time when my people shall be strong, blest with education, purified and made prosperous by virtue and industry."

Many northern teachers, black and white, provided more than the basics of elementary education. Black life and history were occasionally read about and discussed. Abolitionist Lydia Maria Child wrote *The Freedmen's Book,* which offered brief biographies of Benjamin Banneker, Frederick Douglass, and Toussaint Louverture. More often northern teachers, dismayed at the backwardness of the freedmen, struggled to modify behavior and to impart cultural values by teaching piety, thrift, cleanliness, temperance, and timeliness.

Many former slaves came to resent some of these teachers as condescending, self-righteous, and paternalistic. Sometimes the teachers, especially those who were white, became frustrated with recalcitrant students who did not readily absorb middle-class values. Others, however, derived enormous satisfaction from teaching freedmen. A Virginia teacher commented, "I think I shall stay here as long as I live and teach this people. I have no love or taste for any other work, and I am happy only here with them."

BLACK COLLEGES

Northern churches and religious societies established dozens of colleges, universities, academies, and institutes across the South in the late 1860s and the 1870s. Most of these institutions provided elementary and secondary education. Few black students were prepared for actual college or university work. The **American Missionary Association**—an abolitionist and Congregationalist organization—worked with the Freedmen's Bureau to establish Fisk in Tennessee, Hampton in Virginia, Tougaloo in Alabama, and Avery in South Carolina. The primary purpose of these schools was to educate black students to become teachers.

In Missouri, the black enlisted men and white officers of the 62nd and 65th Colored Volunteers raised $6,000 to establish Lincoln Institute in 1866, which would become Lincoln University. The American Baptist Home Mission Society founded Virginia Union, Shaw in North Carolina, Benedict in South Carolina, and Morehouse in Georgia. Northern Methodists helped establish Claflin in South Carolina, Rust in Mississippi, and Bennett in North Carolina. The Episcopalians were responsible for St. Augustine's in North Carolina and St. Paul's in Virginia. These and similar institutions formed the foundation for the historically black colleges and universities.

Black and white land-grant colleges stressed training in agriculture and industry. In this late-nine-teenth-century photograph, Claflin University students learns the craft of wood working.

RESPONSE OF WHITE SOUTHERNERS

White southerners considered black people's efforts to learn absurd. For generations, white Americans had considered people of African descent abjectly inferior. When efforts were made to educate former slaves, white southerners reacted with suspicion, contempt, and hostility.

Countless schools were burned, mostly in rural areas. In Canton, Mississippi, black people collected money to open a school—only to have white residents inform them that the school would be burned and the prospective teacher lynched if it opened. The female teacher at a freedmen's school in Donaldsonville, Louisiana, was shot and killed.

Most white people refused to attend school with black people. No integrated schools were established in the immediate aftermath of emancipation. Most black people were more interested in gaining an education than in whether white students attended school with them. When black youngsters tried to attend a white school in Raleigh, North Carolina, the white students stopped going to it. For a brief time in Charleston, black and white children attended the same school, but they were taught in separate classrooms.

VIOLENCE

In the days, weeks, and months after the end of the Civil War, an orgy of brutality and violence swept across the South. White southerners—embittered by their defeat and unable to adjust to the end of slave labor and the loss of millions of dollars worth of slave property—lashed out at black people. There were beatings, murders, rapes, and riots, often with little or no provocation.

Black people who demanded respect, wore better clothing, refused to step aside for white people, or asked to be addressed as "mister" or "missus" were attacked. In South Carolina, a white clergyman shot and killed a black man who protested when another black man was removed from a church service. In Texas, one black man was killed for not removing his hat in the presence of a white man and another for refusing to relinquish a bottle of whiskey. A black woman was beaten for "using insolent language," and a black worker in Alabama was killed for speaking sharply to a white overseer. In Virginia, a black veteran was beaten after announcing he had been proud to serve in the Union Army.

There was also large-scale violence. In 1865 University of North Carolina students twice attacked peaceful meetings of black people. Near Pine Bluff, Arkansas, in 1866, a white mob burned a black settlement and lynched 24 men, women, and children. An estimated 2,000 black people were murdered around Shreveport, Louisiana. In Texas, white people killed 1,000 black people between 1865 and 1868.

In May 1866 in Memphis, white residents went on rampage after black veterans forced police to release a black prisoner. The city was already beset with economic difficulties and racial tensions caused in part by an influx of rural refugees. White people, led by Irish policemen, destroyed hundreds of homes, cabins, shacks, churches, and schools in the black section of Memphis. Forty-six black people and two white men died.

Little was done to stem the violence. Most Union troops had been withdrawn from the South and demobilized after the war. The Freedmen's Bureau was usually unwilling and unable to protect the black population. Black people left to defend themselves were usually in no position to retaliate. Instead, they sometimes attempted to bring the perpetrators to justice. In Orangeburg, South Carolina, armed black men brought three white men who had been wreaking violence in the community to the local jail. In Holly Springs, Mississippi, a posse of armed black men apprehended a white man who had murdered a freedwoman.

For black people, the system of justice was thoroughly unjust. Although black people could now testify against white people in court, southern juries remained all white and refused to convict white people charged with harming black people. In Texas in 1865 and 1866, 500 white men were indicted for murdering black people. None were convicted.

THE CRUSADE FOR POLITICAL AND CIVIL RIGHTS

In October 1864 in Syracuse, New York, 145 black leaders gathered in a national convention. Some of the century's most prominent black men and women attended, including Frederick Douglass, Henry Highland Garnet, Frances E. W. Harper, William Wells Brown, Francis L. Cardozo, Richard H. Cain, Jonathan J. Wright, and Jonathan C. Gibbs. They embraced the basic tenets of the American political tradition and proclaimed that they expected to participate fully in it.

Even before the **Syracuse Convention,** northern Republicans met in Union-controlled territory around Beaufort, South Carolina, and nominated the state's delegates to the 1864 Republican national convention. Among those selected were Robert Smalls and Prince Rivers, former slaves who had exemplary records with the Union Army. The probability of black participation in postwar politics seemed promising.

But northern and southern white leaders who already held power would largely determine whether black Americans would gain political power or acquire the same rights as white people. As the Civil War ended, President Lincoln was more concerned with restoring the seceded states to the Union than in opening political doors for black people. Yet Lincoln suggested that at least some black men deserved the right to vote. On April 11, 1865, he wrote, "I would myself prefer that [the vote] were now conferred on the very intelligent, and on those who serve our cause as soldiers." Three days later he was assassinated.

PRESIDENTIAL RECONSTRUCTION UNDER ANDREW JOHNSON

Vice President Andrew Johnson then became president and initially seemed inclined to impose stern policies on the white South while befriending the freedmen. He announced that "treason must be made odious, and traitors must be punished and impoverished." In 1864 he had told black people, "I will be your Moses, and lead you through the Red Sea of War and Bondage to a fairer future of Liberty and Peace." Nothing proved to be further from the truth. Andrew Johnson was no friend of black Americans.

Born poor in eastern Tennessee and never part of the southern aristocracy, Johnson opposed secession and was the only senator from the seceded states to remain loyal to the Union. He had nonetheless acquired five slaves and the conviction that black people were so inferior that white men must forever govern them.

Johnson quickly lost his enthusiasm for punishing traitors. Indeed, he began to placate white southerners. In May 1865 Johnson granted blanket amnesty and pardons to former Confederates willing to swear allegiance to the United States. The main exceptions were high former Confederate officials and those who owned property valued in excess of $20,000, a large sum at the time. Yet even these leaders could appeal for individual pardons. By 1866 Johnson had pardoned more than 7,000 high-ranking former Confederates and wealthier southerners. Moreover, he had restored land to those white people who had lost it to freedmen.

Johnson's actions encouraged those who had supported secession, owned slaves, and opposed the Union. He permitted longtime southern leaders to regain political influence and authority only months after the end of America's bloodiest conflict. As black people and radical Republicans watched in disbelief, Johnson appointed provisional governors in the former Confederate states. Leaders in those states then called constitutional conventions, held elections, and prepared to regain their place in the Union. Johnson merely insisted that each former Confederate state formally accept the **Thirteenth Amendment** (ratified in December 1865, it outlawed slavery) and repudiate Confederate war debts.

BLACK CODES

After the election of state and local officials, white legislators gathered in state capitals across the South to determine the status and future of the freedmen. With little debate, the legislatures drafted the so-called **black codes.** Southern politicians gave no thought to providing black people with the political and legal rights associated with citizenship.

The black codes sought to ensure the availability of a subservient agricultural labor supply controlled by white people. They imposed severe restrictions on freedmen. Freedmen had to sign annual labor contracts with white landowners. South Carolina required black people who wanted to establish a business to purchase licenses costing from $10 to $100. The codes permitted black children ages two to 21 to be apprenticed to white people and spelled out their duties and obligations in detail. Corporal punishment was legal. Employers were designated "masters" and employees "servants." The black codes also restricted black people from loitering or vagrancy, using alcohol or firearms, hunting, fishing, and grazing livestock. The codes did guarantee rights that slaves had not possessed. Freedmen could marry legally, engage in contracts, purchase property, sue or be sued, and testify in court. But black people could not vote or serve on juries.

BLACK CONVENTIONS

Alarmed by these threats to their freedom, black people met in conventions across the South in 1865 and 1866 to protest, appeal for justice, and chart their future. Men who had been free before the war dominated the conventions. Many were ministers, teachers, and artisans. These meetings were hardly militant or radical affairs. Delegates respectfully insisted that white people live up to the principles and rights embodied in the Declaration of Independence and the Constitution. At the AME church in Raleigh, North Carolina, delegates asked for equal rights and the right to vote. At Georgia's convention they protested against white violence and appealed for leaders who would enforce the law without regard to color.

Two conventions were held in Charleston, South Carolina—one before and one after the black code was enacted. At the first, delegates stressed the "respect and affection" they felt toward white Charlestonians. They even proposed that only literate men be granted the right to vote if it were applied to both races. The second convention denounced the black code and insisted on its repeal. Delegates again asked for the rights to vote and testify in court: "These two things we deem necessary to our welfare and elevation." They also appealed for public schools and for "homesteads for ourselves and our children." White authorities ignored the black conventions and their petitions. Instead they were confident they had relegated the freedmen to a subordinate role.

By late 1865 President Johnson's Reconstruction policies had aroused black people. One black Union veteran summed up the situation: "If you call this Freedom, what do you call Slavery?" Republicans in Congress also opposed Johnson's policies toward the freedmen and the former Confederate states.

THE RADICAL REPUBLICANS

Radical Republicans, as more militant Republicans were called, were especially disturbed that Johnson seemed to have abandoned the ex-slaves to their former masters. They considered white southerners disloyal and unrepentant, despite their military defeat.

Moreover, radical Republicans—unlike moderate Republicans and Democrats—were determined to transform the racial fabric of American society by including black people in the political and economic system.

Among the most influential radical Republicans were Senators Charles Sumner, Benjamin Wade, and Henry Wilson and Congressmen Thaddeus Stevens, George W. Julian, and James M. Ashley. Few white Americans have been as dedicated to the rights of black people as these men. They had fought to abolish slavery. They were reluctant to compromise. They were honest, tough, and articulate but also abrasive, difficult, self-righteous, and vain.

RADICAL PROPOSALS

To provide freedmen with land, Thaddeus Stevens proposed a bill in Congress in late 1865 to confiscate 400 million acres from the wealthiest 10 percent of southerners and distribute it free to freedmen. The remaining land would be auctioned off in plots no larger than 500 acres. Few legislators supported the proposal. Even those who wanted fundamental change considered confiscation a violation of property rights.

Instead, radical Republicans supported voting rights for black men. They were convinced that black men—to protect themselves and to secure the South for the Republican Party—had to have the right to vote.

Moderate Republicans, however, found the prospect of black voting almost as objectionable as the confiscation of land. They preferred to build the Republican Party in the South by cooperating with President Johnson and attracting loyal white southerners.

The thought of black suffrage appalled northern and southern Democrats. Most white northerners—Republicans and Democrats—favored denying black men the right to vote in their states. After the war, proposals to guarantee the right to vote to black men were defeated in New York, Ohio, Kansas, and the Nebraska Territory. However, five of the six New England states as well as Iowa, Minnesota, and Wisconsin allowed black men to vote.

In December 1865 Congress created the Joint Committee on Reconstruction to determine whether to readmit the southern states to the Union. The committee confirmed reports of widespread mistreatment of black people and white arrogance.

THE FREEDMEN'S BUREAU BILL AND THE CIVIL RIGHTS BILL

In early 1866 Senator Lyman Trumball, a moderate Republican from Illinois, introduced two major bills. The first was to provide more financial support for the Freedmen's Bureau and extend its authority to defend the rights of black people.

The second proposal became the first **Civil Rights Act** in American history. It made any person born in the United States a citizen (except Indians) and entitled them to rights protected by the U.S. government. Black people would possess the same legal rights as white people. The bill was clearly intended to invalidate the black codes.

JOHNSON'S VETOES

Both measures passed in Congress with nearly unanimous Republican support. President Johnson vetoed them. The Johnson vetoes stunned Republicans. Although he had not meant to, Johnson drove moderate Republicans into the radical camp and strengthened the Republican Party. The president did not believe Republicans would oppose him to support the freedmen. He was wrong. Congress overrode both vetoes. The Republicans broke with Johnson in 1866, defied him in 1867, and impeached him in 1868 (failing to remove him from office by only one vote in the Senate).

THE FOURTEENTH AMENDMENT

To secure the legal rights of freedmen, Republicans passed the **Fourteenth Amendment.** This amendment fundamentally changed the Constitution by compelling states to accept their residents as citizens and to guarantee that their rights as citizens would be safeguarded.

Its first section guaranteed citizenship to every person born in the United States. This included virtually every black person. It made each person a citizen of the state in which he or she resided. It defined the specific rights of citizens and protected those rights against the authority of state governments. Citizens had the right to due process (usually a trial) before they could lose their life, liberty, or property.

Eleven years after Chief Justice Roger Taney declared in the *Dred Scott* decision that black people were "a subordinate and inferior class of beings" who had "no rights that white people were bound to respect," the Fourteenth Amendment vested them with the same rights of citizenship other Americans possessed.

The amendment also threatened to deprive states of representation in Congress if they denied black men the vote. The end of slavery had also made obsolete the Three-Fifths Clause in the Constitution, which had counted slaves as only three-fifths (or 60 percent) of a white person in calculating a state's population and determining the number of representatives each state was entitled to in the House of Representatives. Republicans feared that southern states would count black people in their populations without permitting them to vote, thereby gaining more representatives than those states had had before the Civil War. The amendment mandated that if any state, northern or southern, did not allow adult males to vote the number of representatives it was entitled to in Congress would be reduced.

Democrats almost unanimously opposed the Fourteenth Amendment. Andrew Johnson denounced it, although he could not prevent its adoption. Southern states refused to ratify it except for Tennessee. Women's suffragists felt betrayed because the amendment limited suffrage to males. Despite this opposition, the amendment was ratified in 1868.

RADICAL RECONSTRUCTION

By 1867 radical Republicans in Congress had wrested control over **Reconstruction** from Johnson, and they then imposed policies that brought black men into the political system as voters and officeholders. It was a dramatic development, second in importance only to emancipation and the end of slavery.

Republicans swept the 1866 congressional elections despite the belligerent opposition of Johnson and the Democrats. With two-thirds majorities in the House and Senate, Republicans easily overrode presidential vetoes. Two years after the Civil War, Republicans dismantled the state governments established in the South under Johnson's authority. They instituted a new Reconstruction policy.

MAP 12-2 • Congressional Reconstruction Under the terms of the First Reconstruction Act of 1867, the former Confederate states (except Tennessee) were divided into five military districts and placed under the authority of military officers. Commanders in each of the five districts were responsible for supervising the reestablishment of civilian governments in each state.

▶ *In which states by 1868 did black state legislators have sufficient strength to pass legislation over white opposition?*

Republicans passed the first of three **Reconstruction Acts** over Johnson's veto in March 1867. It divided the South into five military districts, each under the command of a general (see Map 12-2). Troops would protect lives and property while new civilian governments were formed. Elected delegates in each state would draft a new constitution and submit it to the voters.

UNIVERSAL MANHOOD SUFFRAGE

The Reconstruction Act stipulated that all adult males in the states of the former Confederacy were eligible to vote, except for those who had actively supported the Confederacy or were convicted felons. Once each state had formed a new government and approved the Fourteenth Amendment, it would be readmitted to the Union with representation in Congress.

The advent of radical Reconstruction was the culmination of black people's struggle to gain legal and political rights. Since the 1864 black national convention in Syracuse and the meetings and conventions in the South in 1865 and 1866, black leaders had argued that one of the consequences of the Civil War should be the inclusion of black men in the body politic. The achievement of that goal was due to their persistent and persuasive efforts, the determination of radical Republicans, and, ironically, the obstructionism of Andrew Johnson, who had played into their hands.

BLACK POLITICS

Full of energy and enthusiasm, black men and women rushed into the political arena in the spring and summer of 1867. Although women could not vote, they joined men at the meetings, rallies, parades, and picnics that accompanied political organizing in the South. For many former slaves, politics became as important as religious activities. Black people flocked to the Republican Party and the new Union Leagues.

The **Union Leagues** had been established in the North during the Civil War, but they expanded across the South as quasi-political organizations in the late 1860s. The Leagues were social, fraternal, and patriotic groups in which black people often, but not always, outnumbered white people. They gave people an opportunity to sharpen leadership skills and gain a political education by discussing issues from taxes to schools.

SIT-INS AND STRIKES

Political progress did not induce apathy, satisfaction, or contentment among black people. Gaining citizenship, legal rights, and the vote generated more expectations and demands for advancement. For example, black people insisted on equal access to public transportation. After a Republican rally in Charleston, in April 1867, black men staged a "sit-in" on a horse-drawn streetcar before they were arrested. In Charleston, black people were permitted to ride only on the outside running boards of the cars. They wanted to sit on the seats inside. Within a month, after military authorities intervened, the streetcar company gave in. Similar protests occurred in Richmond and New Orleans.

Black workers also struck across the South in 1867. Black laborers were usually paid less than white men for the same work, which led to labor unrest during the 1860s and 1870s. Sometimes the strikers won, sometimes they lost. In 1869 a black Baltimore longshoreman, Isaac Myers, organized the National Colored Labor Union.

THE REACTION OF WHITE SOUTHERNERS

White southerners grimly opposed radical Reconstruction. They were outraged that black people could claim the same legal and political rights they possessed. Such a possibility seemed preposterous to people convinced of the absolute inferiority of black people. Benjamin F. Perry, whom Johnson had appointed provisional governor of South Carolina in 1865, captures the depth of this racist conviction. "The African," Perry declared, "has been in all ages, a savage or a slave. God created him inferior to the white man in form, color and intellect, and no legislation or culture can make him his equal . . ."

With the adoption of radical Republican policies, most black men eagerly took part in political activities. Political meetings, conventions, speeches, barbecues, and other gatherings also attracted women and children.

African-American Events	National Events

1862

March 1862	**February 1862**
The Port Royal Experiment in South Carolina begins	Julia Ward Howe publishes the first version of "Battle Hymm of the Republic" in the Atlantic Monthly
	July 1862
	Morrell Land-Grant College Act signed into law

1864

October 1864	**November 1864**
Black national convention in Syracuse, New York	President Lincoln reelected

1865

January 1865	**April 1865**
General Sherman's Special Field Order #15	Lincoln is assassinated; Andrew Johnson succeeds to presidency
March 1865	**May 1865**
Freedmen's Bureau established	Johnson begins presidential Reconstruction
September–November 1865	**June–August 1865**
Black codes enacted	Southern state governments reorganized
	December 1865
	Thirteenth Amendment to the Constitution iratified

1866

February 1866	**November 1866**
Southern Homestead Act	Republicans gain greater than two-thirds majorities in House and Senate
March 1866	
President Johnson vetoes bill to extend the Freedman's Bureau and the Civil Rights bill	
April 1866	
Congress overrides Johnson's veto of the Civil Rights bill	
May 1866	
Memphis riot	

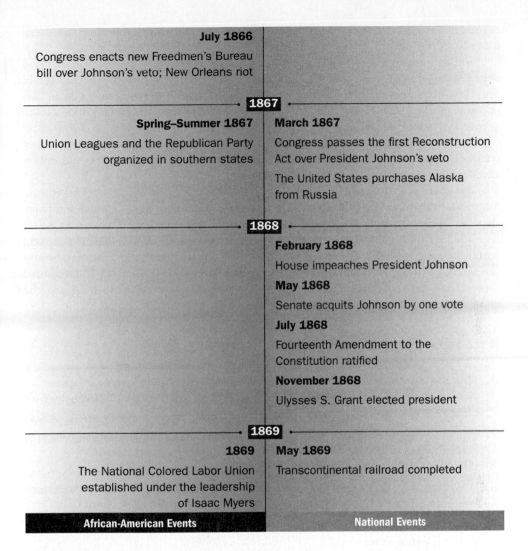

July 1866

Congress enacts new Freedmen's Bureau bill over Johnson's veto; New Orleans riot

1867

Spring–Summer 1867

Union Leagues and the Republican Party organized in southern states

March 1867

Congress passes the first Reconstruction Act over President Johnson's veto

The United States purchases Alaska from Russia

1868

February 1868

House impeaches President Johnson

May 1868

Senate acquits Johnson by one vote

July 1868

Fourteenth Amendment to the Constitution ratified

November 1868

Ulysses S. Grant elected president

1869

1869

The National Colored Labor Union established under the leadership of Isaac Myers

May 1869

Transcontinental railroad completed

African-American Events   **National Events**

Some white people, taking solace in their belief in the innate inferiority of black people, concluded they could turn black suffrage to their advantage. White people, they assumed, should easily be able to control and manipulate black voters just as they had controlled black people during slavery. White southerners who believed this, however, would be disappointed, and their disappointment would turn to fury.

CONCLUSION

Why were black southerners able to gain citizenship and access to the political system by 1868? Most white Americans did not suddenly abandon 250 years of deeply ingrained beliefs that people of African descent were their inferiors. The advances that African Americans achieved fit into a series of complex political developments after the Civil War. Black people themselves had fought and died to preserve the Union, and they had earned the grudging respect of many white people and the open admiration of others. Black leaders in meetings and petitions insisted that their rights be recognized.

White northerners—led by the radical Republicans—were convinced that President Johnson was wrong to support policies that permitted white southerners to retain pre–Civil War leaders while the black codes virtually made freedmen slaves again. Republicans were determined that white southerners realize their defeat had doomed the prewar status quo. Republicans established a Reconstruction program to disfranchise key southern leaders while providing legal rights to freedmen. The right to vote, they reasoned, would enable black people to deal more effectively with white southerners and strengthen the Republican Party in the South.

The result was to make the mid- to late 1860s one of the few high points in African-American history. During this period, not only was slavery abolished, but black southerners were able to organize schools and churches, and black people throughout the South acquired legal and political rights that would have been incomprehensible before the war. Yet black people did not stand on the brink of utopia. Most freedmen still lacked land and had no realistic hope of obtaining much, if any, of it. White violence and cruelty continued almost unabated across much of the South. Still, for millions of African Americans, the future looked more promising than it had ever before in American history.

REVIEW QUESTIONS

1. How did freedmen define their freedom? What did freedom mean to ex-slaves? How did their priorities differ from those of African Americans who had been free before the Civil War?

2. What did the former slaves and the former slaveholders want after emancipation? Were these desires realistic? How did former slaves and former slaveholders disagree after the end of slavery?

3. Why did African Americans form separate churches, schools, and social organizations after the Civil War? What role did the black church play in the black community?

4. How effective was the Freedmen's Bureau? How successful was it in assisting ex-slaves to live in freedom?

5. Why did southern states enact black codes?

6. Why did radical Republicans object to President Andrew Johnson's Reconstruction policies? Why did Congress impose its own Reconstruction policies?

7. Why were laws passed to enable black men to vote?

8. Why did black men gain the right to vote but not possession of land?

9. Did congressional Reconstruction secure full equality for African Americans as American citizens?

PEARSON myhistorylab CONNECTIONS

Reinforce what you learned in this chapter by studying the many documents, images, maps, review tools, and videos available at **www.myhistorylab.com**.

READ AND REVIEW

✔•⎯Study and Review on **myhistorylab.com** STUDY PLAN FOR CHAPTER 12

▯•⎯Read the Document on **myhistorylab.com**

"A Jubilee of Freedom": Freed Slaves March in Charleston, South Carolina (1865)

Address of the Colored State Convention to the People of the State of South Carolina (1865)

Charlotte Forten, Life on the Sea Islands

Mississippi Black Code (1865)

President Johnson's Veto of the Civil Rights Act 1866

The Civil Rights Act of 1866

🔍⎯View the Map on **myhistorylab.com**

Congressional Reconstruction

Milestones in Education

RESEARCH AND EXPLORE

mysearchlab

Consider this question in a short research paper.

Who supported radical Reconstruction? Why?

▯•⎯Read the Document on **myhistorylab.com**

Integration Quest: Race Relations and the Reconstruction Years

Reconstruction: The Struggle to Define the Meaning of Freedom

((•⎯Listen on **myhistorylab.com**

Remembering Slavery #2; newly-released recordings of former slaves talking about slavery

👁⎯Watch the Video on **myhistorylab.com**

Trials of Racial Identity in Nineteenth-Century America

⎯⎯⎯ ((•⎯Listen on **myhistorylab.com** ⎯⎯⎯
Hear the audio files for Chapter 12 at
www.myhistorylab.com.

The Meaning of Freedom: The Failure of Reconstruction • • *1868–1877*

((•─Listen on **myhistorylab.com**
Hear the audio files for Chapter 13 at **www.myhistorylab.com**.

FOCUS QUESTIONS

WHAT POLITICAL offices were black men elected to—and not elected to—during Reconstruction?

WHAT ISSUES most concerned black political leaders?

WHY WERE so many white southerners so opposed to black and white Republicans exercising political power?

WHY WAS the Ku Klux Klan founded and how effective was it?

WHY WAS the Fifteenth Amendment enacted?

HOW AND why did black and white Republicans lose control of every southern state by 1877?

The first African Americans to serve in the U.S. Congress: [standing, left to right] Robert C. DeLarge, representative, South Carolina; Jefferson Long, representative, Georgia; Seated, left to right: U.S. Senator Hiram R. Revels, Mississippi; Benjamin S. Turner, representative, Alabama; Josiah T. Walls, representative, Florida; Joseph H. Rainey, representative, South Carolina; Robert B. Elliott, representative, South Carolina.

I N 1868, FOR THE first time in American history, thousands of black men would elect hundreds of black and white leaders to state and local offices across the South. Would this newly acquired political influence enable freedmen to complete the transition from slavery to freedom? Would political power propel black people into the mainstream of American society? Equally important, would white southerners and northerners accept black people as fellow citizens?

Events from 1867 to 1877 generated hope that black and white Americans might learn to live together on a compatible and equitable basis. But these developments also raised the possibility that black people's new access to political power would fail to resolve the racial animosity and intolerance that persisted in American life after the Civil War.

CONSTITUTIONAL CONVENTIONS

Black men as a group first entered politics as delegates to constitutional conventions in the southern states in 1867 and 1868. Each of the former Confederate states, except Tennessee, which had already been restored to the Union, elected delegates to these conventions. Most southern white men were Democrats. They boycotted these elections to protest Congress's assumption of authority over Reconstruction and the extension of voting privileges to black men. Thus the delegates to the conventions that met to frame new state constitutions to replace those drawn up in 1865 under President Johnson's authority were mostly Republicans joined by a few conservative southern Democrats. The Republicans represented three constituencies. One consisted of white northern migrants who moved to the South after the war. They were disparagingly called **carpetbaggers**, because they were said to have arrived in the South with all their possessions in a single carpetbag. A second group consisted of native white southerners, mostly small farmers in devastated upland regions of the South who hoped for economic relief from Republican governments. Other southern white people denigrated them as scalawags, or scoundrels. African Americans made up the third and largest Republican constituency.

These delegates produced impressive constitutions. Unlike previous state constitutions in the South, the new constitutions ensured that all adult males could vote, and except in Mississippi and Virginia, they did not disfranchise many former Confederates. They conferred broad guarantees of civil rights. In several states they provided the first statewide systems of public education. These constitutions were progressive, not radical. Black and white Republicans hoped to attract support from white southerners for the new state governments these documents created by encouraging state support for private businesses, especially railroad construction.

ELECTIONS

Elections were held in 1868 to ratify the new constitutions and elect officials. Congress required only a majority of those voting—not a majority of all registered voters—to ratify the constitutions. In each state a majority of those voting eventually voted to ratify, and in each state, black men were elected to office.

BLACK POLITICAL LEADERS

Over the next decade, 1,465 black men held political office in the South. Although black leaders individually and collectively enjoyed significant political leverage, white Republicans

Southern black men cast ballots for the first time in 1867 in the election of delegates to state constitutional conventions. The ballots were provided by the candidates or political parties, not by state or municipal officials. Most nineteenth-century elections were not by secret ballot.

dominated politics during Reconstruction. In general, the number of black officials in a state reflected the size of that state's African-American population. (see Table 13.1).

TABLE 13.1 African-American Population and Officeholding during Reconstruction in the States Subject to Congressional Reconstruction

	African-American Population in 1870	African Americans as Percentage of Total Population	Number of African-American Officeholders during Reconstruction
South Carolina	415,814	58.9	314
Mississippi	444,201	53.6	226
Louisiana	364,210	50.1	210
North Carolina	391,650	36.5	180
Alabama	475,510	47.6	167
Georgia	545,142	46.0	108
Virginia	512,841	41.8	85
Florida	91,689	48.7	58
Arkansas	122,169	25.2	46
Texas	253,475	30.9	46
Tennessee	322,331	25.6	20

Source: Eric Foner, Freedom's Lawmakers: A Directory of Black Officeholders during Reconstruction (New York: Oxford University Press, 1993), p. xiv; The Statistics of the Population of the United States, Ninth Census (1873), p. xvii.

Initially, black men chose not to run for the most important political offices because they feared their election would further alienate angry white southerners. But as white Republicans swept into office in 1868, black leaders reversed their strategy, and by 1870 black men had been elected to many key positions. Blanche K. Bruce and Hiram Revels represented Mississippi in the U.S. Senate. Beginning with Joseph Rainey in 1870 in South Carolina, fourteen black men served in the U.S. House of Representatives during Reconstruction. Six men served as lieutenant governors. During Reconstruction, 112 black state senators and 683 black representatives were elected.

Many of these men—by background, experience, and education—were well qualified. Others were not. Of the 1,465 black officeholders, at least 378 had been free before the Civil War, 933 were literate, and 195 were illiterate (we lack information about the remaining 337). Sixty-four had attended college or professional school. In fact, fourteen of the leaders had been students at Oberlin College in Ohio, which began admitting both black and female students before the Civil War.

THE ISSUES

Many, but not all, black and white Republican leaders favored increasing the authority of state governments to promote the welfare of all the state's citizens. Before the

Hiram R. Revels represented Mississippi in the U.S. Senate from February 1870 until March 1871, completing an unexpired term. He went on to serve as Mississippi's secretary of state. He was born free in Fayetteville, North Carolina, in 1822. He attended Knox College in Illinois before the Civil War. In 1874 he abandoned the Republican Party and became a Democrat. By the 1890s he had acquired a sizable plantation near Natchez.

Civil War, most southern states did not provide schools, medical care, assistance for the mentally impaired, or prisons. Such concerns—if attended to at all—were left to local communities or families.

EDUCATION AND SOCIAL WELFARE

Black leaders were eager to increase literacy and promote education among black people. Republicans created statewide systems of public education throughout the South. It was a difficult and expensive task, and the results were only a limited success. Schools had to be built, teachers employed, and textbooks provided. To pay for it, taxes were increased in states still reeling from the war.

In many rural areas, schools were not built. In other places, teachers were not paid. Some people—black and white—opposed compulsory education laws, preferring to let parents determine whether their children should attend school or work to help the family. Some black leaders favored a poll tax on voting to fund the schools. Thus, although Reconstruction leaders established a strong commitment to public education, the results they achieved were uneven.

Furthermore, white parents refused to send their children to integrated schools. Although no laws required segregation, public schools during and after Reconstruction were invariably segregated. Black parents were usually more concerned that their children should have schools to attend than whether the schools were integrated. New Orleans' schools, however, were mixed.

Reconstruction leaders also supported higher education. In 1872 Mississippi legislators took advantage of the 1862 federal Morrill Land-Grant Act, which provided states with funds for agricultural and mechanical colleges, to found the first historically black state university—Alcorn A & M College. The South Carolina legislature created a similar A & M college and attached it to the Methodist-sponsored Claflin University.

Black leaders in the state legislature compelled the University of South Carolina, which had been all white, to admit black students and hire black faculty. Many of the white students and faculty left. Several black politicians enrolled in the law and medical programs at the university.

Despite the costs, Reconstruction leaders also created the first state-supported institutions for the insane, the blind, and the deaf in much of the South. Some southern states during Reconstruction began to offer medical care and public health programs. Orphanages were established. State prisons were built. Black leaders also supported revisions to state criminal codes, the elimination of corporal punishment for many crimes, and a reduction in the number of capital crimes.

CIVIL RIGHTS

Black politicians were often the victims of racial discrimination when they tried to use public transportation and accommodations such as hotels and restaurants. Rather than provide separate arrangements for black customers, white-owned businesses simply excluded black patrons. This was true in the North as well as the South. The Civil War hero Robert Smalls, for example, was ejected from a Philadelphia streetcar in 1864. After protests, the company agreed to accept black riders. In South Carolina, Jonathan J. Wright won $1,200 in a lawsuit against a railroad after he had purchased a first-class ticket but had been forced to ride in the second-class coach.

Black leaders' determination to open public facilities to all people revealed deep divisions between themselves and white Republicans. In several southern states they introduced bills to prevent proprietors from excluding black people from restaurants, barrooms, hotels, concert halls, and auditoriums, as well as railroad coaches, streetcars, and steamboats. Many white Republicans and virtually every Democrat attacked such proposals as efforts to promote social equality and gain access for black people to places where they were not welcome. White politicians blocked these laws in most states. Only South Carolina—with a black majority in the house and many black senators—enacted such a law, but it was not effectively enforced.

ECONOMIC ISSUES

Black politicians sought to promote economic development in general and for black people in particular. For example, white landowners sometimes fired black agricultural laborers near the end of the growing season and then did not pay them. Some of these landowners were dishonest, but others were in debt and could not pay their workers. To prevent such abuses, black politicians secured laws that required laborers to be paid before the crop was sold or when it was sold.

Legislators also enacted measures that protected the land and property of small farmers against seizure for nonpayment of debts. Black and white farmers who lost land, tools, animals, and other property because they could not pay their debts were unlikely to recover financially. "Stay laws" prohibited, or "stayed," authorities from taking property. Besides protecting poor farmers, Republicans hoped these laws would also end the attachment of white yeomen for the Democratic Party.

LAND

Black leaders were unable to provide land to landless black and white farmers. Many black and white political leaders believed the state had no right to distribute land. Again, South Carolina was the exception. Its legislature created a state land commission in 1869 to purchase and distribute land to freedmen.

Although some black leaders were reluctant to use the states' power to distribute land, others had no qualms about raising property taxes so high that large landowners would be forced to sell some of their property to pay their taxes. Abraham Galloway of North Carolina explained, "I want to see the man who owns one or two thousand acres of land, taxed a dollar on the acre, and if they can't pay the taxes, sell their property to the highest bidder … and then we negroes shall become the land holders."

BUSINESS AND INDUSTRY

Black and white leaders had an easier time enacting legislation to support business and industry. Like most Americans after the Civil War, Republicans believed that expanding the railroad network would stimulate employment, improve transportation, and generate prosperity. State governments approved the sale of state-supported bonds to finance railroad construction. In Georgia, Alabama, Texas, and Arkansas, the railroad network did expand. But the bonded debt of these states soared and taxes increased to pay for it.

Frances Ellen Watkin's Sketches of Southern Life

Frances Ellen Watkins Harper (1825–1911) was born free in Baltimore, Maryland. Like Edmonia Lewis (see Chapter 7), her parents died when she was young and she was raised by relatives, in this case, her aunt and uncle. Her uncle, the Reverend William Watkins, had a profound influence on her life. An important member of Baltimore's black community and the founder of a school, Reverend Watkins instilled in Harper a passion for learning, writing, and social activism. Over the course of her life, she would publish poetry, short stories, and a novel. In 1850 Harper moved to Ohio to become the first woman to teach at the Union Seminary, a school established by the AME Church. She joined the American Anti-Slavery Society in 1853, launching a career as public speaker and political activist. Her activism did not end with the abolition of slavery after the Civil War. She continued to fight for civil rights for women and African Americans, as well as for a number of other social causes right up until her death in 1911. During Reconstruction, she toured the South, meeting newly freed blacks and observing the conditions in which they lived. The poems from her *Sketches of Southern Life* (1872) were inspired by that experience. An elderly ex-slave, Aunt Chloe, is the narrator for many of the poems, including the two included below.

Aunt Chloe's Politics

Of course, I don't know very much
    About these politics,
But I think that some who run 'em,
    Do mighty ugly tricks.

I've seen 'em honey-fugle round, And
    talk so awful sweet,
That you'd think them full of kindness,
    As an egg is full of meat.

Now I don't believe in looking
    Honest people in the face,
And saying when you're doing wrong,
    That "I haven't sold my race."

When we want to school our children,
    If the money isn't there,
Whether black or white have took it,
    The loss we all must share.

And this buying up each other
    Is something worse than mean,
Though I thinks a heap of voting,
    I go for voting clean.

Learning to Read

Very soon the Yankee teachers
    Came down and set up school;
But, oh! how the Rebs did hate it,—
    It was agin' their rule.

Our masters always tried to hide
    Book learning from our eyes;
Knowledge didn't agree with slavery—
    'Twould make us all too wise.

But some of us would try to steal
    A little from the book,
And put the words together,
    And learn by hook or crook.

I remember Uncle Caldwell,
    Who took pot liquor fat
And greased the pages of his book,
    And hid it in his hat.

And had his master ever seen
    The leaves upon his head,
He'd have thought them greasy papers,
    But nothing to be read.

And there was Mr. Turner's Ben,
    Who heard the children spell,
And picked the words right up by heart,
    And learned to read 'em well.

Well, the Northern folks kept sending
    The Yankee teachers down;
And they stood right up and helped us,
    Though Rebs did sneer and frown.

And, I longed to read my Bible,
    For precious words it said;
But when I begun to learn it,
    Folks just shook their heads,

And said there is no use trying,
    Oh! Chloe, you're too late;
But as I was rising sixty,
    I had no time to wait.

So I got a pair of glasses,
    And straight to work I went,
And never stopped till I could read
    The hymns and Testament.

Then I got a little cabin
    A place to call my own—
And I felt as independent
    As the queen upon her throne.

What are Aunt Chloe's politics? What problems in Reconstruction politics does she identify? In the poem "Learning to Read," why was literacy so important to slaves and ex-slaves? What light does "Learning to Read" shed on this subject?

Moreover, railroad financing was often corrupt. Most of the illegal money wound up in the pockets of white businessmen and politicians.

So attractive were business profits that some black political leaders formed corporations. In Charleston, 28 black leaders (and two white politicians) formed a horse-drawn streetcar line they called the Enterprise Railroad to carry freight between the city wharves and the railroad terminal. Black leaders in South Carolina also created a company to extract the phosphate used for fertilizer from riverbeds and riverbanks in the low country. Neither business lasted long. Black men found it far more difficult than white entrepreneurs to finance their corporations.

BLACK POLITICIANS: AN EVALUATION

Southern black political leaders on the state level did create the foundation for public education, for state assistance for the blind, deaf, and insane, and for reforming the criminal justice system. They tried, but mostly failed, to outlaw racial discrimination in public facilities. They encouraged state support for economic expansion.

But black leaders could not create programs that significantly improved the lives of their constituents. Because white Republicans almost always outnumbered them, they could not enact an agenda of their own. Moreover, black leaders often disagreed among themselves about issues and programs. Class and prewar status frequently divided them. Those leaders who had not been slaves and had not been raised in rural isolation were less likely to be concerned with land and agricultural labor. More prosperous black leaders showed more interest in civil rights and encouraging business.

REPUBLICAN FACTIONALISM

Disagreements among black leaders paled compared to the conflicts that divided the Republican Party during Reconstruction. Black and white Republicans often disagreed on political issues and strategy, but the lack of party cohesion and discipline was even more harmful. The Republican Party in the South constantly split into factions as groups fought with each other. Most disagreements were over who should run for and hold political office. These bitter and angry contests were based less on race and issues than on the desperate desire to gain an office that would pay even a modest salary. Most black and white Republicans were not well off. Public office assured them a modicum of economic security.

Ironically, these factional disputes led to a high turnover in political leadership and the loss of that very economic security. It was difficult for black leaders (and white leaders too) to be renominated and reelected to more than one or two terms. Few officeholders served three or four consecutive terms in the same office during Reconstruction. This made for inexperienced leadership and added to Republican woes.

OPPOSITION

Even if black and Republican leaders had been less prone to fight among themselves and more effective in adopting a political platform, they might still have failed to sustain themselves for long. Most white southerners led by conservative Democrats remained absolutely opposed to letting black men vote or hold office. For most white southerners, the only acceptable political system was one that excluded black men and the Republican Party.

White southerners were determined to rid themselves of Republicans and the disgrace of having to live with black men who possessed political rights. White southerners would "redeem" their states by restoring white Democrats to power. This meant not just defeating black and white Republicans in elections but removing them from politics entirely. White southerners believed any means—fair or foul—were justified in exorcising this evil.

THE KU KLUX KLAN

If the presence of black men in politics was illegitimate—in the eyes of white southerners—then it was acceptable to use violence to remove them. This thinking gave rise to militant terrorist organizations, such as the **Ku Klux Klan**, the Knights of the White Camellia, the White Brotherhood, and the Whitecaps. Threats, intimidation, beatings, rapes, and murder, such groups believed, would restore conservative white Democratic rule and force black people back into subordination.

The Ku Klux Klan was founded in Pulaski, Tennessee, in 1866. It was originally a social club for Confederate veterans who adopted secret oaths and rituals—similar to the Union Leagues, but with far more deadly consequences. One of the key figures in the Klanrapid growth was former Confederate General Nathan Bedford Forrest, who became its leader or grand wizard. The Klan drew its members from all classes of white society, not merely from among the poor. Businessmen, lawyers, physicians, and politicians were active in the Klan as well as farmers and planters.

The Klan and other terrorist organizations functioned mainly where black people were a large minority and where their votes could affect elections. Klansmen virtually took over areas of western Alabama, northern Georgia, and Florida's panhandle. The Klan controlled the up country of South Carolina and the area around Mecklenburg County, North Carolina. However, in the Carolina and Georgia low country where there were huge black majorities, the Klan rarely, if ever, appeared.

Often wearing hoods and masks to hide their faces, white terrorists embarked on a campaign of violence rarely matched and never exceeded in American history. Mobs of marauding terrorists beat and killed hundreds of black people—and many white people. Black churches and schools were burned. Republican leaders were routinely threatened or killed. As his wife looked on, Jack Dupree—a local Republican leader—had his throat cut and was eviscerated in Monroe County, Mississippi. In 1870 North Carolina Senator John W. Stephens, a white Republican, was murdered. After Alabama freedman George Moore voted for the Republicans in 1869, Klansmen beat him, raped a girl who was visiting his wife, and attacked a neighbor. An Irish-American teacher and four black men were lynched in Cross Plains, Alabama, in 1870. The Texas outlaw John Wesley Hardin openly acknowledged he had killed black Texas state policemen.

White men attacked a Republican campaign rally in Eutaw, Alabama, in 1870 and killed four black men and wounded 54 other people. After three black leaders were arrested in 1871 in Meridian, Mississippi, for delivering what many white people considered inflammatory speeches, shooting broke out in the courtroom. The Republican judge and two of the defendants were killed, and in a wave of violence, 30 black people were murdered, including every black leader in the small community. In the same year, a mob of 500 men broke into the jail in Union County, South Carolina, and lynched eight black prisoners accused of killing a Confederate veteran.

Nowhere was the Klan more active and violent than in York County, South Carolina. Almost the entire adult white male population joined in threatening, attacking, and murdering the black population. Hundreds were beaten and at least eleven killed. Terrified families fled into the woods. Appeals for help were sent to Governor Robert K. Scott.

But Scott did not send aid. He had already sent the South Carolina militia into areas of Klan activity, and even more violence had resulted. The militia was made up mostly of black men, and white terrorists retaliated by killing militia officers. Scott could not send white men to York County because most of them sympathized with the Klan. Thus Republican governors like Scott responded ineffectually. Republican-controlled legislatures passed anti-Klan measures that made it illegal to appear in public in disguises and masks, and they strengthened laws against assault, murder, and conspiracy. But enforcement was weak.

A few Republican leaders did deal harshly and effectively with terrorism. Governors in Tennessee, Texas, and Arkansas declared martial law and sent in hundreds of well-armed white and black men to quell the violence. Hundreds of Klansmen were arrested, many fled, and three were executed in Arkansas. But when Governor William W. Holden of North Carolina sent the state militia after the Klan, he provoked an angry reaction. Subsequent Klan violence in ten counties helped Democrats carry the 1870 legislative elections, and the legislature then removed Holden from office.

THE WEST

By 1860 Native Americans held 7,367 African Americans in slavery. Many of the Indians fought for the Confederacy during the Civil War. Following the war, the former slaves encountered nearly as much violence and hostility from Native Americans as they did from southern white people. Indians were reluctant to share their land with freedmen, and they vigorously opposed policies that favored black voting rights.

Elsewhere on the western frontier, black people struggled for legal and political rights and periodically participated in territorial governments. In the Colorado Territory, William Jefferson Hardin, a barber, campaigned with other black men for the right to vote, and in 1865 they persuaded 137 African Americans (91 percent of Colorado's black population) to petition the territorial governor to abolish a white-only voting provision. In 1867 black men in Colorado finally gained the right to vote. Hardin later moved to Cheyenne and was elected to the Wyoming territorial legislature in 1879.

THE FIFTEENTH AMENDMENT

The federal government under Republican domination tried to protect black voting rights and defend Republican state governments in the South. In 1869 Congress passed the **Fifteenth Amendment,** which was ratified in 1870. It stipulated that a person could not be deprived of the right to vote because of race. Black people, abolitionists, and reformers hailed the amendment as the culmination of the crusade to end slavery and give black people the same rights as white people.

Northern black men were the amendment's immediate beneficiaries because before its adoption, black men could vote in only eight northern states. Yet to the disappointment of many, the amendment said nothing about women voting and did not outlaw poll taxes, literacy tests, and property qualifications that could disfranchise citizens.

THE ENFORCEMENT ACTS

In direct response to the terrorism in the South, Congress passed the **Enforcement Acts** in 1870 and 1871, and the federal government expanded its authority over the states. The 1870 act outlawed disguises and masks and protected the civil rights of citizens. The 1871 act—known as the Ku Klux Klan Act—made it a federal offense to interfere with a person's right to vote, hold office, serve on a jury, or enjoy equal protection of the law. Those accused of violating the act would be tried in federal court. For extreme violence, the act authorized the president to send in federal troops and suspend the writ of **habeas corpus.** (Habeas corpus is the right to be brought before a judge and not be arrested and jailed without cause.)

Armed with this new legislation, the Justice Department and Attorney General Amos T. Ackerman moved vigorously against the Klan. Hundreds of Klansmen were arrested—700 in Mississippi alone. Faced with a full-scale rebellion in late 1871 in South Carolina's up country, President Ulysses S. Grant declared martial law in nine counties, suspended the writ of habeas corpus, and sent in the army. Mass arrests and trials followed, but federal authorities permitted many Klansmen to confess and thereby escape prosecution. The government lacked the human and financial resources to bring hundreds of men to court for lengthy trials. Some white men were tried, mostly before black juries, and were imprisoned or fined. Comparatively few Klansmen, however, were punished severely, especially considering the enormity of their crimes.

THE NORTH AND RECONSTRUCTION

Although the federal government did reduce Klan violence for a time, white southerners remained convinced that white supremacy must be restored and Republican governments overturned. Klan violence did not overthrow any state governments, but it undermined freedmen's confidence in the ability of these governments to protect them. Meanwhile, radical Republicans in Congress grew frustrated that the South and especially black people continued to demand so much of their time and attention year after year. There was less and less sentiment in the North to continue support for the freedmen and involvement in southern affairs.

Many northern Republicans lost interest in civil rights issues and principles and became more concerned with winning elections and the economy. By the mid-1870s there was more discussion in Congress of patronage, veterans' pensions, railroads, taxes, tariffs, the economy, and monetary policy than about rights for black people or the future of the South.

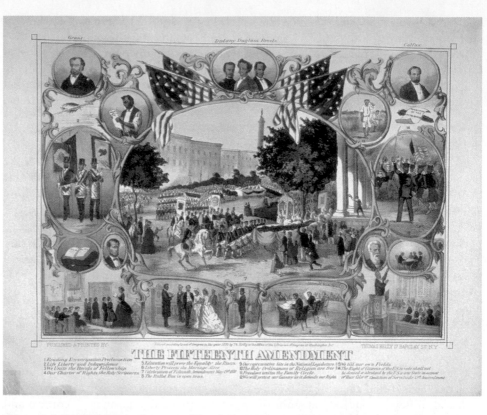

This optimistic 1870 illustration exemplifies the hopes and aspirations generated during Reconstruction as black people gained access to the political system. Invoking the legacy of Abraham Lincoln and John Brown, it suggests that African Americans would soon assume their rightful and equitable role in American society.

The American political system was also awash in corruption by the 1870s, which futher detracted from concerns over the South. Although President Grant was a man of integrity, many men in his administration were not. They were implicated in scandals involving the construction of the transcontinental railroad, federal taxes on whiskey, and fraud within the Bureau of Indian Affairs. Nor was the dishonesty limited to Republicans. William Marcy "Boss" Tweed and the Democratic machine that dominated New York City were notoriously corrupt.

Many Republicans began to question the necessity for more moral, military, and political support for African Americans. They were convinced that African Americans had demanded too much for too long from the national government. Former slaves had become citizens and had the right to vote and hold political office. Therefore, they did not need additional help or legislation from the federal government. Equality for black people would come from their labor as free men, which would produce wealth and acceptance by white people. Federal legislation, many northern white people believed, could not create equality.

Other northern white people, swayed by white southerners' views of black people, began to doubt the wisdom of universal manhood suffrage. Many white people who had nominally supported black suffrage began to believe the exaggerated complaints about corruption among black leaders and the unrelenting claims that freedmen were incapable of self-government. Some white northerners began to conclude that Reconstruction had been a mistake.

Economic conditions contributed to changing attitudes. A financial crisis—the Panic of 1873—sent the economy into a long slump. Businesses and financial institutions failed, unemployment soared, and prices fell. In 1874 the Democrats recaptured a majority in the House of Representatives for the first time since 1860 and also took control of several northern states.

THE FREEDMEN'S BANK

One of the casualties of the financial crisis was the **Freedmen's Savings Bank,** which failed in 1874. Founded in 1865 when hope flourished, the Freedmen's Savings and Trust Company had been chartered by Congress but was not connected to the Freedmen's Bureau. Freedmen and black veterans, churches, fraternal organizations, and benevolent societies opened thousands of accounts in the bank. Most of the deposits totaled under $50, and some amounted to only a few cents.

Although the bank had many black employees, its board of directors consisted of white men. They invested the bank's funds in risky ventures, including Washington, D.C., real estate. With the Panic of 1873, the bank lost large sums in unsecured railroad loans. To restore confidence, its directors persuaded Frederick Douglass to serve as president and invest $10,000 of his own money to help shore up the bank. Douglass lost his money, and African Americans across the South lost more than $1 million when the bank closed in June 1874.

THE CIVIL RIGHTS ACT OF 1875

Before Reconstruction expired, Congress made one final—some said futile—gesture to protect black people from racial discrimination when it passed the **Civil Rights Act of 1875.** Championed by Senator Charles Sumner of Massachusetts, it was originally intended to open public accommodations including schools, churches, cemeteries, hotels, and transportation to all people regardless of race. It passed in the Republican-controlled Senate in 1874. But House Democrats held up passage. It was not enacted until 1875 and then largely as a memorial to Sumner, who had died in 1874. In its final form, the bans on discrimination in churches, cemeteries, and schools were deleted.

After its passage, no attempt was made at enforcement, and in 1883 the Supreme Court declared it unconstitutional. Justice Joseph Bradley wrote that the Fourteenth Amendment protected black people from discrimination by states but not by private businesses. Black newspapers likened the decision to the *Dred Scott* case a quarter century earlier.

THE END OF RECONSTRUCTION

Reconstruction ended as it began—in violence and controversy. Democrats demanded **"redemption"**—a word with biblical and spiritual overtones. They wanted southern states restored to conservative, white political control. By 1875 they had regained authority

VOICES

BLACK LEADERS SUPPORT THE PASSAGE OF A CIVIL RIGHTS ACT

*B*lack *Congressmen Robert Brown Elliott of South Carolina and James T. Rapier of Alabama spoke passionately in favor of the Sumner civil rights bill in 1874. Both men had been free before the war. Both were also, lawyers, and although each accumulated considerable wealth, they died in poverty in the 1880s.*

[James T. Rapier]

I must confess it is somewhat embarrassing for a colored man to urge the passage of this bill, because if he exhibit an earnestness in the matter and expresses a desire for its immediate passage, straightaway he is charged with a desire for social equality, as explained by the demagogue and understood by the ignorant white man. But then it is just as embarrassing for him not to do so, for, if he remains silent while the struggle is being carried on around, and for him, he is liable to be charged with a want of interest in a matter that concerns him more than anyone else, which is enough to make his friends desert his cause. So in steering away from Scylla I may run upon Charybdis. But the anomalous, and I may add the supremely ridiculous, position of the Negro at this time, in this country, compel me to say something. Here his condition is without comparison, parallel alone to itself. Just that the law recognizes my right upon this floor as a law-maker, but that there is no law to secure to me any accommodations whatever while traveling here to discharge my duties as a Representative of a large and wealthy constituency. Here I am the peer of the proudest, but on a steamboat or car I am not equal to the most degraded. Is not this most anomalous and ridiculous?

[Robert Brown Elliott]

The results of the war, as seen in Reconstruction, have settled forever the political status of my race. The passage of this bill will determine the civil status, not only of the Negro but of any other class of citizens who may feel themselves discriminated against. It will form the capstone of that temple of liberty begun on this continent under discouraging circumstances, carried on in spite of the sneers of monarchists and the cavils of pretended friends of freedom, until at last it stands in all its beautiful symmetry and proportions, a building the grandest which the world has ever seen, realizing the most sanguine expectations and the highest hopes of those who in the name of equal, impartial and universal liberty, laid the foundation stone.

■ If black men had the right to vote and serve in Congress, why was a civil rights law needed?

■ Who would benefit most from the passage of this bill?

■ What distinction do the two congressmen draw between social discrimination and political rights?

SOURCES: *Congressional Record*, vol. II, part 1, 43d Congress, 1st session, pp. 565–67; Peggy Lamson, *The Glorious Failure* (New York: Norton, 1973), p. 181.

in all the former Confederate states except Mississippi, Florida, Louisiana, and South Carolina (see Map 13-1). Democrats had redeemed Tennessee in 1870 and Georgia in 1871. Democrats had learned two lessons. First, few black men would vote for the Democratic Party. Second, intimidation and violence would win elections in areas where the number of black and white voters was nearly equal.

VIOLENT REDEMPTION

In Alabama in 1874, black and white Republican leaders were murdered, and white mobs destroyed crops and homes. On election day in Eufaula, white men killed seven and injured nearly 70 unarmed black voters. Black voters were also driven from the polls in Mobile. Democrats won the election and "redeemed" Alabama.

White violence marred every election in Louisiana from 1868 to 1876. After Republicans and Democrats each claimed victory in the 1872 elections, black people seized the small town of Colfax along the Red River to protect themselves against a Democratic takeover. They held out for three weeks. Then on Easter Sunday in 1873, a well-armed white mob attacked the black defenders. At least 105 were killed in the Colfax Massacre, the worst single day of bloodshed during Reconstruction. In 1874 the White League almost redeemed Louisiana in a wave of violence. Black people were murdered, courts were attacked, and white people refused to pay taxes to

On January 6, 1874, Robert Brown Elliott delivered a ringing speech in the U.S. House of Representatives in support of the Sumner civil rights bill. Elliott was responding in part to words uttered the day before by Virginia congressman John T. Harris, who claimed that "there is not a gentleman on this floor who can honestly say he really believes that the colored man is created his equal." P.S. Duval and Son, Come and join us brothers; Civil War; Philadelphia, PA; ca. 1863. Chicago Historical Society ICHi-22051

MAP 13-1 • Dates of Readmission of Southern States to the Union and Reestablishment of Democratic Party Control Once conservative white Democrats regained political control of a state government from black and white Republicans, they considered that state "redeemed." The first states the Democrats "redeemed" were Georgia, Virginia, and North Carolina. Louisiana, Florida, and South Carolina were the last. (Tennessee was not included in the Reconstruction process under the terms of the 1867 Reconstruction Act.)

▶ *In which states did black and white Republicans hold political control for the shortest and longest periods of time?*

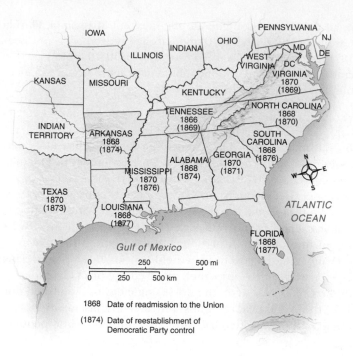

1868 Date of readmission to the Union

(1874) Date of reestablishment of Democratic Party control

the Republican state government. In September, President Grant finally sent federal troops to New Orleans after 3,500 White Leaguers nearly wiped out the black militia and the Metropolitan Police. But the stage had been set for the 1876 campaign.

THE SHOTGUN POLICY

In 1875 white Mississippians, no longer afraid the national government would intervene in force, declared open warfare on the black majority. The masks and hoods of the Klan were discarded. One newspaper proclaimed that Democrats would carry the election, "peaceably if we can, forcibly if we must."

White Mississippi unleashed a campaign of violence known as the **"shotgun policy"** that was extreme even for Reconstruction. Many Republicans fled and others were murdered. In late 1874 an estimated 300 black people were hunted down outside Vicksburg after black men armed with inferior weapons had lost a "battle" with white men. In 1875, 30 teachers, church leaders, and Republican officials were killed in Clinton.

Governor Adelbert Ames appealed for federal intervention, but President Grant refused. The terrorism intensified, and many black voters went into hiding on election day, afraid for their lives and those of their families. Democrats redeemed Mississippi and prided themselves that they—a superior race representing the most civilized of all people—were back in control.

In Florida in 1876, white Republicans noted that support for black people in the South was fading. They nominated an all-white Republican slate and even refused to renominate black congressman Josiah Walls.

THE HAMBURG MASSACRE

South Carolina Democrats were divided between moderate and extreme factions, but they united to nominate former Confederate General Wade Hampton for governor after the **Hamburg Massacre**. The prelude to this event occurred on July 4, 1876—the nation's centennial—when two white men in a buggy confronted the black militia that was drilling on a town street in Hamburg, a small, mostly black town. Hot words were exchanged, and days later, Democrats demanded the militia be disarmed. White rifle club members from around the state arrived in Hamburg and attacked the armory, where 40 black members of the militia defended themselves. The rifle companies brought up a cannon and reinforcements from Georgia. After the militia ran low on ammunition, white men captured the armory. One white man was killed, 29 black men were taken prisoner, and the other eleven fled. Five of the black men identified as leaders were shot down in cold blood. The rifle companies wrecked the town. Seven white men were indicted for murder. All were acquitted.

The Hamburg Massacre incited South Carolina Democrats to imitate Mississippi's "shotgun policy." It also forced a reluctant President Grant to send federal troops to South Carolina. Democrats attacked, beat, and killed black people to prevent them from voting.

As the election approached, black people in the up country of South Carolina knew it would be dangerous if they tried to vote. But in the low country, black people went on the offensive and attacked Democrats. In Charleston, a white man was killed in a racial melee. At a campaign rally at Cainhoy, a few miles outside Charleston, armed black men killed five white men.

A few black men supported Wade Hampton, South Carolina's Democratic candidate for governor. Hampton had a paternalistic view of black people and, although he considered them inferior, he promised to respect their rights. Black leader Martin Delany believed Hampton and the Democrats were more trustworthy than unreliable Republicans. Delany campaigned for Hampton and was later rewarded with an appointment to a minor political post. A few conservative black men during Reconstruction also supported the Democrats and curried their favor and patronage.

THE "COMPROMISE" OF 1877

Threats, violence, and bloodshed accompanied the elections of 1876 in the South, but the national results were confusing and contradictory. Samuel Tilden, the Democratic presidential candidate, won the popular vote by more than 250,000 and had a large lead – 185 to 167 – over Republican Rutherford B. Hayes in the electoral vote. The 20 remaining electoral votes were in dispute. Both Democrats and Republicans claimed to have won in Florida, Louisiana, and South Carolina, the last three southern states that had not been redeemed. (There was also one contested vote from Oregon.) Whoever took the 20 electoral votes of the three contested states (and Oregon) would be the next president (see Map 13-2).

The constitutional crisis over the outcome of the 1876 election was not resolved until shortly before Inauguration Day in March 1877. An informal understanding known as the **Compromise of 1877** ended the dispute. Democrats accepted a Hayes victory, but Hayes let southern Democrats know he would not support Republican governments in Florida, Louisiana, and South Carolina. In 1877 Hayes withdrew the last federal troops from the South, and the Republican administration in those states collapsed. Democrats immediately took control.

MAP 13-2 • The Election of 1876

Although Democrat Samuel Tilden appeared to have won the election of 1876, Rutherford B. Hayes and the Republicans were able to claim victory after a prolonged political and constitutional controversy involving the disputed electoral college votes from Louisiana, Florida, and South Carolina (and one from Oregon). In an informal settlement in 1877, Democrats agreed to accept electoral votes for Hayes from those states, and Republicans agreed to permit those states to be "redeemed" by the Democrats. The result was to leave the entire South under the political control of conservative white Democrats. For the first time since 1867, black and white Republicans no longer effectively controlled any former Confederate state.

▶ *What factors explain the loss of political power by southern Republicans?*

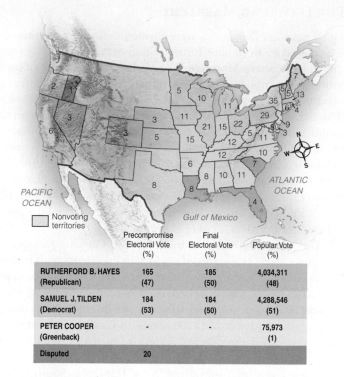

	Precompromise Electoral Vote (%)	Final Electoral Vote (%)	Popular Vote (%)
RUTHERFORD B. HAYES (Republican)	165 (47)	185 (50)	4,034,311 (48)
SAMUEL J. TILDEN (Democrat)	184 (53)	184 (50)	4,288,546 (51)
PETER COOPER (Greenback)	-	-	75,973 (1)
Disputed	20		

CONCLUSION

The glorious hopes that emancipation and the Union victory in the Civil War had aroused among African Americans in 1865 appeared forlorn by 1877. To be sure, black people were no longer slave laborers or property. They lived in tightly knit families that white people no longer controlled. They had established hundreds of schools, churches, and benevolent societies. The Constitution now endowed them with freedom, citizenship, and the right to vote. Some black people had even acquired land.

But no one can characterize Reconstruction as a success. The epidemic of terror and violence made it one of the bloodiest eras in American history. Thousands of black people had been beaten, raped, and murdered since 1865, simply because they had acted as free people. Too many white people were determined that black people could not and would not have the same rights that white people enjoyed. White southerners would not tolerate either the presence of black men in politics or white Republicans who accepted black political involvement. Most white northerners and even radical Republicans grew weary of intervening in southern affairs and became convinced again that black men and women were their inferiors and were not prepared to participate in government. Reconstruction, they concluded, had been a mistake.

Furthermore, black and white Republicans hurt themselves by indulging in fraud and corruption and by engaging in angry and divisive factionalism. But even if Republicans had been honest and united, white southern Democrats would never have accepted black people as worthy to participate in the political system.

Southern Democrats would accept black people in politics only if Democrats could control black voters. But black voters understood this, rejected control by former slave owners, and were loyal to the Republican Party—as flawed as it was.

But as grim a turn as life may have taken for black people by 1877, it would get even worse in the decades that followed.

African-American Events	National Events
1865	**1865**
The Freedmen's Savings Bank and Trust Company is established	Freedmen's Bureau established
	1866
	President Johnson vetoes Freedmen's Bureau and civil rights bills; Congress overrides both vetoes
	Ku Klux Klan founded in Pulaski, Tennessee

1867

African-American Events	National Events
1867–1868	**1867**
Ten southern states hold constitutional conventions	Congress takes over Reconstruction and provides for universal manhood suffrage
1867	**1868**
Howard University established in Washington, D.C.	Fourteenth Amendment to the Constitution ratified
	Ulysses S. Grant elected president
1868	
Black political leaders elected to state and local offices across the South	

1869

African-American Events	National Events
1870	**1869**
Hiram R. Revels elected to the U.S. Senate and Joseph H. Rainey to the U.S. House of Representatives	Knights of Labor founded in Philadelphia
	1870
Congress passes the Enforcement Act	Fifteenth Amendment to the Constitution ratified
	John D. Rockefeller incorporates Standard Oil Co. in Cleveland

African-American Events	National Events
1871	**1871**
Congress passes the Ku Klux Klan Act	William Marcy "Boss" Tweed indicted for fraud in New York City
	Chicago Fire
	1872
	President Grant reelected
	Yellowstone National Park established

1873

1873	**1873**
The Colfax Massacre occurs in Louisiana	Financial panic and economic depression begin

1875

1875	**1875**
Blanche K. Bruce elected to the U.S. Senate	Whiskey Ring exposes corruption in federal liquor tax collections
Congress passes the Civil Rights Act of 1875	
Democrats redeem Mississippi with the "shotgun policy"	
1876	**1876**
Hamburg Massacre occurs in South Carolina	Disputed presidential election between Samuel J. Tilden and Rutherford B. Hayes
	Gen. George A. Custer and U.S. troops defeated by Sioux and Cheyenne in Battle of Little Big Horn

1877

1877	**1877**
Last federal troops withdrawn from South	"Compromise of 1877" ends Reconstruction

REVIEW QUESTIONS

1. What issues most concerned black political leaders during Reconstruction?

2. What did black political leaders accomplish and fail to accomplish during Reconstruction? What contributed to their successes and failures?

3. Were black political leaders unqualified to hold office so soon after the end of slavery?

4. To what extent did African Americans dominate southern politics during Reconstruction? Should we refer to this era as "Black Reconstruction"?

5. Why was it so difficult for the Republican Party to maintain control of southern state governments during Reconstruction?

6. What was "redemption"? What happened when redemption occurred? What factors contributed to redemption?

7. How did Reconstruction end?

8. How effective was Reconstruction in assisting black people to make the transition from slavery to freedom? How effective was it in restoring the southern states to the Union?

myhistorylab CONNECTIONS

Reinforce what you learned in this chapter by studying the many documents, images, maps, review tools, and videos available at **www.myhistorylab.com**.

READ AND REVIEW

✓•⌐**Study** and **Review** on **myhistorylab.com** STUDY PLAN FOR CHAPTER 13

▢•⌐**Read** the **Document** on **myhistorylab.com**

Blanche K. Bruce, Speech in the Senate (1876)

Diary of Joseph Addison Waddell (1865)

Hannah Irwin Describes Ku Klux Klan Ride (Late 1860s)

James T. Rapier, Testimony before U.S. Senate Regarding the Agricultural Labor Force in the South (1880)

Organization and Principles of the Ku Klux Klan (1868)

The New Slavery in the South - An Autobiography (1904)

The Victims of the Ku Klux Klan (1935)

Thirteenth, Fourteenth, and Fifteenth Amendments

⌐**View** the **Map** on **myhistorylab.com**

Dates of Readmission of Southern States to the Union and Reestablishment of Democratic Party Control

RESEARCH AND EXPLORE

mysearchlab

Consider this question in a short research paper.

Why did so many whites in the North lose interest in the situation of blacks in the South?

📖● **Read** the **Document** on **myhistorylab.com**

Exploring America: Did Reconstruction Work for the Freed People?

👁● **Watch** the **Video** on **myhistorylab.com**

The Promise and Failure of Reconstruction

——————— (((●● **Listen** on **myhistorylab.com** ———————

Hear the audio files for Chapter 13 at

www.myhistorylab.com.

EPILOGUE

A Nation within a Nation

Since the first Africans were brought to these shores in the seventeenth century, black people have been a constant and distinct presence in America. During the prolonged course of the Atlantic slave trade, approximately 600,000 Africans were sold into servitude in what became the United States. By the outbreak of the Civil War in 1861 there were nearly four million African Americans in this country. Today black people number over 30 million and make up slightly over 10 percent of the nation's population.

Initially regarded merely as an enslaved labor force to produce cash crops and not as a people who would or could enjoy an equal role in the political and social affairs of American society, African Americans constituted a separate ethnic, racial, and cultural group. For more than two centuries they remained outcasts.

People of African descent developed decidedly ambivalent relationships with the white majority in America. Never fully accepted and never fully rejected, black people relied on their own resources as they created their own institutions and communities. In 1852 Martin Delany declared, "We are a nation within a nation." A half century later W. E. B. Du Bois observed that the black man wanted to retain his African identity and to be an American as well. "He would not Africanize America, for America has too much to teach the world and Africa. He would not bleach his Negro soul in a flood of white Americanism, for he knows that Negro blood has a message for the world. He simply wishes to make it possible for a man to be both a Negro and an American, without being cursed and spit upon by his fellows, without having the doors of Opportunity closed roughly in his face."

Sometimes in desperation or disgust, some black people have been willing to abandon America or reject assimilation. The slaves who engaged in South Carolina's 1739 Stono rebellion attempted to reach Spanish Florida. As early as 1773, slaves in Massachusetts pledged to go to Africa after emancipation. From the 1790s to the start of the Civil War, visions of nationhood in Africa attracted a minority of African Americans. During the 1920s, Marcus Garvey and the Universal Negro Improvement Association glorified Africa while seeking black autonomy in the United States. By the 1950s, Elijah Muhammad, Malcolm X, and the Nation of Islam attracted black people by emphasizing a separate black destiny.

Yet in spite of the horrors of slavery, the indignity and cruelty of Jim Crow, and the unrelenting violence and discrimination inflicted on people of color, most African Americans have not rejected America but worked and struggled to participate fully in the American way of life. African slaves accepted elements of Christianity, and their descendants found solace in their spiritual beliefs. Black Americans have embraced American principles of brotherhood, justice, fairness, and equality before the law that are embedded in the Declaration of Independence and the Constitution. Again and again, African Americans have insisted that America be America, that the American majority live up to its professed ideals and values.

The nation within a nation has never been homogeneous. There have been persistent class, gender, and color divisions. There have been tensions and ideological conflicts among black leaders and organizations as they sought strategies to overcome racial inequities and white supremacy. Some leaders, such as Booker T. Washington, have emphasized self-reliance and economic advancement, while others, including W. E. B. Du Bois and leaders of the NAACP, have advocated full inclusion in the nation's political, economic, and social fabric.

Furthermore, African Americans have been far more than victims, than an exploited labor force, than the subjects of segregation and stereotypes. They have contributed enormously to the development and character of American society and culture. As slaves, they provided billions of hours of unrequited labor to the American economy. Black people established churches, schools, and colleges that continue to thrive. Black people demonstrated a willingness to fight and die for a country that did not fully accept or appreciate their sacrifices. African Americans have made remarkable and innovative contributions to art, music, folklore, science, politics, and athletics that have shaped and enriched American society.

America is no longer what it was in 1700, 1800, or 1900. Chattel slavery ended in 1865. White supremacy is no longer fashionable or openly acceptable. Legal segregation was prohibited a generation ago. The capacity and willingness of Americans of diverse backgrounds and origins to live together in harmony has vastly improved in recent decades. Although we are now in the twenty-first century, the long odyssey of American people of African descent has not ended, nor will it end in the immediate future. The persistence of urban and rural poverty and the disorganized response of public officials to Hurricane Katrina's destruction of New Orleans remind us of that.

While African Americans have been and remain "a nation within a nation," the election of Barack Obama in 2008 represents a remarkable milestone in their odyssey. Michelle Obama gives her husband's presidency an even deeper meaning. She is America's first black first lady, a fact that possesses enormous ramifications for African-American women and for women of color across the globe who have long struggled for recognition, justice, and respect. Now, with African Americans occupying the White House, black people will—as never before—help mold and shape the United States as a nation and a society.

Perhaps a clergyman who had been born a slave and experienced emancipation and the joy of freedom summed it up best 140 years ago when he perceptively observed: "Lord, we ain't what we want to be; we ain't what we ought to be; we ain't what we gonna be, but, thank God, we ain't what we was."

APPENDIX

The Declaration of Independence

When in the course of human events it becomes necessary for one people to dissolve the political bands which have connected them with another and to assume, among the powers of the earth, the separate and equal station to which the laws of nature and of nature's God entitle them, a decent respect to the opinions of mankind requires that they should declare the causes which impel them to the separation.

We hold these truths to be self-evident, that all men are created equal; that they are endowed by their Creator with certain unalienable rights; that among these are life, liberty, and the pursuit of happiness. That, to secure these rights, governments are instituted among men, deriving their just powers from the consent of the governed; that, whenever any form of government becomes destructive of these ends, it is the right of the people to alter or to abolish it, and to institute a new government, laying its foundation on such principles, and organizing its powers in such form, as to them shall seem most likely to effect their safety and happiness. Prudence, indeed, will dictate that governments long established should not be changed for light and transient causes; and, accordingly, all experience hath shown that mankind are more disposed to suffer, while evils are sufferable, than to right themselves by abolishing the forms to which they are accustomed. But when a long train of abuses and usurpations, pursuing invariably the same object, evinces a design to reduce them under absolute despotism, it is their right, it is their duty, to throw off such government and to provide new guards for their future security. Such has been the patient sufferance of these colonies, and such is now the necessity which constrains them to alter their former systems of government. The history of the present King of Great Britain is a history of repeated injuries and usurpations, all having, in direct object, the establishment of an absolute tyranny over these States. To prove this, let facts be submitted to a candid world:

He has refused his assent to laws the most wholesome and necessary for the public good.

He has forbidden his governors to pass laws of immediate and pressing importance, unless suspended in their operation till his assent should be obtained; and, when so suspended, he has utterly neglected to attend to them.

He has refused to pass other laws for the accommodation of large districts of people, unless those people would relinquish the right of representation in the legislature, a right inestimable to them and formidable to tyrants only.

He has called together legislative bodies at places unusual, uncomfortable, and distant from the depository of their public records, for the sole purpose of fatiguing them into compliance with his measures.

He has dissolved representative houses, repeatedly for opposing, with manly firmness, his invasions on the rights of the people.

He has refused, for a long time after such dissolutions, to cause others to be elected; whereby the legislative powers, incapable of annihilation, have returned to the people at large for their exercise; the state remaining, in the meantime, exposed to all the danger of invasion from without and convulsions within.

He has endeavored to prevent the population of these States; for that purpose, obstructing the laws for naturalization of foreigners, refusing to pass others to encourage their migration hither, and raising the conditions of new appropriations of lands.

He has obstructed the administration of justice by refusing his assent to laws for establishing judiciary powers.

He has made judges dependent on his will alone for the tenure of their offices and the amount and payment of their salaries.

He has erected a multitude of new offices and sent hither swarms of officers to harass our people and eat out their substance.

He has kept among us, in time of peace, standing armies, without the consent of our legislatures.

He has affected to render the military independent of, and superior to, the civil power.

He has combined with others to subject us to a jurisdiction foreign to our Constitution and unacknowledged by our laws, giving his assent to their acts of pretended legislation—

For quartering large bodies of armed troops among us;

For protecting them by mock trial, from punishment for any murders which they should commit on the inhabitants of these States;

For cutting off our trade with all parts of the world;

For imposing taxes on us without our consent;

For depriving us, in many cases, of the benefit of trial by jury;

For transporting us beyond seas to be tried for pretended offences;

For abolishing the free system of English laws in a neighboring province, establishing therein an arbitrary government, and enlarging its boundaries, so as to render it at once an example and fit instrument for introducing the same absolute rule into these colonies;

For taking away our charters, abolishing our most valuable laws, and altering, fundamentally, the powers of our governments.

For suspending our own legislatures and declaring themselves invested with power to legislate for us in all cases whatsoever.

He has abdicated government here by declaring us out of his protection and waging war against us.

He has plundered our seas, ravaged our coasts, burnt our towns, and destroyed the lives of our people.

He is, at this time, transporting large armies of foreign mercenaries to complete the works of death, desolation, and tyranny already begun with circumstances of cruelty and perfidy scarcely paralleled in the most barbarous ages, and totally unworthy the head of a civilized nation.

He has constrained our fellow citizens, taken captive on the high seas, to bear arms against their country, to become the executioners of their friends and brethren, or to fall themselves by their hands.

He has excited domestic insurrections amongst us and has endeavored to bring on the inhabitants of our frontiers, the merciless Indian savages, whose known rule of warfare is an undistinguished destruction of all ages, sexes, and conditions.

In every stage of these oppressions, we have petitioned for redress in the most humble terms; our repeated petitions have been answered only by repeated injury. A prince whose character is thus marked by every act which may define a tyrant is unfit to be the ruler of a free people.

Nor have we been wanting in attention to our British brethren. We have warned them, from time to time, of attempts made by their legislature to extend an unwarrantable jurisdiction over us. We have reminded them of the circumstances of our emigration and settlement here. We have appealed to their native justice and magnanimity, and we have conjured them, by the ties of our common kindred, to disavow these usurpations, which would inevitably interrupt our connections and correspondence. They, too, have been deaf to the voice of justice and consanguinity. We must, therefore, acquiesce in the necessity which denounces our separation, and hold them, as we hold the rest of mankind, enemies in war, in peace, friends.

We, therefore, the representatives of the United States of America, in general Congress assembled, appealing to the Supreme Judge of the world for the rectitude of our intentions, do, in the name and by the authority of the good people of these colonies, solemnly publish and declare, that these united colonies are, and of right ought to be, free and independent states: that they are absolved from all allegiance to the British Crown, and that all political connection between them and the state of Great Britain is, and ought to be, totally dissolved; and that, as free and independent states, they have full power to levy war, conclude peace, contract alliances, establish commerce, and to do all other acts and things which independent states may of right do. And, for the support of this declaration, with a firm reliance on the protection of Divine Providence, we mutually pledge to each other our lives, our fortunes, and our sacred honor.

The Constitution of the United States of America

(with clauses pertaining to the status of African Americans highlighted)

We the people of the United States, in order to form a more perfect union, establish justice, insure domestic tranquillity, provide for the common defense, promote the general welfare, and secure the blessings of liberty to ourselves and our posterity, do ordain and establish this Constitution for the United States of America.

ARTICLE I

SECTION 1. All legislative powers herein granted shall be vested in a Congress of the United States, which shall consist of a Senate and House of Representatives.

SECTION 2. 1. The House of Representatives shall be composed of members chosen every second year by the people of the several States, and the electors in each State shall have the qualifications requisite for electors of the most numerous branch of the State legislature.

2. No person shall be a representative who shall not have attained to the age of twenty-five years, and been seven years a citizen of the United States, and who shall not, when elected, be an inhabitant of that State in which he shall be chosen.

3. Representatives and direct taxes[1] shall be apportioned among the several States which may be included within this Union, according to their respective numbers, which shall be determined by adding to the whole number of free persons, including those bound to service for a term of years, and excluding Indians not taxed, three fifths of all other persons.[2] The actual enumeration shall be made within three years after the first meeting of the Congress of the United States, and within every subsequent term of ten years, in such manner as they shall by law direct. The number of representatives shall not exceed one for every thirty thousand, but each State shall have at least one representative; and until such enumeration shall be made, the State of New Hampshire shall be entitled to choose three, Massachusetts eight, Rhode Island and Providence Plantations one, Connecticut five, New York six, New Jersey four, Pennsylvania eight, Delaware one, Maryland six, Virginia ten, North Carolina five, South Carolina five, and Georgia three.

4. When vacancies happen in the representation from any State, the executive authority thereof shall issue writs of election to fill such vacancies.

5. The House of Representatives shall choose their speaker and other officers; and shall have the sole power of impeachment.

SECTION 3. 1. The Senate of the United States shall be composed of two senators from each State, chosen by the legislature

[1]See the Sixteenth Amendment.

[2]See the Fourteenth Amendment.

thereof,[3] for six years; and each senator shall have one vote.

2. Immediately after they shall be assembled in consequence of the first election, they shall be divided as equally as may be into three classes. The seats of the senators of the first class shall be vacated at the expiration of the second year, of the second class at the expiration of the fourth year, and of the third class at the expiration of the sixth year, so that one third may be chosen every second year; and if vacancies happen by resignation, or otherwise, during the recess of the legislature of any State, the executive thereof may make temporary appointments until the next meeting of the legislature, which shall then fill such vacancies.[4]

3. No person shall be a senator who shall not have attained to the age of thirty years, and been nine years a citizen of the United States, and who shall not, when elected, be an inhabitant of that State for which he shall be chosen.

4. The Vice President of the United States shall be President of the Senate, but shall have no vote, unless they be equally divided.

5. The Senate shall choose their other officers, and also a president pro tempore, in the absence of the Vice President, or when he shall exercise the office of the President of the United States.

6. The Senate shall have the sole power to try all impeachments. When sitting for that purpose, they shall be on oath or affirmation. When the President of the United States is tried, the chief justice shall preside: and no person shall be convicted without the concurrence of two thirds of the members present.

7. Judgment in cases of impeachment shall not extend further than to removal from office, and disqualification to hold and enjoy any office of honor, trust or profit under the United States: but the party convicted shall nevertheless be liable and subject to indictment, trial, judgment and punishment, according to law.

SECTION 4. 1. The times, places, and manner of holding elections for senators and representatives, shall be prescribed in each State by the legislature thereof; but the Congress may at any time by law make or alter such regulations, except as to the places of choosing senators.

2. The Congress shall assemble at least once in every year, and such meeting shall be on the first Monday in December, unless they shall by law appoint a different day.

SECTION 5. 1. Each House shall be the judge of the elections, returns and qualifications of its own members, and a majority of each shall constitute a quorum to do business; but a smaller number may adjourn from day to day, and may be authorized to compel the attendance of absent members, in such manner, and under such penalties as each House may provide.

2. Each House may determine the rules of its proceedings, punish its members for disorderly behavior, and, with the concurrence of two thirds, expel a member.

3. Each House shall keep a journal of its proceedings, and from time to time publish the same, excepting such parts as may in their judgment require secrecy; and the yeas and nays of the members of either House on any question shall, at the desire of one fifth of those present, be entered on the journal.

4. Neither House, during the session of Congress, shall, without the consent of the other, adjourn for more than three days, nor to any other place than that in which the two Houses shall be sitting.

SECTION 6. 1. The senators and representatives shall receive a compensation for their services, to be ascertained by law, and paid out of the Treasury of the United States. They shall in all cases, except treason, felony, and breach of the peace, be privileged from arrest during their attendance at the session of their respective Houses, and in going to and returning from the same; and for any speech or debate in either House, they shall not be questioned in any other place.

2. No senator or representative shall, during the time for which he was elected, be appointed to any civil office under the authority of the United States, which shall have been created, or the emoluments whereof

[3]See the Seventeenth Amendment.
[4]See the Seventeenth Amendment.

shall have been increased, during such time; and no person holding any office under the United States shall be a member of either House during his continuance in office.

SECTION 7. 1. All bills for raising revenue shall originate in the House of Representatives; but the Senate may propose or concur with amendments as on other bills.

2. Every bill which shall have passed the House of Representatives and the Senate, shall, before it become a law, be presented to the President of the United States; If he approves he shall sign it, but if not he shall return it, with his objections, to that House in which it shall have originated, who shall enter the objections at large on their journal, and proceed to reconsider it. If after such reconsideration two thirds of that House shall agree to pass the bill, it shall be sent, together with the objections, to the other House, by which it shall likewise be reconsidered, and if approved by two thirds of that House, it shall become a law. But in all such cases the votes of both Houses shall be determined by yeas and nays, and the names of the persons voting for and against the bill shall be entered on the journal of each House respectively. If any bill shall not be returned by the President within ten days (Sundays excepted) after it shall have been presented to him, the same shall be a law, in like manner as if he had signed it, unless the Congress by their adjournment prevent its return, in which case it shall not be a law.

3. Every order, resolution, or vote to which the concurrence of the Senate and the House of Representatives may be necessary (except on a question of adjournment) shall be presented to the President of the United States; and before the same shall take effect, shall be approved by him, or being disapproved by him, shall be repassed by two thirds of the Senate and House of Representatives, according to the rules and limitations prescribed in the case of a bill.

SECTION 8. I. The Congress shall have the power.

1. To lay and collect taxes, duties, imposts, and excises, to pay the debts and provide for the common defense and general welfare of the United States; but all duties, imposts, and excises shall be uniform throughout the United States.

2. To borrow money on the credit of the United States;

3. To regulate commerce with foreign nations, and among the several States, and with the Indian tribes;

4. To establish a uniform rule of naturalization, and uniform laws on the subject of bankruptcies throughout the United States;

5. To coin money, regulate the value thereof, and of foreign coin, and fix the standard of weights and measures;

6. To provide for the punishment of counterfeiting the securities and current coin of the United States;

7. To establish post offices and post roads;

8. To promote the progress of science and useful arts, by securing for limited times to authors and inventors the exclusive right to their respective writings and discoveries;

9. To constitute tribunals inferior to the Supreme Court;

10. To define and punish piracies and felonies committed on the high seas, and offenses against the law of nations;

11. To declare war, grant letters of marque and reprisal, and make rules concerning captures on land and water;

12. To raise and support armies, but no appropriation of money to that use shall be for a longer term than two years;

13. To provide and maintain a navy;

14. To make rules for the government and regulation of the land and naval forces;

15. To provide for calling forth the militia to execute the laws of the Union, suppress insurrections and repel invasions;

16. To provide for organizing, arming, and disciplining the militia, and for governing such part of them as may be employed in the service of the United States, reserving to the States respectively, the appointment of the officers, and the authority of training the militia according to the discipline prescribed by Congress;

17. To exercise exclusive legislation in all cases whatsoever, over such district (not exceeding ten miles square) as may, by cession of particular States, and the acceptance

of Congress, become the seat of the government of the United States, and to exercise like authority over all places purchased by the consent of the legislature of the State in which the same shall be, for the erection of forts, magazines, arsenals, dockyards, and other needful buildings; and

18. To make all laws which shall be necessary and proper for carrying into execution the foregoing powers, and all other powers vested by this Constitution in the government of the United States, or any department or officer thereof.

SECTION 9. 1. The migration or importation of such persons as any of the States now existing shall think proper to admit, shall not be prohibited by the Congress prior to the year one thousand eight hundred and eight, but a tax or duty may be imposed on such importation, not exceeding ten dollars for each person.

2. The privilege of the writ of habeas corpus shall not be suspended, unless when in cases of rebellion or invasion the public safety may require it.

3. No bill of attainder or ex post facto law shall be passed.

4. No capitation, or other direct, tax shall be laid, unless in proportion to the census or enumeration herein-before directed to be taken.[5]

5. No tax or duty shall be laid on articles exported from any State.

6. No preference shall be given by any regulation of commerce or revenue to the ports of one State over those of another: nor shall vessels bound to, or from, one State be obliged to enter, clear, or pay duties in another.

7. No money shall be drawn from the treasury, but in consequence of appropriations made by law; and a regular statement and account of the receipts and expenditures of all public money shall be published from time to time.

8. No title of nobility shall be granted by the United States: and no person holding any office of profit or trust under them, shall,

without the consent of the Congress, accept of any present, emolument, office, or title, of any kind whatever, from any king, prince, or foreign State.

SECTION 10. 1. No State shall enter into any treaty, alliance, or confederation; grant letters of marque and reprisal; coin money; emit bills of credit; make any thing but gold and silver coin a tender in payment of debts; pass any bill of attainder, ex post facto law, or law impairing the obligation of contracts, or grant, any title of nobility.

2. No State shall, without the consent of the Congress, lay any imposts or duties on imports or exports, except what may be absolutely necessary for executing its inspection laws: and the net produce of all duties and imposts laid by any State on imports or exports, shall be for the use of the treasury of the United States; and all such laws shall be subject to the revision and control of the Congress.

3. No State shall, without the consent of the Congress, lay any duty of tonnage, keep troops, or ships of war in time of peace, enter into any agreement or compact with another State, or with a foreign power, or engage in war, unless actually invaded, or in such imminent danger as will not admit of delay.

ARTICLE II

SECTION 1. 1. The executive power shall be vested in a President of the United States of America. He shall hold his office during the term of four years, and, together with the Vice President, chosen for the same term, be elected, as follows:

2. Each State shall appoint, in such manner as the legislature thereof may direct, a number of electors, equal to the whole number of senators and representatives to which the State may be entitled in the Congress: but no senator or representative, or person holding any office of trust or profit under the United States, shall be appointed an elector.

The electors shall meet in their respective States, and vote by ballot for two persons, of whom one at least shall not be an

---

[5]See the Sixteenth Amendment.

inhabitant of the same State with themselves. And they shall make a list of all the persons voted for, and of the number of votes for each; which list they shall sign and certify, and transmit sealed to the seat of the government of the United States, directed to the president of the Senate. The president of the Senate shall, in the presence of the Senate and House of Representatives, open all the certificates, and the votes shall then be counted. The person having the greatest number of votes shall be the President, if such number be a majority of the whole number of electors appointed; and if there be more than one who have such majority, and have an equal number of votes, then the House of Representatives shall immediately choose by ballot one of them for President; and if no person have a majority, then from the five highest on the list the said House shall in like manner choose the President. But in choosing the President, the votes shall be taken by States, the representation from each State having one vote; a quorum for this purpose shall consist of a member or members from two thirds of the States, and a majority of all the States shall be necessary to a choice. In every case after the choice of the President, the person having the greatest number of votes of the electors shall be the Vice President. But if there should remain two or more who have equal votes, the Senate shall choose from them by ballot the Vice President.[6]

3. The Congress may determine the time of choosing the electors, and the day on which they shall give their votes; which day shall be the same throughout the United States.

4. No person except a natural born citizen, or a citizen of the United States, at the time of the adoption of this Constitution, shall be eligible to the office of President; neither shall any person be eligible to the office who shall not have attained to the age of thirty-five years, and been fourteen years a resident within the United States.

5. In case of the removal of the President from office, or of his death, resignation, or

inability to discharge the powers and duties of the said office, the same shall devolve on the Vice President, and the congress may by law provide for the case of removal, death, resignation or inability, both of the President and Vice President, declaring what officer shall then act as President, and such officer shall act accordingly until the disability be removed, or a President shall be elected.

6. The President shall, at stated times, receive for his services a compensation which shall neither be increased nor diminished during the period for which he shall have been elected, and he shall not receive within that period any other emolument from the United States, or any of them.

7. Before he enter on the execution of his office, he shall take the following oath or affirmation:—"I do solemnly swear (or affirm) that I will faithfully execute the office of President of the United States, and will to the best of my ability, preserve, protect and defend the Constitution of the United States."

SECTION 2. 1. The President shall be commander in chief of the army and navy of the United States, and of the militia of the several States, when called into the actual service of the United States; he may require the opinion in writing, of the principal officer in each of the executive departments, upon any subject relating to the duties of their respective offices, and he shall have power to grant reprieves and pardons for offenses against the United States, except in cases of impeachment.

2. He shall have power, by and with the advice and consent of the Senate, to make treaties, provided two thirds of the senators present concur; and he shall nominate, and by and with the advice and consent of the Senate, shall appoint ambassadors, other public ministers and consuls, judges of the Supreme Court, and all other officers of the United States, whose appointments are not herein otherwise provided for, and which shall be established by law; but the Congress may by law vest the appointment of such inferior officers, as they think proper, in the

---

[6]Superseded by the Twelfth Amendment.

President alone, in the courts of laws, or in the heads of departments.

3. The President shall have power to fill up all vacancies that may happen during the recess of the Senate, by granting commissions which shall expire at the end of their next session.

SECTION 3. He shall from time to time give to the Congress information of the state of the Union, and recommend to their consideration such measures as he shall judge necessary and expedient; he may, on extraordinary occasions, convene both Houses, or either of them, and in case of disagreement between them with respect to the time of adjournment, he may adjourn them to such time as he shall think proper; he shall receive ambassadors and other public ministers; he shall take care that the laws be faithfully executed, and shall commission all the officers of the United States.

SECTION 4. The President, Vice President, and all civil officers of the United States, shall be removed from office on impeachment for, and conviction of, treason, bribery, or other high crimes and misdemeanors.

ARTICLE III

SECTION 1. The judicial power of the United States shall be vested in one Supreme Court, and in such inferior courts as the Congress may from time to time ordain and establish. The judges, both of the Supreme and inferior courts, shall hold their offices during good behavior, and shall, at stated times, receive for their services, a compensation, which shall not be diminished during their continuance in office.

SECTION 2. 1. The judicial power shall extend to all cases, in law and equity, arising under this Constitution, the laws of the United States, and treaties made, or which shall be made, under their authority;—to all cases of admiralty and maritime jurisdiction;—to controversies to which the United States shall be a party;[7]—to controversies

between two or more States;—between a State and citizens of another State;—between citizens of different States;—between citizens of the same State claiming lands under grants of different States, and between a State, or the citizens thereof, and foreign States, citizens or subjects.

2. In all cases affecting ambassadors, other public ministers and consuls, and those in which a State shall be party, the Supreme Court shall have original jurisdiction. In all the other cases before mentioned, the Supreme Court shall have appellate jurisdiction, both as to law and fact, with such exceptions, and under such regulations as the Congress shall make.

3. The trial of all crimes, except in cases of impeachment, shall be by jury; and such trial shall be held in the State where the said crimes shall have been committed; but when not committed within any State, the trial shall be such place or places as the congress may by law have directed.

SECTION 3. 1. Treason against the United States shall consist only in levying war against them, or in adhering to their enemies, giving them aid and comfort. No person shall be convicted of treason unless on the testimony of two witnesses to the same overt act, or on confession in open court.

2. The Congress shall have power to declare the punishment of treason, but no attainder of treason shall work corruption of blood, or forfeiture except during the life of the person attained.

ARTICLE IV

SECTION 1. Full faith and credit shall be given in each State to the public acts, records, and judicial proceedings of every other State. And the Congress may by general laws prescribe the manner in which such acts, records and proceedings shall be proved, and the effect thereof.

SECTION 2. 1. The citizens of each State shall be entitled to all privileges and immunities of citizens in the several States.[8]

---

[7]See the Eleventh Amendment.

[8]See the Fourteenth Amendment, Sec. 1.

2. A person charged in any State with treason, felony, or other crime, who shall flee from justice, and be found in another State, shall on demand of the executive authority of the State from which he fled, be delivered up to be removed to the State having jurisdiction of the crime.

3. No person held to service or labor in one State under the laws thereof, escaping into another, shall, in consequence of any law or regulation therein, be discharged from such service or labor, but shall be delivered up on claim of the party to whom such service or labor may be due.[9]

SECTION 3. 1. New States may be admitted by the Congress into this Union; but no new State shall be formed or erected within the jurisdiction of any other State, nor any State be formed by the junction of two or more States, or parts of States, without the consent of the legislatures of the States concerned as well as of the Congress.

2. The Congress shall have power to dispose of and make all needful rules and regulations respecting the territory or other property belonging to the United States; and nothing in this Constitution shall be so construed as to prejudice any claims of the United States, or of any particular State.

SECTION 4. The United States shall guarantee to every State in this Union a republican form of government, and shall protect each of them against invasion; and on application of the legislature, or of the executive (when the legislature cannot be convened) against domestic violence.

ARTICLE V

The Congress, whenever two thirds of both Houses shall deem it necessary, shall propose amendments to this Constitution, or, on the application of the legislatures of two thirds of the several States, shall call a convention for proposing amendments, which in either case shall be valid to all intents and purposes, as part of this Constitution, when ratified by the legislatures of three fourths of the several States, or by conventions in three fourths thereof, as the one or the other mode of ratification may be proposed by the Congress; Provided that no amendment which may be made prior to the year one thousand eight hundred and eight shall in any manner affect the first and fourth clauses in the ninth section of the first article; and that no State, without its consent, shall be deprived of its equal suffrage in the Senate.

ARTICLE VI

1. All debts contracted and engagements entered into, before the adoption of this Constitution, shall be as valid against the United States under this Constitution, as under the Confederation.[10]

2. This Constitution, and the laws of the United States which shall be made in pursuance thereof; and all treaties made, or which shall be made, under the authority of the United States, shall be the supreme law of the land; and the judges in every State shall be bound thereby, any thing in the Constitution or laws of any State to the contrary notwithstanding.

3. The senators and representatives before mentioned, and the members of the several State legislatures, and all executive and judicial officers, both of the United States and of the several States, shall be bound by oath or affirmation to support this Constitution; but no religious test shall ever be required as a qualification to any office or public trust under the United States.

ARTICLE VII

The ratification of the conventions of nine States shall be sufficient for the establishment of this Constitution between the States so ratifying the same.

Done in Convention by the unanimous consent of the States present the seventeenth day of September in the year of our Lord one thousand seven hundred and eighty-seven, and of the independence of the United States

---

[9]See the Thirteenth Amendment.

[10]See the Fourteenth Amendment, Sec. 4.

of America the twelfth. In witness whereof we have hereunto subscribed our names.

[Signatories' names omitted]

Articles in addition to, and amendment of, the Constitution of the United States of America, proposed by Congress, and ratified by the legislatures of the several States, pursuant to the fifth article of the original Constitution.

Amendment I
[First ten amendments ratified December 15, 1791]

Congress shall make no law respecting an establishment of religion, or prohibiting the free exercise thereof; or abridging the freedom of speech, or of the press; or the right of the people peaceably to assemble, and to petition the government for a redress of grievances.

Amendment II
A well regulated militia, being necessary to the security of a free State, the right of the people to keep and bear arms, shall not be infringed.

Amendment III
No soldier shall, in time of peace be quartered in any house, without the consent of the owner, nor in time of war, but in a manner to be prescribed by law.

Amendment IV
The right of the people to be secure in their persons, houses, papers, and effects, against unreasonable searches and seizures, shall not be violated, and no warrants shall issue, but upon probable cause, supported by oath or affirmation, and particularly describing the place to be searched, and the persons or things to be seized.

Amendment V
No person shall be held to answer for a capital or otherwise infamous crime, unless on a presentment or indictment of a grand jury, except in cases arising in the land or naval forces, or in the militia, when in actual service in time of war or public danger; nor shall any person be subject for the same offense to be twice put in jeopardy of life or limb; nor shall be compelled in any criminal case to be a witness against himself, nor be deprived of life, liberty, or property, without due process of law; nor shall private property be taken for public use, without just compensation.

Amendment VI
In all criminal prosecutions, the accused shall enjoy the right to a speedy and public trial, by an impartial jury of the State and district wherein the crime shall have been committed, which district shall have been previously ascertained by law, and to be informed of the nature and cause of the accusation; to be confronted with the witnesses against him; to have compulsory process for obtaining witnesses in his favor, and to have the assistance of counsel for his defense.

Amendment VII
In suits at common law, where the value in controversy shall exceed twenty dollars, the right of trial by jury shall be preserved, and no fact tried by a jury shall be otherwise reexamined in any court of the United States, than according to the rules of the common law.

Amendment VIII
Excessive bail shall not be required, nor excessive fines imposed, nor cruel and unusual punishments inflicted.

Amendment IX
The enumeration in the Constitution of certain rights shall not be construed to deny or disparage others retained by the people.

Amendment X
The powers not delegated to the United States by the Constitution, nor prohibited by it to the States, are reserved to the States respectively, or to the people.

Amendment XI [January 8, 1798]
The judicial power of the United States shall not be construed to extend to any suit in law or equity, commended or prosecuted against one of the United States by citizens

of another State, or by citizens or subjects of any foreign State.

Amendment XII
[September 25, 1804]

The electors shall meet in their respective States, and vote by ballot for President and Vice President, one of whom, at least, shall not be an inhabitant of the same State with themselves; they shall name in their ballots the person voted for as President, and in distinct ballots, the person voted for as Vice President, and they shall make distinct lists of all persons voted for as President and of all persons voted for as Vice President, and of the number of votes for each, which lists they shall sign and certify, and transmit sealed to the seat of the government of the United States, directed to the President of the Senate;—The President of the Senate shall, in the presence of the Senate and House of Representatives, open all the certificates and the votes shall then be counted;—The person having the greatest number of votes for President, shall be the President, if such number be a majority of the whole number of electors appointed; and if no person have such majority, then from the persons having the highest numbers not exceeding three on the list of those voted for as President, the House of Representatives shall choose immediately, by ballot, the President. But in choosing the President, the votes shall be taken by States, the representation from each State having one vote; a quorum for this purpose shall consist of a member or members from two thirds of the States, and a majority of all the States shall be necessary to a choice. And if the House of Representatives shall not choose a President whenever the right of choice shall devolve upon them, before the fourth day of March next following, then the Vice President shall act as President, as in the case of the death or other constitutional disability of the President. The person having the greatest number of votes as Vice President shall be the Vice President, if such number be a majority of the whole number of electors appointed, and if no person have a majority, then from the two highest numbers

on the list, the Senate shall choose the Vice President; a quorum for the purpose shall consist of two thirds of the whole number of Senators, and a majority of the whole number shall be necessary to a choice. But no person constitutionally ineligible to the office of President shall be eligible to that of Vice President of the United States.

Amendment XIII
[December 18, 1865]

SECTION 1. Neither slavery nor involuntary servitude, except as a punishment for crime whereof the party shall have been duly convicted, shall exist within the United States, or any place subject to their jurisdiction.

SECTION 2. Congress shall have power to enforce this article by appropriate legislation.

Amendment XIV [July 28, 1868]

SECTION 1. All persons born or naturalized in the United States, and subject to the jurisdiction thereof, are citizens of the United States and of the State wherein they reside. No State shall make or enforce any law which shall abridge the privileges or immunities of citizens of the United States; nor shall any State deprive any person of life, liberty, or property, without due process of law; nor deny to any person within its jurisdiction the equal protection of the laws.

SECTION 2. Representatives shall be apportioned among the several States according to their respective numbers, counting the whole number of persons in each State, excluding Indians not taxed. But when the right to vote at any election for the choice of electors for President and Vice President of the United States, representatives in Congress, the executive and judicial officers of a State, or the members of the legislature thereof, is denied to any of the male inhabitants of such State, being twenty-one years of age, and citizens of the United States, or in any way abridged, except for participating in rebellion, or other crime, the basis of representation there shall be reduced in the proportion which the number of such male citizens shall bear to the whole number of male citizens twenty-one years of age in such State.

SECTION 3. No person shall be a senator or representative in Congress, or elector of President and Vice President, or hold any office, civil or military, under the United States, or under any State, who having previously taken an oath, as a member of Congress, or as an officer of the United States, or as a member of any State legislature, or as an executive or judicial officer of any State, to support the Constitution of the United States, shall have engaged in insurrection or rebellion against the same, or given aid or comfort to the enemies thereof. But Congress may by a vote of two thirds of each House, remove such disability.

SECTION 4. The validity of the public debt of the United States, authorized by law, including debts incurred for payment of pensions and bounties for services in suppressing insurrection or rebellion; shall not be questioned. But neither the United States nor any State shall assume or pay any debt or obligation incurred in aid of insurrection or rebellion against the United States, or any claim for the loss or emancipation of any slave; but all such debts, obligations, and claims shall be held illegal and void.

SECTION 5. The Congress shall have the power to enforce, by appropriate legislation, the provisions of this article.

Amendment XV [March 30, 1870]
SECTION 1. The right of citizens of the United States to vote shall not be denied or abridged by the United States or by any State on account of race, color, or previous condition of servitude.

SECTION 2. The Congress shall have power to enforce this article by appropriate legislation.

Amendment XVI
[February 25, 1913]
The Congress shall have power to lay and collect taxes on incomes, from whatever source derived, without apportionment among the several States, and without regard to any census or enumeration.

Amendment XVII [May 31, 1913]
The Senate of the United States shall be composed of two senators from each State, elected by the people thereof, for six years; and each senator shall have one vote. The electors in each State shall have the qualifications requisite for electors of the most numerous branch of the State legislature.

When vacancies happen in the representation of any State in the Senate, the executive authority of such State shall issue writs of election to fill such vacancies: Provided, That the legislature of any State may empower the executive thereof to make temporary appointments until the people fill the vacancies by election as the legislature may direct.

This amendment shall not be so construed as to affect the election or term of any senator chosen before it becomes valid as part of the Constitution.

Amendment[11] XVIII
[January 29, 1919]
After one year from the ratification of this article, the manufacture, sale, or transportation of intoxicating liquors within, the importation thereof into, or the exportation thereof from the United States and all territory subject to the jurisdiction thereof for beverage purposes is thereby prohibited.

The Congress and the several States shall have concurrent power to enforce this article by appropriate legislation.

This article shall be inoperative unless it shall have been ratified as an amendment to the Constitution by the legislatures of the several States, as provided in the constitution, within seven years from the date of the submission hereof to the States by Congress.

Amendment XIX [August 26, 1920]
The right of citizens of the United States to vote shall not be denied or abridged by the United States or by any State on account of sex.

Congress shall have the power to enforce this article by appropriate legislation.

---

[11]Repealed by the Twenty-first Amendment.

Amendment XX [January 23, 1933]

SECTION 1. The terms of the President and Vice President shall end at noon on the 20th day of January and the terms of Senators and Representatives at noon on the 3rd day of January, of the years in which such terms would have ended if this article had not been ratified; and the terms of their successors shall then begin.

SECTION 2. The Congress shall assemble at least once in every year, and such meeting shall begin at noon on the 3rd day of January, unless they shall by law appoint a different day.

SECTION 3. If, at the time fixed for the beginning of the term of President, the President-elect shall have died, the Vice President-elect shall become President. If a President shall not have been chosen before the time fixed for the beginning of his term, or if the President-elect shall have failed to qualify, then the Vice President-elect shall act as President until a President shall have qualified; and the Congress may by law provide for the case wherein neither a President-elect nor a Vice President-elect shall have qualified, declaring who shall then act as President, or the manner in which one who is to act shall be selected, and such person shall act accordingly until a President or Vice President shall have qualified.

SECTION 4. The Congress may by law provide for the case of the death of any of the persons from whom, the House of Representatives may choose a President whenever the right of choice shall have devolved upon them, and for the case of the death of any of the persons from whom the Senate may choose a Vice President whenever the right of choice shall have devolved upon them.

SECTION 5. Sections 1 and 2 shall take effect on the 15th day of October following the ratification of this article.

Section 6. This article shall be inoperative unless it shall have been ratified as an amendment to the Constitution by the legislatures of three-fourths of the several States within seven years from the date of its submission.

Amendment XXI [December 5, 1933]

SECTION 1. The Eighteenth Article of amendment to the Constitution of the United States is hereby repealed.

SECTION 2. The transportation or importation into any State, Territory, or possession of the United States for delivery or use therein of intoxicating liquors in violation of the laws thereof, is hereby prohibited.

SECTION 3. This article shall be inoperative unless it shall have been ratified as an amendment to the Constitution by conventions in the several States, as provided in the Constitution, within seven years from the date of the submission thereof to the States by the Congress.

Amendment XXII [March 1, 1951]

No person shall be elected to the office of the President more than twice, and no person who has held the office of President, or acted as President, for more than two years of a term to which some other person was elected President shall be elected to the office of the President more than once.

But this article shall not apply to any person holding the office of President when this article was proposed by the Congress, and shall not prevent any person who may be holding the office of President, or acting as President, during the term within which this article becomes operative from holding the office of President or acting as President during the remainder of such term.

This article shall be inoperative unless it shall have been ratified as an amendment to the Constitution by the legislatures of three-fourths of the several States within seven years from the date of its submission to the States by the Congress.

Amendment XXIII [March 29, 1961]

SECTION 1. The District constituting the seat of Government of the United States shall appoint in such manner as the Congress may direct.

A number of electors of President and Vice President equal to the whole number of Senators and Representatives in Congress to which the District would be entitled if it were a State, but in no event more than the least populous State; they shall be in addition to those appointed by the States, but they shall be considered, for the purposes of the election of President and Vice President, to be electors appointed by a State; and they shall meet in the District and perform such duties as provided by the twelfth article of amendment.

SECTION 2. The Congress shall have power to enforce this article by appropriate legislation.

Amendment XXIV
[January 23, 1964]

SECTION 1. The right of citizens of the United States to vote in any primary or other election for President or Vice President, for electors for President or Vice President, or for Senator or Representative in Congress, shall not be denied or abridged by the United States or any State by reason of failure to pay any poll tax or other tax.

SECTION 2. The Congress shall have power to enforce this article by appropriate legislation.

Amendment XXV
[February 10, 1967]

SECTION 1. In case of the removal of the President from office or of his death or resignation, the Vice President shall become President.

SECTION 2. Whenever there is a vacancy in the office of the Vice President, the President shall nominate a Vice President who shall take office upon confirmation by a majority of both Houses of Congress.

SECTION 3. Whenever the President transmits to the President pro tempore of the Senate and the Speaker of the House of Representatives his written declaration that he is unable to discharge the powers and duties

of his office, and until he transmits to them a written declaration to the contrary, such powers and duties shall be discharged by the Vice President as Acting President.

SECTION 4. Whenever the Vice President and a majority of either the principal officers of the executive departments or of such other body as Congress may by law provide, transmit to the President pro tempore of the Senate and the Speaker of the House of Representatives their written declaration that the President is unable to discharge the powers and duties of his office, the Vice President shall immediately assume the powers and duties of the office as Acting President.

Thereafter, when the President transmits to the President pro tempore of the Senate and the Speaker of the House of Representatives his written declaration that no inability exists, he shall resume the powers and duties of his office unless the Vice President and a majority of either the principal officers of the executive departments or of such other body as Congress may by law provide, transmit within four days to the President pro tempore of the Senate and the Speaker of the House of Representatives their written declaration that the President is unable to discharge the powers and duties of his office. Thereupon Congress shall decide the issue, assembling within forty-eight hours for that purpose if not in session. If the Congress, within twenty-one days after receipt of the latter written declaration, or, if Congress is not in session, within twenty-one days after Congress is required to assemble, determines by two-thirds vote of both Houses that the President is unable to discharge the powers and duties of his office, the Vice President shall continue to discharge the same as Acting President; otherwise, the President shall resume the powers and duties of his office.

Amendment XXVI
[June 30, 1971]

SECTION 1. The right of citizens of the United States who are eighteen years of

e or older to vote shall not be denied or
ridged by the United States or by any State
account of age.

CTION 2. The Congress shall have power
enforce this article by appropriate
islation.

Amendment XXVII
[May 7,12 1992]

No law, varying the compensation for services of the Senators and Representatives, shall take effect until an election of Representatives shall have intervened.

---

ames Madison proposed this amendment in 1789 together with the ten amendments that were adopted he Bill of Rights, but it failed to win ratification at the time. Congress, however, had set no deadline for ratification, and over the years—particularly in the 1980s and 1990s—many states voted to add it to the nstitution. With the ratification of Michigan in 1992 it passed the threshold of three-fourths of the states uired for adoption, but because the process took more than 200 years, its validity remains in doubt.

PRESIDENTIAL ELECTIONS

Year	Number of States	Candidates	Party	Popular Vote*	Electoral Vote†	Percenta of Popul Vote
1789	11	GEORGE WASHINGTON	No party designations		69	
		John Adams			34	
		Other Candidates			35	
1792	15	GEORGE WASHINGTON	No party designations		132	
		John Adams			77	
		George Clinton			50	
		Other Candidates			5	
1796	16	JOHN ADAMS	Federalist		71	
		Thomas Jefferson	Democratic-Republican		68	
		Thomas Pinckney	Federalist		59	
		Aaron Burr	Democratic-Republican		30	
		Other Candidates			48	
1800	16	THOMAS JEFFERSON	Democratic-Republican		73	
		Aaron Burr	Democratic-Republican		73	
		John Adams	Federalist		65	
		Charles C. Pinckney	Federalist		64	
		John Jay	Federalist		1	
1804	17	THOMAS JEFFERSON	Democratic-Republican		162	
		Charles C. Pinckney	Federalist		14	
1808	17	JAMES MADISON	Democratic-Republican		122	
		Charles C. Pinckney	Federalist		47	
		George Clinton	Democratic-Republican		6	
1812	18	JAMES MADISON	Democratic-Republican		128	
		DeWitt Clinton	Federalist		89	
1816	19	JAMES MONROE	Democratic-Republican		183	
		Rufus King	Federalist		34	
1820	24	JAMES MONROE	Democratic-Republican		231	
		John Quincy Adams	Independent-Republican		1	
1824	24	JOHN QUINCY ADAMS	Democratic-Republican	108,740	84	30.5
		Andrew Jackson	Democratic-Republican	153,544	99	43.1
		William H. Crawford	Democratic-Republican	46,618	41	13.1
		Henry Clay	Democratic-Republican	47,136	37	13.2

*Percentage of popular vote given for any election year may not total 100 percent because candidates receiving le than 1 percent of the popular vote have been omitted.

†Prior to the passage of the Twelfth Amendment in 1904, the electoral college voted for two presidential candida the runner-up became Vice-President. Data from *Historical Statistics of the United States, Colonial Times to 1957* (196: pp. 682–683, and *The World Almanac*.

PRESIDENTIAL ELECTIONS (CONTINUED)

Year	Number of States	Candidates	Party	Popular Vote*	Electoral Vote†	Percentage of Popular Vote
828	24	ANDREW JACKSON	Democrat	647,286	178	56.0
		John Quincy Adams	National Republican	508,064	83	44.0
832	24	ANDREW JACKSON	Democrat	687,502	219	55.0
		Henry Clay	National Republican	530,189	49	42.4
		William Wirt	Anti-Masonic	33,108	7	2.6
		John Floyd			11	
336	26	MARTIN VAN BUREN	Democrat	765,483	170	50.9
		William H. Harrison	Whig		73	
		Hugh L. White	Whig		26	
		Daniel Webster	Whig	739,795	14	49.1
		W. P. Mangum	Whig		11	
340	26	WILLIAM H. HARRISON	Whig	1,274,624	234	53.1
		Martin Van Buren	Democrat	1,127,781	60	46.9
344	26	JAMES K. POLK	Democrat	1,338,464	170	49.6
		Henry Clay	Whig	1,300,097	105	48.1
		James G. Birney	Liberty	62,300		2.3
348	30	ZACHARY TAYLOR	Whig	1,360,967	163	47.4
		Lewis Cass	Democrat	1,222,342	127	42.5
		Martin Van Buren	Free Soil	291,263		10.1
352	31	FRANKLIN PIERCE	Democrat	1,601,117	254	50.9
		Winfield Scott	Whig	1,385,453	42	44.1
		John P. Hale	Free Soil	155,825		5.0
356	31	JAMES BUCHANAN	Democrat	1,832,955	174	45.3
		John C. Frémont	Republican	1,339,932	114	33.1
		Millard Fillmore	American ("Know Nothing")	871,731	8	21.6
360	33	ABRAHAM LINCOLN	Republican	1,865,593	180	39.8
		Stephen A. Douglas	Democrat	1,382,713	12	29.5
		John C. Breckinridge	Democrat	848,356	72	18.1
		John Bell	Constitutional Union	592,906	39	12.6
364	36	ABRAHAM LINCOLN	Republican	2,206,938	212	55.0
		George B. McClellan	Democrat	1,803,787	21	45.0
68	37	ULYSSES S. GRANT	Republican	3,013,421	214	52.7
		Horatio Seymour	Democrat	2,706,829	80	47.3
72	37	ULYSSES S. GRANT	Republican	3,596,745	286	55.6
		Horace Greeley	Democrat	2,843,446	*	43.9

cause of the death of Greeley, Democratic electors scattered their votes.

PRESIDENTIAL ELECTIONS (CONTINUED)

Year	Number of States	Candidates	Party	Popular Vote*	Electoral Vote†	Percenta of Popul Vote
1876	38	RUTHERFORD B. HAYES	Republican	4,036,572	185	48.0
		Samuel J. Tilden	Democrat	4,284,020	184	51.0
1880	38	JAMES A. GARFIELD	Republican	4,453,295	214	48.5
		Winfield S. Hancock	Democrat	4,414,082	155	48.1
		James B. Weaver	Greenback-Labor	308,578		3.4
1884	38	GROVER CLEVELAND	Democrat	4,879,507	219	48.5
		James G. Blaine	Republican	4,850,293	182	48.2
		Benjamin F. Butler	Greenback-Labor	175,370		1.8
		John P. St. John	Prohibition	150,369		1.5
1888	38	BENJAMIN HARRISON	Republican	5,447,129	233	47.9
		Grover Cleveland	Democrat	5,537,857	168	48.6
		Clinton B. Fisk	Prohibition	249,506		2.2
		Anson J. Streeter	Union Labor	146,935		1.3
1892	44	GROVER CLEVELAND	Democrat	5,555,426	277	46.1
		Benjamin Harrison	Republican	5,182,690	145	43.0
		James B. Weaver	People's	1,029,846	22	8.5
		John Bidwell	Prohibition	264,133		2.2
1896	45	WILLIAM McKINLEY	Republican	7,102,246	271	51.1
		William J. Bryan	Democrat	6,492,559	176	47.7
1900	45	WILLIAM McKINLEY	Republican	7,218,491	292	51.7
		William J. Bryan	Democrat; Populist	6,356,734	155	45.5
		John C. Woolley	Prohibition	208,914		1.5
1904	45	THEODORE ROOSEVELT	Republican	7,628,461	336	57.4
		Alton B. Parker	Democrat	5,084,223	140	37.6
		Eugene V. Debs	Socialist	402,283		3.0
		Silas C. Swallow	Prohibition	258,536		1.9
1908	46	WILLIAM H. TAFT	Republican	7,675,320	321	51.6
		William J. Bryan	Democrat	6,412,294	162	43.1
		Eugene V. Debs	Socialist	420,793		2.8
		Eugene W. Chafin	Prohibition	253,840		1.7
1912	48	WOODROW WILSON	Democrat	6,296,547	435	41.9
		Theodore Roosevelt	Progressive	4,118,571	88	27.4
		William H. Taft	Republican	3,486,720	8	23.2
		Eugene V. Debs	Socialist	900,672		6.0
		Eugene W. Chafin	Prohibition	206,275		1.4

PRESIDENTIAL ELECTIONS (CONTINUED)

Year	Number of States	Candidates	Party	Popular Vote*	Electoral Vote†	Percentage of Popular Vote
1916	48	WOODROW WILSON	Democrat	9,127,695	277	49.4
		Charles E. Hughes	Republican	8,533,507	254	46.2
		A. L. Benson	Socialist	585,113		3.2
		J. Frank Hanly	Prohibition	220,506		1.2
1920	48	WARREN G. HARDING	Republican	16,143,407	404	60.4
		James M. Cox	Democrat	9,130,328	127	34.2
		Eugene V. Debs	Socialist	919,799		3.4
		P. P. Christensen	Farmer-Labor	265,411		1.0
1924	48	CALVIN COOLIDGE	Republican	15,718,211	382	54.0
		John W. Davis	Democrat	8,385,283	136	28.8
		Robert M. La Follette	Progressive	4,831,289	13	16.6
1928	48	HERBERT C. HOOVER	Republican	21,391,993	444	58.2
		Alfred E. Smith	Democrat	15,016,169	87	40.9
1932	48	FRANKLIN D. ROOSEVELT	Democrat	22,809,638	472	57.4
		Herbert C. Hoover	Republican	15,758,901	59	39.7
		Norman Thomas	Socialist	881,951		2.2
1936	48	FRANKLIN D. ROOSEVELT	Democrat	27,752,869	523	60.8
		Alfred M. Landon	Republican	16,674,665	8	36.5
		William Lemke	Union	882,479		1.9
1940	48	FRANKLIN D. ROOSEVELT	Democrat	27,307,819	449	54.8
		Wendell L. Willkie	Republican	22,321,018	82	44.8
1944	48	FRANKLIN D. ROOSEVELT	Democrat	25,606,585	432	53.5
		Thomas E. Dewey	Republican	22,014,745	99	46.0
1948	48	HARRY S. TRUMAN	Democrat	24,105,812	303	49.5
		Thomas E. Dewey	Republican	21,970,065	189	45.1
		J. Strom Thurmond	States' Rights	1,169,063	39	2.4
		Henry A. Wallace	Progressive	1,157,172		2.4
1952	48	DWIGHT D. EISENHOWER	Republican	33,936,234	442	55.1
		Adlai E. Stevenson	Democrat	27,314,992	89	44.4
1956	48	DWIGHT D. EISENHOWER	Republican	35,590,472	457†	57.6
		Adlai E. Stevenson	Democrat	26,022,752	73	42.1
1960	50	JOHN F. KENNEDY	Democrat	34,227,096	303‡	49.9
		Richard M. Nixon	Republican	34,108,546	219	49.6

‡Harry F. Byrd received 15 electoral votes.
†Resigned August 9, 1974: Vice President Gerald R. Ford became President.

PRESIDENTIAL ELECTIONS (CONTINUED)

Year	Number of States	Candidates	Party	Popular Vote*	Electoral Vote†	Percenta of Popul Vote
1964	50	LYNDON B. JOHNSON	Democrat	42,676,220	486	61.
		Barry M. Goldwater	Republican	26,860,314	52	38.
1968	50	RICHARD M. NIXON	Republican	31,785,480	301	43.
		Hubert H. Humphrey	Democrat	31,275,165	191	42.
		George C. Wallace	American Independent	9,906,473	46	13.
1972	50	RICHARD M. NIXON‡	Republican	47,165,234	520**	60.
		George S. McGovern	Democrat	29,168,110	17	37.
1976	50	JIMMY CARTER	Democrat	40,828,929	297***	50.
		Gerald R. Ford	Republican	39,148,940	240	47.
		Eugene McCarthy	Independent	739,256		
1980	50	RONALD REAGAN	Republican	43,201,220	489	50.
		Jimmy Carter	Democrat	34,913,332	49	41.
		John B. Anderson	Independent	5,581,379		
1984	50	RONALD REAGAN	Republican	53,428,357	525	59.
		Walter F. Mondale	Democrat	36,930,923	13	41.
1988	50	GEORGE H. W. BUSH	Republican	48,901,046	426****	53.
		Michael Dukakis	Democrat	41,809,030	111	45.
1992	50	BILL CLINTON	Democrat	43,728,275	370	43.
		George H.W. Bush	Republican	38,167,416	168	37.
		H. Ross Perot	United We Stand, America	19,237,247		19.
1996	50	BILL CLINTON	Democrat	45,590,703	379	49.
		Robert Dole	Republican	37,816,307	159	41.
		H. Ross Perot	Reform	7,866,284		8.
2000	50	George W. Bush	Republican	50,459,624	271	47.
		Albert Gore, Jr.	Democrat	51,003,328	266	49.
		Ralph Nader	Green	2,882,985		2.
2004	50	George W. Bush	Republican	62,040,610	286*****	50.
		John F. Kerry	Democrat	59,028,444	251	48.
2008	50	Barack H. Obama	Democrat	69,456,897	365	52.
		John McCain	Republican	59,934,814	173	45.

**John Hospers received 1 electoral vote.
***Ronald Reagan received 1 electoral vote.
****Lloyd Bentsen received 1 electoral vote.
*****John Edwards received 1 electoral vote.

GLOSSARY OF KEY TERMS AND CONCEPTS

54th Massachusetts Regiment: This all-black volunteer infantry regiment was recruited in the Northern states for service with Union military forces in the Civil War. It was made up almost entirely of black men who had been free. It was commanded by white officers.

Abolitionists: Those who sought to end slavery within their colony, state, nation, or religious denomination. By the 1830s the term best applied to those who advocated immediate rather than gradual emancipation.

Acculturation: Change in individuals who are introduced to a new culture.

Affirmative action: Civil rights policy or program that seeks to redress the effects of past discrimination due to race or gender by giving preference to women and minorities in education and employment.

African Methodist Episcopal (AME) Church: Founded in Philadelphia in 1816, it was the first and became the largest independent black church.

Afrocentricists: Scholars who view history from an African perspective.

Afrocentricity: A philosophy of culture that celebrates Africa's role in history and stresses the enduring African roots and identity of black America.

Age of Revolution: A period in Atlantic history that began with the American Revolution in 1776 and ended with the defeat of Napoleonic France in 1815.

Agricultural Adjustment Act (AAA): A federal program that provided subsidies to farmers to grow less to help stabilize prices.

American and Foreign Anti-Slavery Society (AFASS, 1840–1855): An organization of church-oriented abolitionists.

American Anti-Slavery Society (AASS, 1833–1870): The umbrella organization for immediate abolitionists during the 1830s and the main Garrisonian organization after 1840.

American Colonization Society (ACS, 1816–1912): An organization founded in Washington, D.C., by prominent slaveholders. It claimed to encourage the ultimate abolition of slavery by sending free African Americans to its West African colony of Liberia.

American Convention for Promoting the Abolition of Slavery and Improving the Condition of the African Race (1794–1838): A loose coalition of state and local societies, dominated by the Pennsylvania Abolition Society, dedicated to gradual abolition.

American Missionary Association: This religious organization sent teachers and clergymen throughout the South following the Civil War to tend to the spiritual and educational needs of former slaves. It was instrumental in establishing dozens of schools, including Fisk, Hampton, and Avery.

Amistad: A Spanish schooner on which West African Joseph Cinque led a successful slave revolt in 1839.

Animism: The belief that inanimate objects have spiritual attributes.

Asiento: The monopoly over the slave trade from Africa to Spain's American colonies.

Battery Wagner: This defensive fortification guarded Fort Sumter near the entrance to Charleston Harbor in South Carolina. It was the scene in July 1863 of a major Union assault by the 54th Massachusetts Regiment, a black unit. The assault failed, but the bravery and valor of the black troops earned them fame and glory.

Benevolent Empire: A network of church-related voluntary associations designed to fight sin and save souls. It emerged during the 1810s in relationship to the Second Great Awakening.

Berbers: A people native to North Africa and the Sahara Desert.

Black arts movement: Artistic movement that seeks to promote black art by black artists for black people.

Black Cabinet: Informal group of highly placed African-American advisors to President Franklin D. Roosevelt.

Black codes: Laws that were passed in each of the former Confederate states following the Civil War that applied only to black people. While conceding such rights as the right to marry, to contract a debt, or to own property, the codes severely restricted the rights and opportunities of former slaves in terms of labor and mobility.

Black Committee: An organization of prominent black men in the North who assisted in recruiting African Americans to fight for the Union in the Civil War.

Black English (or African-American Vernacular English): A variety of American English that is influenced by West African grammar, vocabulary, and pronunciation.

Black laws: Laws passed in states of the Old Northwest during the early nineteenth century banning or restricting black settlement and limiting the rights of black residents.

Black nationalism: A belief held by some African Americans that they must seek their racial destiny by establishing separate institutions and, perhaps, migrating as a group to a location (often Africa) outside the United States.

Black Panther Party: Black militant organization set up in 1966 by Huey P. Newton and Bobby Seale.

Black studies: Scholarly study of the history and experiences of persons of African descent.

Border ruffians: Pro-slavery advocates and vigilantes from Missouri who crossed the border into Kansas in 1855–1857 to support slavery in Kansas by threatening and attacking antislavery settlers.

Brooks-Sumner Affair: South Carolina congressman Preston Brooks attacked and severely beat Massachusetts Senator Charles Sumner on the floor of the U.S. Senate after Sumner had denounced the proslavery position of Brooks's uncle, South Carolina Senator Andrew Butler.

Brotherhood of Sleeping Car Porters (BSCP): Black men and women who worked on Pullman passenger coaches on the nation's railroads organized this labor union in 1925 with A. Philip Randolph as its leader. It struggled until the passage in 1935 of the National Labor Relations Act, after which it became one of the powerful unions within the American Federation of Labor (AFL). In 1978 it was absorbed into the Brotherhood of Railway and Airline Clerks.

Brown v. Board of Education of Topeka: Decision by the Supreme Court in 1954 that overturned the "separate but equal" doctrine.

Brownsville Affair: In 1906, a shooting in Brownsville, Texas, was blamed on black soldiers from the 25th Infantry Regiment. President Theodore Roosevelt summarily dismissed 167 black men from the U.S. Army. Later investigations exonerated the men.

Buffalo soldiers: Four regiments of black soldiers that served with the U.S. Army on the western frontier from the 1870s to the 1890s. The Plains Indians called them the buffalo soldiers.

Call-and-response: An African-American singing style rooted in Africa. A solo call tells a story to which a group responds, often with repeated lyrics.

Carpetbagger: The derogatory term used during Reconstruction to describe Northerners who came South following the Civil War to take advantage of political and economic opportunities. They were labeled "carpetbaggers" because they ostensibly carried all of their possessions in a solitary carpetbag.

Cash crop: A crop grown for sale rather than subsistence.

Chattel slavery: A form of slavery in which the enslaved are treated legally as property.

Chicago Renaissance: Flourishing of the arts that made Chicago the center of black culture in the 1940s.

Church of England: A Protestant church established in the sixteenth century as the English national or Anglican church with the English monarch as its head. After the American Revolution, its American branch became the Episcopal Church.

Civil Rights Act, 1866: This act nullified the black codes and made African Americans citizens with the basic rights of life, liberty, and due process. It was passed over President Andrew Johnson's veto. Its main features were subsequently embedded in the Fourteenth Amendment to the Constitution.

Civil Rights Act of 1875: This federal legislation outlawed racial discrimination in public accommodations such as hotels and restaurants, and in transportation, including railroad coaches and steamboats. The Supreme Court invalidated it in 1883.

Civil Rights Act of 1964: Federal law banning discrimination in places of public accommodation.

Civil Rights Act of 1968: Federal law banning discrimination in housing.

Coffle: A file of slaves chained together that was typical of the domestic slave trade.

Colored American (New York, 1837–1842): The leading African-American newspaper of its time.

Colored Farmers' Alliance: A large organization of black southern farmers in the 1880s and 1890s that had as many as one million members who agitated for improved conditions and income for black landowners, renters, and sharecroppers.

Committee for Industrial Organization (CIO): Labor organization that was committed to inter-racial and multiethnic organizing.

Communist Party: Political party formed to promote communism.

Community Action Programs (CAPS): Anti-poverty programs involving "maximum feasible participation" by the poor themselves.

Compromise of 1850: An attempt by the U.S. Congress to settle divisive issues between the North and South, including slavery expansion, apprehension in the North of fugitive slaves, and slavery in the District of Columbia.

Compromise of 1877: This informal arrangement between national Democrats and Republicans settled the disputed presidential election of 1876 by permitting Republican Rutherford B. Hayes to become president while allowing Democrats to complete redemption by taking political control of Louisiana, Florida, and South Carolina.

Congress of Racial Equality: Protest group committed to nonviolent direct action.

Continental Army: The army created by the Continental Congress in June 1775 to fight British troops. George Washington was its commander in chief.

Continental Congress: A representative assembly that first met in October 1775 and served as the de facto central government of the United States during the Revolutionary War.

Contraband: Slaves who escaped to the Union or were captured by Union troops early in the Civil War were considered enemy property or contraband.

Convict lease system: Southern states and communities leased prisoners to privately operated mines, railroads, and timber companies. These businesses forced the prisoners, who were usually black men, to work in brutal, unhealthy, and dangerous conditions. Many convicts died of abuse and disease.

Cotton gin: A simple machine invented by Eli Whitney in 1793 to separate cotton seeds from cotton fiber. It greatly speeded this task and encouraged the westward expansion of cotton-growing in the United States.

Creole: An American brig on which Madison Washington led a successful slave revolt in 1841.

Creoles: Persons of African and/or European descent born in the Americas.

Crop lien: Black and white farmers purchased goods on credit from local merchants. The merchant demanded collateral in the form of a lien on the crop, typically cotton. If the farmer failed to repay the loan, the merchant had the legal right to seize the crop.

Disfranchisement: White southern Democrats devised a variety of techniques in the late nineteenth and early twentieth centuries to prevent black people from voting. Those techniques included literacy tests, poll taxes, and the grandfather clause as well as intimidation and violence.

Divination: A form of magic aimed at telling the future by interpreting a variety of signs.

Domestic slave trade: A trade dating from the first decade of the nineteenth century in American-born slaves purchased primarily in the border South and sent overland or by sea to the cotton-growing regions of the Old Southwest.

Double V campaign: Slogan during World War II that stood for victory over fascism abroad and over racism at home for blacks.

Dred Scott v. Sanford: The 1857 U.S. Supreme Court case that ruled against Missouri slave Dred Scott by declaring that black people were not citizens, that they possessed no constitutional rights, and were considered to be property.

Economic Opportunity Act of 1964: Federal law creating the Office of Economic Opportunity and a number of programs aimed at poor communities.

Emancipation Proclamation: President Abraham Lincoln issued the Preliminary Emancipation Proclamation on September 22, 1862. It declared that slaves in states or portions of states still in rebellion 100 days later would be freed. On January 1, 1863, the Emancipation Proclamation freed slaves in areas of the Confederate states not under Union control.

Enforcement Acts: Also known as the Force Acts, these measures were passed by Congress in the early 1870s to undermine the Ku Klux Klan and other terrorist organizations by authorizing the president to use military force and to suspend the writ of habeas corpus.

Executive Order #8802: Order issued by President Franklin D. Roosevelt in 1941 banning discrimination in employment in defense industries and the federal government.

Executive Order #9346: Order establishing a new Committee on Fair Employment Practices, with greater resources, and direct oversight by the Executive Office of the President.

Executive Order #9981: Order issued by President Harry Truman in 1948 desegregating the armed forces.

Exodusters: Black migrants who left the South during and after Reconstruction and settled in Kansas, often in all-black towns.

Factory: A headquarters for a European company that traded for slaves or engaged in other commercial enterprises on the West African coast.

Fair Employment Practices Committee (FEPC): A committee created by Franklin Roosevelt to investigate complaints of discrimination.

Fair Play Committee: Organization formed to promote black actors in the movie industry and improve the image of blacks in film.

Family Assistance Plan (FAP): Plan giving financial assistance to families with no wage earner.

Federal Arts Project: New Deal agency formed to promote the creation of public art.

Federal Elections bill, 1890: A measure, also known as the Force bill, to protect the voting rights of black men in the South by providing federal supervision of elections. It passed in the House of Representatives but failed in the Senate.

Fetish: A natural object or an artifact believed to have magical power. A charm.

Fifteenth Amendment, 1870: This constitutional amendment stipulated that the right to vote could not be denied on account of race, color, or because a person had been a slave.

First South Carolina Volunteers: This black military unit consisted of former slaves recruited in the South Carolina and Georgia low country in 1862 and 1863 for service with Union military forces in the Civil War.

Fort Pillow: This fort on the east bank of the Mississippi River north of Memphis, Tennessee, was the scene of a massacre of black Union troops as well as some white soldiers and officers by Confederate cavalry in April 1864.

Forty-Niners: The men and women who rushed to California in 1849 after gold had been discovered there.

Fourteenth Amendment, 1868: This amendment ratified during Reconstruction made any person born in the United States a citizen of the United States and of the state in which they lived. It guaranteed citizens the rights of life, liberty, and due process—usually a trial or judicial proceeding—as well as equal protection of the law. It also contained a provision reducing a state's representation in Congress if that state denied the right to vote to any adult males.

Free labor: Mid-nineteenth-century Americans who were free and worked for income or compensation to advance themselves, as opposed to slave labor, which was work done with no financial compensation by people who were not free.

Free papers: Proof of freedom that free black people had to carry at all times in the southern states prior to emancipation. The papers, issued by state governments, identified an individual by name, age, sex, color, height, and so forth.

Free-Soil Party (1848–1853): An almost entirely northern political coalition opposed to the expansion of slavery into western territories. It included former supporters of the Whig, Democratic, and Liberty parties.

Freedmen's Bureau: Congress established the Bureau of Refugees, Freedmen, and Abandoned Lands in February 1865 to assist black and white Southerners left destitute by the Civil War.

Freedmen's Savings Bank: A private financial institution chartered by Congress in 1865. Many black people and organizations deposited funds in the bank, which went bankrupt in 1874.

Freedom Rides: Effort in 1961 to desegregate interstate bus and rail travel.

Freedom suits: Legal cases in which slaves sued their master or master's heirs for freedom.

French and Indian War: A war between Great Britain and its American Indian allies and France and its American Indian allies, fought between 1754 and 1763 for control of the eastern portion of North America.

Fugitive Slave Act of 1793: An act of Congress permitting masters to recapture escaped slaves who had reached the free states and, with the authorization of local courts, return with the slave or slaves to their home state.

Fugitive Slave Law, 1850: Part of the Compromise of 1850. It required law enforcement officials as well as civilians to assist in capturing runaway slaves.

Gang system: A mode of organizing labor that had West African antecedents. In this system American slaves worked in groups under the direction of a slave driver.

Gansta rap: A genre of rap music characterized by violent and sexist lyrics.

Gary Convention: Meeting of black leaders and organizations in Gary, Indiana to develop an agenda for black empowerment.

Grandfather clause: A method southern states used to disfranchise black men. It stipulated that only men whose grandfathers were eligible to vote were themselves eligible to vote. The U.S. Supreme Court invalidated the grandfather clause in 1915.

Great Dismal Swamp: A heavily forested area on the Virginia–North Carolina border that served as a refuge for fugitive slaves during the eighteenth and nineteenth centuries.

Griot: A West African self-employed poet and oral historian.

Guinea Coast: The southward-facing coast of West Africa, from which many of the people caught up in the Atlantic slave trade departed for the Americas.

Habeas corpus: A court order that a person arrested or detained by law enforcement officers must be brought to court and charged with a crime and not held indefinitely.

Hamburg Massacre: White Democrats attacked black Republicans in July 1876 in the village of Hamburg, South Carolina. Five black men were murdered as the Democrats began a violent effort to redeem the state.

Harlem Renaissance: As New York City became a destination for black migrants before, during, and after World War I, most of them settled in Harlem—a large neighborhood in the northern portion of Manhattan Island—which by the 1920s became a center of

African-American cultural activities including literature, art, and music.

Harpers Ferry: *See* John Brown's raid.

Hierarchical: Refers to a social system based on class rank.

Hieroglyphics: A writing system based on pictures or symbols.

Hip-Hop: The back up music for rap. It is also the term for the youth culture that developed with the rise of rap music.

House of Burgesses: A representative body established at Jamestown, Virginia, in 1619.

House Un-American Activities Committee (HUAC): Congressional committee formed to investigate the activities of communists and "communist sympathizers" in America.

Humanism: The belief that human achievement and interests are more important than theological issues.

Hunting and gathering societies: Small societies dependent on hunting animals and collecting wild plants rather than on agriculture.

Import duties: Taxes on goods brought into a country or colony.

Impressment: During the Civil War, Southern states and the Confederate government required slave owners to provide slaves to work on such public projects as fortifications, roads, and wharves. The owners (not the slaves) were usually compensated for the work.

Incest taboos: Customary rules against sexual relations and marriage within family and kinship groups.

Indigo: A bluish-violet dye produced from the indigo plant.

Industrial Revolution: An economic change that began in England during the early eighteenth century and spread to Continental Europe and the United States. Industry rather than agriculture became the dominant form of enterprise.

Jim Crow: Jump Jim Crow was a nineteenth-century dance ridiculing black people that was transformed by the twentieth century into a term meaning racial discrimination and segregation.

John Brown's raid: Brown's raid on Harpers Ferry, Virginia, in October 1859 failed to lead to a major slave insurrection, but it inflamed the controversy over slavery in the North and South.

Joint-stock companies: Primitive corporations that carried out British and Dutch colonization in the Americas during the seventeenth century.

Kansas-Nebraska Act, 1854: Legislation introduced by Democratic Senator Stephen Douglas to organize the Kansas and Nebraska territories. It provided for "popular sovereignty," whereby settlers would decide whether slavery would be legal or illegal.

"Know-Nothing Party": The nickname applied to members of the American Party, which opposed immigration in the 1850s.

Ku Klux Klan: A secret society founded by former Confederates in Pulaski, Tennessee, in 1866. It transformed itself into a terrorist organization during Reconstruction to drive black and white Republicans from political power in southern states. It disappeared by the late nineteenth century but was revived near Atlanta, Georgia, in 1915, as a powerful, white, Anglo-Saxon, Protestant political force in many states outside the South. It was revived again in the 1950s to oppose the civil rights movement.

Liberty Party (1840–1848): The first antislavery political party. Most of its supporters joined the Free-Soil Party in 1848, although its radical New York wing maintained a Liberty organization into the 1850s.

Lincoln-Douglas debates: Abraham Lincoln and Stephen Douglas debated seven times in the 1858 U.S. Senate race in Illinois. They spent most of their time arguing over slavery, its expansion, the *Dred Scott* decision, and the character of African Americans. Douglas won the election.

Lineage: A type of clan, typical of West Africa, in which members claim descent from a single ancestor.

Lowndes County Freedom Organization (LCFO): Political organization founded in 1965 by Stokely Carmichael.

Loyalists: Those Americans who, during the Revolutionary War, wished to remain within the British Empire.

Lynching: Killing by a mob without the benefit of a trial or conviction.

Manifest Destiny: A doctrine, prevalent during the nineteenth century, holding that God intended the United States to expand territorially over all of North America and the Caribbean islands, or over the entire Western Hemisphere.

Manumission: The act of freeing a slave by the slave's master.

March on Washington Movement (MOWM): Movement created by A. Philip Randolph to pressure the federal government to end discrimination in the defense industry and government.

Market revolution: The process between 1800 and 1860 by which an American economy based on subsistence farming, production by skilled artisans, and local markets changed into an economy marked by commercial farming, factory production, and national markets.

Master class: Slaveholders.

Matrilineal: Descent traced through the female line.

Middle Passage: The voyage of slave ships (slavers) across the Atlantic Ocean from Africa to the Americas.

Mississippi Freedom Democratic Party: Interracial group set up to challenge Mississippi's all-white delegation to the Democratic National Convention in 1964.

Missouri Compromise, 1820: A congressional attempt to settle the issue of slavery expansion in the United States by permitting Missouri to enter the Union as a slave state, admitting Maine as a free state, and banning slavery in the rest of the Louisiana Purchase north of the 36° 30′ line of latitude.

Montgomery Bus Boycott: Refusal from 1955 to 1957 of African Americans in Montgomery, Alabama to ride the city's buses until the bus lines were desegregated.

Moral suasion: A tactic endorsed by the American Anti-Slavery Society during the 1830s. It appealed to slaveholders and others to support immediate emancipation on the basis of Christian principles.

Moynihan Report: Report attributing many of the problems of poor black communities to the breakdown of the "lower-class" black family.

Nation of Islam: Religious movement that combines Islam with black nationalism.

National Industrial Recovery Act (NIRA): Federal law intended to promote the revival of manufacturing by allowing for cooperation among industries.

National Negro Congress (NCC): Organization founded in 1926 to unite African-American protest groups.

Negro National League: A professional baseball league for black players and teams organized in 1912.

New Deal: Set of policies proposed by the Roosevelt administration in response to the Great Depression.

New York City draft riot: In early July 1863 in opposition to the forthcoming military draft, rioting erupted in New York City. Many of the victims were black men, women, and children.

North Atlantic Treaty Organization: Military alliance formed to counter the threat posed by the Soviet Union and its allies.

North Star: A weekly newspaper published and edited by Frederick Douglass from 1847 to 1851. *Fredrick Douglass's Paper* (1851–1860) succeeded it.

Northwest Ordinance, 1787: Based on earlier legislation drafted by Thomas Jefferson, it organized the Northwest Territory, providing for orderly land sales, public education, government, the creation of five to seven states out of the territory, and the prohibition of slavery within the territory.

Nuclear family: A family unit consisting solely of one set of parents and their children.

Nullification Crisis (1832–1833): Arose when the South Carolina legislature declared the United States tariff "null and void" within the state's borders. President Andrew Jackson denounced the action as treasonous and threatened to use military force to uphold national supremacy.

Pan-Africanism: A movement of people of African descent from sub-Saharan Africa in the early twentieth century that emphasized their identity, shared experiences, and the need to liberate Africa from its European colonizers.

Patriarchal: A society ruled by a senior man.

Patrilineal: Descent through the male line.

Patriots: Those Americans who, during the Revolutionary War, favored independence.

Peace Mission Movement: Religious movement led by Father Major Jealous Divine.

Pennsylvania Society for Promoting the Abolition of Slavery (Pennsylvania Abolition Society: 1787–present): An antislavery organization centered in Philadelphia and based on an earlier Quaker society. Exclusively white, it promoted gradual abolition, black self-improvement, freedom suits, and protection of African Americans against kidnapping.

Peonage: The system that forbade southern farmers, usually sharecroppers and renters, who accumulated debts to leave the land until the debt was repaid—often an impossible task. The U.S. Supreme Court outlawed peonage, but many landowners and merchants still forced farmers to remain on the land.

Philadelphia Female Anti-Slavery Society (1833–1870): A biracial abolitionist organization aligned with the American Anti-Slavery Society. White Quaker women dominated the society, but it included a significant number of black women.

Phonetic script: A writing system based on symbols representing a single sound.

Pidgin: A simplified mixture of two or more languages used to communicate between people who speak different languages.

Plessy v. Ferguson: In 1896 in an 8-to-1 decision, the U.S. Supreme Court ruled that segregation did not violate the equal protection clause of the Fourteenth Amendment. The "separate but equal" doctrine remained the supreme law of the land until the 1954 *Brown vs. Board of Education* decision overturned *Plessy.*

Polygynous family: A family unit consisting of a man, his wives, and their children.

Polytheism: The worship of many gods.

Poor People's Campaign: Project supported by Martin Luther King involving the march of tens of thousands of poor people on Washington.

Popular sovereignty: The residents of a territory (such as Kansas) would vote to legalize or prohibit slavery in that territory.

Populist Party: Also known as the Peoples' Party, the Populists supported inflation, the free and unlimited coinage of silver and gold, government ownership of railroads, telephone, and telegraph companies, and an eight-hour workday. They won state and congressional elections but lost the presidential contests in 1892 and 1896.

Port Royal Experiment: An effort by Northern white missionaries, educators, and businessmen in the Sea Islands near Beaufort, South Carolina, to transform former slaves into educated, reliable, and industrious wage earners. Most of the freedmen did not acquire the land they worked.

Prince Hall Masons: A black Masonic order formed in 1791 in Boston under the leadership of Prince Hall. He became its first grand master and promoted its expansion to other cities.

Project 100,000:   Military project with the goal of reducing the number of African Americans rejected by the military.

Race films: Movies made for African-American audiences in the 1930s and 1940s.

Radical Republicans: Members of the Republican Party during Reconstruction who vigorously supported the rights of African Americans to vote, hold political office, and to have the same legal and economic opportunities as white people.

Rain forest: A dense growth of tall trees characteristic of hot, wet regions.

Rainbow Coalition: Political coalition of African Americans, workers, liberals, feminists, gay people, environmentalists, and others formed by Jesse Jackson in the 1980s.

Reconstruction: The twelve years (1865–1877) following the Civil War, during which the former Confederate states were restored to the Union and former slaves became citizens and gained the right to vote and hold political office. It was also a time of violence and terrorism as many southern white people resisted the change in the status of African Americans.

Reconstruction Acts, 1867:   Led by Radical Republicans, Congress divided the South into five military districts. Each former Confederate state (except Tennessee) was to frame a new state constitution and establish a new state government. The first Reconstruction Act provided for universal manhood suffrage, which granted the right to vote to all adult males, including black men.

Red Scare: The widespread fear among any Americans in the years immediately after World War I from about 1918 to about 1924 that Russia's 1917 Bolshevik Revolution might result in communists attempting to take over the U.S. government.

Redemption: The term used for the process, often violent, by which white conservative Democrats regained political control of a southern state from black and white Republicans during Reconstruction.

Renaissance: A humanist and artistic movement that began in Italy during the late fourteenth century and spread across Europe.

Rochester Convention, 1853:   African-American leaders assembled in Rochester, New York, to discuss slavery, abolition, the recently passed Fugitive Slave Law, and their prospects for life in America.

Savannah: A flat, nearly treeless grassland typical of large portions of West Africa.

Scalawag: The derogatory term used during Reconstruction to identify a native white southerner who supported black and white Republicans. They were considered traitors to their people and the Democratic Party.

Scottsboro Boys: Nine young African-American men unjustly accused of raping two white women in Alabama in 1931. The Supreme Court overturned their convictions in 1937.

Seasoning: The process by which newly arrived Africans were broken in to slavery in the Americas.

Second Great Awakening (1790s–1830s):   A widespread religious revival, centered in the North and upper South, that encouraged reform movements.

Secret societies: Social organizations that have secret ceremonies that only their members know about and can participate in.

Secularism: The belief that the present public welfare should predominate over religion in civil affairs.

Segregation: The separation of people based on their race in the use of such public facilities as hotels, restaurants, restrooms, drinking fountains, parks, and auditoriums. In many instances segregation meant the exclusion of black people.

Semitic: Refers to people who speak languages, such as Arabic and Hebrew, native to southwest Asia.

Sharecropping: The system following the Civil War in which former slaves worked land owned by white people and "paid" for the use of the land and for tools, seeds, fertilizer, and mules by sharing the crop—usually cotton—with the owner.

Shotgun policy: In Mississippi in 1875 white men resorted to violence and intimidation against black and white Republicans to regain political control of the state for conservative Democrats.

Slave power: A term used to indicate the political control exercised by slaveholders over the U.S. government before the Civil War.

Slaver: A ship used to transport slaves from Africa to the Americas.

Sons of Liberty: A secret American organization formed in the Northeast during the summer of 1765 and committed to forcible opposition to the Stamp Act.

Southern Christian Leadership Conference (SCLC): Organization spearheaded by Martin Luther King, Jr. to provide an institutional base for the Civil Rights Movement.

Southern Homestead Act, 1866: Congress passed this measure that set aside over 3 million acres of land for former slaves and loyal white Southerners to farm following the Civil War. Most of the land was not fertile or suitable for agriculture, and the act largely failed.

Southern Regional Council (SRC): Organization that conducted research and focused attention on social, political, and educational inequality in the South.

Spanish Armada: A fleet that unsuccessfully attempted to carry out an invasion of England in 1588.

Special Field Order #15: General William Tecumseh Sherman issued this military directive in January 1865. It set aside lands along the coast from Charleston, South Carolina, to Jacksonville, Florida, for former slaves. President Andrew Johnson revoked the order six months later.

Spirit possession: A belief rooted in West African religions that spirits may possess human souls.

Student Non-Violent Coordinating Committee (SNCC): Civil rights organization founded by black college students in 1960 at the initiative of Ella Baker.

Syracuse Convention, 1864: A meeting of black leaders in Syracuse, New York, to discuss the future of African Americans following the abolition of slavery. They insisted that black people had earned and deserved the same political and legal rights as white Americans.

Talented Tenth: Term coined by W. E. B. Du Bois for the educated black elite of the late nineteenth and early twentieth centuries. The upper 10 percent was supposed to assume responsibility for the leadership and advancement of the remaining 90 percent of African Americans.

Term slavery: A type of slavery prevalent in the Chesapeake from the late 1700s to the Civil War in which slaves were able to purchase their freedom from their masters by earning money over a number of years.

Terrell law: The Terrell law was a Texas law banning African-American participation in the Democratic primary.

The Great Society: Programs created in response to the problems of poor Americans championed by President Johnson.

Thirteenth Amendment, 1865: This amendment to the U.S. Constitution outlawed slavery and involuntary servitude.

Three-Fifths Clause: A clause in the U.S. Constitution providing that a slave be counted as three-fifths of a free person in determining a state's representation in Congress and the electoral college and three-fifths of a free person in regard to per capita taxes levied by Congress on the states.

Tuskegee Airmen: All-black combat air unit during World War II.

Tuskegee Machine: As the president of Tuskegee Institute, Booker T. Washington developed an extensive network of contacts that gave him extraordinary influence with white political leaders and philanthropists as well as with black businesspeople, journalists, and college presidents.

Tuskegee Study: A medical study by the U.S. Public Health Service of the effects of syphilis on 622 black men. The study ran from 1932 to the 1970s, and the men were given only placebos and no treatment for the disease.

Uncle Tom's Cabin: This antislavery novel by Harriet Beecher Stowe was a best seller in the 1850s and it helped inflame the controversy over slavery.

Underground Railroad: Refers to several loosely organized, semisecret biracial networks that helped slaves escape from the border South to the North and Canada. The earliest networks appeared during the first decade of the nineteenth century; others operated into the Civil War years.

Union League: A social and fraternal organization that stirred political interest and support among black and white Republicans in the South during Reconstruction.

Universal Negro Improvement Association (UNIA): Established in 1914 in Jamaica by Marcus Garvey, it fostered racial pride, African heritage, Christian faith, and economic uplift.

Voting Rights Act of 1965: Federal law banning the methods that had systematically excluded African Americans from registering or voting in southern elections.

Wilmot Proviso: A measure introduced in Congress in 1845 to prohibit slavery in any lands acquired from Mexico. It did not pass.

PHOTO CREDITS

Chapter 13: Courtesy of the Library of Congress, pp. 282–283; The Granger Collection, NYC—All rights reserved, 285, 286; Courtesy of the Library of Congress, 289, 294; P.S. Duval and Son, Come and join us brothers; Civil War; Philadelphia, Pa.; ca. 1863. Chicago History Museum ICHi-22051, 297.

Chapter 14: Nebraska State Historical Society, pp. 306–307; © Bettmann/Corbis, 315; (c) Collection of The New-York Historical Society, Negative #: 51391, 317; North Carolina Department of Cultural Resources, 320; Courtesy of the Library of Congress, 322; Courtesy of the Library of Congress, 324, 326 (all photos).

Chapter 15: Amon Carter Museum of American Art, Fort Worth, Texas, © Erwin E. Smith Foundation, LC.S611.015, pp. 334–335; Courtesy of the Library of Congress, 339, 344; Montana Historical Society, Helena, 347; Museum of the American West Collection, Autry National Center; 87.61.2, 350; Madam C.J. Walker Collection, Indiana Historical Society., M0399., 354 (first photo); Courtesy of the Library of Congress, 354 (second two photos), 359.

Chapter 16: Courtesy of the Library of Congress, pp. 366–367; Courtesy of the Library of Congress, 369; The Granger Collection, NYC—All rights reserved, 373; Schomburg Center/Art Resource, NY, 375; Courtesy of the Library of Congress, 381; Research Division of the Oklahoma Historical Society, 387; Courtesy of the Library of Congress, 394 (photos in second column); The Chicago Defender, 394 (photo in first column).

Chapter 17: Courtesy of the Library of Congress, pp. 400–401; The Granger Collection, NYC—All rights reserved, 403; © Bettmann/Corbis, 407; National Archives and Records Administration, 411; Beinecke Rare Book and Manuscript Library, Yale University, 413; © Bettmann/Corbis, 417 (bottom photo in first column); Fred Ramage/Hulton Archive/Getty Images, 417 (bottom photo in second column); Courtesy of the Rutgers Institute of Jazz Studies, 417 (top photo in first column); © Culver Pictures, Inc./SuperStock, 417 (top photo in second column).

Chapter 18: Margaret Bourke-White//Time Life Pictures/Getty Images, pp. 424–425; University of South Carolina, 430; Courtesy of the Library of Congress, 432; Courtesy Mary McLeod Bethune Council House National Historic Site, Washington, DC., 434; Courtesy of the Library of Congress, 439; Courtesy of the Library of Congress, 444 (all photos), 445.

Chapter 19: © Bettmann/Corbis, pp. 452–453; Courtesy of the Library of Congress, 458; Vivian G. Harsh Research Collection of Afro-American History & Literature at the Chicago Public Library donated by Ms. Clarice Durham. Photo by Dion A. Stams, Sr., 460; Courtesy of the Library of Congress, 461; © David Lees/Corbis, 467; Courtesy of the Library of Congress, 470; © Bettmann/Corbis, 472.

Chapter 20: National Archives and Records Administration, pp. 478–479; Courtesy of the Library of Congress, 483, 485; National Archives and Records Administration, 487; Courtesy of the Library of Congress, 488; National Archives and Records Administration, 496 (bottom photos); National Baseball Hall of Fame Library, Cooperstown, N.Y., 496 (top photo).

Chapter 21: © Bettmann/Corbis, pp. 502–503, 506; Courtesy of the Library of Congress , 507, 510; ullstein bild/The Image Works, 516; Jack Moebes/Corbis, 518; All rights reserved to Joe Alper Photo Collection LLC. The photograph may not be reproduced in any manner whatsoever without the written permission of the Joe Alper Photo Collection LLC., 522; John F. Kennedy Library, National Archives, document MS 2003-036, 525.

Chapter 22: © Bettmann/Corbis, pp. 534–535; Courtesy of the Library of Congress, 537; © Bettmann/Corbis, 539; Leonard Freed/Magnum Photos, 540; Courtesy of the Library of Congress, 543; AP Images, 553; Courtesy of the Library of Congress, 560 (top photo); AP Images/Bill Hudson, 560 (middle photo); www.jofreeman.com, 560 (bottom two photos).

Chapter 23: ©David Grossman/The Image Works, pp. 568–569; © Viviane Moos/Corbis, 574; Woodfin Camp & Associates, Inc., 578; Lynn Goldsmith/Corbis, 581 (bottom photo in first column); Frank Micelotta/Getty Images, 581 (bottom photo in second column); AP Images/Al Behrman, 584; Manny Ceneta/Getty Images, 587.

Chapter 24: Damon Winter/The New York Times/Redux, pp. 596–597; © Bettmann/Corbis, 600; Najlah Feanny/Corbis News/Corbis Saba, 603; © Paul Conklin/PhotoEdit, 605; ZUMA Archive/ZUMA Press/Newscom, 607; AP Images/Gerald Herbert, 612 (top photo); © Gary Hershorn/Reuters/Corbis, 612 (bottom photo in second column); Courtesy of Democratic National Committee, 612 (bottom photo in first column); Marko Georgiev/Getty Images, 616.

INDEX

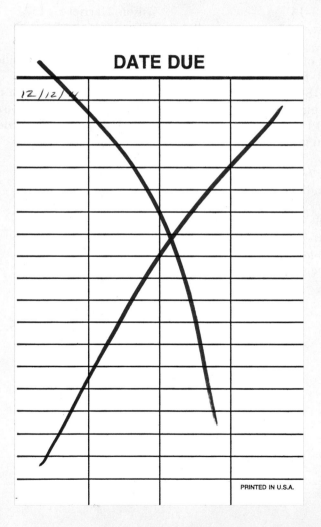